Microsoft® Office SharePoint® Designer 2007 Bible

Microsoft® Office SharePoint® Designer 2007 Bible

Vikram Kartik

WILEY

Wiley Publishing, Inc.

Microsoft® Office SharePoint® Designer 2007 Bible

Published by
Wiley Publishing, Inc.
10475 Crosspoint Boulevard
Indianapolis, IN 46256
www.wiley.com

Copyright © 2009 by Wiley Publishing, Inc., Indianapolis, Indiana

Published by Wiley Publishing, Inc., Indianapolis, Indiana

Published simultaneously in Canada

ISBN: 978-0-470-38644-6

Manufactured in the United States of America

10 9 8 7 6 5 4 3 2 1

For general information on our other products and services or to obtain technical support, please contact our Customer Care Department within the U.S. at (800) 762-2974, outside the U.S. at (317) 572-3993 or fax (317) 572-4002.

Library of Congress Control Number: 2008941630

About the Author

Vikram Kartik is a support escalation engineer with Microsoft Customer Support Services for SharePoint and SharePoint Designer technologies. Based in Microsoft's Global Technical Support Center in India, he has been working on FrontPage client and server technologies since August 2003. Besides actively engaging with Microsoft's customers, partners, and vendors on support issues, he's also involved in the evaluation of Microsoft's support knowledge base articles for FrontPage and SharePoint Designer products.

This book is dedicated to my father, the question "What did you give back to this world in return?" and to the people who love to do what they're doing but still yearn to do something else.

Credits

Acquisitions Editor
Laura Sinise

Project Editor
Christopher Stolle

Technical Editor
Patricia DiGiacomo Eddy

Copy Editor
Kim Heusel

Editorial Manager
Robyn Siesky

Business Manager
Amy Knies

Senior Marketing Manager
Sandy Smith

Vice President and Executive Group Publisher
Richard Swadley

Vice President and Executive Publisher
Barry Pruett

Project Coordinator
Lynsey Stanford

Graphics and Production Specialists
Reuben W. Davis
Christin Swinford

Quality Control Technician
Amanda Graham

Proofreading
Context Editorial Services

Indexing
Broccoli Information Management

Contents

Contents

Contents

Contents

Contents

Part VII: Managing and Publishing Web Sites   509

Acknowledgments

My mother is an iconic figure in my life and a source of inspiration. However, this book wouldn't have been possible without the support and understanding of my wife, Shweta Sharma. As I toiled to meet the deadlines on this project, she didn't raise a brow to the pressures we were going through in our personal lives during this time. It was her uncompromising love, affection, and care that kept me dedicated to the effort that was put into writing this book.

Also, I can't help but acknowledge the contribution that Microsoft has had to my professional and personal lives. I'm extremely emotional about the support I have received from Microsoft during the tougher times. Being able to work with this company has been one of my greatest pleasures.

Lastly, I want to thank my friends; my brothers Varun Kartik, Vipul Kartik, and Ashish R. Mohan; and the small town of Tuljapur. You continue to have a deep influence on my perception of life and this world.

Introduction

SharePoint Designer is Microsoft's premier offering for Web designers, information workers, and business users to be able to interactively design collaborative SharePoint-based Web applications. It has its roots in FrontPage technologies and is considered the product of choice for users who want to work specifically on SharePoint Web applications.

This book tries to align its content to the development life cycle of a Web site or application. From the initial decisions about the server technologies to be used for Web site development to the actual Web application design and implementation and finally to the Web site maintenance and housekeeping, all facets of SharePoint Designer are covered in simple and easy-to-follow chapters.

This book strives to introduce readers to most of the server-side aspects of SharePoint Designer. Because SharePoint Designer relies on a number of server technologies, such as Internet Information Services (IIS), FrontPage Server Extensions (FPSE), and SharePoint, a substantial portion of this book is devoted to helping develop understanding on how these technologies work individually and in relation to SharePoint Designer. Before the book starts to explore the SharePoint Designer functionality, it offers insight into the server products that SharePoint Designer can interact with. Throughout the book, you find notes and tips about features provided by the server technologies that SharePoint Designer either relies on or interacts with. Overall, one of the intentions of this book is to simplify understanding of SharePoint Designer's interaction with the server technologies to help troubleshoot common issues with remote authoring and publishing.

After a deep dive into SharePoint Designer's remote authoring internals, readers are exposed to the SharePoint Designer tools and features that they can exploit to design Web pages on SharePoint and non-SharePoint Web sites. Easy-to-follow exercises help you understand the power of SharePoint Designer in laying out Web pages, using ASP.NET controls and FrontPage Web components, and working with data and SharePoint-specific features, such as data forms and workflows.

Finally, the later parts of this book focus on SharePoint Designer's ability to help administer SharePoint and non-SharePoint Web applications. I also discuss in detail how to use SharePoint Designer to export and import sites, publish Web applications, and perform site analysis.

As a personal note to readers, it's recommended that you go through the exercises in this book by actively using SharePoint Designer. These exercises are designed to introduce you to the SharePoint Designer user interface. Also, it's a good idea to read through the text in SharePoint Designer dialog boxes. A lot of useful information and hints are written right on them.

Ultimately, I hope you find that this book encourages your Web design capabilities and gives you confidence to design creative, interactive, and successful Web pages and Web sites.

Part I

Understanding the Technologies

Chapter 1

Becoming Familiar with SharePoint Designer

The Internet has long been one of the favorite mechanisms of expression because of the wide reach, connection, and exposure it offers. It's one of the basic means of communication in the 21st century and has drawn people closer in unique ways. Having a presence on the Internet is a pivotal requirement for any organization, irrespective of its size, nature, or range of operations. Web sites on the Internet provide the canvas that organizations can use to explain their missions and goals, advertise their products, perform business transactions, and communicate with their customers and partners.

It's apparent that the Internet as a medium offers tremendous prospects and opportunities. To exploit this medium, Web site designers have a range of Internet technologies to choose from. From simple markup languages (such as HTML) to complex application development technologies (such as ASP. NET), there are a variety of platforms on which you can base your Web site application. To achieve the most from these technologies without having to re-create a lot of work, many Web site development tools and products are available to you. Microsoft's key offerings for these tools and products have been FrontPage and Visual Studio. While Visual Studio is targeted to Web developers and complex Web application development, FrontPage is designed to provide a simpler no-code-based software development tool that helps Web site designers focus on designing Web sites rather than have to deal with the complex code that goes behind Web site development and still be able to create complex Web sites.

FrontPage offers Web site designers a number of components and What You See Is What You Get (WYSIWYG) features that help in building important sections of Web sites. It provides wizard-based interfaces that aid in developing Web pages without having to write a lot of code behind the Web pages and creating key Web site features, such as site navigation, data collection

IN THIS CHAPTER

Introducing SharePoint Designer

Understanding SharePoint Designer basics

Exploring hidden metadata and raw Webs

Maintaining Web sites

forms, dynamic effects, and graphics and animation. Along with that, it offers a number of Web site management features that provide for ease in managing Web sites as well as importing, exporting, and publishing content to Web servers.

With the advent of SharePoint technologies, FrontPage has been replaced primarily because of the need to address the requirements of Web site designers in the SharePoint and non-SharePoint environments. FrontPage 2003 is the last version of FrontPage, and FrontPage is now available as two separate products: Expression Web (for non-SharePoint development) and SharePoint Designer (for SharePoint development). While SharePoint Designer falls into the Microsoft Office suite (although it's not part of any Office 2007 suite and is sold separately), Expression Web is part of the new Expression Studio suite of products, which includes Expression Blend, a program once called Interactive Designer.

In this chapter, I introduce you to SharePoint Designer and help familiarize you with some basics for developing Web pages and Web sites using SharePoint Designer. Although I try to keep this chapter simple, if you run across a term, feature, or component that sounds confusing, don't be concerned because I cover these elements in more depth throughout this book.

Introducing SharePoint Designer

SharePoint is one of the fastest-growing Microsoft products and offers a platform for developing enterprise-level Web applications that focus on the sharing and collaboration of content and documents. In its most basic of definitions, SharePoint provides the infrastructure for creating and maintaining Web sites that can be used for a variety of Internet-based operations besides sharing Office or non-Office content and collaboration. You can later customize these Web sites that SharePoint creates to suit your business needs, format, or branding.

SharePoint Designer is Microsoft's premier product for Web site designers who are tasked with customizing and branding SharePoint Web sites. Although SharePoint Designer in its current release can be used for non-SharePoint Web site development, its full capability is exposed when you work with SharePoint Web sites. However, before I discuss SharePoint Designer and its features, I want to briefly mention its predecessor, FrontPage, and the origins of SharePoint Designer.

Exploring the legacy of FrontPage technologies

Microsoft acquired FrontPage quite a few years ago from a company called Vermeer Technologies Incorporated (VTI, an acronym you encounter a lot when exploring the internals of SharePoint Designer later in this chapter). FrontPage's Web site authoring and management techniques were really ahead of their time and allowed Web site developers to easily create Web sites on local computers and then push them to Web servers or even work directly on the Web site residing on the Web server. The underlying authoring techniques of FrontPage were exploited by a lot of other Microsoft products, such as Visual InterDev, Office, and Visual Studio.

The concept was simple: The FrontPage program installed on the client computer provided the *client-side component* that could be used for creating Web pages and designing Web sites. The Web server was set up with a *server-side component* — namely, FrontPage Server Extensions (FPSE) — that would communicate with the client-side component for providing the basic infrastructure for three operations:

- Moving content from the client machine to the Web server
- Authoring or modifying content directly on the Web server
- Enabling certain Web components that provide functionality for Web sites

These authoring technologies that FrontPage introduced are still very much alive and used by SharePoint Designer, Expression Web, and Office 2007 products when working with SharePoint and non-SharePoint sites.

CROSS-REF For more on these authoring mechanisms and protocols, see Chapter 3.

FrontPage could be used to create Web pages and design Web sites by using a set of Web components and features offered with the product. These features included components such as hit counters, shared borders, link bars based on the navigation structure, and many more. The list of these components grew with each new version of FrontPage.

On the server side, FPSE provided the basis for the first SharePoint implementation offered with Office XP/2002. This release of SharePoint was called SharePoint Team Services (STS) and stemmed from a less-used ASP-based Office 2000 document management feature called Office Server Extensions (OSE). STS allowed developers to create Web sites by using Web site templates that were provided with the product. These Web sites provided basic collaboration and document management features, including document libraries and lists.

FrontPage XP/2002 became the client-side tool for customizing and modifying Web pages inside STS sites. FrontPage 2002 also provided for the interface that could be used to create new document libraries and lists (SharePoint content) as well as new SharePoint Web pages and Web sites, publishing STS sites from one Web server to another. All these SharePoint features were enabled in FrontPage 2002 only when an STS site was open in it and were not available for non-SharePoint sites.

This client-server relationship was thus established as the basis for the next versions of FrontPage and SharePoint. FrontPage 2003 was offered as the client-side designing tool for working with Windows SharePoint Services 2.0 (WSS v2). It could be used to develop SharePoint content and exploit the features offered by WSS v2 sites.

Following this relationship, SharePoint Designer was introduced as the designing tool for the current version of SharePoint, WSS v3, and Microsoft Office SharePoint Server (MOSS). Although SharePoint Designer is backward-compatible to a certain extent with the previous versions of SharePoint, its complete set of features are exposed only when using it with WSS v3 and MOSS sites.

Comparing SharePoint Designer with FrontPage 2003

As discussed earlier, SharePoint Designer is the designing tool for the current release of SharePoint. SharePoint Designer inherits many of its features from FrontPage 2003. Besides these features and enhancements, SharePoint Designer makes available a set of new technologies and features, such as workflows, page layouts, etc., that SharePoint v3 exposes.

While I highlight key improvements in SharePoint Designer as compared to FrontPage 2003 throughout this book, Table 1.1 compares some of the major features and components available in FrontPage 2003 and SharePoint Designer.

TABLE 1.1

Comparing SharePoint Designer with FrontPage 2003

Features	FrontPage 2003	SharePoint Designer
Task panes	Introduced in FrontPage 2003 for working with various features, such as layers, behaviors, layouts, etc.	Extensively uses dockable task panes to manage features, such as CSS, Tag Properties, Data Sources, Reports, etc. Property grids provide a Visual Studio–like interface for working with tag and control properties.
Cascading Style Sheets (CSS)	Interface available to create new styles and implement style sheets on Web pages	Brand-new intuitive CSS application and management interface using toolbars and task panes that can be used to create and manage styles. CSS layout templates also available.
Master pages	Not available	Ability to create, attach, and detach master pages and content regions. Reporting for master pages is also available
ASP.NET 2.0 controls	Not available	Available with .NET Framework 2.0 installed on the machine
Database wizards	Used to create Web pages for interfacing with databases	Deprecated and replaced by ASP.NET 2.0 data controls
SharePoint content	Can be used to create and manage content with WSS v2 sites. Limited backward-compatibility also available for STS sites	Can be used to create content for and manage WSS v2 and WSS v3 sites
Workflows	Not available in WSS v2	Workflow Designer available for creating and deploying declarative workflows for WSS v3 sites
Data views	Available for showing data from databases, SharePoint sources, XML files, etc.	Available for showing data from databases, SharePoint sources, XML files, etc. Extends the FrontPage 2003 capabilities by allowing for creation of forms that can be used to insert and update data besides showing it

Features	FrontPage 2003	SharePoint Designer
Web components	A number of FPSE- and WSS v2–based components available, such as hit counters, confirmation fields, etc.	Inherits these Web components from FrontPage 2003
Dynamic Web templates	Ability to create, attach, and detach dynamic Web templates and manage editable regions	Inherits this feature from FrontPage 2003
Data forms	Not available. List forms can be modified to a certain extent by using Collaborative Application Markup Language (CAML) features.	Can be used to create advanced data forms for SharePoint list and document libraries, databases, etc., using the new and advanced Data Form Web Part
Reporting for Web sites	Site and usage reporting available depending on the server setup	Advanced CSS error and usage reporting, accessibility, and compatibility reporting available using task panes
Code and design features	IntelliSense and auto code completion available for HTML and client-side scripts	Visual and formatting marks for HTML tags and ASP.NET 2.0 controls in the Design view. IntelliSense for HTML, JavaScript, and ASP.NET 2.0
Data sources	SharePoint data sources available through the Data Source Library task pane	SharePoint and non-SharePoint data sources available through the Data Source Library task pane. Aggregate data sources available for linking data sources together
Re-ghosting SharePoint pages	Not available	User interface available to selectively re-ghost SharePoint Web pages

Some of the differences shown throughout this book are apparent; SharePoint Designer is the newer version and exploits many features that the new SharePoint 3.0 itself has to offer. Workflows, for example, is a new technology that SharePoint 3.0 exposes to SharePoint Designer for creating advanced logic-based processes that could help in implementing common business actions and purposes. The ability to use ASP.NET 2.0 controls through a wizard-based approach is also new for SharePoint Designer, which now offers a simpler Visual Studio/Visual InterDev–like interface to work with ASP.NET 2.0 control properties. Some features, such as the Database Results Wizard and shared borders, are deprecated and have been replaced in favor of newer and better technologies. Throughout this book, I talk about these differences while also discussing the new features.

Although SharePoint Designer offers its full capabilities for SharePoint sites, you could be a Web site designer concentrating totally on non-SharePoint Web sites. In that case, the SharePoint features of SharePoint Designer might just be useless to you until you start developing for SharePoint, and you might want to invest in a trimmed-down version of SharePoint Designer, such as the current release of Expression Web, which is a subset of SharePoint Designer.

Choosing between Expression Web and SharePoint Designer

This choice is quite simple: If you as a Web site designer need to concentrate primarily on SharePoint sites, the obvious choice is SharePoint Designer. However, if you don't develop content for SharePoint sites, you can invest in Expression Web. Expression Web offers almost all the non-SharePoint features of SharePoint Designer, such as ASP.NET 2.0 controls, master pages, and CSS, but has the limitation that it can't open SharePoint sites. It lacks all the SharePoint capabilities that SharePoint Designer offers. So, if a non-SharePoint Web server hosts your Web site and you have no plans to develop SharePoint content, Expression Web can provide you with all the tools you need for your Web site development. The non-SharePoint interface for the current release of Expression Web and SharePoint Designer is essentially similar and thus you can also use this book as a reference for Expression Web.

Understanding SharePoint Designer Basics

In this section, I discuss some basic concepts and terminology about Web site designing from the SharePoint Designer perspective, helping you feel more comfortable as you read the rest of this book. Most of the concepts surrounding SharePoint Designer are based on FrontPage technology, so if you're already familiar with FrontPage 2003, this might just emphasize your knowledge about SharePoint Designer.

Meeting the requirements

Although the basic SharePoint Designer setup is fairly simple and doesn't require much user interaction, you might want to have these prerequisites set up on your computer before you install SharePoint Designer so that all its features are readily available to you:

- .NET Framework 2.0
- .NET Framework 3.0

You can download these from the Microsoft Web site at www.microsoft.com/downloads.

Having these tools downloaded to your computer prior to installing SharePoint Designer ensures that you can properly use the elaborate ASP.NET 2.0 features of SharePoint Designer. But you can also download them after installing SharePoint Designer.

Prior to installing SharePoint Designer, you also need to ensure that your machine meets these basic system requirements:

- **Processor:** 700 megahertz (MHz) processor or higher
- **Memory:** 512 megabyte (MB) RAM or higher

- **Hard drive:** 1.5 gigabyte (GB); a portion of this disk space is freed after installation if you remove the original download package from the hard drive.

- **Drive:** CD-ROM or DVD drive

- **Display:** 1024 × 768 or higher resolution monitor

- **Operating system:** Microsoft Windows XP with Service Pack (SP) 2, Windows Server 2003 with SP1, or later operating system

If you work with SharePoint Designer on SharePoint sites, then you need to have a Web server set up for WSS or MOSS.

The setup process for SharePoint Designer is fairly simple and is similar to the Office 2007 setup process. The Setup Wizard allows you to choose to either set up the basic installation by using the Install Now button or customize the setup using the Customize button. The Customize button, as shown in Figure 1.1, allows you to change the installation directory for SharePoint Designer and pick features that you want to install during setup.

FIGURE 1.1

Customization options during setup for SharePoint Designer

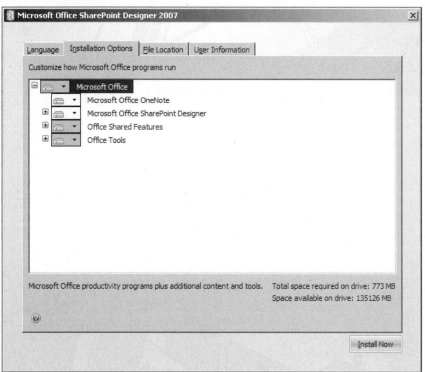

After you install SharePoint Designer on your computer, choose Start ➪ Control Panel ➪ Add or Remove Programs to change (add or remove features), repair, or remove SharePoint Designer. On Windows Vista machines, this is accessible by choosing Start ➪ Control Panel ➪ Programs and Features. The first time you open SharePoint Designer, you're asked whether you want to make SharePoint Designer your default program for Web site development. If you choose to use SharePoint Designer as the default program, it's set up so that Web content (HTML or ASP.NET pages, style sheets, etc.) on your computer opens with SharePoint Designer.

TIP Setup administrators might want to skip the introductory messages that are shown the first time SharePoint Designer opens and allow their users to directly start using SharePoint Designer rather than having to make these choices. You can learn more about turning off these messages at `http://support.microsoft.com/kb/929767`.

The SharePoint Designer setup can also be configured using Office policy templates, which allow administrators to control the features available within SharePoint Designer to their users.

NOTE The Microsoft support article at the following Web site provides information about how administrators can use Microsoft Office templates with Microsoft Office 2007 programs (including SharePoint Designer): `http://support.microsoft.com/kb/924617`.

After your SharePoint Designer setup is complete, you might also want to install the SharePoint Designer Service Pack (SP) 1 from the Microsoft Web site at www.microsoft.com/downloads.

Understanding the structure of Web pages and Web sites

The structure of Web pages in general is pretty flexible and spans to the imagination of a Web site designer. As a designer, you have the power to decide how you want to lay out your Web pages. SharePoint Designer provides you with templates that you can use for starting up.

CROSS-REF For more on working with basic Web page components, see Chapter 5.

From the SharePoint Designer perspective, it's important to understand that a Web page essentially has a Design view and a Code view. The Code view shows the code (HTML, JavaScript, ASP.NET code, etc.) of the Web page and allows direct modification by using features such as IntelliSense and auto code completion. When you click the Design view tab of a Web page, SharePoint Designer renders the code associated with the Web page into a WYSIWYG format that assists in designing and previewing the page layout. Some files, such as style sheets, don't need a Design view, so only a Code view is displayed for them.

SharePoint Designer's complex rendering logic also renders ASP.NET 2.0 controls, the master page application, and the style sheet application on Web pages. While rendering Web pages for the Design view, SharePoint Designer also stores the properties and attributes of the tags and controls present in the code of the Web page. These properties are then presented in the various task panes for modification.

NOTE All task panes are accessible under the Task Panes menu.

CROSS-REF For more on property grids and task panes, see Chapters 4 and 6.

I now take you through the steps for creating a simple Web site and then adding some content to that Web site.

One important thing to understand while using SharePoint Designer to create Web pages is that Web pages by nature reside inside Web sites. Although you can save your Web pages wherever you want on your computer, it's always best that you create a folder for your Web site and store all Web pages and other content inside that folder. Such a folder is called the root folder of your Web site. Creating a root folder assists you in better management of Web pages and other content that you create during the course of building a Web site:

1. **Create a root folder for your Web site at the location of your choice on your computer.** This ensures that you remember the location where your Web pages and content are stored. Ensure that your root folder is empty.

2. **Open SharePoint Designer and then choose File ➪ New.** The New dialog box opens. This dialog box is new to SharePoint Designer and provides a consolidated interface to create new Web content (pages, JavaScript file, style sheets, etc.).

CROSS-REF For more on the New dialog box, see Chapter 4.

3. **Click the Web Site tab.** This tab allows you to choose from a list of Web site templates available in SharePoint Designer. For this exercise, use the One Page Web Site template.

4. **Click Browse, which is next to the Specify the location of the Web site dropdown menu.** Using the New Web Site Location dialog box, specify the location of the root folder that you created in step 1.

5. **Click OK.** SharePoint Designer opens your Web site at the root folder and automatically places a `default.htm` file (because you selected the One Page Web Site template) inside the root folder. The folder is now listed in the Folder List task pane (which can be toggled on or off by pressing Alt+F1), which is displayed in the left corner of the SharePoint Designer window by default.

After following these steps, the icon for your root folder inside Windows Explorer changes to a folder icon with a globe on it, indicating that it's a Web site (a disk-based Web site). SharePoint Designer Web sites are basically one of two types:

■ **Disk-based:** The content of this Web site resides inside a folder on your local computer. You work on the disk-based Web site locally and then publish the content you create locally to a Web server–based location that might reside either on your local computer (if your computer is a Web server itself) or a remote Web server computer (a site-hosting service provider, for example). The folder icon with a globe on it (an `fpdbw.ico` file stored in the `_vti_pvt` folder) indicates this type of Web site.

■ **Server-based:** The content of this Web site is located on a remote Web server and is accessible to the SharePoint Designer client for modification by using a remote-authoring mechanism, such as FPSE, SharePoint, FTP, or WebDAV. SharePoint Designer now allows for remote authoring (also called live editing) of server-based FTP and WebDAV sites. SharePoint sites also fall into this category of Web sites.

When you open the root folder of your Web site, SharePoint Designer has created a number of other files and folders inside the root folder.

NOTE   **Many of these files and folders are hidden by default, so you have to enable the viewing of hidden folders in Windows Explorer by choosing Tools ➪ Folder Options ➪ View. Click the Show hidden files and folders radio button in the Advanced Settings list.**

The two folders that result from the previous steps are the _vti_cnf and the _vti_pvt folders. The reason for having these folders is that they provide the underlying infrastructure files for many features that SharePoint Designer exposes. For example, in the _vti_pvt folder is a file called structure.cnf. This file stores the navigation structure of the Web site, which can be created by using the Navigation pane in SharePoint Designer. So, essentially, if someone deletes this file or folder using Windows Explorer, the navigation structure of your Web site is lost, and any Web components based on the navigation structure are useless.

CROSS-REF   **For more on the Navigation pane, see Chapter 14.**

NOTE   **The folders that have the prefix _vti_ aren't displayed in SharePoint Designer. So, if you want to hide the contents of a folder from being edited using the SharePoint Designer interface, you can do so by adding the _vti_ prefix to it.**

The other important thing to understand about these folders is that they're used for the FPSE-based features of SharePoint Designer. Also, a number of other folders — such as _derived, _overlay, and _themes — are created in the root folder when you use FPSE features. If you delete these folders, any FPSE-based components that depend on these folders and the files inside them stop working.

Exploring Hidden Metadata and Raw Webs

Files and folders inside the root folder of a SharePoint Designer Web site are collectively called the hidden metadata of the Web site. The metadata inside the root folder keeps track of whether the Web site is a disk-based Web site or a server-based Web site. It also stores information about the list of subsites that the root site might contain. The metadata is a vital resource for performing a number of site management operations, such as hyperlink recalculation and creating the navigation structure.

If you decide to move away from using the FPSE features of SharePoint Designer, you might not need this metadata and can configure SharePoint Designer to not create the hidden metadata. A SharePoint Designer Web site that doesn't have metadata in it is called a raw Web. To convert your Web site to a raw Web, follow these steps:

1. **In SharePoint Designer, open the Web site you created earlier in this chapter by choosing File ⇨ Open Site.** The Open Site dialog box opens, with the Web Sites pane selected in the left Navigation pane. The Web Sites pane shows the list of Web sites that you've created.

2. **Choose your Web site and then click Open.**

3. **Choose Site ⇨ Site Settings.** The Site Setting dialog box opens.

4. **Deselect the Manage the Web site using hidden metadata files check box.** As indicated in the explanation text next to this check box, SharePoint Designer adds hidden metadata files to your root folder to enable and maintain certain features.

5. **Click OK.** A dialog box asks you for confirmation. The warning message indicates that if you elect to not use hidden metadata, you lose the navigation of your Web site and many FrontPage Web components stop being updated.

6. **Click Yes if you want to continue.**

After you deselect this option, the root folder of your Web site no longer has any _vti folders in it. This means that SharePoint Designer now has no ability to track FrontPage Web components and features. These features are thus disabled from the SharePoint Designer user interface when this option is deselected. For example, if you choose Insert ⇨ Web Component and then open the Insert Web Component dialog box, most of the features are disabled when you deselect the hidden metadata usage check box. Also, the Recalculate Hyperlinks menu option is no longer available in the Site menu.

CROSS-REF For more on Recalculate Hyperlinks, see Chapter 23.

If you later need to use the SharePoint Designer features that rely on the hidden metadata files, you can click the Manage the Web site using hidden metadata files check box again. SharePoint Designer then adds new hidden metadata to your Web site and starts using it for maintaining cross-page dependencies and other FrontPage Web components.

CAUTION Any metadata that's removed by deselecting the hidden metadata check box is completely lost and isn't recoverable. When you click the check box again, new metadata is created, and you have to rebuild the components.

The ability to remove hidden metadata has long been asked for by Web site developers who don't use FrontPage-based components and want to see cleaner Web site content directories. Because SharePoint Designer now offers the capability to use ASP.NET 2.0 controls and features extensively, most of the FrontPage legacy functionality can be obtained by newer, advanced ASP.NET 2.0 controls. Raw Webs provide these advantages for Web site developers:

- Developers now have a mechanism to ensure that they don't inadvertently use any FrontPage legacy features.

- Because SharePoint Designer now offers the capability of live editing using FTP and WebDAV, developers can choose not to use FPSE as a remote-authoring mechanism.

- They don't have to manage the hidden metadata when moving Web content from one location to another.

Creating basic Web pages

Continuing with efforts to understand the basics involved in Web content development, I take you through some steps that you generally follow in SharePoint Designer when creating Web pages. I want you to become familiar with the SharePoint Designer terminology in this chapter so that you don't feel uncomfortable when you delve into more complicated Web site designing concepts.

Follow these steps to create simple Web pages using various templates that SharePoint Designer offers:

1. **In SharePoint Designer, open the disk-based Web site you created earlier in this chapter.** Ensure that the Manage the Web site using hidden metadata files check box is selected.

2. **Choose File ⇨ New to open the New dialog box.**

3. **Click HTML under the Page tab to create a blank HTML Web page and then click OK.** The Design view of the newly created HTML page is shown.

4. **Choose File ⇨ Save or press Ctrl+S to save the page.** The Save As dialog box opens, with your currently opened Web site listed in the Save dropdown menu.

5. **Using the File name text field, type a name for your Web page and then click Save.** HTML pages have the extension .htm or .html. You can save the Web page by using either extension.

6. **Choose File ⇨ New to open the New dialog box.** You can now create a new CSS from the existing templates in SharePoint Designer.

CROSS-REF   **For more on Cascading Style Sheets (CSS), see Chapter 12.**

7. **Click Style Sheets and then click the Downtown style sheet template.** A new CSS based on the Downtown template opens. This template appears in the Code view.

8. **Press Ctrl+S to open the Save As dialog box and then save the style sheet with the name of your choice.** Style sheets have the extension .css, so make sure that you keep this extension when saving a style sheet. Because you're saving these files into the Web site's root folder, the newly created Web page and the style sheet are listed in the Folder List task pane.

9. **Using the Folder List task pane, double-click the Web page you created in the previous steps to open it in SharePoint Designer.**

10. **Choose Format ⇨ CSS Styles ⇨ Attach Style Sheet to open the Attach Style Sheet dialog box.** You use this dialog box to attach to the Web page the style sheet you previously created.

11. **Click Browse next to the URL text field to open the Select Style Sheet dialog box, click the style sheet file you created in the previous steps, and then click Open.** Ensure that the Current Page radio button is selected so that the style sheet applies only to the current page.

12. **Click OK to apply the style sheet to the Web page.**

The look and feel of the Web page changes after the application of the style sheet. The Web page now has a new background, and if you type some text on the Web page, the color of the text is white. The SharePoint Designer Design view renders the Web page in the Design view by combining the formatting implemented in the style sheet attached to it.

The New dialog box that you worked with in the previous exercise is the interface that consolidates the creation of all Web content within SharePoint Designer. This is different from FrontPage 2003 and the previous versions where page and Web content creation were scattered around in different task panes. Having a single interface for creating all SharePoint and non-SharePoint content is advantageous because it eliminates the need to search around the user interface for developing content.

The New dialog box can be used to create HTML and ASPX Web pages, JavaScript files, CSS, master pages and dynamic Web templates (DWTs), XML, and TXT files. Also, it offers the Web Site tab, which can be used to create Web sites (SharePoint and non-SharePoint) based on templates.

NOTE   If you open a SharePoint site in SharePoint Designer, the New dialog box also shows a tab called SharePoint Content. This tab can be used to create SharePoint-based content, such as lists, document libraries, workflows, and page layouts. Also, for SharePoint sites, the Web Site tab lists a number of templates that you can choose from for your new SharePoint sites.

Apart from using the New dialog box, you can also use the Folder List task pane to create new Web pages and content. If you right-click in the empty area inside the Folder List task pane, a popup menu appears that has the New menu option that allows for the creation of Web pages and CSS. You can use this menu to create new folders and subsites.

Follow these steps to use the existing frame templates that SharePoint Designer provides to create a set of Web pages:

CROSS-REF   For more on frames, see Chapter 5.

1. In SharePoint Designer, open your Web site and then choose File ⇨ New to open the New dialog box.

2. **In the Page tab, click Frames Pages and then click the Header, Footer and Contents template.** As indicated in the description text, the template creates header and footer frames for navigation.

3. **Click OK.** This creates a frameset page, as shown in Figure 1.2, that's displayed in the Design view in SharePoint Designer.

4. **Save this page inside the root folder of your Web site.**

5. **Click the New Page button on all the four frames inside the frameset page.** This creates new pages that fill up the frames present in the frameset page. Remember the order in which you clicked the New Page buttons. This is required to name the pages in the next step to keep track of which page is displayed in which frame.

FIGURE 1.2

A frameset page in the SharePoint Designer Design view

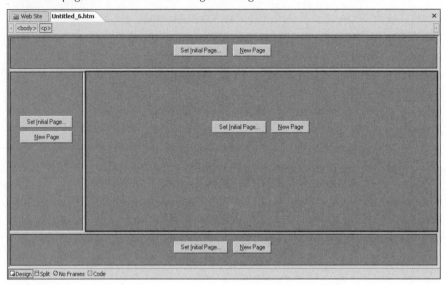

6. **Press Ctrl+S, and you're asked to save all the HTML pages inside the frames one after the other in the order they were created.** Because there are four frames, you have four new Web pages in the root after you save the frames pages. You can name the page for the left frame as `Left.htm`, the top frame as `Top.htm`, etc.

Your frameset page is now ready for the content that you want to put on the frames pages. For example, you could use the top frame page for a banner picture, and the left frame could be used to create hyperlinks that switch pages in the Contents frame of the frameset.

Right now, I want to divert your attention to the newly created pages from the previous exercise. The Folder List task pane lists these newly created Web pages in the root folder of your Web site. If you right-click on a Web page in the Folder List task pane, a popup menu opens with these options:

- **Open:** Opens the Web page in the SharePoint Designer Design view (or Code view)

- **Open With:** Allows you to choose the program that you want to open the Web page in

- **Open in New Window:** Opens the Web page in a new instance of SharePoint Designer

- **Set as Default Master Page:** If you've selected a master page, you can use this option to set the selected master page as the default master page for the Web site. If you don't have a master page selected, this option is grayed out.

CROSS-REF For more on master pages, see Chapter 13.

- **New From Existing Page:** Creates a new page based on the selected page
- **Preview in Browser:** Opens the Web page in the default browser for previewing
- **Cut, Copy and Paste menu options:** Allows for moving Web pages from one folder location to another inside the Web site
- **Set as Home Page:** Sets the Web page as the default home page for the Web site
- **Rename:** Allows you to rename the Web page
- **Delete:** Deletes the Web page after requesting confirmation from the user
- **Publish Selected Files:** Opens the publishing page that can be used to publish the Web page to a new location. Web page publishing is discussed later in this chapter.
- **Don't Publish:** Marks the Web page so that it's not included when a publishing operation is performed on the Web site
- **Properties:** Opens the Properties dialog box, which can be used to view general properties of the Web page and choose categories (if hidden metadata is allowed) for the Web page

Options in this popup menu might change depending on the type of selection you make in the Folder List task pane and the type of Web site that you have open in SharePoint Designer. For example, if you have document checking enabled on a Web site (discussed later in this chapter), the Check Out menu option becomes available.

Right-click on the Web page after opening it in the Design view and then choose Page Properties from the popup menu. This opens the Page Properties dialog box, as shown in Figure 1.3, which can be used to set up a number of properties for the Web page. These properties include the title, background sound, background picture, etc.

The Page Properties dialog box has the following tabs that allow for setting a number of properties for a Web page. Most of these settings provide a user interface for applying HTML tags and attributes or style elements that define the look and feel of the Web page:

- **General:** Allows the user to set the `<Title>` tag, the `<Base>` tag, keywords, and description meta tags for the Web page. It also allows you to set the default target frame and background sound for a Web page.
- **Formatting:** Provides the interface to set the background picture or configure the background picture as a watermark on a Web page. This also allows for setting the background color, text color, and colors for hyperlinks.
- **Advanced:** Used to set margins for a Web page. This is done by applying the margin styles to the `<Body>` tag of the Web page.
- **Custom:** Allows for creating HTML meta tags, such as `Refresh`, `Keywords`, and `Description`, that define the behavior of the Web page or provide directions to the Web browser
- **Language:** Provides the interface to set the `Content-Type` and `Content-Language` meta tags for the Web page. These meta tags define the page's language and HTML encoding.
- **Workgroup:** Allows the Web site designer to create categories of Web pages and assign Web pages to those categories. These categories can then be used to create a categorized table of contents. This feature requires the hidden metadata to be enabled.

FIGURE 1.3

The Page Properties dialog box

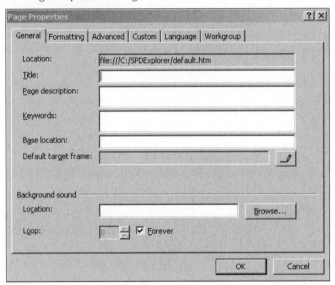

Follow these steps to use the Page Properties dialog box to set some properties for the Web page that define the way the Web page looks and behaves:

1. **Choose File ➪ New to open the New dialog box and then create a new HTML Web page.** The new page opens in the Design view.

2. **Right-click on the Web page and then choose Page Properties from the popup menu.** The Page Properties dialog box opens.

3. **In the General tab, type the title for the Web page in the Title text field.**

4. **Click the Formatting tab, and in the Colors section, choose a background color for the Web page by using the Background dropdown menu.**

5. **Click the Custom tab.** In the next steps, you use this tab to create a new system variable (an HTML meta tag) that refreshes the page every 5 seconds when viewed in a browser.

6. **Click the Add button next to the System variables list.**

7. **In the Name text field, type** Refresh, **and in the Value text field, type** 5 **(for a refresh every 5 seconds).**

8. **Click OK.** Your choices have been saved for this HTML page.

9. **Save the Web page.** You can now browse to the page by either right-clicking on it in the Folder List task pane and then choosing Preview in Browser from the popup menu or pressing F12.

The title you set for the Web page shows in the title bar of the Web browser. The background color of the Web page changes to the one you set. Also, the browser reloads the Web page every 5 seconds because of the Refresh meta tag that you created in the previous steps. The SharePoint Designer interface allows you to set the basic properties for a Web page without having much understanding of the code involved in the back end. Obviously, SharePoint Designer offers many other ways to manage these properties for Web pages, and I discuss those options throughout the rest of this book.

Working with simple Web sites

A Web site is basically a collection of resources that help realize the goals of an organization on the Internet. The resources for Web content are Web pages, pictures, supporting files (style sheets, JavaScript files, etc.) and programs (.exe, .dll, etc.) that contain logic and perform business operations. A Web site is accessible on the Internet through a Web server. The role of the Web server is to be a host for Web site content and process Web page requests made by Web browsers. A single Web server can host a large number of Web sites.

Now that you know how to create a simple Web site and add Web pages and style sheets to it, it's time to learn how to open and delete Web sites, create subsites, and establish general settings for Web sites inside SharePoint Designer.

Creating subsites within a Web site by using SharePoint Designer essentially involves the same steps you would follow to create a new Web site. That is, choosing File ⇨ New ⇨ Web Site allows you to pick the template you want to use for the subsite. However, just before you click OK, you need to click the Add to current web site check box. It's important to note that subsites inherit the server configuration of the parent Web site. This means that subsites inside SharePoint sites are always SharePoint subsites. Similarly, subsites inside FPSE parent sites are always FPSE subsites.

To open a Web site in SharePoint Designer, simply choose File ⇨ Open Site. The Open Site dialog box opens, with a number of panes that allow you to look for the Web site that you want to open. The Web Sites pane in the left Navigation pane shows the list of all Web sites that you've created or opened on the machine that has SharePoint Designer installed.

The Current Site pane, as the name suggests, is only available if you already have a site open in SharePoint Designer before you open the Open Site dialog box. It shows the list of folders and files for the Web site that's currently open and can be used to open subsites within the site. The My SharePoint Sites pane lists the SharePoint sites that you created or opened by using SharePoint Designer.

If you've previously opened the Web site in SharePoint Designer, try to see if you can find it in the recently opened list of Web sites by choosing File ⇨ Recent Sites.

NOTE SharePoint Designer also maintains a list of recently opened sites and Web pages in the Windows registry at C:\My Computer\HKEY_CURRENT_USER\Software\ Microsoft\Office\12.0\SharePoint Designer. SharePoint Designer uses this registry hive for saving user settings, including recently opened sites and Web pages, the default save location for Web sites, and the state of various SharePoint Designer user interface components.

If the Web site that you want to open doesn't already exist in the aforementioned lists, you can simply type the complete URL of the Web site in the Site Name text field. SharePoint Designer tries to establish a connection to the remote Web server and, if it finds the Web server hosting the Web site and can successfully authenticate to it, then opens the Web site for remote authoring.

CROSS-REF For more on remote authoring, see Chapter 3.

While choosing File ⇨ Open Site takes you to the Open Site dialog box, which allows you to open Web sites, choosing File ⇨ Open brings you to the Open File dialog box, which is used to open files and documents inside Web sites. If your page or document resides inside a Web site, SharePoint Designer opens the Web site itself. You can choose File ⇨ Close Site to close the Web site.

SharePoint Designer supports live editing and remote authoring for a number of Web server types. You can work directly on a Web site in SharePoint Designer if the Web server hosting the Web site supports one of these remote-authoring technologies:

- FTP
- WebDAV
- FPSE
- SharePoint

Depending on the remote-authoring technology that your Web server supports, some of the features of SharePoint Designer are disabled. SharePoint Designer offers its full capability for SharePoint sites. The SharePoint Designer features that rely on SharePoint aren't available for FPSE sites. Similarly, the features and components that rely on FPSE aren't available on FTP or WebDAV sites.

After you open a Web site in SharePoint Designer, you can use the Site Settings dialog box to determine the type of Web server that hosts the Web site. As with many other dialog boxes in SharePoint Designer, many of the options in this dialog box might be disabled depending on the Web site that you open. To open the Site Settings dialog box, as shown in Figure 1.4, choose Site ⇨ Site Settings.

Within the Site Settings dialog box are several tabs:

- **General:** This tab is used to display the version information about the Web server and version information about the FPSE or SharePoint installed on the Web server. You can use this tab to disable the use of hidden metadata for non-SharePoint and non-FPSE sites. Also, you can enable lightweight document check-in and check-out using this tab.
- **Preview:** You can use this tab to specify if you want to use the Microsoft ASP.NET Development Server to preview ASP.NET Web pages on your machine. SharePoint Designer installs the Microsoft ASP.NET Development Server during its setup. This option is useful if you don't have a Web server machine (ASP.NET pages need a Web server for processing) and would like to see a browser-based preview of the ASP.NET pages you create with SharePoint Designer.

CROSS-REF For more on ASP.NET, see Chapter 10.

- **Parameters:** Allows you to create FPSE-based parameters for your Web site. These parameters can be used later by FrontPage components, such as substitution components. This tab isn't useful for Web sites that don't allow hidden metadata.

- **Advanced:** Allows you to set the default validation script language for FrontPage validation components. Also, it provides a check box to show hidden files and folders (certain metadata files) inside the Web site. Also, this tab isn't useful for Web sites that have hidden metadata disabled.

- **Language:** Allows you to set the default page encoding for the Web site. For Web sites with hidden metadata, this tab allows you to set the language of the server messages.

- **Navigation:** Allows you to customize the text labels on FrontPage link bar components. This tab isn't available for Web sites with disabled hidden metadata.

CROSS-REF For more on FrontPage components, see Chapter 9.

- **Database:** This tab is for backward-compatibility with Web sites that have Database Results Wizard pages in them.

FIGURE 1.4

The Site Settings dialog box

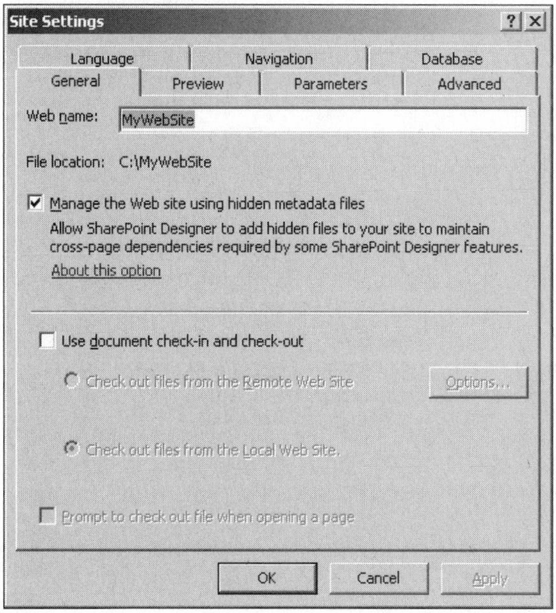

Maintaining Web Sites

After you create a Web site, you likely want to manage it properly so that you don't lose the work you've completed and don't have to re-create anything. However, Web site maintenance isn't just about backing up and publishing content. You also have to decide which content to publish, which Web pages to keep, and which version of files to delete.

SharePoint Designer offers a number of options for Web site maintenance. Depending on the type of Web site that you're working on, you have a set of tools available in SharePoint Designer to perform housekeeping and Web site management.

Understanding basic site management for non-SharePoint sites

The first operation that you need to perform when your Web site is ready is to publish it to a remote Web server by using an Internet address (URL) that your hosting provider or Web site administrator grants for your Web site. Publishing is the process of making the Web site content available for viewing by others. SharePoint Designer allows you to publish content from one Web server to another, from a disk-based location on the local computer to a Web server, or from a Web server–based location to a folder on your local computer (called reverse publishing).

CROSS-REF For more on managing non-SharePoint sites, see Chapter 23.

Publishing

SharePoint Designer offers an easy-to-use, intuitive mechanism for publishing content from one location to another. You can access the SharePoint Designer publishing interface by choosing File ⇨ Publish Site. The Remote Web Site Properties dialog box, as shown in Figure 1.5, opens in the foreground, and the Remote Publishing pane opens in the background of the SharePoint Designer environment.

The Web site that you have open in SharePoint Designer becomes the local Web site for publishing and is displayed in the Local Web Site section of the Remote Publishing pane. You then use the Remote Web Site Properties dialog box to specify the type of remote Web server, the location of the remote Web site, and the settings for the publishing operation.

After the remote Web site is set up, you can either publish from local to remote, publish from remote to local (reverse publishing), or synchronize the content of the two Web sites.

FIGURE 1.5

The Remote Web Site Properties dialog box

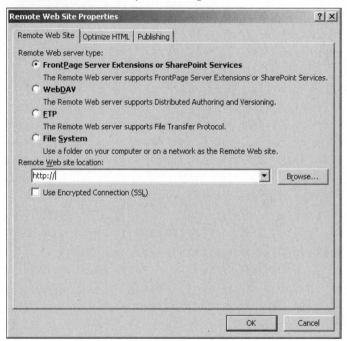

Import and export content

SharePoint Designer provides two mechanisms for importing and exporting content, which are available by choosing File ➪ Import or File ➪ Export:

- **Import Site Wizard:** Use this wizard to import content from a variety of locations. Choosing to use FPSE, WebDAV, or FTP as an import location in this wizard links you back to the Remote Publishing pane for SharePoint Designer. However, the HTTP option allows you to download Web pages and content from any HTTP location on the Internet.

- **Personal Web Packages:** This allows you to package a Web site into a compressed file (.fwp) that can then be exported into another site. While exporting and importing contents of a Web site, SharePoint Designer allows you to choose the content you want to compress in the package for exporting and then choose content you want to import.

Versioning

Depending on the nature of a Web site, the SharePoint Designer interface allows a designer to check-out a document so that it becomes locked — preventing others from working on the Web site — modify and update the document, and save and then check-in the document so that the updated document is available for other users.

Versioning and document check-in and check-out features in SharePoint Designer mostly rely on the Web server configuration and type. Although basic check-in and check-out are available for disk-based (using hidden metadata), FTP, and WebDAV sites, the advanced versioning features are provided by Web sites that use FPSE or SharePoint. For example, you can enable basic document check-in and check-out (if you have hidden metadata allowed) by clicking the Use document check-in and check-out check box in the General tab of the Site Settings dialog box.

Reporting

You use the Reports pane in SharePoint Designer to access many of the reports that it generates for Web sites. Choose Site ➪ Reports to open the Reports pane. Besides site and usage reporting, SharePoint Designer also offers these reporting features:

CROSS-REF   For more on the Reports pane, see Chapter 25.

- **CSS reports:** You can have SharePoint Designer generate reports that show details about unused styles, undefined classes, mismatched cases, and CSS usage while implementing CSS. These reports help in consolidating the style sheets being used inside the Web site more efficiently.

- **Accessibility reports:** Using the Accessibility Checker in SharePoint Designer, you can find out if your Web pages are compatible with the accessibility Web standards. You can use the report generated to correct issues and improve accessibility.

- **Compatibility reports:** You can use these reports to find out if your Web pages are compatible with the Web browser and CSS schema you're targeting your Web site for.

Authoring SharePoint sites

With SharePoint sites, although most site management operations are performed using the SharePoint administration Web sites and tools, limited backup and restore and import and export capabilities are offered by SharePoint Designer.

In the user interface, SharePoint Designer treats SharePoint sites almost like any other Web site. So, you can perform most authoring and site management operations on SharePoint sites in manners similar to non-SharePoint sites. However, SharePoint Designer provides a lot of new features in collaboration with SharePoint that make the authoring and management experience a lot more different and enriching.

Here's a brief introduction to some SharePoint-specific features of SharePoint Designer:

- **SharePoint content:** SharePoint Designer allows the creation of almost all SharePoint content, including sites and subsites, page layouts and master pages, lists and document libraries, and surveys. It also offers the Document Library View Page Wizard and List View Page Wizard that assist in creating view pages for SharePoint document libraries and lists.

- **Workflows:** SharePoint Designer has an advanced Workflow Designer that can be used to create, compile, and deploy declarative workflows for SharePoint sites.

- **Data forms:** With SharePoint sites, SharePoint Designer enables a complete menu called Data View that offers capabilities to work with data sources provide by SharePoint. It offers the Data Form Web Part that can be used to create views and forms for SharePoint data sources.

- **Web parts and SharePoint controls:** SharePoint Designer allows for inserting and modifying properties of SharePoint Web parts and Web part zones. Also, it exposes a number of SharePoint controls as well as page and content fields that can be used on SharePoint Web pages.

- **Contributor settings:** These settings allow SharePoint administrators to enable or disable certain features and menu options in SharePoint Designer based on the permissions that a user has on a SharePoint Web site.

- **Back up and restore Web sites:** The publishing feature of SharePoint Designer isn't useable with SharePoint sites. Instead, you can use SharePoint Designer to package, back up, and restore SharePoint Web sites.

 **For more on authoring and site management, see Chapters 5, 12, and 21.**

Summary

In this chapter, you learned about the origins and birth of SharePoint Designer. You also learned about how to use SharePoint Designer to create basic Web pages and manage settings for Web sites. You learned how SharePoint Designer creates and manages hidden metadata for Web sites and whether to use raw Webs. You were also exposed to the remote-authoring abilities of SharePoint Designer as well as SharePoint and non-SharePoint authoring and site management features.

Chapter 2

Understanding Related Server Technologies

I n the previous chapter, you learned some basic concepts about creating simple Web pages and Web sites by using SharePoint Designer. This chapter focuses on server-related technologies because they form the foundation and support for the Web content and Web sites that you design in SharePoint Designer. Understanding these technologies is important, and this information helps you decide how best to exploit the features of SharePoint Designer, including which features to use and which ones to avoid. It also helps you understand the internals of Web site administration and management from the perspective of a Web server and helps you build some concepts around Web server management so that you can troubleshoot issues and problems when working with these technologies by using SharePoint Designer.

Simply put, a Web server is a machine that hosts Web sites. When you use a Web browser to visit a Web site, you're actually requesting some Web content from a Web server that hosts the Web site. It's the job of a Web server to serve requests for Web pages and other Web-based content in a timely, scalable, and performance-optimized fashion. The Web server processes the code associated with the Web pages and delivers the resulting output to a Web browser for display.

Besides processing Web pages for display, Web servers also support a variety of technologies that facilitate content management and publishing. Software such as SharePoint Designer relies on the capabilities of Web server computers to provide their publishing features to Web site developers.

Although a number of Web server products are available for you to choose from, I mostly concentrate on Microsoft's Internet Information Services (IIS) Web server. While SharePoint Designer can be used with Web sites hosted by other Web server products, IIS provides the complete package for

SharePoint Designer as a Web server. Apart from supporting development technologies such as ASP.NET 2.0 (which is heavily exposed in SharePoint Designer), IIS supports all Web content management and publishing technologies exploited by SharePoint Designer. These include FTP, WebDAV, FPSE, and SharePoint. As a matter of fact, SharePoint 3 can only be installed with IIS 6.0 and above as the Web server platform.

Exploring the Basics of Internet Information Services

Internet Information Services (IIS) is Microsoft's premier Web server offering. As a product, it's available with almost all professional and enterprise versions of Microsoft's Windows operating system (OS). Table 2.1 lists the versions of IIS available with the various Windows OS versions.

TABLE 2.1

Versions of IIS Available with Different Windows Versions

Windows (OS) Version	Available IIS Version
Windows 2000	IIS 5.0
Windows XP Professional Edition	IIS 5.1
Windows Server 2003 Family (Windows 2003 Web, Standard, Datacenter, and Enterprise editions)	IIS 6.0 (which can also be run in IIS 5.0 isolation mode)
Windows Vista and Windows Server 2008	IIS 7.0

Throughout this section, I discuss the concepts, settings, and configuration of IIS 6.0. Although at the time of this writing IIS 7.0 was available for use as a Web server, it was not heavily deployed, and most organizations were still developing strategies for possible upgrades and migration. I use IIS 6.0 as the Web server platform for this book simply because of its wide acceptance, its success, and its ability to host SharePoint environments. Also, while I discuss the most important concepts for IIS 6.0 (which help you understand SharePoint Designer components and features better), a detailed discussion of IIS 6.0 architecture and functionality is beyond the scope of this text.

The IIS 6.0 release for the Windows 2003 server family of operating systems is by far the most reliable, scalable, and secure version of IIS. It provides unparallel reliability and uptime to Web applications (and Web sites) through its application isolation environment, which allows Web applications to run in their own process space without interfering with each other. It includes a number of security features that ensure the protection and integrity of Web content and data presented by your Web sites. Also, it offers support for the latest Web standards, including HTTP 1.1, TCP/IP, FTP, SMTP, NNTP, and WebDAV.

Understanding basic concepts

The first question that might come to the mind of a Web site designer when discussing IIS is how to configure Web sites for use with SharePoint Designer. However, hold on to this feeling while I talk about some basic IIS concepts. I can assure you that once these concepts are clear, you should feel more comfortable working with the IIS interface. Obviously, you would want to know what an application pool is before you go ahead and create one.

Web site identification

As discussed later in this chapter, IIS can host multiple Web sites on a single Web server computer. Although that sounds fairly simple, identifying these multiple Web sites on a single computer as separate when viewed from the Internet involves some work on the part of site administrators.

To distinguish among multiple Web sites on a single computer and ensure that user requests for a Web site can be served from the correct physical location, IIS provides the identification options shown in Figure 2.1:

- **Multiple IP addresses:** An IP address identifies a computer on a given network. If your Web server computer is configured for multiple IP addresses, you can set up Web sites using these multiple addresses. However, this approach requires that you have one unique, static IP address for each Web site hosted on the Web server. Because public static IP addresses are difficult to obtain, this approach might not necessarily be your one solution for identifying multiple Web sites on a single server. You can open a Web site configured with an IP address in SharePoint Designer by using the site name `http://serveripaddress` — for example, `http://192.164.52.16`.

- **Multiple ports:** The standard port for Web-based HTTP operations is port 80. If a port is not specified manually, it's assumed that port 80 should be used. However, there are a number of TCP/IP ports that can be specified for Web site identification. For example, you can have three Web sites use a single IP address but three different ports. The downside of using this approach is that the Web site user needs to denote the IP address (or the name of the server) followed by the port number to reach the Web site. To open a Web site configured with a TCP port in SharePoint Designer, use the format `http://serverip address:portnumber` — for example, `http://192.164.52.16:8000` — for the site name.

- **Multiple host headers names:** This is the most recommended approach and is commonly followed by Internet-facing Web server machines. The host header is a friendly name (such as `www.wiley.com`) that can be associated with a Web site. Each Web site on the Web server can have a set of host headers associated with it that helps IIS identify the Web site when user requests are made. If your Web site is configured with a host header, you can open it in SharePoint Designer by using the site name format `http://hostheader` — for example, `http://www.wiley.com`.

This *signature*, or identification, of a Web site — which includes the combination of an IP address, a port, and a host header — is called the Web site's server binding and is stored in the IIS configuration file (called the *metabase file*).

FIGURE 2.1

These dialog boxes offer advanced Web site identification features.

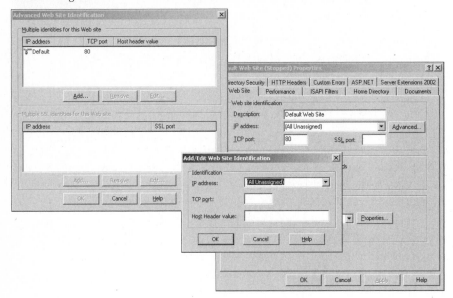

Later in this chapter, I take you through the steps for configuring multiple Web sites on a single Web server machine. As a matter of fact, you use this approach to set up four separate Web sites with FTP, WebDAV, FPSE, and SharePoint and then later use them to understand related SharePoint Designer features.

Authentication and authorization

When you open a protected Web site in SharePoint Designer, you're prompted for a username and password, which are used by the Web server to identify you and then determine the operations that you can perform. The process of identifying a user before granting access to a resource is called authentication. Authorization, on the other hand, is the process of determining the level of access an authenticated user has. IIS offers these authentication mechanisms, as shown in Figure 2.2:

- **Anonymous authentication:** Allows IIS to determine the kind of access for users who aren't known, such as those who don't have a username or password that can be used for authentication. If anonymous access is allowed, IIS uses the built-in IUSER_ Machinename account (set up during the IIS installation process) for authentication.

- **Windows integrated authentication:** This is the most secure form of authentication because users must use their Windows accounts to identify themselves with IIS 6.0. This form of authentication is point to point; that is, the user credentials can't be passed on from one machine to another. For example, once the Web server identifies the user with a username and password, it can't *double-hop*, which is using the credentials to connect to a different resource or computer on the network. Due to this, Windows integrated authentication is not suitable for Internet use, where the request might have to hop from one machine to another before reaching a Web server.

NOTE A type of integrated authentication called Kerberos authentication can be set up to bypass this double-hop issue.

- **Basic authentication:** As the name suggests, this is the most basic form of authentication, where the username and password are sent as clear text and are easily susceptible to security breaches and attacks. However, it's the most simple to set up and maintain and is the most common form of authentication used on the Internet. To increase protection, basic authentication is always used on a Secured Socket Layer (SSL) encryption channel.

- **Digest authentication:** This offers functionality similar to basic authentication but increases security by providing better encryption of the user credentials across the network.

- **Passport authentication:** This provides a .NET-based single sign-in service, where users have to type their credentials only once and then gain access to all Web sites and related resources.

FIGURE 2.2

Authentication mechanisms in IIS

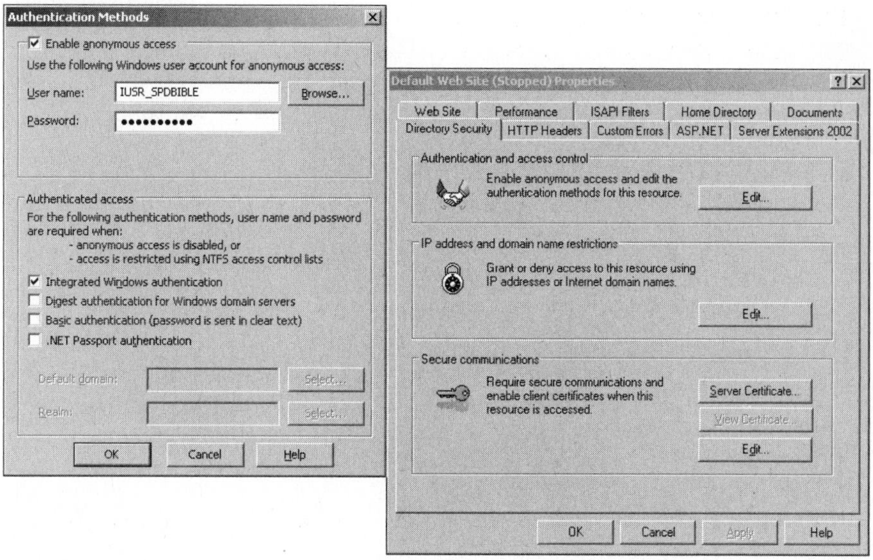

While authentication is mostly provided to Web sites and Web applications by IIS 6.0, authorization can be either done manually or, as in the case of FPSE and SharePoint, by using a custom application. The most basic authorization involves adding (or removing) users and granting (or denying) them access by using the Security tab inside the folder's Properties dialog box in Windows Explorer, as shown in Figure 2.3.

Application isolation and protection

In previous IIS versions, Web sites and Web applications were loosely packed; that is, Web applications could interfere with each other, and faulty code running in one Web application could bring down other Web applications running along with it or, in worst cases, IIS itself. IIS 6.0 introduced the concept of application isolation (worker process isolation mode) and allows Web site developers and administrators to separate Web sites and applications into application pools.

Worker process isolation mode ensures the protection and separation of the IIS base processes (such as `inteinfo.exe`) from the Web application processes. All Web sites and Web applications run inside separate worker processes (`w3wp.exe`) that can't interfere with the root functionality of IIS. So, if a Web application crashes or hangs because of faulty code, only the worker process associated with the Web application is affected, and other processes can still run and serve requests without problems.

FIGURE 2.3

The Security tab in the MyWebSite Properties dialog box

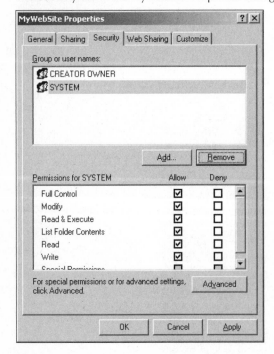

You implement application protection by creating application pools and associating Web applications with application pools. (You can have an application pool that hosts one or more Web sites.) All the Web sites associated with an application pool run in a single worker process (or in multiple worker processes, in the case of Web gardening). If the application pool stops or becomes unhealthy, only Web sites associated with that particular application pool are affected.

For example, you can define the properties of the MSSharePointAppPool application pool by using the MSSharePointAppPool Properties dialog box, as shown in Figure 2.4. Using this dialog box, you can set up the recycling, performance, and health settings of the application pool. You can also define the credentials under which the worker process associated with the application pool run.

> **NOTE** IIS 5.0 isolation mode is a mechanism offered by IIS 6.0 to emulate IIS 5.0 behavior and operational architecture. SharePoint doesn't support IIS 6.0 running in IIS 5.0 isolation mode (provided in IIS 6.0 for backward-compatibility) and can only work with IIS 6.0 configured in the worker process isolation mode.

One more level of protection that's available to you for Web sites is to control the execute permissions for Web site content. These options are available under the Home Directory tab in the Web Site Properties dialog box, as shown in Figure 2.5:

- **None:** No Scripts (ASP, ASP.NET, etc.) or executables (`.exe`, `.dll`, etc.) can be run.
- **Scripts Only:** Only scripts can be run.
- **Scripts and Executables:** Both scripts and executables can be run.

FIGURE 2.4

The Recycling settings options in the MSSharePointAppPool Properties dialog box

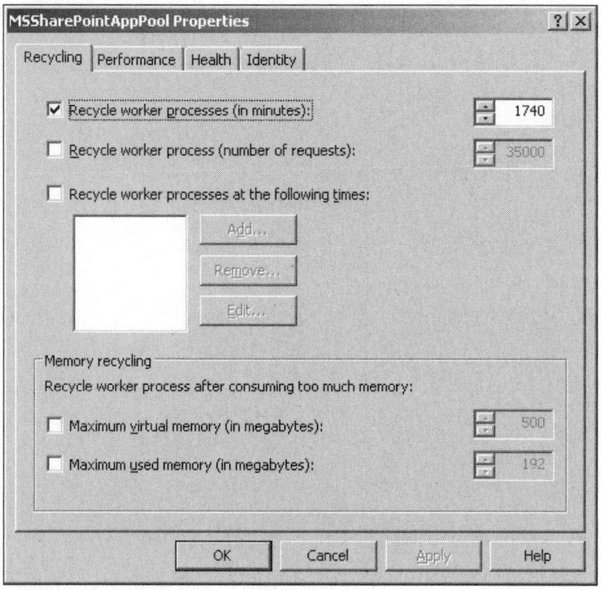

You use the execute permissions to determine the level of code execution that can be performed on a Web site. These options provide an added level of security for Web sites so that unwanted content can't run on the Web sites without proper configuration.

Web Service extensions

One more level of protection that IIS 6.0 offers is that it provides an interface to easily allow or prohibit any known or unknown Web Service extension. Web Service Extensions is a generic name for all Common Graphical Interface (CGI) and Internet Server Application Programming Interface (ISAPI) applications that can be installed and configured on IIS. Common ISAPI applications are ASP.NET, FPSE, and SharePoint. As shown in Figure 2.6, you can easily allow or prohibit Web Service extensions by using the IIS 6.0 interface.

IIS 6.0 follows the locked-down configuration so that all ISAPI extensions must be manually enabled before using them. Extensions such as WebDAV are disabled at the server level by default, and you have to manually enable them by using the Web Service Extensions interface before they can be used.

FIGURE 2.5

The Default Web Site (Stopped) Properties dialog box

FIGURE 2.6

The Web Service Extensions Properties dialog box

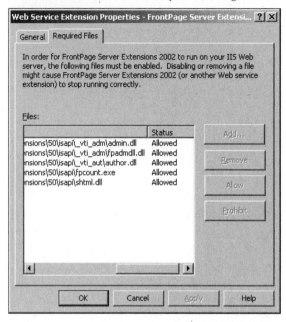

Installing and configuring IIS

You can install IIS 6.0 on a Windows 2003 server using the following steps. While you're installing IIS 6.0, these steps also guide you to install the FTP service and FPSE 2002 on the machine:

> **NOTE** You might be requested to provide the Windows 2003 or Windows 2003 Service Pack (SP) 1 installation media during the installation of IIS 6.0.

1. **Choose Start ➪ Control Panel ➪ Add or Remove Programs and then click Add/Remove Windows Components.** The Windows Components Wizard opens. Use this wizard to install IIS with the FTP service and FPSE 2002.

2. **Choose Application Server from the list of components and then click Details.** The Application Server dialog box opens.

3. **Along with the options selected by default, ensure that the ASP.NET check box is selected.**

4. **Click Internet Information Services (IIS) and then click Details.** The Internet Information Services (IIS) dialog box, as shown in Figure 2.7, opens.

5. Select the File Transfer Protocol (FTP) service and FrontPage 2002 Server Extensions check boxes, including the options selected by default, and then click OK twice to return to the Windows Components Wizard.

6. Click Next to allow the wizard to install the requested components.

FIGURE 2.7

The Internet Information Services dialog box

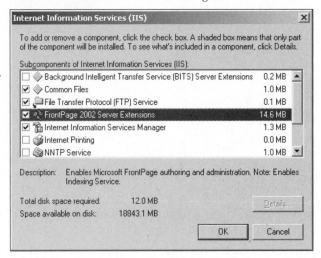

After the setup is complete, the new Internet Information Services (IIS) Manager shortcut appears inside Start ⇨ Administrative Tools. The IIS administrative interface, as shown in Figure 2.8, is called the Internet Information Services (IIS) Manager and is a snap-in added to the Microsoft Management Console (MMC). You can also access the IIS Manager by typing **inetmgr** in the Start ⇨ Run dialog box. The console provides the interface to change Web server settings for IIS, create and manage Web sites and virtual directories, set up application pools, and perform other management operations for the Web server.

Although the IIS Manager can be used to connect to the IIS Web Service running on any computer (right-click on Internet Information Services in the left pane and then choose Connect from the popup menu), it connects to the IIS Web Service running on your local computer by default. So, when you open the IIS Manager on your Web server, it displays the list of application pools and Web sites hosted by the local Web server in a treeview under the machine name.

FIGURE 2.8

The Internet Information Services (IIS) Manager

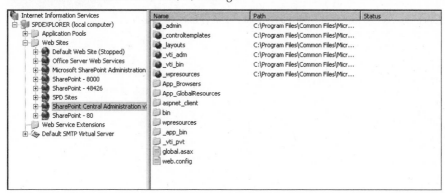

You can enable the Web Service Extensions that you want to use on the Web server by clicking on the `Web Service Extensions` folder in the left pane of the IIS Manager. Right-clicking on the extension opens a popup menu that allows you to enable/disable the extension.

CAUTION The All Unknown CGI Extensions and All Unknown ISAPI Extensions are prohibited for increasing the security and excluding unknown extensions from being run on the Web server. You shouldn't unnecessarily allow them. Instead, selectively allow the extensions you want to use.

The master properties that affect all new Web sites and application pools for the Web sites (and application pools) can be set by right-clicking on the `Web Sites` (and `Application Pools`) folder in the left pane of the IIS Manager and then choosing Properties from the popup menu. When you create a new Web site (or an application pool), these properties are copied to form the properties of the newly created Web site (or application pool).

Setting up Web sites

To create a new Web site by using the IIS Manager, follow these steps:

1. **Right-click on the** `Web Sites` **folder and then choose New ⇨ Web Site from the popup menu.** The Web Site Creation Wizard, as shown in Figure 2.9, opens.

2. **Click Next to start the wizard.**

3. **Type a name for your Web site in the Description text field in the Web Site Description window and then click Next.**

FIGURE 2.9

The Web Site Creation Wizard dialog box

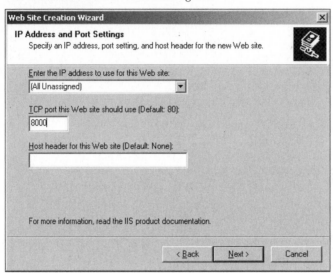

4. **In the IP Address and Port Settings window, specify the IP address, port, or host header that you want to use to identify the Web site.** For example, for this exercise, set the IP address to All Unassigned, change the port to 8000, and leave the host header blank. This makes the server binding so that the Web site is accessible by using the address `http://servername:8000`.

5. **Click Next.**

6. **In the Web Site Home Directory window, specify the folder that you want to set as the root folder for the Web site.** You can use the Browse button to either choose the location or create a new folder at the location of your choice. Keep the Allow anonymous access to this Web site check box selected if you want to allow anonymous access to Web sites.

7. **Using the Web Site Access Permissions window, you can set the execute permissions for the Web site.** For this exercise, click the Read and Run Scripts (such as ASP) check boxes.

8. **Click Next and then click Finish to complete the creation of your Web site.**

If your Web site's server binding already exists — that is, if another Web site uses the IP address, port, and host header combination you specified for your Web site — you receive a message indicating that a Web site already exists. Although the Web site is created in such a case, it can't be started until the server binding is unique.

By default, the new Web site inherits the master properties configured for new Web sites by using the IIS Manager. If you use the default master properties for Web sites, the new Web site is configured to use the DefaultAppPool application pool (created by default during initial IIS configuration). To create a new application pool and associate your Web site with the new application pool, follow these steps:

1. **Right-click on the `Application Pools` folder in the left page in IIS Manager and then choose New ⇨ Application Pool from the popup menu.** The Add New Application Pool dialog box, as shown in Figure 2.10, opens.

FIGURE 2.10
_____

The Add New Application Pool dialog box

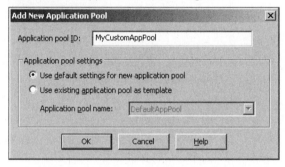

2. **Using the Application Pool ID text field, type a name for the application pool.** Using the application pool settings, you can choose whether to use the master application pool settings or use settings of an existing application pool for new application pool creation.

3. **Click OK.** The new application pool appears in the list of application pools under the `Application Pools` folder. Click the new application pool, and the right pane in the IIS Manager is empty. This indicates that the application pool doesn't yet have a Web site associated with it.

4. **Right-click on the Web site you just created in the previous steps and then choose Properties from the popup menu.** The Properties dialog box for the new Web site opens.

5. **Click the Home Directory tab.** In the Application Settings, click the Application pool dropdown menu and then click the newly created application pool.

6. **Click Apply and then click OK.**

The newly created Web site appears in the right pane of the IIS Manager when you click the newly created application pool. This list always shows all the Web sites that use the application pool. If you right-click on the application pool on the left pane in the IIS Manager, you can start, stop, or recycle the application pool. Recycling the application pool is a process where the application pool is restarted without actually causing the associated Web applications to stop working. IIS does this by creating a new worker process for the application pool before terminating the existing one. After the new worker process is created, all user requests are redirected to the new worker process, and the old one is then terminated. This configuration helps in increasing the uptime for the Web sites while the application pools remain healthy and badly used resources recovered.

You can specify recycling settings for an application pool by right-clicking on it and then choosing Properties from the popup menu. The Properties dialog box allows you to perform these operations:

- **Recycling:** Provides the settings for configuring the recycling of worker processes associated with the application pool
- **Performance:** Offers the settings to enable CPU monitoring and Web gardening
- **Health:** Allows you to configure settings for rapid-fail protection for application pools. Rapid-fail protection facilitates that the application pool can be disabled after it fails for a particular number of times.
- **Identity:** Allows you to set up the user account that the worker process associated with the application pool runs under

If you need to change the properties of a Web site itself, you can do so by using the Web Site Properties dialog box (which you can open by right-clicking on the Web site and then choosing Properties from the popup menu). Using the Web Site Properties dialog box, you can change these settings:

- **Web Site:** Offers an interface to change the Web site's server binding and enable IIS logging for the Web site
- **Performance:** Allows you to set bandwidth throttling and change the number of allowed Web site connections
- **ISAPI Filters:** Shows (and allows addition/removal of) the ISAPI filters that are active for the Web site
- **Home Directory:** Allows you to change the Web site root folder location, set general application settings, change application pools association, and set execute permissions for the Web site
- **Documents:** Allows you to set a list of default documents for a Web site. If it exists in the site content location, the top document in this list becomes the home page of the Web site.
- **Directory Security:** Allows you to change the authentication mechanisms that the Web site uses, configure restrictions, and set up SSL
- **HTTP Headers:** Lists the custom HTTP headers and provides settings for content expiration, rating, and MIME types

- **Custom Errors:** Lists the default error messages that IIS shows when an issue occurs while accessing a Web site. You can use this tab to change the default Web pages associated with the various IIS error codes.

- **ASP.NET:** Allows you to set the version of ASP.NET to be used for the Web site

- **Server Extensions 2002:** If the Web server is configured with FPSE 2002, this tab provides the mechanism to open the administration Web pages for configuring FPSE settings related to the Web site.

Although you just created a Web site by using the IIS Manager, the Web site still isn't completely ready for SharePoint Designer because this Web site doesn't have a publishing or remote authoring mechanism set up for it. You can't yet open or publish this site in SharePoint Designer with an Internet-based HTTP address.

The best you can do as far as pushing Web content into this Web site is to copy the Web pages and files you created with SharePoint Designer from your local root folder to the root folder of this Web site. However, this isn't a recommended method, especially when you're using FPSE features, and it's not applicable for SharePoint sites.

Investigating the Nature of FTP and WebDAV Sites

File Transfer Protocol (FTP) is one of the most commonly used mechanisms for transferring Web content from a machine where it's developed (for example, a SharePoint Designer client machine) to a location on the Web server. In a common scenario, an administrator might create an FTP site whose content location is the same as a normal HTTP site. An author would then publish the content by using FTP as a communication mechanism between the client software (such as SharePoint Designer) and the Web server (such as IIS). Although using the FTP approach might have some security issues, it's a very simple and standard way to move content to the Web server.

You have to install the FTP service by using the Add/Remove Programs function prior to creating FTP Web sites in IIS. To set up an FTP site in IIS, follow these steps:

1. **Open the IIS Manager by choosing Start ⇨ Administrative Tools.** If you have the FTP service installed, an `FTP Sites` folder appears in the left pane in the Microsoft Management Console.

2. **Right-click on the `FTP Sites` folder and then choose New ⇨ FTP Site from the popup menu.** The FTP Site Creation Wizard, as shown in Figure 2.11, opens.

FIGURE 2.11

The FTP Site Creation Wizard

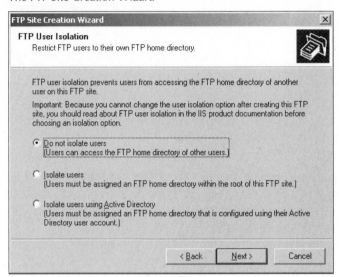

3. Click Next and then type the description for your FTP site in the Description text field.

4. Click Next.

5. **On the next screen, specify the IP address and port for use by the FTP site.** When you installed the FTP service, a default FTP site was created for you and uses port 21. If you want to create a new FTP site, you can either specify a different IP address or a different port.

6. Click Next.

7. **In the FTP User Isolation window, click Isolate users and then click Next.** FTP User Isolation Settings provides you with a mechanism that can be used to isolate FTP directories based on users. The Isolate Users option ensures that users can't view directories that they don't have permissions to see and are directly taken to their folders and files within the FTP site.

8. **Specify the root folder location of your FTP site and then click Next.**

9. **In the FTP Access Permissions screen, keep the Read check box selected and then click Next.** You can change these settings later by using the Home Directory tab in the FTP Site Properties dialog box.

10. Click Next and then click Finish.

CAUTION   The FTP site you created stops if the IP address and port (server binding) being used by the site is already being used by another site. You must change these settings to be unique before you can use the FTP site.

You can now create directories within the root content location of this Web site for various users and set up permissions using the Security tab in the Folder Properties dialog box so that users are directed only to the folders where they have permissions. Once the FTP site is set up, you can use the Current Sessions button in the FTP Site tab of the site properties to determine the users that are connected to your FTP site.

While FTP is a simple way to transfer files to a Web server, it has a number of security and management issues. IIS also supports another Web standard for remote authoring called WebDAV. WebDAV adds on to the HTTP protocol (the main Internet communication protocol) and provides features that allow client programs to list files and directories on a Web server, add and delete files from a Web server, check-in or check-out files, etc. So, once a Web site is configured for WebDAV, you can access it in a Windows Explorer–like view in a client program, such as Internet Explorer, Firefox, Opera, etc. By default, in IIS 6.0, WebDAV is prohibited. So, in order to enable it for use on an HTTP site, you have to follow these steps:

1. **Open the IIS Manager and then click the** Web Service Extensions **folder in the left pane, as shown in Figure 2.12.** By default, WebDAV is prohibited.

FIGURE 2.12

The Web Service Extension folder and its contents

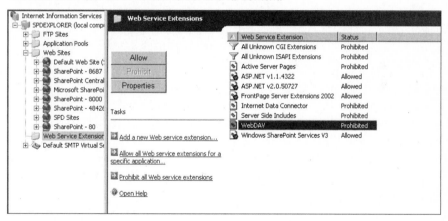

2. **Click WebDAV and then click Allow.**

3. **In the left pane in the IIS Manager, right-click on the Web site (or a folder inside the Web site) that you want to configure for use as a WebDAV site and then choose Properties from the popup menu.**

4. **Click the Home Directory tab and then click the Write and Directory Browsing check boxes.**

This is all you need to do to enable WebDAV on an IIS Web site (or folder). Based on the permissions that you set on the Web site folders, users should be able to access and modify the site contents in a folder-like view in a Web browser or SharePoint Designer.

Working with FPSE-Based Web Sites

FrontPage Server Extensions (FPSE) is one of the oldest publishing and remote-authoring mechanisms offered for Web sites developed using FrontPage and Visual Studio. The current Microsoft-supported versions of FPSE are:

- FPSE 2000, available as an IIS 5.1 component with Windows XP
- FPSE 2002, available as an IIS 6.0 component with Windows 2003

NOTE   There's also a version of FPSE 2002 for IIS 7.0 on Windows Vista machines supported by RTR (Ready-to-Run) that's available for download at www.rtr.com.

In cases of both Windows XP and Windows 2003, FPSE can be installed from the Add/Remove Windows Components section in the Add or Remove Programs dialog box. As discussed earlier, you can elect to install FPSE binaries and files as components while installing IIS on the machine.

Understanding FPSE

FPSE is an ISAPI-based authoring and publishing mechanism that provides the backbone for Web-based clients (such as FrontPage, Expression Web, and SharePoint Designer) to open content from remote Web sites for authoring and publishing content from one location to another. Besides remote authoring and publishing, FPSE also enables features such as version control, permissions management, etc., and provides support for a variety of Web components (such as Web search, form-based components, hit counters, etc.) available in FrontPage and inherited by Expression Web and SharePoint Designer.

IIS 6.0 supports the most updated and robust version of FPSE (FPSE 2002), which provides a Web-based site management and administration console. After you choose and install FPSE 2002 as a component with IIS 6.0, a Web site called Microsoft SharePoint Administration is created for you and is used to administer FPSE 2002 Web sites on the Web server.

NOTE   Don't be confused by the naming of Microsoft SharePoint Administration for this Web site. It's so called because if SharePoint Team Services (STS) is installed on the machine, this Web site provides an interface for the administration of STS Web sites along with serving as an administration tool for FPSE 2002 Web sites.

If you open the properties of this Web site using the IIS Manager, the important thing to notice (in the Home Directory tab) is that this Web site uses `C:\Program Files\Common Files\ Microsoft Shared\Web Server Extensions\50\ISAPI\_VTI_ADM` as the root folder. All the FPSE 2002 binaries and support files are stored at `C:\Program Files\Common Files\ Microsoft Shared\Web Server Extensions\50`.

Also, it has the execute permissions set to Scripts and Executables (allowing for the execution of `.dll` and `.exe`) and uses a new application pool called MSSharePointAppPool. This application pool is also created when FPSE 2002 is installed on a machine.

Before you can use FPSE 2002 on your Web sites, you must ensure that it's enabled as a Web Service extension in IIS. You can do this by using the Web Service Extensions pane in the IIS Manager. If the status of FPSE 2002 shows as being prohibited, simply right-click on it and then choose Allow from the popup menu to enable it for use.

Extending and configuring Web sites

To perform many of the FPSE 2002 configuration and management operations, you must be an administrator on the Web server machine. You use the Microsoft SharePoint Administration Web site for configuring Web sites in IIS with FPSE 2002. The main Web page of the Microsoft SharePoint Administration Web site, as shown in Figure 2.13, shows the list of Web sites and indicates whether they're configured with FPSE 2002.

FIGURE 2.13

The Microsoft SharePoint Administration home page

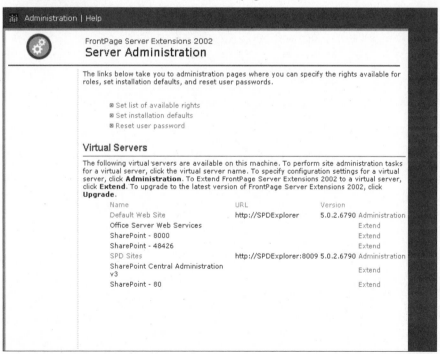

The process of configuring FPSE 2002 on a Web site is called extending a Web site. To extend a Web site with FPSE 2002, follow these steps:

1. **Using the IIS Manager, create a new Web site.** Ensure that the root folder for the Web site is empty. While creating a root folder for an FPSE 2002–based Web site, keep in mind that FPSE 2002 itself manages permissions for users and groups. It's best that you use the FPSE 2002 administration Web site to add or remove users and groups rather than directly managing them by using Windows Explorer (via the Security tab). To start with, when you create the root folder, ensure that the folder doesn't inherit permissions from its parent folder, and set Administrators and System accounts to have full control.

2. **In the IIS Manager, right-click on the Web site and then choose All Tasks⇨ Configure Server Extensions 2002 from the popup menu.** This takes you to the Extend virtual server with the FPSE 2002 Web page inside the Microsoft SharePoint Administration Web site. You can also reach this page by clicking the Extend link next to the Web site on the home page of the Microsoft SharePoint Administration Web site.

NOTE The Configure Server Extensions 2002 option isn't enabled if you already have the Web site extended with FPSE 2002 or if the root folder of the Web site contains hidden metadata.

3. **Ensure that the Administrator user name is correct and then click Submit.** This begins the process of extending the Web site, and once complete, you return to the home page of the Microsoft SharePoint Administration Web site. The URL and Version columns are updated with the URL of the Web site and the version of FPSE 2002 on the Web site. Also, the Extend link has now changed to Administration.

If you go to the root folder of the Web site (by right-clicking on it in the IIS Manager and then choosing Open from the popup menu) after it has been extended with FPSE 2002, a number of _vti folders now exist inside the Web site. These folders contain files that store the hidden metadata necessary for operating FPSE 2002.

CAUTION These folders are important for the proper operation of FPSE 2002 on the Web site. Deleting any of these folders can result in the corruption of FPSE 2002.

Also, if you expand the Web site in the IIS Manager, the _vti_bin virtual directory appears, with the root folder at C:\Program Files\Common Files\Microsoft Shared\Web Server Extensions\50\ISAPI. This virtual directory contains the binary files that enable the remote authoring and publishing features of FPSE 2002 on the Web site. It exists in every site or subsite (also called subweb) that's configured to be an FPSE 2002 Web site.

NOTE A virtual directory is a virtual folder inside a Web site, the content of which doesn't reside inside the root folder of the Web site. You use virtual directories to share files and folders across multiple Web sites.

By default, the virtual directory uses the same application pool as the Microsoft SharePoint Administration Web site (MSSharePointAppPool) and has the execute permissions set to Scripts and Executables. If this virtual directory is missing or isn't set up properly, FPSE 2002 authoring and publishing features can't work.

Now that you have FPSE 2002 set up for your Web site, you can use SharePoint Designer to open the Web site for live editing of Web pages and other files, use FPSE 2002–based Web components, and publish content to and from the Web site. To open your FPSE 2002–based Web site in SharePoint Designer, simply choose File⇨Open Site and then type the URL of the Web site in the site name text field. Your best bet for the Web site's correct URL would be the URL indicated in the URL column for the Web site in the home page of the Microsoft SharePoint Administration Web site.

Managing and administrating sites

After you extend your Web site with FPSE 2002, you need to set some configuration settings to provide functionality to Web components that you insert on pages by using SharePoint Designer. Most of these configuration settings can be done using the Microsoft SharePoint Administration Web site, although FPSE 2002 offers a command-line tool called owsadm.exe — mostly used for performing bulk operations on a number of Web sites using batch files — to perform these operations.

Change configuration settings

Some configuration settings for FPSE 2002 that you make using the Microsoft SharePoint Administration Web site apply to all the Web sites that are extended with FPSE 2002 on the Web server. These settings include the list of available rights and installation defaults for FPSE 2002 and are available at the home page of the Microsoft SharePoint Administration Web site.

Besides these, several settings apply specifically to Web sites. You can access these by clicking on the Administration link next to the Web site in the home page of the Microsoft SharePoint Administration Web site. Using the Virtual Server Administration page, you can perform these operations:

- **Visit the Web site–specific administration pages:** Using these administration pages, you can add or remove users and roles, perform server health checks, and create subwebs.

- **Uninstall FPSE 2002:** You can choose to either completely remove FPSE 2002 or just remove the binaries from the Web site. As indicated in the description text, a full uninstall removes all virtual directories, subweb information, hidden metadata files, and folders.

- **Upgrade the virtual server with FPSE 2002:** This allows you to perform an upgrade of the hidden metadata of the Web site in case an update or service pack updates the FPSE 2002 binaries.

- **Change the configuration settings:** As shown in Figure 2.14, these settings allow you to set up the SMTP mail server settings for use by the FrontPage form components, enable or disable authoring, log authoring actions, etc.

- **Configure user accounts limits:** This allows you to set a limit to the number of users that can be created via the FPSE 2002 user management console.

FIGURE 2.14

The Change Configuration Settings Web page

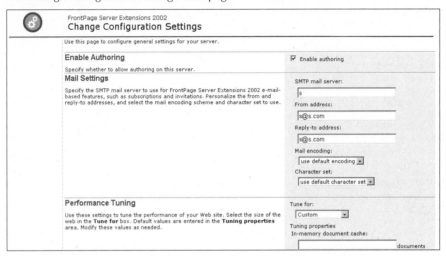

Adding users and roles

FPSE 2002 allows you to add or remove users and groups by using the Microsoft SharePoint Administration Web site and manages the actual New Technology File System (NTFS) (folder and file level) security and permissions for the users and groups itself.

It does so by managing roles for users and groups. A role is a list of rights and privileges that are given to the members of the role. For example, the Administrator role has a list of rights that allow its members to view, add, and change all server content and manage server settings and accounts.

Using the Manage Roles Web page, as shown in Figure 2.15, you can view the roles available by default and add/remove roles.

FIGURE 2.15

The Manage Roles Web page

To access the Manage Roles administration Web page, click the link that's the name of the Web site in the Microsoft SharePoint Administration Web site home page. This takes you directly to the site-specific administration pages, where you can use the Manage Roles link in the Users and Roles section.

After the roles are created, you can add users and groups to these roles by using the Manage Users Web page accessible from the Users and Roles section.

NOTE When you add a user (or group) to a specific role by using the FPSE 2002 administration Web site, FPSE 2002 in the background creates a local security group (with the prefix ows_) and adds the user (or group) to the local group. FPSE 2002 then adds this local group with appropriate permissions to the NTFS Access Control Lists (ACL) of the Web site folders.

FPSE 2002 stores the roles and permissions associated with the roles in files called roles.ini at C:\Documents and Settings\All Users\Application Data\Microsoft\Web Server Extensions\50. These files are used to reapply the security settings to FPSE 2002 Web sites in operations such as checking a server's health.

Checking a server's health

The Check Server Health Web page, as shown in Figure 2.16, is a single operation that can be used on FPSE 2002 Web sites to detect and repair problems with security; reapply security settings stored in roles.ini files; and check, verify, and repair FPSE 2002 on subsites inside a Web site. It can also be used to re-create any missing _vti_bin directories, provided that the hidden metadata for the Web site is intact.

CAUTION It's important to understand that the Check Server Health operation removes all existing NTFS security on the Web site's folders and files and reapplies the security settings stored in the roles.ini files. So, if you've added any users (or groups) directly to the NTFS security by using Windows Explorer (or other means), these permissions are lost. Therefore, it's recommended that you perform all security operations on FPSE 2002 Web sites by using the Microsoft SharePoint Administration Web site so that they're saved in the roles.ini files for repair.

FIGURE 2.16

The Check Server Health Web page

FrontPage Server Extensions 2002 - Site Administration for "http://spdexplorer:8009"
Check Server Health

Use this page to detect and repair potential problems on your Web server.

Detect and Repair

Choose which areas of server health to detect possible problems in, and whether to repair any problems found.

Select the actions to perform:

	Detect	Repair
Reapply file security settings		☐ Repair
Verify existence of webs	☑ Detect	☐ Repair
Check roles configuration	☑ Detect	☐ Repair
Tighten security	☑ Detect	☐ Repair
Check anonymous access	☑ Detect	

OK   Cancel

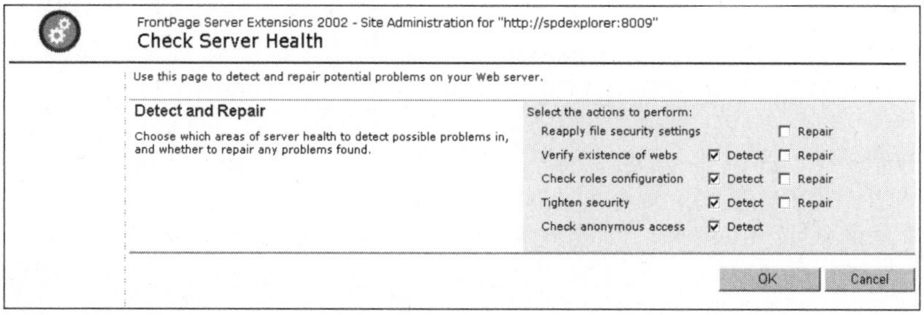

Introducing WSS and MOSS Technologies

The current version of SharePoint (including WSS v3 and MOSS) is the third generation of office document management, collaboration, and publishing products offered by Microsoft. As discussed earlier, this lineage started with SharePoint Team Services (supported by FPSE 2002) offered with Office XP and has now grown into a robust, scalable, and extendable platform for Web-based application development for intranet, extranet, and Internet scenarios.

Out-of-the-box installation of SharePoint provides for a large number of features that can be configured and used just as they are or exploited by application developers for custom implementation and business logic architecture.

Comparing WSS and MOSS offerings

When choosing between WSS and MOSS, know that WSS is freely downloadable on Microsoft's Web site (www.microsoft.com/downloads). MOSS relies on the infrastructure that WSS provides for SharePoint sites, so that when you install MOSS, the setup program first installs WSS by itself on the machine.

However, while WSS only provides you with basic collaboration features, MOSS offers a more complete collaboration and publishing feature set and includes advanced functionality for enterprise-level implementation. These features include user profiles and personal sites; audience targeting; advanced search capabilities; and add-on services, such as Excel Services, Form Services, and Business Data Catalogs.

Understanding basic SharePoint site interface, layout, and settings

Although discussion about the detailed setup, configuration, and architecture of SharePoint (WSS v3 and MOSS) is beyond the scope of this book, keep in mind the following about SharePoint configuration:

- The SharePoint server farm consists of one or more Web Front End Web servers (WFEs), one or more application servers (servers that provide indexing, search services, and offer various SharePoint features, such as user profiles, My Sites, Excel Services, Form Services, etc.), and one or more database servers.

- The SharePoint setup is a two-step process. First, you use the setup executable to install the SharePoint binaries and supporting files. Then, you use the SharePoint Configuration Wizard to set up the SharePoint farm settings, secure resources, and create the configuration database and provisions for the SharePoint Central Administration Web site.

- Like the FPSE 2002 Microsoft SharePoint Administration Web site, the SharePoint Central Administration Web site serves as the operations and application management console for SharePoint. You can use this Web site to create Web applications, site collections, etc., and configure settings for all SharePoint features.

- Unlike non-SharePoint sites, SharePoint stores most of the Web site content (including content of Web pages, list and document library data, pictures, etc.) in the SQL Server database. Only shared templates and supporting files are stored in the file system.

In this section, I take you through the steps to set up WSS v3 in a single-server farm environment on a Windows 2003 server and create a Web application and a site collection. Later, I discuss the interface of a SharePoint site to familiarize you with the key components that later help you in customizing SharePoint Designer.

Setting up WSS v3 on a Web server

WSS v3 is available for download on the Microsoft Web site at www.microsoft.com/ downloads. The setup for WSS v3 includes the installation files for SQL Server 2005 Express edition, which is used as the database back end for a single-server basic installation. You need to be an administrator to successfully install and configure WSS v3 on a Web server. Along with that, you need to ensure that IIS 6.0 is installed and running in the worker process isolation mode.

The one-click installation of WSS v3 is fairly simple and requires no specific user input except clicking on the setup executable and then clicking the Basic installation radio button. Once the setup is complete, the SharePoint Configuration Wizard automatically runs to provision the SharePoint Central Administration Web site. You perform all the SharePoint server-level Web application and operations management by using the Central Administration Web site, as shown in Figure 2.17.

The setup also installs the SQL Server 2005 Express edition and uses it as the default database server for WSS v3.

FIGURE 2.17

The SharePoint Central Administration Web site

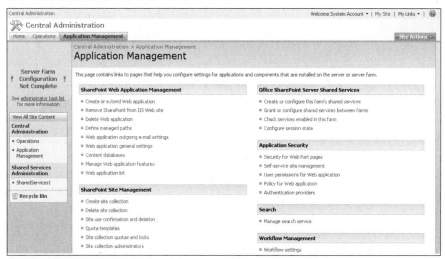

Create a SharePoint Web application

After you install and configure WSS v3, you can use the SharePoint Central administration Web site to create a SharePoint Web application by using these steps:

1. **Choose Start ➪ Administrative Tools ➪ SharePoint Central Administration to open the SharePoint Central Administration Web site.**

2. **Click the Application Management tab.** The Application management Web page opens, allowing you to perform a number of operations related to Web application management.

3. **Click Create or Extend Web Application.** The Create or Extend Web Application dialog box opens.

4. **Click Create New Web Application.** The Create New Web Application Web page, as shown in Figure 2.18, opens, allowing you to create a new IIS Web site for the SharePoint Web application, create an application pool for the Web site, and define security configurations for the Web site.

FIGURE 2.18

The Create New Web Application Web page

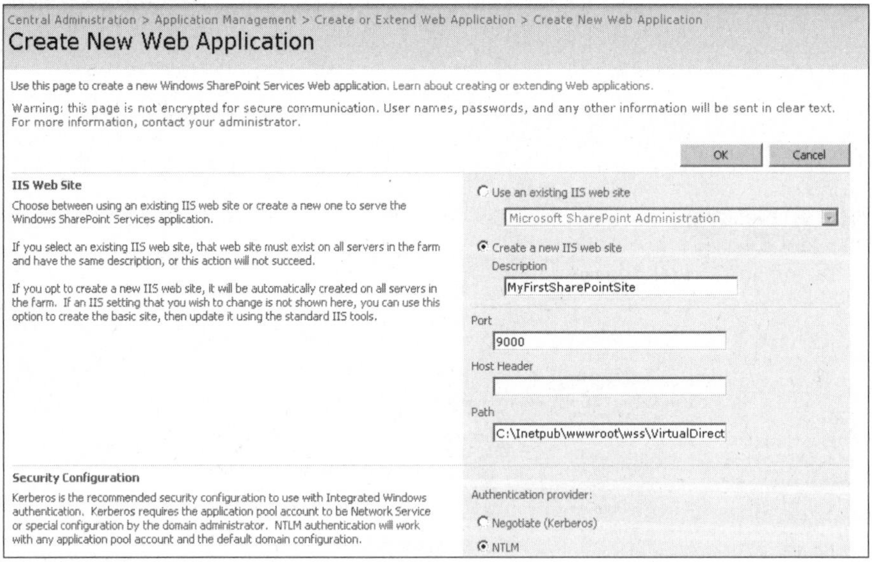

5. **Type the name of the SharePoint Web application in the Description text field and then use the Port, Host Header, and Path text fields to specify a TCP/IP port, host header, and root folder for the Web application.**

6. **Use the default settings for the Security Configuration and the Load Balanced URL section.**

7. In the Application Pool section, create a new application pool for the Web application, type the name for the application pool in the Application Pool name text field, and then use the username and password text fields to set the credentials that the application pool will run as.

8. Keep the defaults for the Database Name and Authentication sections.

9. Click OK.

When the Web application setup is complete, the new Web site and application pool are now listed in the IIS Manager. Also, the newly created SharePoint Web application is shown in the Web Application List available in the Application Management tab of the SharePoint Central Administration Web site.

Creating a site collection in the SharePoint Web application

After the SharePoint Web application is set up, you need to create a root *site collection* in the Web application. Simply put, a site collection is a set of SharePoint Web sites, features, and permissions that's centrally managed at the site collection level. You can create a site collection using these steps:

1. **In the Application Management tab in the SharePoint Central Administration Web site, click Create Site Collection.** The Create Site Collection page, as shown in Figure 2.19, opens, allowing you to set some general settings and choose a site template for use for the root site collection SharePoint site.

FIGURE 2.19

The Create Site Collection Web page

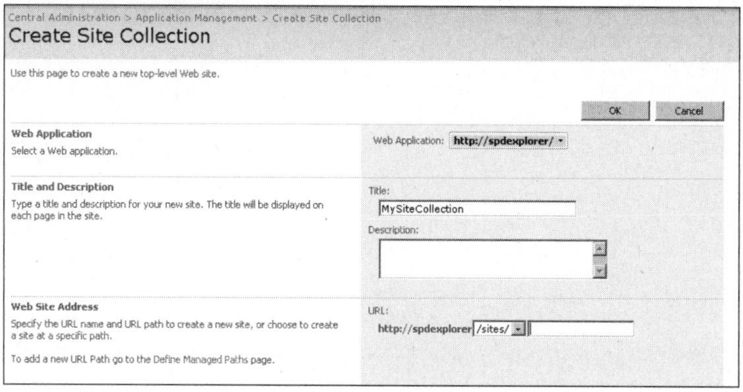

2. **Ensure that the Web Application dropdown menu shows the Web application in which you want to create the site collection.** If not, you can change the Web application by using the Change Web Application option.

3. **Type a title and description for the site collection.**

4. **Using the Web Site Address section, specify the URL for the site collection.** Click /
   in the dropdown menu if you want to create the site collection at the root path of the
   Web application.

5. **Click the site template to use for the site collection by using the Select a template
   list.** For this exercise, choose the Team Site template.

6. **Specify the site administrator's username in the User Name text field in the Primary
   Site Collection Administrator text field.**

7. **Use the defaults for the Quota Template section.**

8. **Click OK.**

When your site collection is created, you can browse to the root site of the site collection by using
the URL specified in the previous steps.

To be able to intelligently modify and develop SharePoint sites with SharePoint Designer, you need
to understand some key components of a SharePoint Web page. The interface for a WSS v3 site
based on the Team Site template is shown in Figure 2.20.

FIGURE 2.20

A SharePoint site based on the Team Site template

The layout of the default page of the SharePoint site based on the Team Site template consists of
some key elements:

- Toward the top-left corner of the Web page is a tab-based link bar (or navigation bar) that
  has the links to the Web sites inside the site collection. While creating new Web sites inside
  the site collection, you have the option to add the link for the Web site in this Top Link bar.

- In the same horizontal pane, toward the right, is the Site Actions dropdown menu. This menu allows you to navigate to Web pages to allow you to create new content and change site settings. For sites using the Collaboration or Publishing templates (available with MOSS), the list of menu options in the Site Actions dropdown changes.

- Just above the Site Actions menu is the search box Web part that includes a scopes dropdown.

- On the left of the Web page is the Quick Launch bar that, among other selections, has the links to the lists and document libraries. You have the option to add links to this bar while creating lists, document libraries, and other SharePoint content.

- In the main content region of the Web page is a set of Web parts that provide views for various lists (Announcement, Calendar, Links, etc.). An image Web part that shows the Windows SharePoint Services logo is also there.

Choose Site Actions ⇨ Edit Page to see the edit mode view of the Web page. This view allows you to add or remove Web parts. Also, this Web page has two Web part zones: Left and Right. Based on the template being used to create the site, the layout changes.

NOTE   SharePoint 3.0 (WSS v3 and MOSS) follows the concept of context-based security trimming. Thus, all menus and interfaces that SharePoint sites expose are shown only if you have the required permissions to see and use them.

To add a Web part to the Web page by using the browser interface, simply click Add Web Parts. The Add Web Parts Web page dialog box opens, allowing you to choose from a list of Web parts available from WSS v3. Again, this list changes if you have MOSS installed or if there are any custom Web parts installed on the WFE. Clicking on the Advanced Web Part gallery and options link opens the Add Web Parts task pane in the right corner of the Web page. Here, you can search Web part galleries, choose Web parts, and add them to the Web part zone of your choice.

You exit the edit mode view by clicking on the Exit Edit Mode link just below the Site Actions menu.

Working with SharePoint sites and site collections

Choose Site Actions ⇨ Site Settings to open the Site Settings page for the site collection, as shown in Figure 2.21. You use this page to make general settings for the site collection:

- **Users and Permissions:** The settings in this section allow you to set up the permissions for the site collection. You can use these settings to add or remove users and groups and specify site collection administrators.

- **Look and Feel:** Most of the settings in this section are useful while working with SharePoint Designer on the Web site. These settings allow you to change the site's theme, change settings for the Top Link bar and the Quick Launch bar, and save the SharePoint site as a template. You use these settings in later chapters, along with SharePoint Designer features, to change the look and feel of the site.

- **Galleries:** This lists the various SharePoint content galleries, such as Master Pages, Content Types, Site Columns, Web Parts, etc.

- **Site Administration:** The settings in this section allow you to view and set SharePoint settings for alerts, Really Simple Syndication (RSS), and site usage reports. This section also allows you to create new sites and workspaces.

- **Site Collection Administration:** As the name indicates, the settings in this section apply at the site collection level and provide configuration settings for the SharePoint recycle bin, audit log reports, site collection features, etc.

FIGURE 2.21

The Site Settings Web page

To create new sites inside the site collection, you can click Sites and Workspaces in the Site Administration section of the Site Settings Web page. You can also follow these steps to create new sites inside the site collection:

1. **Choose Site Actions ⇨ Create.** The Create Web page, as shown in Figure 2.22, opens, providing a consolidated interface for creating SharePoint content of many types. You can create custom lists, document libraries, and Web pages and sites.

2. **Click Sites and Workspaces in the Web Pages section.** The New SharePoint Site Web page opens.

3. **Type the Title and Description as well as the URL for the new Web site.**

4. **Click the site template for the SharePoint site by using the Select a Template list in the Template Selection section.**

5. Using the Navigation and Navigation Inheritance sections, specify whether you want to add the site to the Top Link bar and the Quick Launch bar.

6. Click Create.

You can also create SharePoint sites by using templates provided by SharePoint in SharePoint Designer by choosing File ⇨ New. However, SharePoint Designer doesn't allow you to create site collections. After you create a SharePoint site or site collection, you can open the site in SharePoint Designer for customization either by using SharePoint Designer's File ⇨ Open Site dialog box or simply by browsing to the Web site in Internet Explorer (IE 6.0 and later) and using the IE menu option at File ⇨ Edit with SharePoint Designer.

FIGURE 2.22

The Create Web page

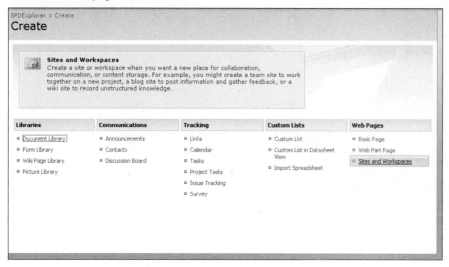

Using SharePoint lists and libraries

You can also choose Site Actions ⇨ Create to create SharePoint lists and libraries. A list in SharePoint is a container that allows you to store data and records in a flexible manner. A record inside a SharePoint list is called a list item. Lists provide the infrastructure to maintain list items in the form of views that can be used to view the list items and forms that can be used to add, edit, and delete list items. You can create new list views by using the SharePoint interface and then customize the list forms by using SharePoint Designer.

CROSS-REF For more on creating custom list forms, see Chapter 17.

Document libraries (form libraries, picture libraries, slides libraries, etc.) are special lists that can be used to store content (documents, pictures, and forms) and provide features for management of such content. They also provide special views that show the content they store in a more comprehensible manner.

Every SharePoint list (or library) has a set of actions and settings available for it. These actions are accessible by using the Actions menu in the list (or library) views. Figure 2.23 shows the Actions menu for the My Pictures library.

The actions available might change depending on the list (or library) you're working with. Libraries also have an Upload menu that can be used to upload one or more items. The Settings menu allows you to access the settings for the list (or library) so you can set permissions and manage advanced settings, including versioning, RSS, and workflows. You can also use the Settings menu to create new columns and views for the list (or library).

 SharePoint 3.0 supports item-level permissions, which can be set by using the Actions menu, which you access by clicking on the item inside a list view.

FIGURE 2.23

The My Pictures library Actions menu

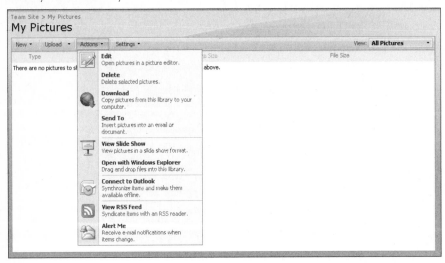

Using SharePoint Web parts

A SharePoint Web part is a Web user control that can be used to perform specific operations on SharePoint sites. SharePoint out of the box offers a number of Web parts that are available in the site's Web Parts Gallery. SharePoint application developers can use the SharePoint object model to create new Web parts and deploy them for use in SharePoint, thus providing custom Web parts to the site's users.

You can add Web parts to a SharePoint Web page in its edit mode by using the Add Web Parts interface. Also, you can use the edit mode to delete, close Web parts, and set up Web part connections. SharePoint Designer offers the interface to add Web parts and Web part zones to Web pages. It also allows you to change properties for Web parts.

 **For more on Web part modifications, see Chapter 11.**

Summary

In this chapter, I discussed a number of technologies and software that form the server-side piece to the SharePoint Designer authoring framework. You learned about the basic IIS user interface and settings for Web, FTP, and WebDAV sites. You also set up and configured FPSE and SharePoint sites on IIS Web sites. Understanding these technologies should help you when I discuss remote authoring and publishing to such sites in SharePoint Designer.

Chapter 3

Exploring the Internals of Remote Authoring

While the process of opening Web sites, live editing of Web pages, or publishing Web content in SharePoint Designer looks simple and straightforward on the surface, these procedures are quite complex, and a lot of client-server communication technologies are employed to accomplish even the most basic of operations. It's important as a Web site designer that you have some understanding of these underlying client-server communication protocols and technologies so that you can diagnose and troubleshoot problems associated with content authoring in SharePoint Designer. In this chapter, I introduce you to some of the key underlying communication protocols that SharePoint Designer uses for its site authoring and management operations. I also explain how some of the Windows (OS) components are used by SharePoint Designer to allow for its remote authoring and publishing features. Finally, I discuss some remote-authoring protocols and technologies that provide the foundation for SharePoint Designer capabilities of working with FPSE and SharePoint sites.

Throughout this chapter, you capture the client-server communication between SharePoint Designer and the Web server hosting the Web site content to develop understanding on the background processes and mechanisms used. Before I begin, I want to familiarize you with the Fiddler tool, which I use for capturing client-server communication.

Fiddler is a proxy-based HTTP debugging tool that allows you to capture HTTP (or HTTPS for HTTP over a secure socket) traffic originating from and finishing at a machine where Fiddler is installed and run. It provides an intuitive user interface that can be used to easily capture and understand HTTP-based communication.

The latest release of Fiddler at the time of this writing is Fiddler 2 and is available for download at www.fiddler2.com. The setup requirements, installation steps, and basic operations guide for Fiddler are also available at this Web site.

IN THIS CHAPTER

Understanding the basics of remote authoring

Working with Web Folders and Web clients

Understanding FrontPage Remote Procedure Call

Understanding Simple Object Access Protocol and Web Services basics

To better understand how to use Fiddler, the following steps help capture the client-server traffic that occurs when you open a WSS v3 team site in Internet Explorer. To reduce the captured traffic, ensure that all Web browsers and other Web-based applications installed on your computer are closed before you begin these steps. Also, ensure you have downloaded and installed Fiddler 2 before doing the following:

1. **Open the Fiddler tool by choosing Start ⇨ All Programs ⇨ Fiddler.** If no Web-based programs already run on your machine, the left Web Sessions pane in Fiddler just shows a request to the Fiddler Web site (indicated in red).

2. **Choose Edit ⇨ Remove ⇨ All Sessions to clear the Web Sessions pane.**

3. **While keeping Fiddler running, open Internet Explorer (or any other Web browser, such as Firefox, Opera, etc.) and then browse to a WSS v3 Web site based on the Team Site template.**

CROSS-REF For more on Web site templates, see Chapters 2 and 4.

4. **After the default page of the Web site displays in the browser, switch back to the Fiddler tool.** The Web Sessions pane in Fiddler is now filled with rows of HTTP sessions.

5. **Choose File ⇨ Capture Traffic (or press F12) to direct Fiddler to stop capturing HTTP traffic.** A Web session in Fiddler is basically composed of two components: an HTTP request from the client machine for a resource (such as a Web page, style sheet, picture, JavaScript, etc.) and the HTTP response from the server machine for the request. As shown in Figure 3.1, the Result column in the Web Sessions pane shows the HTTP response code for the request, the Host column shows the Web site URL, and the URL column shows the relative URL of the resource being requested.

6. **In the list of captured Web sessions, find the one where the Result column shows 200 and the URL column shows** /default.aspx. The result 200 here implies a successful Web server response. This Web session corresponds to the request for the default Web page of the WSS v3 site you opened in IE in the previous step and the response from the SharePoint Web server for it.

7. **Double-click the Web session to activate the Session Inspector tab on the right pane of Fiddler.** You use the Session Inspector tab to see the actual text of the HTTP request and the HTTP response associated with the Web session. The top window in the Session Inspector shows the HTTP request, and the bottom window shows the HTTP response.

8. **On the menu inside the Session Inspector window, click the Raw button to view the raw HTTP request and the response associated with the Web session.** The top window of the Session Inspector shows the request to GET (an HTTP verb) the default. aspx page by using the HTTP 1.1 Web protocol. The request also includes a number of HTTP headers (User-Agent, Authorization, Set-Cookie, etc.) that the Web server uses to identify the Web browser, retrieve the user credentials for authentication, and perform other operations.

FIGURE 3.1

A Fiddler capture while opening the default page of a SharePoint site

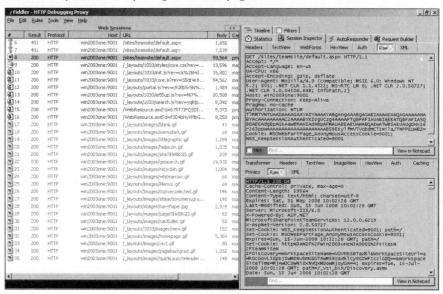

The bottom window shows the HTTP response from the Web server. In the previous exercise, the server responded with an HTTP 200 OK response (indicating that the request was properly authenticated and processed), some HTTP response headers, and the complete HTML code of the `default.aspx` Web page (obtained by the server-side processing of the ASP.NET code of the Web page) that's actually interpreted and displayed by a Web browser.

While the previous steps should help in understanding how to use the Fiddler tool to capture HTTP traffic, I use this tool later in this chapter to help you understand the internals of SharePoint authoring in SharePoint Designer.

Understanding the Basics of Remote Authoring

In this section, you learn some of the basic components that form the foundation of the remote-authoring features of SharePoint Designer. It's important to understand that remote authoring (or live editing) is not a SharePoint Designer–only feature. SharePoint Designer is mostly an intelligent consumer of the remote-authoring technologies provided by the client computer on which it's installed and the Web server computer where the remote Web site resides.

Client: the SharePoint Designer machine

From a user's perspective, SharePoint Designer is all you need on the client machine to be able to edit (or publish to) remote Web sites and SharePoint Web applications. However, SharePoint Designer relies on a number of other services offered by the operating system to successfully perform its operations. These services cumulatively become the client side of the remote-authoring features of SharePoint Designer.

Internet Explorer

SharePoint Designer relies on IE (`WinINet.dll`) for its HTTP settings, proxy server configuration, and authentication support. If you open SharePoint Designer, choose Tools ➪ Application Options, and then click the General tab, you find the Proxy Settings button. This button actually opens the Internet Properties dialog box, as shown in Figure 3.2, in the Connections tab and allows you to set settings for the proxy server to be used.

Also, SharePoint Designer respects the IE security zone settings for security and user authentication as well as advanced settings for HTTP 1.1 and passive FTP.

FIGURE 3.2

The Internet Properties dialog box

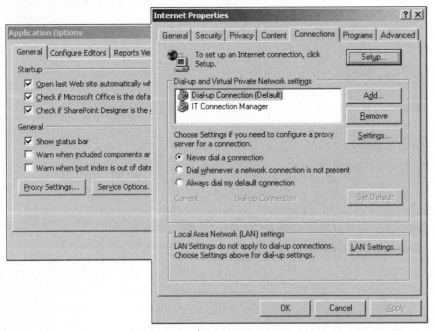

Web Client service

The Web Client service offered by the Windows XP, Windows Server 2003, and Windows Vista operating systems allows Web-based HTTP addresses (for example, `http://webservername`) to be accessed as Uniform Naming Convention (UNC) paths (`\\webservername\folder name`). This feature provides a mechanism to map network drives to Web-based addresses.

Web Folders

Web Folders offers the underlying infrastructure that allows you to open your remote Web sites in a Windows Explorer–like interface. If Web Folders is properly configured on your client machine and your Web server supports remote authoring, it can be used to manage the Web site content and add, remove, view, and copy files and folders to and from your remote Web site.

I discuss the Web Client service and Web Folders in more detail later in this chapter.

Web server: the site-hosting machine

The Web server (IIS for this discussion) is the machine that hosts the Web sites and Web applications.

While I previously discussed the components that enable remote authoring on a Web server, I must mention that in order to enable live editing of Web sites in SharePoint Designer, the Web server must support one of these technologies:

- FTP
- WebDAV
- FPSE
- SharePoint

Client-server communication protocols

HTTP is the base communication protocol that SharePoint Designer uses to converse with a Web server. All other application protocols that SharePoint Designer exploits — for example, FrontPage Remote Procedure Call (RPC), which is discussed later in this chapter — are HTTP-based.

HTTP protocol is not just limited in use for SharePoint Designer. It is, in fact, the standard communication protocol for interaction between a Web client (for example, a Web browser) and a Web server. When you type an address in a Web browser to view a Web site, the browser creates an HTTP request and sends it to the Web server for processing. When the processing is complete, the Web server sends an HTTP response back, which the browser interprets and then displays as a Web page. The HTTP request is usually composed of these parts:

- A request line, such as GET /_vti_bin/author.dll HTTP/1.1, which requests the file author.dll from the /_vti_bin directory. Here, GET is the HTTP verb being used to indicate that the browser wants to retrieve the requested resource. Commonly used HTTP verbs are GET, HEAD, POST, OPTIONS, etc.

> **NOTE** WebDAV expands the set of standard HTTP verbs and allows for the use of verbs such as `LOCK`, `UNLOCK`, `PROPFIND`, `PROPPATCH`, etc. These verbs enable the remote authoring and live editing features for clients such as SharePoint Designer.

- Headers, such as `Accept-Language: en`. These headers provide a way for a browser to tell the Web server about itself and the technologies that it supports.

- An empty line

- An optional message body. This is usually the place in the HTTP request where the FrontPage Remote Procedure Call (RPC) methods and SharePoint Simple Object Access Protocol (SOAP) messages are sent. FPSE (and SharePoint SOAP Web Services) reads this section to determine the action that needs to be performed for framing the HTTP response to the Web browser for the request.

Similar to the HTTP request, the HTTP response also has these sections:

- Response line, such as `HTTP/1.1 200 OK`, which indicates the result of the processing done by the Web server for the HTTP request. If the processing fails for some reason, the response code (for example, `401`, `500`, etc.) indicates the type of failure.

- Headers, such as `Content-Length: 438`. Like in the case of the HTTP request, the headers in the response allow the Web server to specify information about itself and the response that it just sent.

- An empty line

- A message body; this is the actual response that's parsed by the browser and displayed for a user's viewing. In the case of FPSE and SharePoint sites, this section might also contain information that SharePoint Designer can use for various purposes, such as displaying folder lists, rendering Web site content, working with Web parts, etc.

As discussed later in this chapter, FPSE (and SharePoint) sends a lot of optional information in the HTTP request body. This information usually contains a Web method (with parameters and values), which is executed on the Web server by FPSE (or SharePoint) to form an HTTP response that SharePoint Designer can utilize to perform its functions. Obviously, if the execution fails and the HTTP response indicates a failure, SharePoint Designer functionality relying on the response also fails.

Working with Web Folders and Web Clients

While SharePoint Designer provides a smart design and development interface for working with remote Web site content, it's not the only interface that you can use for accessing remote Web site content. Windows itself offers you the infrastructure that allows you to access remote Web site content much like a local folder on your computer. In fact, SharePoint Designer and other Office 2007 programs internally use this infrastructure as a basis for providing their remote-authoring features. A problem in this infrastructure can cause the remote-authoring functionality of these programs to fail.

The two main components offered by Windows for facilitating remote authoring are the Web Client service and Web Folders.

Understanding client-side components for remote authoring

The Web Client service (also known as the WebDAV Client Redirector) is a Windows service that allows you to access content in Web sites (that support WebDAV) from a client machine in a Windows Explorer–like interface. With this service enabled and running, you can access a folder inside a Web site in Windows Explorer by using a UNC path (`\\webservername\foldername`). You can also map network drives to folders inside Web sites. It's a really useful tool for accessing Web content on an intranet where you know the name of the Web server where your Web content resides.

The Web Client service is enabled and running by default on Windows XP and Vista client machines. However, it's disabled on a Windows 2003 server. You can enable or disable the Web Client service by using the Services management console. To access the Services console, type **Services.msc** in the Run dialog box (accessible by choosing Start ➪ Run). If the Web Client service is disabled, you can enable it by right-clicking on it and then choosing Properties from the popup menu. In the General tab of the WebClient Properties dialog box that opens, as shown in Figure 3.3, select Manual in the StartUp Type dropdown menu and then click Start. This should enable and start the Web Client service on the computer.

FIGURE 3.3

The WebClient Properties dialog box

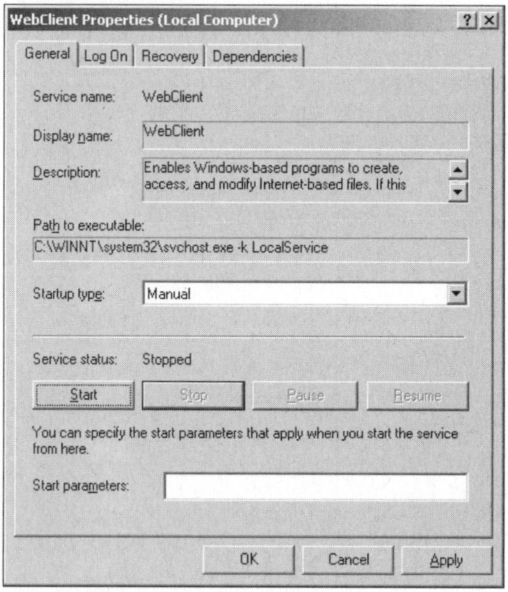

To access a folder inside a WebDAV-enabled site in Windows Explorer by using the Web Client service and then map a network drive to that folder, follow these steps:

1. **Open Windows Explorer and then type the location inside the Web site that you want to open by using the** `\\webservername\foldername` **format.** The contents of the folder are displayed in the right pane inside Windows Explorer, and the Folders pane on the left shows the other folders inside the site.

2. **To map a network drive to a folder inside the Web site, click Start, right-click on My Computer (Computer on Windows Vista machines), and then choose Map Network Drive from the popup menu to open the Map Network Drive dialog box, as shown in Figure 3.4.**

FIGURE 3.4

The Map Network Drive dialog box

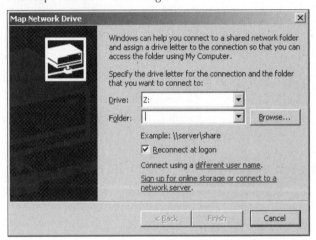

3. **Using the Drive dropdown menu, choose a name for this drive.**

4. **Type the UNC path** (`\\servername\foldername`) **of the folder in the Folder dropdown menu.**

5. **Click Finish.** A new drive with the name you chose is created in Windows Explorer. You can now access the content of the folder inside the Web site by clicking on the mapped drive. You can also use SharePoint Designer to modify content inside this mapped network drive by choosing File ➪ Open Site to display the Open Site dialog box. The Open Site dialog box makes available the mapped network drive to be used for opening the Web site in SharePoint Designer.

Because SharePoint sites support WebDAV, the Web Client service can be very useful for accessing document libraries inside SharePoint sites in a Windows Explorer–like interface, which can be used to perform bulk copy/paste operations inside document libraries. Office 2007 programs also use this service to directly open Office documents residing in Web sites for modification.

CAUTION Mapping network drives to folders inside SharePoint sites and then opening them in SharePoint Designer for editing isn't recommended.

Using Web Folders in Windows XP and Windows Vista clients

Web Folders is the other component offered by Windows for supporting remote authoring. Like the Web Client service, the Web Folders technology provides the local infrastructure to open remote sites in a Windows Explorer–like view. However, Web Folders is a relatively older technology, and newer Windows operating systems, such as Windows Vista, don't ship it by default. To create a local Web folder for a Web site on a Windows XP machine, follow these steps:

1. **Open Windows Explorer and then click My Network Places.** This interface allows you to create and view Web Folders.

2. **Click Add a network place to open the Add Network Place Wizard and then click Next.**

3. **Ensure that the Choose another network location option is selected and then click Next.**

4. **Type the complete HTTP address of the Web site in the Internet or network address text field and then click Next.**

5. **Specify a name for the Web folder in the Type a name for this network place text field.**

6. **Click Next and then click Finish.**

Files and folders inside your Web site are displayed in a Windows Explorer–like interface. Also, inside My Network Places is the newly created Web folder in the corresponding section. You can also create and access a Web folder using IE. The Open dialog box in IE (accessible by choosing File ⇨ Open) has the Open as Web Folder check box that allows you to open a Web site as a Web folder.

Web Folders is installed by default on Windows XP machines. On Windows 2003 and Windows Vista, the Web Client service is used by default to implement the Add a network place operation. If the Web Client service is disabled, it falls back to Web Folders (if it's installed).

NOTE On Windows 2003 and Windows Vista machines, Web Folders isn't installed, but you can use the Web Client windows service instead. However, you can download and install Web Folders on Windows 2003 and Vista machines from www.microsoft.com/downloads/details.aspx?FamilyId=17C36612-632E-4C04-9382-987622ED1D64&displaylang=en.

If your Web Folders installation becomes corrupted, you might experience issues where SharePoint Designer fails to open any sites for remote authoring, publish sites, etc. After you install Web Folders on a machine, you can update and repair the associated files by using the `webfldrs.msi` setup file:

1. **Choose Start ⇨ Run and then type** webfldrs.msi **in the Run dialog box.** The WebFldrs Welcome Dialog box opens. You use this dialog box to add or remove features and remove or reinstall Web Folders.

2. **Click Reinstall.** The WebFldrs Reinstall Mode dialog box opens, allowing you to choose from a set of reinstall options.

3. **Select all options and then click OK.** All the files required for Web Folders to work properly on the machine are now installed and registered.

Understanding FrontPage Remote Procedure Call

When you open an FPSE-extended Web site (or a SharePoint site) for live editing, SharePoint Designer internally has to perform a lot of operations, such as discovering the remote-authoring mechanism supported by the Web site, opening the site, listing the files and folders of the Web site, and determining the properties associated with the files. Even more such background operations need to be performed to implement other SharePoint Designer features, such as saving Web pages, publishing content, etc.

SharePoint Designer accomplishes these operations by using an HTTP-based protocol called FrontPage Remote Procedure Call (RPC). This protocol is the key component enabled for use on a Web site when you extend it with FPSE (or set up a SharePoint site).

The remote-authoring operations are performed in the FrontPage RPC protocol by using *Web methods*. A Web method, simply put, is a function implemented by the remote-authoring mechanism (FPSE or SharePoint) that performs a specific operation. For example, the `Open Service` Web method offered by FPSE provides the necessary metadata information about a Web site that SharePoint Designer can later use to open the Web site.

Investigating basic HTTP communication

To understand FrontPage RPC better, I take you through the operations performed when you open an FPSE-extended Web site in SharePoint Designer and then discuss the Web methods involved:

1. **Open Fiddler and then choose File ⇨ Capture Traffic to ensure that Fiddler is set to capture HTTP traffic.** You use this tool to capture HTTP Web sessions while opening an FPSE site in SharePoint Designer.

2. **Open SharePoint Designer and then choose File ⇨ Open Site to open a Web site extended with FPSE.** Fiddler captures the Web sessions that take place during the processing of opening the site, as shown in Figure 3.5. Unless you receive an error while opening the site in SharePoint Designer, for this exercise, you need to concentrate only on the HTTP Web sessions in Fiddler that show 200 in the Results column.

> **NOTE** Depending on whether this is the first time you've opened this site in SharePoint Designer, you might see that some of the Web sessions discussed might be missing. SharePoint Designer caches information received from some Web methods to reduce the HTTP traffic and improve efficiency.

3. **Click the Web session with /_vti_inf.html in the URL column.** This Web page is in the root folder of your Web site after you extend it with FPSE. The HTTP response to this request for _vti_inf.html tells SharePoint Designer about the relative URLs of the various server executables (primarily shtml.dll, author.dll, and admin.dll) that enable remote authoring. These executables are installed with FPSE and SharePoint. SharePoint Designer uses these relative URLs to formulate its next requests for the open site operation.

4. **Click the Web session with /_vti_bin/shtml.dll/_vti_rpc in the URL column.** If you view the raw HTTP request in the top pane inside the Session Inspector tab for this session, the use of the Server Version Web method appears at the end of the HTTP request. The FrontPage RPC Web methods are always sent at the end of the Web request after the HTTP headers. The response to this Web method tells SharePoint Designer about the version of FPSE the Web site is extended with. SharePoint Designer uses this version to formulate the next HTTP request.

FIGURE 3.5

An HTTP Web session captured by Fiddler for the SharePoint Designer open site process

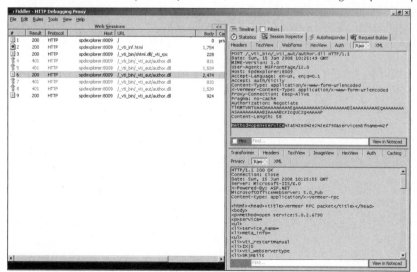

5. **Click the first Web session with** `/_vti_bin/_vti_aut/author.dll` **in the URL column.** The `author.dll` is the executable that provides the main server remote-authoring functionality for SharePoint Designer. In the HTTP request, the `Open Service` Web method response tells SharePoint Designer metadata information about the Web site it needs to open.

6. **Click the next Web session with** `/_vti_bin/_vti_aut/author.dll` **in the URL column.** This HTTP request has the `List Documents` Web method. The Web server's HTTP response to this Web method tells SharePoint Designer about the list of files and folders inside the Web site and the metadata information about the files and folders.

As indicated by these steps, FrontPage RPC Web methods are heavily used by SharePoint Designer to provide even the most basic functionality. Troubleshooting remote-authoring issues with SharePoint Designer usually involves determining which Web method is being executed at the time the problem occurs.

Exploring FrontPage RPC

If you examine an HTTP request in the last step in the previous exercise, after the initial verb and the header information, SharePoint Designer sends this RPC method:

```
method=list+documents%3a5%2e0%2e2%2e6790&service%5fname=&listHidd
    enDocs=true&listExplorerDocs=false&listRecurse=false&listFiles
    =true&listFolders=true&listLinkInfo=true&listIncludeParent=tru
    e&listDerived=false&listBorders=false&listChildWebs=true&listT
    hickets=false&initialUrl=&platform=WinI386
```

The name of this method is `List Documents`, and it takes the parameters `service name`, `listHiddenDocs`, `listExplorerDocs`, `listRecurse`, `listFiles`, `listFolders`, etc. The whole text is URL-encoded for fidelity across the Internet connection. As evident, SharePoint Designer uses this Web method to request FPSE on the Web server to send folder information about the Web site. The Web server HTTP response (that FPSE helps formulate) contains the information and metadata about the files and folders inside the Web site. SharePoint Designer then uses this information to display the list of files and folders inside the Web site.

Understanding the use of FrontPage RPC methods

Like `Open Service` and `List Documents` RPC methods, FPSE has a number of other Web methods that are used by SharePoint Designer (and other Office applications) to enable their features. Table 3.1 lists some of the important FrontPage RPC methods. Because SharePoint sites also have their FPSE lineage, these proprietary Web methods are also used when authoring against SharePoint sites in SharePoint Designer.

TABLE 3.1

Common FrontPage RPC Methods

RPC Method	Description
Server version	Requests for the version of FPSE or SharePoint installed on the Web site
Open service	Retrieves the information about the Web site for use in the client application
URL to Web URL	Converts the given URL into the URL of the Web site containing the given URL
List documents	Provides the list of documents and folders inside the Web site. Also provides the metadata, such as creation time, modified time, author, etc., associated with the files for display in the client application
Get document	Retrieves the document specified in the RPC method to the client for display
Get documents	Provides the list of documents asked for in the parameter information of the RPC method to the client application

While SharePoint Designer internally uses these methods, you can also consume these RPC methods in a custom program to query information and perform operations related to FPSE and SharePoint.

 **For a more complete reference to FrontPage RPC methods, visit this Web site:** `http://msdn.microsoft.com/en-us/library/ms954084.aspx`.

Understanding Simple Object Access Protocol and Web Services Basics

Along with using FrontPage RPC Web methods, SharePoint Designer relies on a number of Web methods and functions exposed by SharePoint ASP.NET–based Web Services for the remote authoring of SharePoint sites. SharePoint Designer uses Simple Object Access Protocol (SOAP) to communicate with SharePoint Web Services for performing basic operations on SharePoint sites, including opening Web pages, rendering SharePoint content in the Design view, and implementing advanced features, such as Data Forms and Web Parts.

To be able to understand the background processes involved when working with SharePoint sites in SharePoint Designer, it's important to have some basic understanding of SOAP and ASP.NET Web Services. In this section, I discuss Web Services and SOAP as a communication protocol to converse with Web Services.

Understanding SOAP technology

To put it in simple terms, SOAP allows a client program to remotely execute a method exposed by a Web Service being hosted on a Web server. Unlike the FrontPage RPC methods discussed earlier, the syntax of SOAP-based communication is mostly driven by XML-based messages. These XML messages are sent in the body of the HTTP request to the Web Service on the Web server. The Web Service processes the request based on the information in the HTTP request and formulates an HTML/XML response for use by the client.

Web Services are programs with an `.asmx` file extension that, once developed by using an application such as Visual Studio, can be installed on the Web server machine to provide the functionality they offer to a Web site. Besides running their isolated server-side tasks, Web Services also provide for a mechanism of Web methods that allows for the invocation of tasks from a remote client. These Web methods are exposed by a Web Service and are discoverable by the client programs by using a Web Services Description Language (WSDL) file.

For example, SharePoint installs a Web Service called `Lists.asmx`. If you browse to this Web Service in a Web browser (by using the URL `http://servername/_vti_bin/lists.asmx`), as shown in Figure 3.6, you can see the Web methods that this service exposes.

If you click on any of the Web methods, a sample of the HTTP request and response appears.

FIGURE 3.6

A description of the `Lists.asmx` Web Service

Lists

The following operations are supported. For a formal definition, please review the **Service Description**.

- **AddAttachment**
- **AddDiscussionBoardItem**
- **AddList**
- **AddListFromFeature**
- **ApplyContentTypeToList**
- **CheckInFile**
- **CheckOutFile**
- **CreateContentType**
- **DeleteAttachment**
- **DeleteContentType**
- **DeleteContentTypeXmlDocument**
- **DeleteList**
- **GetAttachmentCollection**
- **GetList**
- **GetListAndView**

Exploring Web Services and Web Methods

When you open a SharePoint site in SharePoint Designer, the client requests a lot of information about the Web site by using a combination of FrontPage RPC methods and SharePoint Web Services. While most of the FrontPage RPC methods are served by the `author.dll` that SharePoint installs, the Web methods are processed by the corresponding SharePoint Web Service.

To understand the nature of the SOAP HTTP session that SharePoint Designer makes with a SharePoint site, I discuss the `GetWebPartPage` Web method exposed by the `WebPartPages.asmx` SharePoint Web Service. This Web method is used when you open a SharePoint Web page for editing in SharePoint Designer. Figure 3.7 shows the HTTP request captured by Fiddler that shows the use of this Web method.

FIGURE 3.7

The `GetWebPartPage` SOAP Web method being used by SharePoint Designer

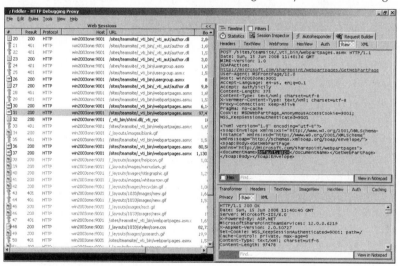

The `POST` verb is used to post information to the `WebPartPages.asmx` Web Service:

```
POST /sites/teamsite/_vti_bin/webpartpages.asmx HTTP/1.1
```

In the header section is the SOAP action header, which defines the Web method that's being requested for execution by the client:

```
SOAPAction: http://microsoft.com/sharepoint/webpartpages/
    GetWebPartPage
```

Later in the body of the HTTP request, the `GetWebPartPage` Web method was called with the `documentName` parameter set to `default.aspx`. This indicates that SharePoint Designer is requesting SharePoint to help it open the `default.aspx` page for editing:

```
<?xml version="1.0" encoding="utf-8"?>
<soap:Envelope xmlns:xsi="http://www.w3.org/2001/XMLSchema-instance"
    xmlns:xsd="http://www.w3.org/2001/XMLSchema" xmlns:soap="http://
    schemas.xmlsoap.org/soap/envelope/"><soap:Body><GetWebPartPage
    xmlns="http://microsoft.com/sharepoint/webpartpages"><documentNam
    e>default.aspx</documentName></GetWebPartPage></soap:Body></
    soap:Envelope>
```

The HTTP response to this request has the actual code of the `default.aspx` page, which is displayed in the Code view of SharePoint Designer and rendered for display in the Design view.

Examining SharePoint Web Services for SharePoint Designer authoring support

SharePoint provides the remote-authoring support for SharePoint sites to SharePoint Designer by using a number of Web Services. While the most used Web Service is `WebPartPages.asmx`, Table 3.2 lists some of the Web Services that SharePoint Designer uses while working with SharePoint sites.

TABLE 3.2

SharePoint Web Services for SharePoint Designer Remote Authoring

Web Service	Web Method
`WebPartPages.asmx`	Provides a large number of Web methods, such as `GetWebPartPage`, `GetAssemblyMetaInfo`, `ExecuteProxyUpdates`, `GetDataFrom DataSourceControl`, etc. This Web Service provides most of the SharePoint capabilities of SharePoint Designer.
`UserGroup.asmx`	Provides the `GetRolesAndPermissionsForCurrentUser` method that's used by SharePoint Designer to fetch user permissions from SharePoint
`Sites.asmx`	Exposes the `GetSiteTemplates` used to show the list of available SharePoint site templates in SharePoint Designer
`Lists.asmx`	Exposes a number of Web methods for performing various SharePoint lists–related operations

After you become comfortable using Fiddler to understand HTTP requests and responses, you find that many of the SharePoint-related operations of SharePoint Designer use these Web Services. If the Web Services don't properly respond or the HTTP response from SharePoint indicates a failure, SharePoint Designer has no choice but to fail. Understand that these Web methods can help find important clues to troubleshooting SharePoint authoring issues.

Summary

Because SharePoint Designer can work as a remote-authoring tool for a number of Web server types, the number of communication protocols it supports is enormous. This chapter focused on providing you with some details on all these internal protocols, such as HTTP, FrontPage RPC, and SOAP services. This should help you narrow down many issues you might run into while working with these server types in SharePoint Designer.

Part II

Developing Web Page Components

Chapter 4

Exploring the SharePoint Designer Environment

Although the current release of SharePoint Designer keeps the basic FrontPage 2003 user interface, it also includes a large number of enhancements to improve output and productivity for developing both SharePoint and non-SharePoint Web sites. The SharePoint Designer user environment focuses on consolidating similar features into dialog boxes, toolbars, and dockable task panes. It provides you with the flexibility to morph its environment to suit your style and design needs. You can customize the interface to keep the task panes and toolbars that you most commonly use in the front for easy access and hide the less commonly used user interface.

In this chapter, I begin by familiarizing you with the SharePoint Designer environment and then take you through some exercises and help you understand how to customize the user interface to suit your needs. Also, I mention some of the most commonly used user interface features that you encounter every time you work with a Web site in SharePoint Designer. Later in this chapter, I talk about the page-editing and application options that help you make decisions about how certain user interface components should behave and set default settings and schemas for use on Web pages.

When you open SharePoint Designer the first time after it's installed, the default interface layout is shown. Because there's no Web site or Web page open, most of the menu options and task panes in the interface are disabled. The environment is divided into four sections:

- **The top section** has the main commands menu bar and toolbars (the Common toolbar is enabled by default).

- **The left section** shows the Folder List task pane along with additionally enabled task panes.

- **The center section** is either empty (if no page is open) or shows a page view (Design or Code view) for a Web page.

- **The right section** has a set of task panes enabled by default.

Figure 4.1 shows the key components of the SharePoint Designer interface.

FIGURE 4.1

The SharePoint Designer environment

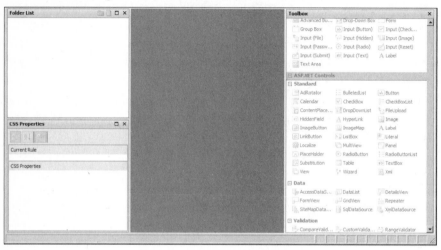

It's important to understand that while this interface is the default interface, SharePoint Designer allows you to customize it to a large extent. So, for example, if you feel more comfortable having the Folder List task pane on the right side of the environment, you can move it there.

The first operation that you usually perform is to create or open a site. Choose File ➪ Open Site to open a site in SharePoint Designer. For illustration purposes, I use a WSS v3 site, open it in SharePoint Designer, and then open its `default.aspx` page by double-clicking it in the Folder List task pane. Figure 4.2 displays the SharePoint Designer user interface after opening a WSS v3 site in it.

The interface becomes live after you open the site in SharePoint Designer. The Folder List task pane in the left section shows the list of subsites, lists, document libraries, folders, and files, with icons representing the type and nature of the content.

The center section has a tabbed interface. The Web Site tab allows you to switch between a set of Web Site panes, which I discuss later in this chapter. Then, depending on the number of pages open for editing, you see multiple tabs, each allowing you to activate the associated page for editing. When you activate a Web page for editing, you can choose from a set of page views, which allow you to edit the design and layout of the page or the code associated with the Web page.

FIGURE 4.2

A WSS v3 site open in SharePoint Designer

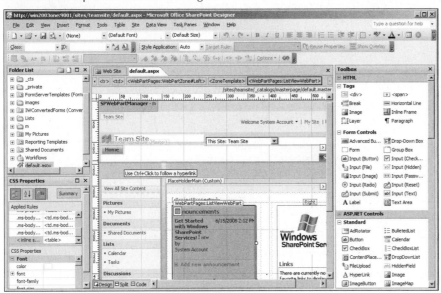

CROSS-REF   **For more on page views, see Chapter 6.**

In the right section is the Toolbox task pane, which is mostly disabled when you have the Web Site tab open in the center section. However, when you switch to a Web page, the Toolbox task pane becomes enabled and allows you to insert a number of HTML, ASP.NET, and SharePoint controls on the Web page. I talk about the various task panes in detail when discussing the corresponding features in various chapters in this book. However, later in this chapter, I show how you can reposition task panes to customize the SharePoint Designer environment to suit your needs.

Using the New Dialog Box

One major improvement that SharePoint Designer offers compared to FrontPage 2003 is that it provides a single interface to create all content associated with SharePoint and non-SharePoint sites. The New dialog box, as shown in Figure 4.3, provides an integrated user interface that allows you to create Web pages, Web sites, and SharePoint-related content.

Depending on the type of Web site being worked on in SharePoint Designer, the New dialog box shows and hides the user interfaces available to you.

FIGURE 4.3

The New dialog box

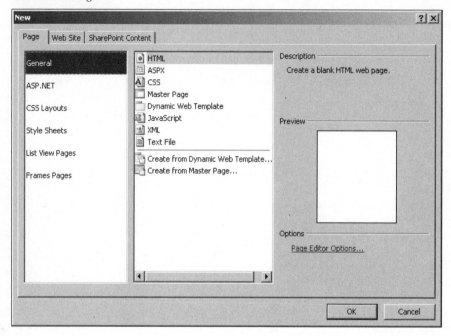

Creating Web content and files

The Page tab in the New dialog box allows you to create Web pages and other file types by using a list categorized by the nature of the Web content:

- **General:** Allows you to choose from a list of general Web content types, such as HTML, ASPX, CSS, ASP.NET master pages, dynamic Web templates, JavaScript, XML, and text files. It also allows you to create new content based on existing dynamic Web templates or master pages. You can also specify the programming language to be used while creating ASP.NET content.

- **ASP.NET:** Filters the General list to ASP.NET–specific Web content. Also allows you to create new ASP.NET `web.config` files, site maps, and Web user controls

- **CSS Layouts:** Allows you to choose from a list of CSS layout templates that can be used to lay out Web pages based on style sheets

- **Style Sheets:** Allows you to choose from a list of style sheet templates

- **List View Pages:** Available only for SharePoint sites, this allows you to create new view pages for SharePoint document libraries and lists. A view page, usually just called a View, is a customized or filtered view of the items in a list or document library.

- **Frames Pages:** Provides you with page templates that can be used to create Web pages based on HTML frames

Using Web site templates

You use the Web Site tab in the New dialog box to create new SharePoint and non-SharePoint Web sites from scratch or based on available templates. Here are the available options:

- **General:** Allows you to create a new Web site based on the One Page Web Site or Empty Web Site templates or by using the Import Web Site Wizard

- **Templates:** Empty in the case of SharePoint Designer. In the case of Expression Web, provides a list of non-SharePoint Web site templates

- **SharePoint Templates:** Allows you to create a Web site based on a list of templates provided by your SharePoint site

The Add to Current Web site and Use Encrypted Connection (SSL) check boxes are available if you already have a Web site open prior to opening the New dialog box.

NOTE The interface to list and use SharePoint templates can be a little confusing. This is because SharePoint Designer lists the SharePoint site templates by making SOAP requests to the `Sites.asmx` Web service inside the SharePoint site you type in the Specify the location of the new Web site dropdown list box. When you click the Web Site tab, it's not necessary that the URL of the Web site typed in this text field be for a SharePoint site; thus, you might have to follow a series of steps to show the available SharePoint site templates.

To list the site templates available for a SharePoint site in the New dialog box, follow these steps:

1. **Open SharePoint Designer and ensure that there's no Web site open in it.** If a site is open, choose File ⇨ Close Site to close the open site.

2. **Choose File ⇨ New to open the New dialog box, as shown in Figure 4.4, and then click the Web Site tab.**

3. **In the Specify the location of the new Web site dropdown menu, type the HTTP address of your SharePoint Web application.** Note again that you can't use SharePoint Designer to create SharePoint site collections. You need to create a Web application and site collection by using the SharePoint interface before you can use SharePoint Designer to create sites inside the site collection.

4. **Click the SharePoint Templates list option in the Web Site tab.** If this is already selected, first click another option in the list (such as General) before clicking back to SharePoint Templates. This process forces SharePoint Designer to make an HTTP-based SOAP request to the `Sites.asmx` and then retrieve the list of site templates provided by the SharePoint site.

FIGURE 4.4

The New dialog box

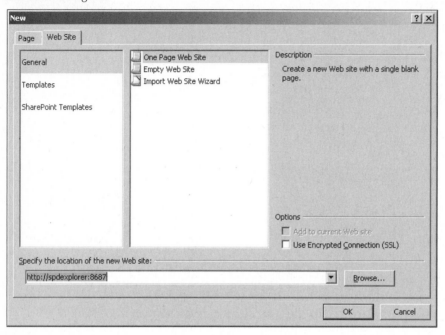

You can now click a site template from the available list and then create a new site inside the SharePoint site that you typed in the Specify the location of the new Web site dropdown menu.

Exploring SharePoint content

After you open a SharePoint Web site in SharePoint Designer, a new tab called SharePoint Content appears in the New dialog box, as shown in Figure 4.5. This tab can be used to create new SharePoint content, such as lists, document libraries, surveys, and workflows:

- **Lists:** SharePoint Designer retrieves the available list templates from the SharePoint site being edited. You can then use these templates to create new lists inside a Web site.
- **Document Libraries:** Allows you to create new libraries based on the templates provided by the SharePoint site being edited
- **Surveys:** Allows you to create new SharePoint survey lists
- **Workflows:** Links to the Workflow Designer that can be used to create workflows on SharePoint sites
- **SharePoint Publishing:** Available only for MOSS Web sites, this option allows you to create new page layouts based on the available SharePoint content types.

The SharePoint Content tab in the New dialog box

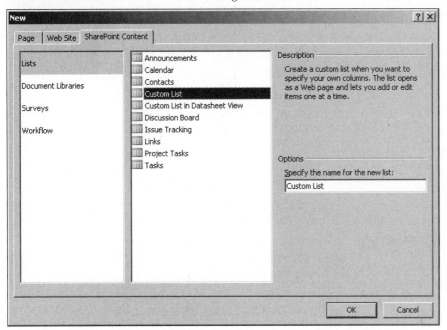

While the New dialog box offers the combined interface for all content creation, shortcuts in SharePoint Designer allow you to create Web content without having to open the New dialog box. For example, in the File menu, if you just hover over the New menu option, another menu opens that either lets you create Web content directly or opens the New dialog box.

Also, in the Web Site tab discussed earlier, a New Page icon in the top-right corner allows you to create a new Web page (the document type of which is defined in the Page Editor Options).

Working with Page Views

The page-editing interface of SharePoint Designer offers three main views that you can use to design and code for your Web page: the Design view, the Code view, and the Split view. Figure 4.6 shows the Split view of a Web page in SharePoint Designer. You can switch views by clicking the tabs located near the lower-left corner.

To become familiar with the page views, follow these steps to create a simple SharePoint Web page using SharePoint Designer:

1. **Choose File ⇨ Open Site to open a WSS v3 site in SharePoint Designer.** This exercise creates a new Web page based on the default master page of a WSS v3 site.

CROSS-REF   For more on master pages, see Chapter 13.

2. **Choose File ⇨ New to open the New dialog box.** Under the Page tab in the General list, click Create from Master Page. Keep C# as the Programming Language for the Web page.

3. **Click OK.** The Select a Master Page dialog box opens.

4. **Keep the defaults in the Select a Master Page dialog box and then click OK.** SharePoint Designer now creates a new Web page and applies the Web site's default master page to it. When the default master page is applied to the new Web page, SharePoint Designer renders the Web page in the Design view.

5. **Press Ctrl+S or choose File ⇨ Save As to save the Web page inside the root folder of the Web site.**

FIGURE 4.6

The Split view for a page in SharePoint Designer

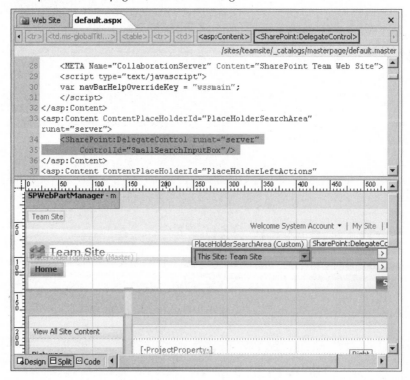

The Design view is the canvas you use to develop your Web pages and see the first preview of how your Web page would look. The Design view renders HTML tags and controls, ASP.NET 2.0, and SharePoint controls in a manner very similar to the way they would look in a Web browser (hence, WYSIWYG). It enables design features, such as visual aids and formatting marks, that assist you in managing the design and layout of a Web page, and provides the user interface to selectively access control properties and common control tasks.

To view the code associated with the Web page, open it the Code view, which you do by clicking the Code tab at the bottom-left corner of the Web page. The Code view in SharePoint Designer provides a rich, enhanced Visual Studio–like experience to aid in code writing. It supports features such as IntelliSense and auto code completion for HTML, client-side scripts, and ASP.NET 2.0. It also provides features such as code hyperlinks and incremental search that developers can use to easily manage code on their Web pages.

The Split view allows designers to view both the Design and Code views of the Web page in a single view. This view is particularly useful in quickly locating code associated with a tag or control in the Code view. Simply clicking on the control in the Design view highlights the associated code in the Code view.

To see this with the Web page that you just created in the previous exercise, follow these steps:

1. **With the Web page open in the Design view, hover over the search box control in the top-right corner of the Web page.** A button with an arrow on it is enabled for the search box control. This button is called the control's Common Tasks button and is used to open the Common Control Tasks menu, which allows you to change control properties.

2. **Click the Common Tasks button and then click Create Custom Content.** Now click the Quick Launch bar on the left to move the focus away from the search box control.

3. **Click the Split view tab of the Web page and then click the search box control again.**

The code associated with the search box control is highlighted in the Code view. This ability is very useful in locating code associated with a particular control, especially when the Code view of the Web page has a large number of lines in it.

 **For more on page views, see Chapter 6.**

Understanding Web Site Panes

The Web Site tab shown in Figure 4.7 provides another set of standard panes in SharePoint Designer to manage certain site-level components, such as site hyperlinks, reports, and navigation:

FIGURE 4.7

The Web Site panes in SharePoint Designer

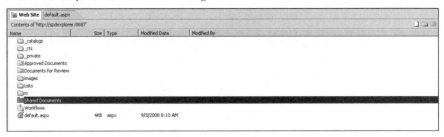

- **Folders:** Like the Folder List task pane, this pane shows the list of folders and files inside the Web site. Again, the icons for the files and folders indicate the type of content.

- **Remote Web Site:** Allows the use of SharePoint Designer publishing features for non-SharePoint Sites. This pane is not available for SharePoint sites.

- **Reports:** The option provides the interface for viewing and managing a SharePoint Designer site and usage reports for a Web site.

- **Navigation:** Displays the navigation structure of the Web site (for Web sites that use hidden metadata). Allows you to add and remove pages from the Web site's navigation structure and set page titles

- **Hyperlinks:** This displays a visual representation and allows management of the hyperlinks inside the selected Web page.

Using Toolbars and Task Panes

SharePoint Designer makes most of its designing and development features available through toolbars and task panes. You can enable or disable toolbars in SharePoint Designer by choosing View ⇨ Toolbars. The Task Panes menu in SharePoint Designer can be used to enable and disable the task panes. One of the really cool features of SharePoint Designer task panes is that they can be docked in and out of the user interface. This feature allows SharePoint Designer users to lay out the environment as they want it. So, if a designer is working heavily on data views, he or she can modify the interface so that the task panes and toolbars associated with data views are enabled and activated for easy access.

Laying out your SharePoint Designer interface

While the default view of the SharePoint Designer environment has the task panes and toolbars located in a specific manner, the interface is very flexible and allows you to modify it to keep the most frequently used task panes activated.

You can easily drag and dock task panes to either corner of the center section (which displays the Web Site panes) or drag them to another screen if you're working with multiple monitors and running out of screen real estate. Toolbars and the menu bar can also be docked around any corner of the screen. Figure 4.8 shows such a customized view of the SharePoint Designer environment.

The Style and Style application toolbars can be seen in the top section, the CSS Properties task pane is activated in the left section, the CSS reports in the center section, and the Manage Styles and Apply Styles task panes are enabled in the right section. This environment is set up for ease of operation when working with CSS.

FIGURE 4.8

A customized view of the SharePoint Designer environment

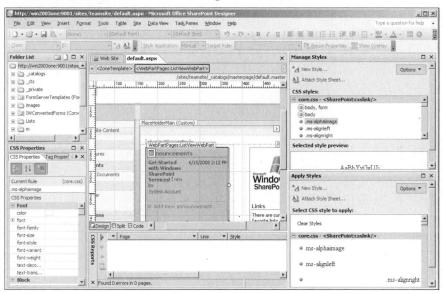

Using the Customize dialog box

The Customize dialog box, as shown in Figure 4.9, provides the Commands well for SharePoint Designer, which is used to host menus, menu options, commands, etc. These menu options and commands can be dragged and dropped into new or existing menus and toolbars to customize the SharePoint Designer environment to suit your needs.

FIGURE 4.9

The Commands well in the Customize Dialog box

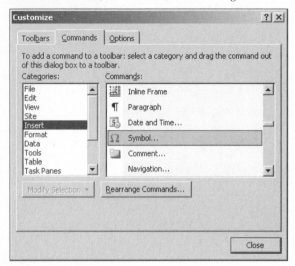

NOTE SharePoint Designer stores the customizations you make to its interface in a state file called `CMDUI.PRF` stored in the user's profile at `C:\Documents and Settings\<username>\Application Data\Microsoft\SharePoint Designer\State`.

In the next exercise, I take you through the steps to create a new toolbar for SharePoint Designer by using the Customize dialog box:

1. **Choose View ⇨ Toolbars ⇨ Customize to open the Customize dialog box.**

2. **In the Toolbars tab, click the New button.** Type the name for your custom toolbar in the New Toolbar dialog box, as shown in Figure 4.10.

FIGURE 4.10

The New Toolbar dialog box

3. **Click OK.** The new toolbar without any buttons is shown. The next step is to add buttons to the toolbar by using the Commands well.

4. **To access the Commands well, click the Commands tab.** Here, the left list shows the command categories, and the right list shows the list of available commands.

5. **Locate the commands you want to add to your new toolbar.** Drag and drop the commands into the newly created toolbar. After you drop a command inside the new toolbar, the Modify Selection button becomes enabled. This button can be used to change the name, image, and text of the command in the toolbar.

> **TIP** The Customize dialog box is especially useful for providing command buttons to expose the functionality that developers might have created through macros by using the SharePoint Designer object model. You can use the Assign Macro option (found after clicking the Modify Selection button) to assign a macro to a command button. The macro can then be run by just clicking the command button.

> **NOTE** You can learn more about macros at this Web site: `http://msdn.microsoft.com/en-us/library/bb149050.aspx`.

When the toolbar is complete, you can drag and dock it to any of the four corners of the SharePoint Designer environment.

Modifying Page-Editing and Application Options

SharePoint Designer comes with some default general application settings that define its behavior when it's open. These settings can be controlled by the Application Options dialog box, as shown in Figure 4.11, which is accessible by choosing Tools ⇨ Application Options. The Application Options dialog box has four tabs:

■ **General:** Allows you to establish application startup options that check whether SharePoint Designer is the default editor for Web pages and Office documents, toggle the SharePoint Designer status bar (displayed at the bottom of the SharePoint Designer interface), show warnings in the status bar for expired FrontPage Include components, etc.

■ **Configure Editors:** This tab allows you to associate programs with various file extensions or change existing associations. You can also add, modify, or delete extensions.

■ **Reports View:** Allows you to set some settings that apply to the site reports generated for Web pages by SharePoint Designer

■ **FTP:** Allows you to choose whether a file extension is transferred via FTP in binary or ASCII format

The Application Options dialog box

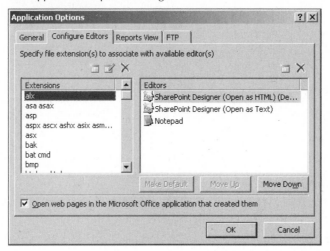

The Page Editor Options dialog box, as shown in Figure 4.12, which can be accessed by choosing Tools ⇨ Page Editor Options or via the Page Editor Options link in the New dialog box, is the interface that allows you to set master properties for a number of SharePoint Designer components and features. These properties include general settings for HTML tags, Code view options, picture and auto thumbnail settings, IntelliSense and code formatting options, CSS settings, etc. The Page Editor Options dialog box has several tabs:

CROSS-REF   For more on page-editor options, see Chapters 6, 7, and 12.

- **General:** This allows you to establish general settings for HTML tags and set spelling options and Code view options.

- **Auto Thumbnail:** This allows you to change the width, height, and border thickness of thumbnails created by SharePoint Designer during various picture operations.

- **Default Fonts:** This allows you to set the default font settings and the fonts for text display in the Design and Code views of SharePoint Designer. The font settings here for the Design view don't actually apply to the text of the Web page. While the preview on the page in Design view uses the font settings you make here, the actual page text uses the font specified using text formatting via HTML, CSS, etc. For example, if you set the default font to Calibri, the portion of text that has Verdana applied to it in the HTML code is displayed in the Design view in Verdana. However, a portion of text that has no HTML, CSS, etc., applied to it is shown in Calibri.

FIGURE 4.12

The Page Editor Options dialog box

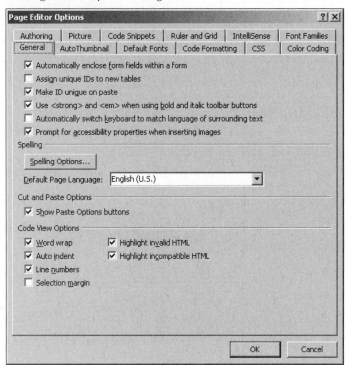

- **Code Formatting:** This allows you to set a number of options for the Code view of SharePoint Designer.

CROSS-REF   For more on code formatting, see Chapter 6.

- **CSS:** This allows you to set how CSS styles are applied to the various HTML tags.

- **Color Coding:** Settings in this tab allow you to specify the colors used to indicate various SharePoint Designer components in the Design view. Also, you can set colors to differentiate code in the Code view. While the default settings here usually work best, you can change settings in case you're accustomed to a different set of code colors.

- **Authoring:** This allows you to set default new document types for non-SharePoint and SharePoint sites. Also, you can set the document type declaration, Internet Explorer and CSS schemas to be used for IntelliSense, auto code completion, and indicating errors in code.

- **Picture:** This provides the interface for setting default file types for pictures and picture conversion.
- **Code Snippets:** This allows you to add or remove code snippets. Code snippets is a feature offered by SharePoint Designer that allows you to quickly add frequently used code pieces to the code of the Web page.
- **Ruler and Grid:** This can be used to specify settings for rulers and grids in the Design view.
- **IntelliSense:** This provides settings for auto code completions and code hyperlinks for the SharePoint Designer Code view.
- **Font Families:** This allows you to add fonts and create font families.

These options are discussed throughout the rest of this book.

Summary

By the end of this chapter, you have seen SharePoint Designer enough to be familiar with the layout and placement of the various features. What makes this interface so easy is that most of the functionality is easily accessible by using task panes and toolbars. As you work more with SharePoint Designer, you start remembering shortcuts that make it even simpler to use. Have you already figured out that pressing Ctrl+N creates a new page and opens it in one of the views? More such shortcuts follow throughout the rest of this book.

Chapter 5

Working with Basic Web Page Components

I n this chapter, I elaborate on Web page design and development. This chapter focuses primarily on Web page development by using HTML technology.

The default Web pages that come with SharePoint sites use a variety of complex page design and development technologies. To avoid overload, I use non-SharePoint sites to discuss Web page design and formatting concepts. Once you understand these basic concepts, you can apply them to SharePoint Web pages with relative ease. Although profound discussion on HTML is beyond the scope of this text, I introduce you to some basic HTML concepts and tags as you move along and design HTML Web pages by using SharePoint Designer tools and features. Also, many page-formatting features of SharePoint Designer rely heavily on CSS. I also discuss the SharePoint Designer no-code implementation of such features.

CROSS-REF For more on Web page development by using DHTML and ASP.NET 2.0, see Chapters 8 and Chapter 10. For more on internal CSS implementation, see Chapter 12.

HTML is the principal language for developing Web pages. Even if you use a server-side script, such as ASP.NET, to write the actual code of your Web page, the code that a browser renders is always HTML. HTML provides its features through a number of tags that you can set attributes for to define your usage. For example, the <a> tag is used to create a hyperlink, and the HREF attribute of the <a> tag is used to define the location of the hyperlink.

SharePoint Designer allows you to implement many of the commonly used formatting techniques without having to write or understand the HTML coding that goes with it.

IN THIS CHAPTER

Understanding basic formatting and positioning

Understanding frames

Creating hyperlinks and bookmarks

Using tables and table layouts

Working with layers

Understanding Basic Formatting and Positioning

In this section, I help you understand some of the very basic formatting features of SharePoint Designer. Later, you might decide to implement functionality provided by these features by using separate CSS styles. However, this section should help you develop understanding about how these features work and also explore some code behind the implementation.

Setting fonts for text

Fonts and font styles help implement text formatting on Web pages. You implement basic font formatting in SharePoint Designer by using the Font dialog box, as shown in Figure 5.1. You access the Font dialog box by either choosing Format ➪ Font or by simply right-clicking on the Web page in the Design view and then choosing Font from the popup menu.

FIGURE 5.1

The Font dialog box with the Font tab selected

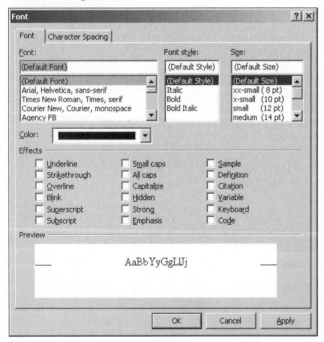

To apply a font to text on a Web page, follow these steps:

1. **Open the Web page in the Design view and then select the text to which you want to apply a font.** Double-clicking a word in a line of text selects that word. Clicking three times successively selects a whole paragraph.

2. **Right-click on the selected text and then choose Font from the popup menu.** The Font dialog box opens, allowing you to choose the font, font style, and size you want to apply to your text.

3. **Using the Font list in the Font tab, choose the font that you want to apply to the selected text.** The Font list displays the font families and the fonts installed and available for use on Web pages. Your selection is shown in the box just above the Font list. For this exercise, choose Tahoma from the Font list.

> **NOTE** You can press Ctrl+Z to undo any changes made to a Web page. Ctrl+Y can be used to reapply the last change made. This comes in handy if you need to change only certain aspects of a page and don't want to access the Font dialog box for each change.

4. **Use the Font style list to choose the style for the selected text.** You can choose to display the text in bold, italics, both, or neither. Choose the (Default Style) option (which actually means neither) in the Font style list for this exercise.

5. **You can use the Size box and list to either specify a size (in points) or choose from a set of predefined sizes.** Choose a small size (such as 12 points) for the selected text.

6. **Click the Color dropdown menu to choose a color for the text.** You can either choose from the standard colors shown in the default palette, custom colors that you created, or document colors that already exist in the document. You can also click More Colors to specify or create another color.

7. **Choose More Colors from the Color dropdown menu to open the More Colors dialog box, as shown in Figure 5.2.** Here, you can specify the hex value that defines the color, create a custom color by using the Custom button, or choose from the hexagonal palette of colors by clicking Select. Also, a preview in the bottom-right corner of the dialog box shows the New and Current colors.

8. **Click Select to enable selection from the hexagonal palette in the dialog box.** Choose the color you want to use by clicking on it in the hexagonal palette. The Value text field shows the hex code associated with the color, the Name text field shows the color name, and the preview shows the selected color.

9. **Click OK to view the preview of the selected color in the Preview section of the Font dialog box.**

10. **In the Effects section, click the Underline, Overline, Strong, and Variable check boxes.** The Effects section allows you to choose from some default effects that have been prepared for use. When you make a selection in the Effects section, some of the font styles may change. For example, clicking the Strong check box changes the selection in the Font style list to Bold.

11. **Click OK to apply the font to the selected text.**

While the Design view of the Web page now shows the font formatting applied to the text, the interesting aspect is how SharePoint Designer applies this formatting. You can view the code that SharePoint Designer wrote for the previous steps by choosing the Code view of the Web page:

■ **Style section:**

```
<style type="text/css">
    .style1 {
        font-family: Verdana;
        font-size: small;
        color: #CC6699;
        text-decoration: overline underline;
    }
    .style2 {
        font-style: normal;
    }
</style>
```

■ **HTML section:**

```
<p class="style1"><var class="style2"><strong>test</strong></
    var></p>
```

FIGURE 5.2

The More Colors dialog box

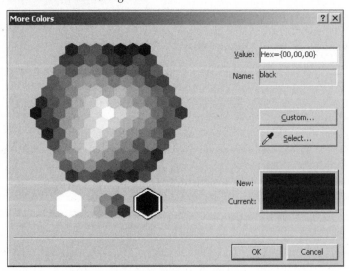

As indicated in the Code view, fonts are implemented by using a combination of CSS and HTML technologies. The font size, color, etc., are applied by using CSS styles (indicated by the `class="style"` code), and the Strong effect is applied by using the `<strong>` tag.

Many of the formatting options provided by the Font dialog box are also available by using the Common and Formatting toolbars, as shown in Figure 5.3. For example, you can use the Formatting toolbar to quickly choose a font for the selected text, define the font size and apply font styles, specify the background and foreground colors for lines and paragraphs, create borders for lines and paragraphs, etc.

FIGURE 5.3

The Common (top) and Formatting (bottom) toolbars

TIP You can specify whether to use the `<strong>` tags for bolds and italics by using the Use `<strong>` and `<em>` when using bold and italics toolbar buttons check box in the General tab of the Page Editor Options dialog box, which you access by choosing Tools ➪ Page Editor Options. If you deselect this check box, SharePoint Designer uses the `<b>` tag to bold text.

You can also use the Character Spacing tab in the Font dialog box to specify settings for the spacing between the words and characters in the text. By default, the character spacing is set to normal. However, you can choose to either expand (or condense) the characters and specify the measure (by using the By list box) of the expansion (or condensation). In the next exercise, I help you understand how you can position the text by using the options in the Character Spacing tab:

1. **Create a new HTML Web page with some text paragraphs inside your Web site and open it in the Design view.**

2. **Select a line of text in the paragraph on the Web page.** Right-click on the selected text and then choose Font from the popup menu to open the Font dialog box, as shown in Figure 5.4.

3. **Click the Character Spacing tab, and in the Spacing dropdown menu, choose Expanded.** Use the By list box to specify the amount of expansion.

4. **In the Position dropdown menu, choose Super.**

5. **Click OK.**

The selected text in the Design view appears positioned a little above the normal text of the paragraph. If you investigate the Code view of the Web page, this functionality is again implemented by using CSS with `vertical-align` and `letter-spacing` properties:

■ CSS section:

```
<style type="text/css">
.style1 {
    letter-spacing: 5pt;
    vertical-align: super;
}
</style>
```

■ HTML section:

```
<p>Show me how to <span class="style1">superscript</span></p>
```

FIGURE 5.4

The Font dialog box with the Character Spacing tab selected

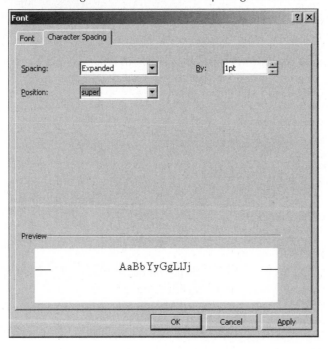

Because all the fonts might not be available on the machine where your Web page is being viewed or supported by the browser being used to view the Web page, it's useful to apply fonts by using the font families. Font families allow you to apply fonts to text on Web pages by using a set of fonts rather than a single font. If one font isn't available, a browser can display the text by using another font in the font family. You can create font families in SharePoint Designer by using the Font Families tab in the Page Editor Options dialog box, as shown in Figure 5.5.

To create a new font family and use it to format the text on your Web page, follow these steps:

1. Choose Tools ⇨ Page Editor Options to open the Page Editor Options dialog box and then click the Font Families tab.

2. In the Select font family list, click the (New Font Family) option.

3. Choose Arial from the Add font list and then click Add. Repeat this step to also add Calibri, Tahoma, and Verdana to the new font family you just created.

4. Click OK.

The new font family is now created and is available for use in the Font dialog box or the Common and Formatting toolbars.

CAUTION The Default Fonts tab in the Page Editor Options dialog box specifies the default fonts to use for displaying text in the Design and Code views. The fonts you set here are for display purposes only and don't apply to the page itself. When you view the Web page in a browser, fonts that are actually applied to the text using the Font dialog box (or other features) are used.

FIGURE 5.5

The Font Families tab in the Page Editor Options dialog box

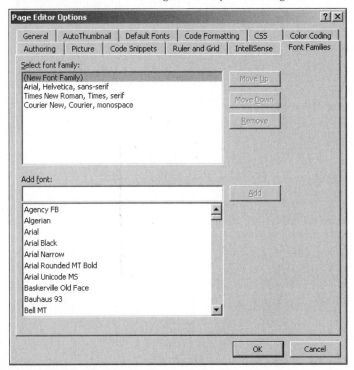

Working with paragraphs and indentation

By default, SharePoint Designer allows you to format text by using paragraphs. Whenever you press Enter on a Web page in SharePoint Designer, a <p> tag is inserted and a new paragraph is started. Most of the paragraph formatting that can be applied by using the SharePoint Designer user interface applies to the <p> tag by using CSS styles.

In the next exercise, you use the Paragraph dialog box, as shown in Figure 5.6, to implement paragraph formatting to selected text on a Web page:

1. **In the Design view, open or create a Web page that has text paragraphs.**

2. **Select a paragraph of text in the Design view and then choose Format ➪ Paragraph to open the Paragraph dialog box.**

3. **Choose Center from the Alignment dropdown menu.** This aligns the selected text in the center of the Web page.

4. **In the Indentation section, type the values of the indentation for the paragraph from the left and the right sides as well as the indentation of the first line in the paragraph.**

5. **In the Spacing section, type the spacing you want before and after the paragraph and between words in the paragraph.** Also, type the spacing between the lines of the paragraph by using the Line Spacing dropdown menu. The preview at the bottom of the dialog box shows how the settings you make for the paragraph look.

6. **Click OK and then save the Web page.**

If you investigate the Code view of the page where you applied the settings using the Paragraph dialog box, you see that most of the settings have been implemented by using CSS, with properties such as `text-align`, `line-height`, `word-spacing`, `margin-left`, etc.

One interesting feature provided by the Common and Formatting toolbars is to quickly format text lines and paragraphs by using predefined HTML and CSS styles. If you click the dropdown menu that has the Paragraph option selected, a list of available HTML tags, such as Headings (<h1>, <h2>, etc.) and Lists (<ul>, <ol>, etc.), are available for use on a paragraph. These tags format text in different ways, allowing you to choose the best formatting for representing the text. For example, the <ul> tag allows you to create a bulleted list in the text, while the <ol> tag allows you to create a numbered list.

NOTE   You can also increase or decrease the indentation of a paragraph or a line of text by using the Increase Indent Position (Ctrl+M) and Decrease Indent Position (Ctrl+Shift+M) buttons in the Common and Formatting toolbars.

FIGURE 5.6

The Paragraph dialog box

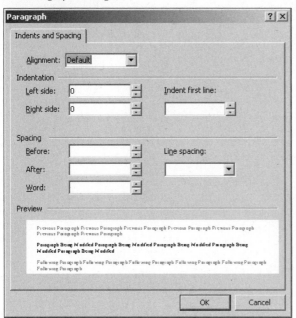

Choose Format ⇨ Borders and Shading to apply borders and specify background colors and patterns for your text lines and paragraphs. In the next exercise, you use the Borders and Shading dialog box, as shown in Figure 5.7, to apply borders to a paragraph of text inside your Web page:

1. **In the Design view, open or create a Web page that has text paragraphs.**

2. **Select a paragraph of text and then choose Format ⇨ Borders and Shading to open the Borders and Shading dialog box.**

3. **In the Setting section under the Borders tab, click Custom.** The Settings section allows you to choose from Default (no borders), Box (creates a border on all four boundaries of the selected text), and Custom (allows you to choose on which boundary the border should be applied).

4. **In the Style list, choose double.** The Style list allows you to choose from a list of styles that you can use for borders.

5. **Choose a color for the border by using the Color dropdown menu and then specify a width (in pixels) for the border.**

FIGURE 5.7

The Borders and Shading dialog box

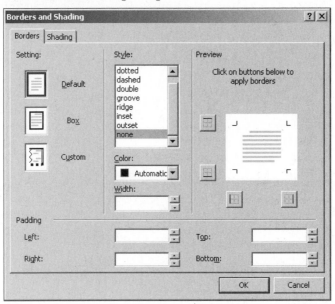

6. **In the Padding section, type the values (in pixels) in the Left and Right boxes for applying padding to the left and right boundaries of the text paragraph.** Padding specifies the amount of space from the border where the text begins.

7. **In the Preview section, click the appropriate buttons to apply the left and right borders to the text.** The preview shows how the borders appear inside the Web page. You can also click in the Preview box to set the borders.

8. **Click the Shading tab and then choose the background and foreground colors by using the Fill section.** The Preview section shows a minor preview of the background color that's applied to the paragraph. If you want to specify a background picture for the paragraph, you can do so by using the Patterns section.

9. **Click OK and then save the Web page.**

The formatting is again applied in the Design view of the Web page. The borders and shading formatting is also applied by using inline styles.

NOTE   It's important to understand that most of the borders and shading formatting is implemented by using CSS styles. When the formatting is applied, it's not necessary for the Borders and Shading dialog box to pick the settings back from the Web page for modification with full fidelity (which might result in some confusion). To change the formatting, it's best that you clear the exiting style by using the Apply Styles task pane and apply a new one instead. To clear the existing style, select the associated text line or paragraph, and in the Apply Styles task pane, click Clear Styles. For more on the Apply Styles task pane, see Chapter 12.

If you used the Pattern section in the Borders and Shading dialog box to set a background picture for the selected text, you might be asked to save the picture locally inside your Web site if the picture doesn't reside inside the Web site. You can simply specify the folder location inside your Web site where you want to save the picture.

Using bullets and numbering

SharePoint Designer implements bulleted lists and numbered lists by using the `<ul>` and `<ol>` HTML tags. To create a bulleted list and specify settings for it, follow these steps:

1. **Create a Web page in SharePoint Designer and then open it in the Design view.**

2. **Place the cursor (or the insertion point) at the beginning of the line of text where you want to begin the bulleted list.**

3. **Choose Format ⇨ Bullets and Numbering to open the Bullets and Numbering dialog box, as shown in Figure 5.8, and then click the Plain Bullets tab.**

FIGURE 5.8

The Plain Bullets tab in the Bullets and Numbering dialog box

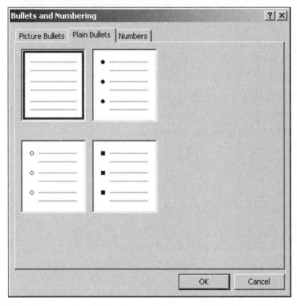

4. **Choose the bullet style and then click OK.** SharePoint Designer creates a bulleted list by using the bullet format you chose.

5. To create new bullet points in this bulleted list, simply press Enter right after the end of a line of bulleted text.

6. To remove a bullet point from the list, place the cursor at the beginning of the line of text corresponding to the bullet and then press Backspace. Or you can right-click on the line of text corresponding to the bullet, choose List Item Properties from the popup menu to open the Bullets and Numbering dialog box, and then choose the No bullets option.

You can also create sublists inside the bulleted list by using these steps:

1. In your existing bulleted list, create a new bullet point by pressing Enter right after the end of a line of bulleted text.

2. Press Ctrl+M or click the Increase Indent Position button on the Common and Formatting toolbar. This creates a child bullet list inside the existing bullet list. To add new bullet points to this child list, press Enter right after the end of a line of bulleted text.

3. To remove a bullet point from the child list, press Ctrl+Shift+M or click the Decrease Indent Position button on the Common and Formatting toolbar.

Using the previous steps, you can create inherited lists of multiple levels. In the Code view of the Web page, SharePoint Designer uses the <ul> tags for creating the bulleted list. The list items are created by using the <li> tag. Also, the style created while creating the list uses the list-style-type property to specify the style of the bullet being used.

> **NOTE** The <ul> tag represents the unordered list and is used to create bulleted lists. The <ol> tag, on the other hand, represents the ordered list and is used to create numbered lists.

If you want to add your own pictures instead of the existing bullets, use the Picture Bullets tab in the Bullets and Numbering dialog box:

1. On the bulleted list you created by using the previous exercise, click the line of text corresponding to the bullet point where you want to change the bullet to a picture of your choice.

2. Choose Format ⇨ Bullets and Numbering to open the Bullets and Numbering dialog box, as shown in Figure 5.9, and then click the Picture Bullets tab.

3. In the Picture section, click the Specify Picture radio button and then click Browse to locate the picture you want to use instead of a bullet point.

4. Click OK and then save the Web page.

> **TIP** Because a picture appears instead of bullet points, make sure that you choose a picture of smaller dimensions. This ensures that the Design view of the list doesn't become confusing and unmanageable when the picture is selected for the list.

FIGURE 5.9

The Picture Bullets tab in the Bullets and Numbering dialog box

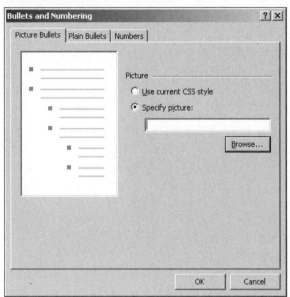

You can create numbered lists instead of bulleted lists in the same manner by selecting the format by using the Numbers tab in the Bullets and Numbering dialog box. You can also mix the numbered list with the bulleted lists. In other words, you can create a parent list as a numbered list and then a child list (created by using the Increase Indent Position button) inside it as a bulleted list or vice versa.

Positioning Web content

The Position dialog box (accessed by choosing Format ➪ Position), as shown in Figure 5.10, allows you to position content on the Web page by using a set of positioning CSS styles and HTML tags. It also provides the option for you to overlap content on Web pages, which enables you to create callouts and screen tips.

FIGURE 5.10

The Position dialog box

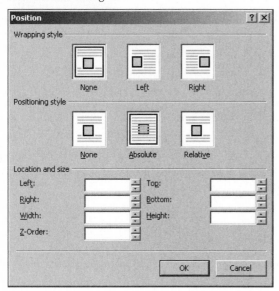

It's really important to understand the various positioning options available in CSS to choose which one is best for your design. Here are the CSS positioning options:

- **Static:** By default, when a browser displays the contents of a Web page, the object has a static position in the display window.

- **Absolute:** With this option, you can specify the top, left, right, and bottom distances from the parent's position where the object should be placed.

- **Relative:** This option allows you to position the object relative to its original position inside a Web page. The object's original position is marked by an anchor sign in the Design view.

- **Fixed:** This option allows a browser to identify content with respect to the main window so that the object maintains its position relative to the window even if the content is scrolled.

The Position dialog box also allows you to specify the location of the object by using the left, right, top, and bottom dimensions as well as set the change in width and height of the location. You can also specify the overlapping position of the content by using the Z-Order box.

Understanding Frames

Frames in HTML provide Web page designers with a means to divide their page layout into sections and then use these sections to manage content. A typical scenario is to divide the Web page into a header, a footer, a left navigation section, and a contents section. Hyperlinks in one section can then be used to display contents in another section. For example, you can create a navigation hyperlink set in the left section so that clicking on the hyperlinks changes the Web page displayed in the contents sections.

Frames are implemented by using a frameset page that becomes the backbone page on which the frames are laid out. Then, the Web pages for each frame within the frameset page are set. To create a new Frames Page, follow these steps:

1. **Choose File ➪ New to open the New dialog box.**

2. **Click the Page tab and then click Frames Pages.** Under this option, choose the Header, Footer and Contents template.

3. **Click OK.** The selected template opens in the Design view, as shown in Figure 5.11

FIGURE 5.11

A template open in the Design view

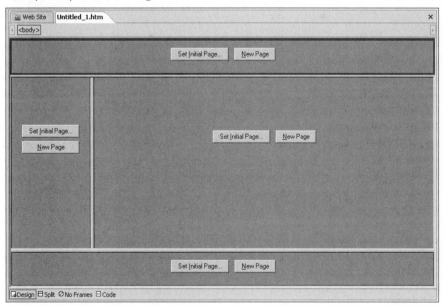

Along with the Design, Code, and Split views, there's now another view called No Frames view. This view indicates the display of the Web page for Web browsers that don't support frames. If you click the Code view tab, you can see the Code view of the frameset page.

As mentioned before, this page provides the frames skeleton that hosts other pages shown inside the frames. You can use the Design view to change the dimensions of the frames inside the frameset page by dragging the frame boundaries to your preferred width and height.

If you want to split a frame, press Ctrl while dragging the frame boundary to the required width or height. This splits the existing frame into two frames. You can change the width of the splitting lines by right-clicking on the frameset page and then choosing Page Properties from the popup menu. The Frames tab, as shown in Figure 5.12, then appears in the Page Properties dialog box.

FIGURE 5.12

The Frames tab in the Page Properties dialog box

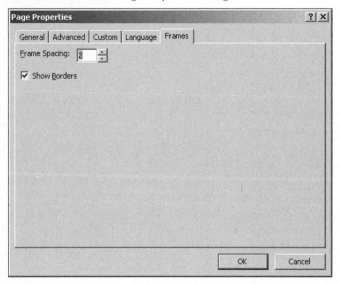

You can use the Frame Spacing box to change the width of the splitting lines. Also, you can deselect the Show Borders check box if you don't want to show the splitting lines. You can also access the Frames tab by clicking Frames Page in the Frame Properties dialog box, as shown in Figure 5.13. You access this dialog box by right-clicking on the frame in the Design view.

You can use the Frame Properties dialog box to set the name, title, initial page, and description associated with a frame. The name of a frame is used when targeting hyperlinks to specific frames inside the frameset page. You can also choose whether to show the scrollbars if the contents of the page inside the frame extend beyond the frame's width and height. Keep the Resizable in browser check box selected if you want Web page viewers to be able to resize the frame in the browser window.

FIGURE 5.13

The Frame Properties dialog box

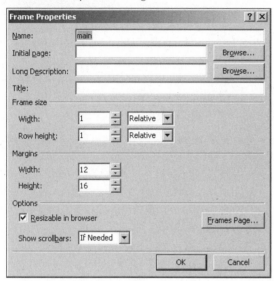

Creating pages using frames

In this exercise, I take you through the steps for creating a navigation-based frameset page. If you completed the other exercises, you should already have at least three Web pages that can be displayed in frames:

1. **Choose File ⇨ New to open the New dialog box, click the Page tab, and then click Frames Pages to choose the Header template.**

2. **Click OK.** The Header frame in this template hosts a page that contains hyperlinks that open the corresponding Web page in the main section. The frames page created by using the Header template has two frames: the header frame (on the top) and the main frame.

3. **Right-click on the frameset page and then choose Page Properties from the popup menu.** The Page Properties dialog box opens.

4. **Click the Frames tab, deselect the Show Borders check box, and then click OK.**

5. **Click the New Page button in the Header frame to create a new page.** You use this page to create hyperlinks for navigation.

6. **Right-click on the newly created header and then choose Hyperlink from the popup menu to open the Insert Hyperlink dialog box.**

7. **In the Text to display box, type a display name for the hyperlink.**

8. **Type the location of the initial Web page of the main frame by using the Address text field or by choosing the Web page from the Look in box.**

9. **Click OK to finish creating the hyperlink.** Clicking on this hyperlink opens the first page in the main frame.

10. **Repeat steps 5 and 6 to create two more hyperlinks in the header for displaying the second and third Web pages.**

11. **Click Set Initial Page in the main frame to set the frame page as the page you used for creating the first hyperlink in step 8 and then click OK when you finish.**

12. **Press Ctrl+S to save the frames page and the header page.**

When you browse to this page, clicking on the links in the header frame opens the corresponding Web page in the main frame. The page created by using the Header template is designed so that every hyperlink link opens in the main frame. In other words, the main frame is the target frame for all hyperlinks.

Using inline frames on Web pages

As discussed earlier, when you use frames for designing Web pages, you have to create a skeleton page that hosts all the frames. However, there may be cases where you might want to show the contents of a Web page inside an existing Web page without using a separate frameset page. You can accomplish this using inline frames.

Inline frames behave like standard frames except they can be placed directly inside the Web page you're designing. To insert and configure an inline frame on a Web page, follow these steps:

1. **Create a new Web page by using SharePoint Designer.**

2. **Choose Insert ➪ HTML ➪ Inline Frame to insert an inline frame on the Web page.** The inline frame opens in the Design view, allowing you to set the initial page.

3. **Right-click on the inline frame and then choose Inline Frame Properties from the popup menu.** The Inline Frame Properties dialog box, as shown in Figure 5.14, opens, allowing you to set the name, title, initial page, and description. You can also change the display text to be shown for browsers that don't support inline frames, set the scrollbar settings, and choose whether to display a frame border.

4. **Close the Inline Frame Properties dialog box.**

5. **Set the Web page to be displayed in the inline frame by clicking the Set Initial Page button.**

6. **Click OK.**

Inline frames are implemented by using the `<iframe>` HTML tag. If you click the Code view tab after you set the properties, the attributes for the inline frame appear with `<iframe>` tags.

FIGURE 5.14

The Inline Frame Properties dialog box

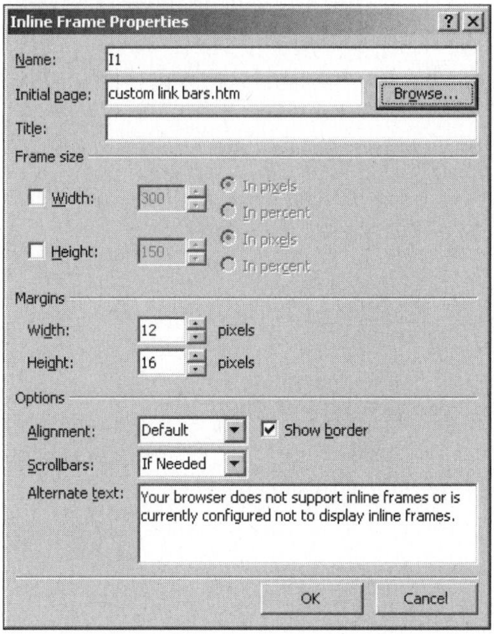

Creating Hyperlinks and Bookmarks

One of the most common operations that you perform on a Web page is to create hyperlinks to content. Hyperlinks provide navigation for Web sites and link content placed at different locations inside a Web site. The basic attributes of a hyperlink include display text and a URL that the hyperlink points to. When you click hyperlinked display text, the Web browser directs you to the URL connected to that hyperlink. You can create hyperlinks to almost any type of content, including pictures, Web pages, documents, executables (`.exe`, `.dll`, etc.), and bookmarks.

You create hyperlinks in SharePoint Designer by using the Insert Hyperlink dialog box, as shown in Figure 5.15. You access this dialog box by choosing Insert ➪ Hyperlink or pressing Ctrl+K. This dialog box is also used for editing hyperlinks (although the name changes to Edit Hyperlink).

The Insert Hyperlink dialog box allows you to create hyperlinks by using these panes:

- **Existing File or Web Page:** The default pane allows you to choose a file from the Current Folder, Browsed Pages, or the Recent Files list. The files or Web pages that are currently open in SharePoint Designer show up with (open) at the end of the filename. You can use the Look in dropdown menu to locate the content you want to create a hyperlink for.

■ **Place in This Document:** Allows you to create hyperlinks to bookmarks on the Web page you currently have open in SharePoint Designer. If no bookmarks have been created, the list is empty.

■ **Create New Document:** Allows you to create a hyperlink to a new document. The interface allows you to change the location of the new document and then specify a target frame for the hyperlink. You can also choose whether you want to edit the newly created document right after creation or later.

■ **E-mail Address:** This option allows you to create a hyperlink to an e-mail address and specify parameters.

FIGURE 5.15

The Insert Hyperlink dialog box

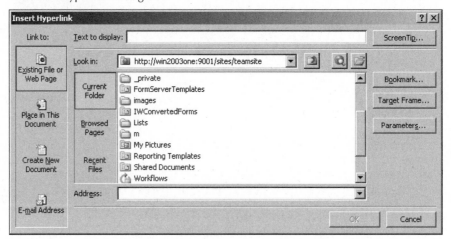

Also, there are a number of buttons in the Insert Hyperlinks dialog box that allow for these operations:

■ **Screen Tip:** Allows you to specify the screen tip displayed when you hover over a hyperlink. A screen tip can be used to display information about the content that the hyperlink points to.

■ **Bookmark:** Displays the list of bookmarks present on the document that you've chosen as the URL for the hyperlink and allows you to add the bookmark to the hyperlink

■ **Target Frame:** Allows you to choose the frame where the target document of the hyperlink should open

- **Parameters:** Allows you to specify parameters sent along with the hyperlink. These parameters form the query string in the hyperlink and can be used by the target document for performing various operations. This is especially useful in performing form-based operations by using ASP, ASP.NET, and FrontPage components.

- **Remove Link:** Removes the link from the Web page

Bookmarks act as anchors that you can insert on Web pages at specific locations of interest and later use hyperlinks to navigate to those locations. They're especially useful if you have a long Web page and you want a Web browser to be able to go directly to a location on the Web page rather than have a user scroll down to the location. You can create a bookmark on a Web page by following these steps:

1. **Place the cursor at the location on the Web page where you want to create the bookmark.**

2. **Press Ctrl+G or choose Insert ⇨ Bookmark to open the Bookmark dialog box, as shown in Figure 5.16.** You use this dialog box to manage the bookmarks on the Web page.

FIGURE 5.16

The Bookmark dialog box

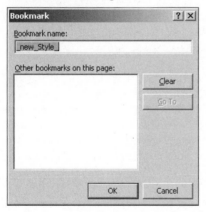

3. **Type the name of the bookmark and then click OK.**

When you view the Code view after inserting a bookmark, the bookmark is just an <a> tag with a Name attribute specified for it. To create a hyperlink to your newly created bookmark, follow these steps:

1. **Select the text on which you want to create a hyperlink.** This could be a word or line of text at the top of your Web page. When you click the hyperlink, the browser takes you to the location on the Web page where the bookmark was placed.

2. **Right-click on the selected text and then choose Hyperlink from the popup menu.** Or you can click the Hyperlink button on the Common toolbar to open the Insert Hyperlink dialog box. The Text to display box shows the text you selected on the Web page for creating the hyperlink on.

3. **In the Existing File or Web Page pane, choose the Web page where the bookmark exists.**

4. **Click the Place in This document icon.** The Select Place in Document dialog box opens, displaying all the bookmarks in the document selected in step 3.

5. **Choose the bookmark you want to use with the hyperlink and then click OK.** The bookmark is indicated in the hyperlink by its name after the # sign.

6. **Click OK.**

To preview the Web page in a browser, press F12. If the page is long enough (to activate scrollbars in the browser), when you click the newly created hyperlink, the page automatically scrolls to the location of the bookmark.

Creating parameters in hyperlinks

Sometimes, you might want to send some information with hyperlinks. This information could be used by scripts running on the target Web page to perform operations. For example, you can send values of variables that could be used by an ASP target page to retrieve information from a database.

Sending parameters in a hyperlink involves creating a query string along with the hyperlink. A query string is a string concatenation of name-value pairs of variables that you want to send with the request for the target Web page. The target Web page can use these name-value pairs for operations by using client- or server-side scripts. To understand the SharePoint Designer interface for creating parameters, the following steps take you through the process of creating a hyperlink that has three parameters: ID, Name, and ZipCode:

1. **Select the text on the Web page on which you want to create a hyperlink.**

2. **Right-click on the highlighted text and then choose Hyperlink from the popup menu to open the Insert Hyperlink dialog box.**

3. **Choose the target Web page of the hyperlink by using the Existing File or Web Page pane and then click Parameters.** The Hyperlink Parameters dialog box, as shown in Figure 5.17, opens.

4. **In the Query String section, click the Add button.** The Add Parameter dialog box opens.

5. **Type ID in the Name text field, type value 1 in the Value text field, and then click OK.**

FIGURE 5.17

The Hyperlink Parameters dialog box

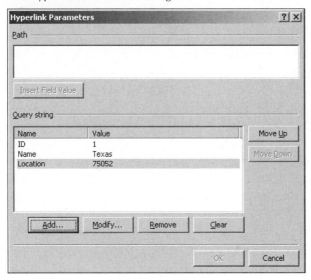

6. **Repeat step 5 to add a** `Name` **parameter with value** Texas **and a** `ZipCode` **parameter with value** 75052.

7. **Click OK to return to the Insert Hyperlink dialog box.** The complete target URL of the hyperlink is in the Address box.

8. **Click OK.**

The hyperlink that's created as a result of the previous steps has this code after the name of the target Web page:

```
?ID=1&Name=Texas&ZipCode=75052
```

This portion of the URL forms the query string that's passed on to the target Web page in the GET request for the target Web page. A script on the target Web page can retrieve parameters from this query string and then use them for performing its business.

Although in this exercise you created only static parameters with fixed values, you can create ASP or ASP.NET Web pages where these parameters can have values filled dynamically (such as from a database).

CROSS-REF For more on ASP.NET controls, see Chapter 10.

Targeting frames in Web pages

Using the Target Frame dialog box, as shown in Figure 5.18, while inserting hyperlinks, you can specify which frame window the target page should open in. You have these options available by default in the Common Targets list:

- **Page Default:** No target frame is specified.

- **Same Frame:** Uses `target=_self` attribute to indicate that the target page opens in the same frame window as the page containing the hyperlink

- **Whole Page:** Uses `target=_top` to specify that the target page opens in the main browser window

- **New Windows:** Uses `target=_blank` to specify that the target page opens in a new browser window

- **Parent Frame:** Uses `target=_parent` to specify that the target frame opens in the parent frame of the frame in which the current Web page is open

Other than the default options, the Common Target list also displays the frames that exist in the current page where the hyperlink is being created. The Set as page default check box allows you to set a particular frame as a default frame type for all hyperlinks in a Web page. This is done by adding a `<base>` tag in the `<head>` section of the Web page, indicating that the default frame should be used.

FIGURE 5.18

The Target Frame dialog box

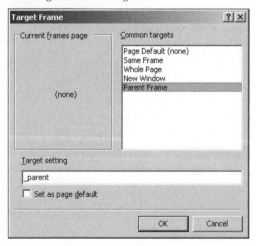

Using Tables and Table Layouts

Tables have been widely accepted as a versatile tool for laying out Web pages for the Internet. Using tables, you can design the structure of a Web page and then fill in the content pieces as needed. The use of tables also reduces formatting and positioning issues that might occur because of the differences in computer screen size and resolution.

SharePoint Designer provides three main interface components to work with tables and related features:

- **Table menu:** Allows you to insert, modify, and delete tables on Web pages. You can also use this menu to convert text to tables and vice versa.

- **Layout Tables task pane:** Allows you to create table layouts for Web pages and provides an intuitive interface to format and resize tables and cells. The task pane also allows you to choose from a set of table layout templates on which to base your table layout.

- **Table toolbar:** This provides shortcuts to the most commonly used tasks in the Table menu and the Layout Tables task pane.

To create a table on a Web page, follow these steps:

1. **In the Design view, open the Web page in which you want to create the table.**

> **NOTE** If you want to ensure that new tables created in SharePoint Designer are assigned unique IDs for identification, click the Assign unique IDs to new tables check box in the General tab of the Page Editor Options dialog box. This ensures that when you copy and paste tables in the Design view, the unique IDs are used for easy identification of tables.

2. **Choose Table ⇨ Insert Table to open the Insert Table dialog box, as shown in Figure 5.19.** The Insert Table dialog box allows you to set the properties for the new table.

3. **In the Size section, specify the number of rows and columns you want for the table.** You can type a rough estimate, as the number of columns and rows can be changed later.

4. **In the Layout section, specify the text alignment, width, and height of the table and cells.** You can also set the cell padding and cell spacing values in this section. Cell padding specifies the amount of space from the border of the cell where text can be placed. Cell spacing determines the amount of space between adjoining cells of the table.

5. **In the Borders section, specify the width and color of the table border.** You can also click the Collapse table border check box if you want the adjacent borders of the table and cells to overlap.

6. **In the Background section, specify the background color to use for the table.** If you want to enable the layout tools for tables (discussed later in this chapter), click the Enable layout tools check box. Also, you can click the Set as default for new tables check box if you want to keep the settings you made in the previous steps for new tables

7. **Click OK.** A new table using the settings specified in the Insert Table dialog box is created.

FIGURE 5.19

The Insert Table dialog box

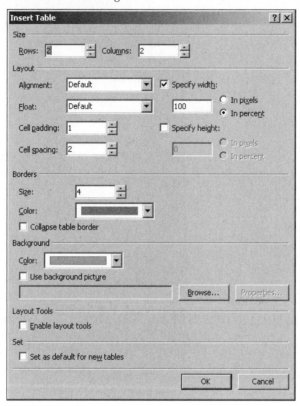

After the table is created, you can modify its properties by right-clicking on the table and then choosing Table Properties from the popup menu. When you right-click on the table, the Cell Properties menu option also appears. As shown in Figure 5.20, you can use the Cell Properties dialog box to modify the properties of the corresponding cell in the table.

Besides the ability to set formatting properties such as width, height, and text alignment, these settings for the cells are also available:

- **Header cell:** You can specify whether the corresponding cell is a table header. Table headers are cells specified with the <th> tag and have special formatting applied to them (such as center alignment and bold text).

- **No wrap:** Keep the No wrap check box deselected if you want the noncontiguous text in the cell to be wrapped once the table width is reached. If this check box is selected, the width of the table is increased to accommodate the text without wrapping it.

FIGURE 5.20

The Cell Properties dialog box

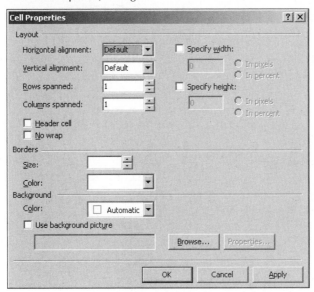

Also, when you right-click on a table, a set of menu options is available for inserting, selecting, modifying, and deleting the rows and columns of the table:

- **Insert:** Allows you to add a column, row, or cell to the left side or the right side of the column, row, or cell where the cursor exists in the Design view
- **Select:** Allows you to choose the row, cell, or column where the cursor is active
- **Delete:** Allows you to delete the row, column, or cell in the table
- **Modify:** Allows you to merge or split cells and tables, apply predefined formatting to tables, and auto-fit the tables to text inside them

In the next exercise, you use the auto-format feature to automatically format tables by using some predefined formatting templates:

1. Choose Table ⇨ Insert Table to open the Insert Table dialog box and then create a new table with the number of rows and columns of your choice.

2. Open the Table AutoFormat dialog box by either right-clicking on the table and then choosing Modify ⇨ Table AutoFormat from the popup menu or clicking on the Table AutoFormat button on the Tables toolbar, as shown in Figure 5.21.

FIGURE 5.21

The Tables toolbar

3. **Choose the format that you want to use for your table by using the Formats list in the Table AutoFormat dialog box, as shown in Figure 5.22.** Choosing a format shows a preview of the format in the Table AutoFormat dialog box.

FIGURE 5.22

The Table AutoFormat dialog box

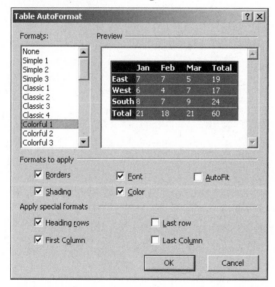

4. **Use the Formats to apply and Apply special formats sections to specify where you want to apply the styles configured in the format selected in step 3.**

5. **Click OK.** A new table with auto formatting is created.

When you apply auto formatting to the table, a number of CSS styles are created inside the Web page. These styles are used to implement the formatting applied to the table and can be modified by using the CSS SharePoint Designer interface.

SharePoint Designer also inherits the FrontPage 2003 feature for creating and managing tables and cells called Table Layouts. A layout table or cell is nothing but an HTML table or cell that has SharePoint Designer layout tools enabled for it. Layout tools provide for resizing and management of the tables. As mentioned earlier, you can have the layout tools enabled for a table inserted by choosing Table ⇨ Insert Table and then clicking the Enable layout tools check box in the Layout Tools section.

You can insert layout tables and cells by using the Layout Tables task pane, as shown in Figure 5.23. You access this task pane by choosing Task Panes ⇨ Layout Tables.

The Layout Tables task pane has some default layout plans for tables that you can use to design your Web pages. These layout tables are listed in the Table layout section of the Layout Tables task pane. To insert a layout table based on a template, simply open a Web page, place the cursor at the location where you want the layout table to be placed on the page, and then click the template in the task pane.

The following exercise can help you understand how you can use the layout tools to design your tables in SharePoint Designer. If used correctly, layout tools can be of great help in resizing and formatting table layouts. In this exercise, you use the Layout Tables task pane to create a new layout table and then insert and resize layout cells in it:

1. **Create a new HTML page by choosing File ⇨ New.** The New dialog box opens. Ensure that the Layout Tables task pane is enabled by using the Task Panes menu option.

2. **Click the Insert Layout Table button in the Layout Tables task pane.** A new table with one row and one column, with layout tools enabled, appears on the Web page. By default, a layout table is represented with a green border in the Design view when you hover over the table border. You can click the green border to see the resizing tools. You can view the properties of this table by using the Table Properties dialog box, just like with any other HTML table. On all four sides of the table, you have dropdown menus showing the width of that side. Clicking on the dropdown menu on the top or the bottom of the table shows these options:

    - **Change Column Width:** Allows you to change the width of the selected column

    - **Make Column Autostretch:** Specifies the width in percentages and uses it to auto-stretch the columns based on the width of the page

    - **Use Column Spacer Image:** Inserts a placeholder image (a white-colored image of the width and height of the column) in the table cell

3. **Click the dropdown menu for the top table side and then choose Make Column AutoStretch.** The display text of the dropdown menus on the top and bottom sides changes to reflect the percentage of page width being used.

4. **Place the cursor inside the layout table you just inserted and then click the Insert Layout Cell button on the Layout Tables task pane to open the Layout Cell dialog box.**

FIGURE 5.23

The Layout Tables task pane

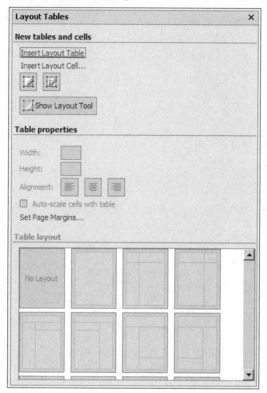

5. **Keep the defaults in the Layout Cell dialog box and then click OK.** The one cell that exists in the layout table is now converted into the Layout Cell. By default, a layout cell is represented by a blue border in the Design view. You can click the blue border to enable the resizing tool for the layout cell.

6. **Use the resizing boxes (small square boxes) on the blue border to resize the layout cell to half the height and width of the layout table.**

7. **Ensure that the layout cell is selected (a blue border shows with the resizing boxes) and then click the Insert Layout Cell button on the Layout Tables task pane.** The Insert Layout Cell dialog box opens.

8. **In the Insert Layout Cell dialog box, click the Vertical radio button in the Layout section and then click OK.** This ensures that the new layout cell is inserted vertically next to the existing layout cell.

9. **Using the resizing boxes, change the height of the new layout cell to half the height of the layout table.**

10. Click the layout cell inserted in step 8 and then click the Insert Layout Cell button in the Layout Tables task pane to insert another layout cell in the table.

11. Keep the defaults in the Insert Layout Cell dialog box and then click OK.

12. Change the width of the newly created cell to half the width of the table.

13. Click the Insert Layout Cell button again to insert another layout cell vertically after the cell inserted in step 10. In the Insert Layout Cell dialog box, click the Vertical radio button in the Layout section.

14. Click OK.

TIP Avoid randomly resizing the layout cells and columns, as that may create unwanted new cells in the layout table. Instead, make room for the new cell by systematically resizing the existing cells and then fill the empty table space (indicated by a gray background) with a new cell.

You now have a layout table with four layout cells in it. If you click the Code view tab, SharePoint Designer recognizes layout tables by using HTML comments placed inside the HTML code of the table and the cell:

```
<table cellpadding="0" cellspacing="0" style="width: 986px; height:
    450px">
<!-- MSTableType="layout" -->
<tr>
        <td valign="top">
        <!-- MSCellType="empty" -->
         </td>
        <td valign="top" style="height: 213px">
        <!-- MSCellType="empty" -->
         </td>
</tr>
<tr>
        <td valign="top" style="width: 537px">
        <!-- MSCellType="empty" -->
         </td>
        <td valign="top" style="height: 237px; width: 449px">
        <!-- MSCellType="empty" -->
         </td>
</tr>
</table>
```

As highlighted in the previous code, there's one layout table and four layout cells.

NOTE It's important to understand that you can't resize a cell if there's no room for the resizing. For example, using the layout table you created in the previous steps, if you try to resize the bottom-right cell from the top or the left outline, it won't resize because there's no space to resize. Instead, resize the adjacent cells to make room for the cell and then resize it accordingly.

Working with Layers

A layer in SharePoint Designer is basically a `<div>` tag that's absolutely positioned inside the Web page. You can drag and drop layers anywhere around the Web page with relative ease and thus layers provide a very simple design surface for laying out Web pages.

You use the Layers task pane shown in Figure 5.24 to work with layers. You access this task pane by choosing Task Panes ➪ Layers.

FIGURE 5.24

The Layers task pane

To create a new layer and configure its settings, follow these steps:

1. **Open a Web page and then place the cursor where you want to insert the layer.** To easily understand the layer positioning, choose View ➪ Formatting Marks ➪ Show.

2. **Choose View ➪ Formatting Marks and ensure that all menu options except Show and Positioned Absolute are disabled.**

3. **Click the Insert Layer button in the Layers task pane.** A layer (a `<div>` tag) is created on the Web page. Also, the anchor formatting mark appears, showing the location where the layer was actually inserted. The newly created layer is displayed in the Layers list in the Layers task pane.

4. **Drag the layer to the location where you want to place it for absolute positioning.**

5. **To create another layer inside the Web page, place the cursor outside the existing layer and then click the Insert Layer button.**

6. **To create a nested layer (a layer inside the existing layer), place the cursor inside the existing layer and then click the Insert Layer button.**

 You can also nest layers by using the Layers task pane to drag the layer you want to nest into the parent layer. To un-nest the layer, simply drag the layer into the Layer list header.

7. **You can now place your text, pictures, or other content inside the layer and then position it by using Layers.** Using this method, you can easily lay out and format Web pages.

NOTE It's important to understand that because layers are absolutely positioned, any content on the page that's not absolutely positioned might appear to have moved when you view the Web page in a browser. It's best that when you use layers heavily, you absolutely position all content on the Web page to maintain formatting.

The cool feature about layers is that along with the ability to position them in the horizontal plane, they can also be positioned vertically — in other words, you can overlap them (in the Z dimension). Every time a layer is created, a `z-index` attribute is set for it. The layers with higher `z-index` values appear on top of layers with lower `z-index` values.

The Z column in the Layer task pane shows the `z-index` value for a layer. You can change this value by right-clicking on a layer in the Layer task pane and then choosing Modify Z-Index from the popup menu, which also has these options:

- **Cut, Copy and Paste:** Allows you to cut, copy, and paste the layer from one location to another
- **Visibility:** You can choose whether you want the layer to be visible or hidden by using this menu option. The menu options set the visibility style (such as `visibility:hidden`) for the `<div>` tag associated with a layer. If a layer is set to be hidden, it's represented with a closed eye in the first column in the Layers list. If it's set to visible, it's represented with an open eye.
- **Modify Z-Index:** Used to modify the Z order of the layer
- **Modify ID:** Used to modify the ID for the layer
- **Borders and Shading:** Opens the Borders and Shading dialog box for setting properties for layer borders and background
- **Positioning:** Opens the Position dialog box

The real functionality of setting layer visibility becomes apparent when you change the visibility of a layer to show or hide it dynamically. SharePoint Designer provides a feature called Behaviors that enables you to implement such functionality without having to manually write code.

CROSS-REF For more on Behaviors, see Chapter 8.

Summary

In this chapter, I discussed the basic page layout features of SharePoint Designer. You learned about the font and paragraph formatting of Web content. I also discussed how you can use the borders, shading, bullets, and numbering features of SharePoint Designer to enhance the look of text on Web pages. Later in this chapter, I took you through a number of exercises to help you use tables and layers to lay out Web pages.

Chapter 6

Exploring the Design and Code Editing Features

From your exposure to the SharePoint Designer interface in the previous chapters, you should be comfortable with the Design and Code views. However, some features of these views can help you further enhance your designing capabilities with SharePoint Designer.

In this chapter, I discuss the designing aids and tools that SharePoint Designer provides for ease of designing Web pages and placing content in the Design view. I show you how you can use the Quick Tag Selector to quickly locate and highlight components and sections on Web pages. I also discuss special tools, such as Format Painter, Paste Special, etc., that provide ways to replicate formatting across Web pages.

Also, I take you through features, such as IntelliSense and code checking, offered by the Code view in SharePoint Designer that give developers a reference that they can use while writing code for Web pages in the Code view. Later in this chapter, I talk about Find and Replace and how you can use this awesome tool to quickly find and replace content, HTML tags, and code across an entire Web site.

SharePoint Designer offers Web site developers a number of tools that provide the ability to easily reuse content without having to re-create all the formatting associated with it. You can import content from other applications, such as Microsoft Word, and still retain the formatting applied to the content. This special copy and paste feature allows you to develop content by using the program of your choice and still maintain the formatting to a large extent. Along with this, you also have an option to repeat the formatting applied to one section of the content to another section. These features provide the flexibility, speed, and simplicity needed when designing Web content with other applications.

IN THIS CHAPTER

Working in the Design view

Working in the Code view

Using the Find and Replace features

Working with the Quick Tag Selector

I begin by taking you through an exercise that helps you understand how you can use SharePoint Designer features to move content with formatting from one page to another or from a document to a Web page:

1. **Using an advanced text editor, such as Microsoft Word, open or create a document with text that has some formatting applied to it.**

2. **Press Ctrl+C or choose Edit ⇨ Copy to select and copy the contents of the document so that they're placed in the Clipboard.** Choose Task Panes ⇨ Clipboard to show the Clipboard task pane and view current and previous contents of the Clipboard.

3. **In SharePoint Designer, open the Web page where you want to move the copied content.**

4. **Place the cursor at the location on the Web page where you want to paste the content and then press Ctrl+V or choose Edit ⇨ Paste to paste the copied content.** The content is placed on the Web page, and the formatting applied in the original document is retained. Also, the small Paste Options menu appears beside the content that you just pasted.

5. **Click the Paste Options menu to show these menu options, which appear as radio buttons:**

   ▪ **Keep Source Formatting:** Retains the formatting applied to the content being pasted

   ▪ **Remove Formatting:** Removes the formatting applied to the content being pasted

   ▪ **Keep HTML Only:** Only formatting applied as HTML is kept. Other formatting, such as styles, isn't retained.

   ▪ **Keep Text Only:** Opens the Paste Text dialog box (also accessible by choosing Edit ⇨ Paste Text), where you can specify whether the paragraph, line breaks, and rows should be retained

If you don't want to use the Paste Options menu and want to hide it, you can do so by deselecting the Show Paste Options Buttons check box (in the Cut and Paste Options section) in the General tab of the Page Editor Options dialog box.

While the Paste Options menu allows you to specify whether you want to keep the formatting applied to the text, there might be cases where you just want to keep the formatting but not the text or content. To replicate formatting applied at one location to another in the same Web page or across different Web pages, you can use the Format Painter. The Format Painter is available as a button in the Standard toolbar, which can be enabled by choosing View ⇨ Toolbars.

To use the Format Painter to replicate the formatting used on text in one location and apply it to text in another location, follow these steps:

1. **Open the source Web page that contains the content with formatting you want to replicate and then open the destination Web page where you want to apply the formatting.**

2. **In the Design view of the source Web page, place the cursor at the location where you want to copy the formatting from.**

3. **Click the Format Painter button in the Standard toolbar.** The mouse pointer changes to a paintbrush. SharePoint Designer has now copied the formatting that was applied to the text at the location where the cursor was placed.

4. **Click the destination Web page in SharePoint Designer by using the tabbed interface.** The mouse pointer is still shown as a paintbrush.

5. **Using the mouse, highlight the content where you want to apply the formatting you copied in step 3.** The formatting that SharePoint Designer copied is applied to the content in the destination Web page.

Working in the Design View

Before discussing the Design view features of SharePoint Designer that enhance your designing experience, I want to discuss the Color Coding tab, as shown in Figure 6.1, in the Page Editor Options dialog box.

FIGURE 6.1

The Color Coding tab in the Page Editor Options dialog box

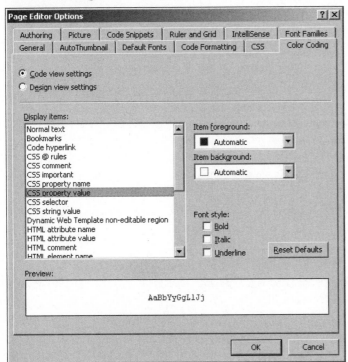

As shown in previous chapters, various SharePoint Designer layout tools, components, and controls are represented by certain colors in the Design view. For example, the layout table is represented with a green border, the layout table cell with a blue border, etc.

The Color Coding tab in the Page Editor Options dialog box allows you to set colors that represent these features in the Design view. If you don't feel comfortable with the default color settings, you can change the colors in the Color Coding tab. If you want to revert the changes you make to the colors here, click Reset Defaults.

Using visual aids and formatting marks

The View menu in SharePoint Designer allows you to enable visual aids and formatting marks in the Design view. You use these two tools to obtain a detailed visual look at tags, placeholders, spaces, carriage returns, etc., on a Web page in the Design view. It's especially useful to indicate and locate components and content formatting that normally hide in the Design view, such as layers with the visibility style set to hidden.

Choose View ➪ Visual Aids to choose from these menu options:

- **Show:** Shows the visual aids selected in the Visual Aids menu in the Design view. You can press Ctrl+/ to show all the selected visual aids. By default, all visual aids are selected.
- **Block Selection:** Displays a dotted rectangle around certain tags
- **Visible Borders:** Makes the borders visible only for reference in the Design view when the borders have been disabled for a component
- **Empty Containers:** Displays a dotted rectangle around empty objects in the page
- **Margins and Padding:** Displays the margins and padding applied to a Web page, tables, paragraphs, etc., in the Design view
- **CSS Display:none Elements:** Displays the elements (HTML tags or controls) that have the `display:none` style applied to them
- **CSS Visibility:hidden Elements:** Displays and indicates the location of the elements that have `visibility:hidden` style applied to them
- **ASP.NET Non-visual Controls:** Displays the ASP.NET controls that don't have a visual interface — for example, data source controls, such as SQLDataSource, for reference — on a Web page
- **ASP.NET Control Errors:** Displays the errors in the Design view for ASP.NET controls that error out while rendering the Web page
- **Template Region Labels:** Displays the names of the editable regions when working with Dynamic Web templates (DWTs)

CROSS-REF For more on Dynamic Web templates (DWTs), see Chapter 13.

NOTE Visual aids might affect the formatting and positioning of your Web page in the Design view to a certain extent but shouldn't affect the Web page itself, as the visual aids aren't shown in the browser.

You can also toggle visual aids on or off by using the Visual Aids panel in the status bar of SharePoint Designer. As previously discussed, you can enable or disable the status bar via the Application Options dialog box, which you access by choosing Tools ➪ Application Options.

Like Visual Aids menu, the Formatting Marks tool shows the locations in the Design view of HTML tags and other formatting applied on a Web page. Choose View ➪ Formatting Marks to choose from these menu options:

- **Show:** Shows the formatting marks selected in the Formatting Marks menu in the Design view. You can press Ctrl+Alt+/ to show all the selected formatting marks. By default, all formatting marks are selected.

- **Tag Marks:** Shows the HTML tags in the Design view

CAUTION The Layout Tables task pane is disabled when you enable Tag Marks.

- **Paragraph Marks:** Shows the location of the end of a paragraph
- **Line Breaks:** Shows in the Design view where the <BR> tags are present
- **Spaces:** Indicates the location of empty spaces ( ) inside a Web page
- **Comments:** Shows where the HTML comments are located inside a Web page. HTML comments aren't rendered in the Design view, so this option can help you quickly identify where in the Web page code HTML comments have been placed.
- **Script Blocks:** Indicates the location of the script blocks in the Web page code
- **Positioned Absolute:** Displays an anchor that shows the location of the content, such as layers with absolute positioning
- **CSS Display:none:** Indicates tags on which the display:none style has been used for reference in the Design view
- **Hidden Form Fields:** Shows the location of the hidden form fields on a Web page

TIP Enabling formatting marks can act as a great way to learn about the HTML tags associated with the components that you can insert by using the SharePoint Designer user interface. However, they might cause confusion if you enable them on large Web pages.

Using rulers and grids

The Ruler and Grid functionality offered by SharePoint Designer allows you to quickly position components, such as tables and layers, on Web pages. Choose View ➪ Ruler and Grid to enable the Ruler and Grid menu for the Design view. The Ruler and Grid menu has these options:

- **Show Ruler:** Displays a ruler at the top and left edges of a Web page. You can use this ruler to quickly determine the top and left position of content on the Web page. It also helps you determine the width and height of pictures, tables, layers, etc., on a Web page. By default, the display unit of the ruler is pixels. You can change the measurement by choosing View ⇨ Ruler and Grid ⇨ Configure.

- **Show Grid:** This displays a grid on the Design view of the Web page, which, combined with the ruler, allows you to position content relative to each other.

- **Snap to Grid:** When selected, this option snaps the content to the grid when resizing in the Design view.

- **Set Origin from Selection:** This sets the origin of the ruler from the selection in the Design view; that is, the ruler begins from the left margin of the selection you make in the Design view.

- **Reset Origin:** This resets the beginning of the ruler to the default settings.

- **Configure:** This opens the Page Editor Options dialog box for modifying the settings for the ruler and grid.

The Configure menu option in the Ruler and Grid menu takes you to the Ruler and Grid tab, as shown in Figure 6.2, in the Page Editor Options dialog box.

You can use this tab to configure these attributes of the ruler and grid for the Design view:

- **Ruler and grid units:** Allows you to specify the units to use for the ruler and grid

- **Display Grid:** Provides settings that allow you to modify the spacing, line style, and line color

- **Snapping Grid:** Allows you to change the distance by which the content is snapped when the Snap to Grid option is enabled (which you access by choosing View ⇨ Ruler and Grid ⇨ Snap to Grid)

Using and configuring the tracing image

Tracing images is one of the features introduced in FrontPage 2003 that has been carried over to SharePoint Designer. The concept behind designing Web pages by using a tracing image is to provide a way to put an image in the background of the Design view interface, allowing the image to be used as a reference for placing and sizing the actual content of a Web page.

In scenarios exploiting a tracing image feature, a Web designer would create the layout for the Web page in the form of an image by using the tool of his or her choice. The designer would provide the image to the Web page developers, who then place the image as a tracing image in the background of the Design view in SharePoint Designer. They can then easily set the content of a Web page so that it fits the tracing image.

You can configure the tracing image you want to use for a Web page by choosing View ⇨ Tracing Image ⇨ Configure, which opens the Tracing Image dialog box, as shown in Figure 6.3.

FIGURE 6.2

The Ruler and Grid tab in the Page Editor Options dialog box

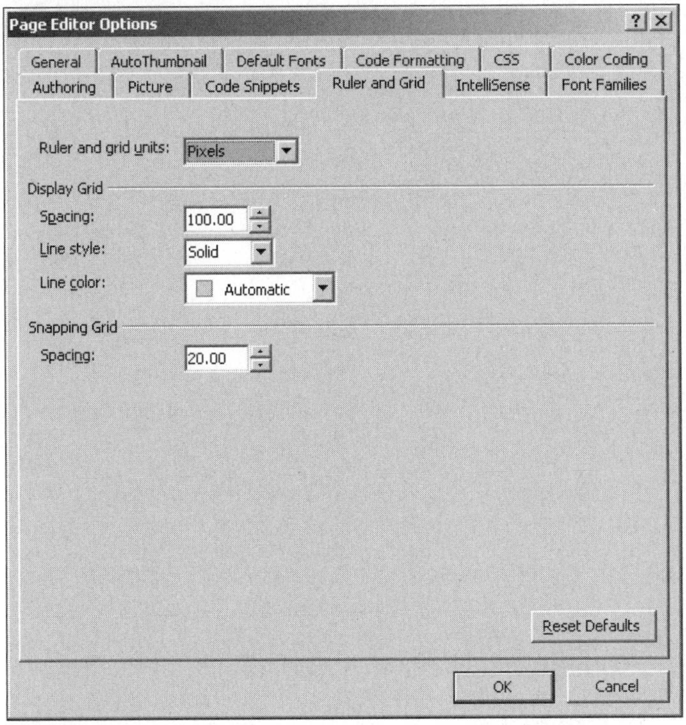

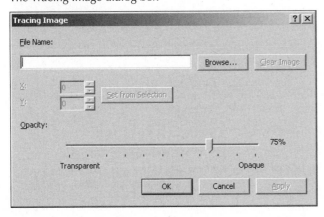

FIGURE 6.3

The Tracing Image dialog box

In the File Name text field, specify the location of the tracing image to be used. In the X and Y text fields, set the coordinates (top and left) for where on a Web page the tracing image should be placed. Also, the Opacity slider allows you to specify the transparency of the tracing image.

Working in the Code View

SharePoint Designer exposes a number of tools for the Code view to help developers with coding for Web pages in an intuitive Visual Studio–like environment. Along with the Tag Properties task pane, the Code view in SharePoint Designer can be used to write code blocks and set properties and attributes of tags, controls, and components.

Like the Design view, the color coding settings of the Code view of SharePoint Designer can also be changed using the Color Coding tab in the Page Editor Options dialog box. Although the default settings here work just fine, the Color Coding tab simply provides a way for you to customize the colors used for various types of code blocks in case you're not comfortable with the default color settings.

While working in the Code view, it's really useful to enable the Code View toolbar, as shown in Figure 6.4. This toolbar exposes many buttons in a single, easily accessible location, helping you avoid having to go through menus to access these features.

FIGURE 6.4

The Code View toolbar

Starting from left to right, the Code View toolbar offers these buttons for the Code view:

- **List Members (Ctrl+L):** Displays the properties and events associated with the control where the cursor is placed. For example, if you want to list all the HTML attributes associated with a table tag, just place the cursor on any of the attributes (or the space between the attributes) and then press Ctrl+L.

- **Parameter Info (Ctrl+Shift+spacebar):** Displays the parameters of the function being used

- **Complete Word (Ctrl+spacebar):** Provides suggestions for auto-completing a tag or control. Press Ctrl+spacebar to auto-complete words.

- **Code Snippets (Ctrl+Enter):** Opens a list where you can choose the code snippets you created by using the Code Snippets tab in the Page Editor Options dialog box. Press Ctrl+Enter to access the code snippets list at the location where the cursor is placed in the Code view.

CROSS-REF For more on code snippets, see Chapter 4.

- **Follow Code Hyperlink(Ctrl+[):** A code hyperlink is a link in the Code view that takes you to the location where the code block associated with the code that's marked as a hyperlink exists.

- **Next Code Hyperlink (Alt+←):** Takes you to the next available code hyperlink

- **Previous Code Hyperlink (Alt+→):** Takes you to the previous code hyperlink

- **Function Lookup:** This dropdown menu in the Code view lists the client-side script functions, if any, present on a Web page open in SharePoint Designer. Choosing a function takes you to the corresponding function definition in the open Web page.

- **Toggle Bookmark (Ctrl+F2):** Creates a bookmark on the Code view of the Web page. Code view bookmarks can be used to identify lines of code and quickly jump from one section of code marked by a bookmark to another.

- **Next Bookmark (F2):** Jumps to the next available bookmark

- **Previous Bookmark (Shift+F2):** Jumps to the previous bookmark

- **Clear Bookmarks:** Removes all bookmarks from the Code view

- **Select Tag (Ctrl+:):** Selects the tag along with the inner HTML and the contents

- **Find Matching Tag (Ctrl+;):** Finds the matching starting or ending tag that corresponds to the tag selected

- **Select Block (Ctrl+'):** Selects the code block

- **Find Matching Brace (Ctrl+]):** Finds the matching starting or ending brace in the code block

- **Insert Start Tag (Ctrl+,):** Provides the angle brackets to place the starting tags

- **Insert End Tag (Ctrl+.):** Provides the angle brackets to place the end tags

- **Insert HTML Comments (Ctrl+/):** Provides the angle brackets that can be used to place HTML comments in a Web page

- **Options:** Provides an interface to enable or disable code wrapping, line numbers, code checking, etc., for the Code view

- **Microsoft Scripting Editor:** Opens the Microsoft Script Editor, which can be used to write code in an environment similar to Visual Studio

Most of these options are also available by choosing Edit ➪ Code View, choosing Edit ➪ IntelliSense, or by right-clicking on a Web page while in the Code view. However, the Code View toolbar consolidates these features for easy use. Remembering the shortcuts associated with these options can also greatly expedite your development time.

The Page Editor Options dialog box also provides a set of tabs for provisioning various settings for the Code view in SharePoint Designer.

General tab

The Code View Option section in the General tab provides the same check boxes that are also available via the Options button in the Code View toolbar:

- **Word wrap:** Enables or disables word wrapping for the code blocks in the Code view
- **Auto indent:** Automatically indents the code inside the Web page to show hierarchy
- **Line numbers:** Displays the line number in a margin on the left side of the Code view
- **Selection margin:** Provides a margin on the left side of the Code view to help with selection
- **Highlight invalid HTML:** Underlines HTML that's deemed invalid based on the selected document type declaration and schema. When you hover over invalid code, the Code view shows a screen tip indicating the reason behind the invalidity.
- **Highlight incompatible HTML:** Underlines HTML that's not compatible with the selected document type declaration and schema

Code Formatting tab

The settings provided in this tab don't make any real changes to the Web page code except formatting it in ways that make the Code view more comprehendible. Most of these settings determine how the HTML tags and their attributes are formatted for viewing in the Code view. For example, selecting the Tag names are lowercase check box ensures that the Code view shows the tags as lowercase.

You can also specify the size of a tab (in character space units), the size of an indentation, and the size of the right margins in the Code view. Also, you have a list of HTML tags for which you can define the code formatting and line breaks.

NOTE The Use shorthand properties when generating styles check box at the bottom of the Code Formatting tab allows SharePoint Designer to create styles by using shorthand — for example, font size: 120; font color: red; and font weight: bold can be shortened to: 120, red, bold.

Code Snippets tab

The Code Snippets tab allows you to create, modify, and delete code snippets. Code snippets offer a mechanism where you can create blocks of code that you would commonly reuse while writing Web pages. You can then insert the code blocks at the required location by just pressing Ctrl+Enter and then choosing the code block you want to insert.

By default, a number of code blocks are already available in the Code Snippets tab, as shown in Figure 6.5.

FIGURE 6.5

The Code Snippets tab in the Page Editor Options dialog box

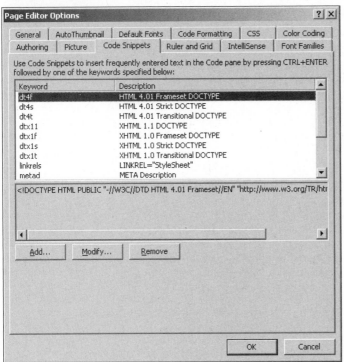

When you create a new code snippet, you define a keyword (and description) to identify the code block associated with the snippet and then specify the code block text for the code snippet. In the Code view, when you press Ctrl+Enter to choose the code snippet for insertion, you only see the keyword and description associated with the code block.

IntelliSense tab

The IntelliSense tab, as shown in Figure 6.6, allows you to make settings for auto code completion in the Code view. It offers several options that you can have IntelliSense enable:

- **Auto Popup:** The check boxes available here allow you to enable the automatic popup of code reference boxes for HTML, CSS, ASP.NET, and client-side scripting.

- **Auto Insert:** The options available in this section allow you to configure the automatic insertion of closing tags and quotes around the HTML, CSS, and ASP.NET attributes.

- **Code Hyperlinks:** These check boxes allow you to enable code hyperlinks for CSS, scripting, and Web page content, such as pictures, Web pages, etc.

FIGURE 6.6

The IntelliSense tab in the Page Editor Options

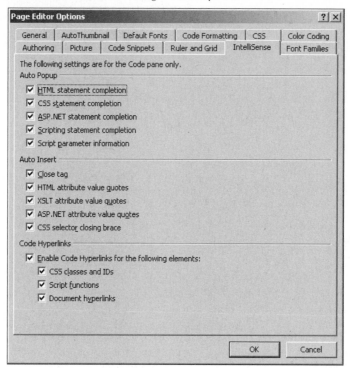

Understanding code hyperlinks

Code Hyperlinks is a feature that assists Web developers working on large projects to quickly jump from one section of code to another related section. It saves time by helping you locate actual code being referenced by a code hyperlink.

In the Code view, a code hyperlink looks just like a normal hyperlink that can be clicked to navigate to the code being referenced at the location of the hyperlink. SharePoint Designer allows you to use code hyperlinks to locate code and functions within the same Web page, different Web pages, style sheets or script files, and other documents.

When you hover over a code hyperlink in the Code view, a screen tip indicates that you can press Ctrl+click to jump to the code being referenced at the location. Clicking the code hyperlink in this manner opens the associated file and highlights the code section for review.

Using IntelliSense for auto code completion

IntelliSense is a feature shared by many Microsoft application development programs, providing you with a ready reference to simplify the code-writing process. Like in most applications, in the Code view, just by pressing Ctrl+spacebar at the location where you're writing code (HTML, Script, ASP.NET, and CSS), a dropdown menu appears, allowing you to choose from a contextual menu of functions, attributes, and properties.

Also, IntelliSense provides for the automatic completion of code, such as HTML tags, script braces, etc. For example, you don't have to manually complete tags or care about quoting attributes when IntelliSense is turned on. To see how IntelliSense works, follow these steps:

1. **Open a Web page in the Code view.**

2. **Find the <body> tag inside the Code view, place the cursor after the ending angle bracket of the <body> tag, and then press Enter.**

3. **Place a starting angle bracket (<) at the cursor location.** A popup menu appears with a list of HTML tags that you can choose from.

4. **Choose the <a> tag from the popup menu and then press the spacebar.** Another contextual menu opens, showing you all the attributes and events associated with the <a> tag.

5. **Choose href from the popup menu.** SharePoint Designer automatically places the attribute with quotes and provides you with a button to pick a URL.

6. **Click the Pick URL button to open the Insert Hyperlink dialog box and then choose a file for the hyperlink.**

7. **Place a closing angle bracket (>) at the end of the inserted code.** The closing tag (</a>) is placed automatically to close the <a> tag.

8. **Between the <a> and </a> tags, you can place the display text of the hyperlink.**

You just created a hyperlink by using the IntelliSense feature of SharePoint Designer's Code view. Although this exercise was fairly simple, you can gauge the usability of this feature when working with complex code.

Using the Find and Replace Features

SharePoint Designer offers an advanced Find and Replace tool that allows you to find and replace content and code in the Design and Code views. This feature provides for searching in a Web page, a set of Web pages, or all across a Web site open in SharePoint Designer. You can match content to be searched by using expressions created with the regular expression syntax. Also, you can create rules for specifying search criteria to match HTML tags and then choose to replace a tag, an attribute within a tag, or the inner content of a tag.

The user interface for Find and Replace is composed of the Find and Replace dialog box and the Find 1 and Find 2 task panes.

Working with the Find, Replace, and HTML Tags tabs

You can access the Find and Replace dialog box, as shown in Figure 6.7, by choosing Edit ⇨ Find or Edit ⇨ Replace. To begin with, you can enable the Find 1 and Find 2 menus by using the Task Panes menu. A Play button on both these panes also takes you to the Find and Replace dialog box. The Find 1 and Find 2 task panes provide for running and comparing two search operations at the same time.

CAUTION The Replace functionality of SharePoint Designer is an irreversible operation. You can't undo the replacement once it occurs. SharePoint Designer warns about this before it runs the replacement operation on a Web site.

FIGURE 6.7

The Find and Replace dialog box

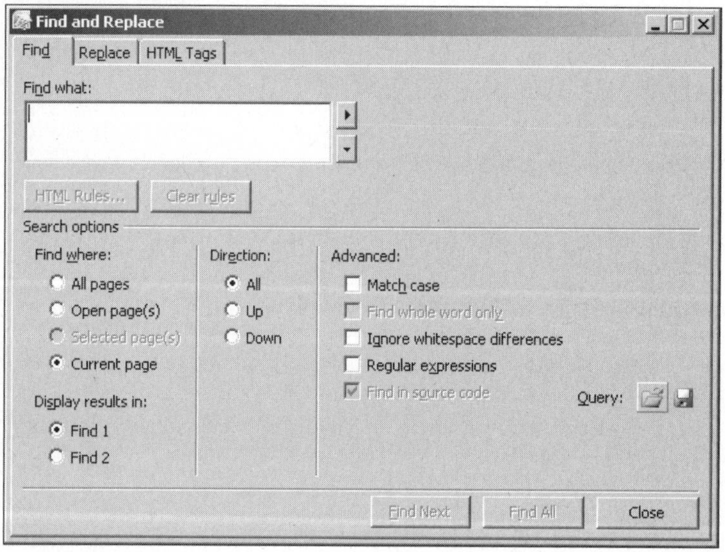

The Find and Replace dialog box exposes its features using three tabs: Find, Replace, and HTML Tags. All three tabs have a Search Options section that allows you to choose from a set of options to define the scope and direction and set other settings.

Find tab

The Find tab allows you to specify the text you want to search. You can also choose to create search queries by using HTML rules and regular expressions, which are discussed later in this chapter. To find some text or code, simply type it in the Find what text box and then click Find All. The Find task pane shows the list of Web pages where your search is successful. Also, the Matched Text column highlights in red the text you typed in the Find what text box.

Replace tab

The Replace tab adds the interface to the Find tab for specifying the replacement text and options. Considering that replacement is irreversible, it's recommended that you choose to find first to understand the results retrieved and then run the replacement later. You need to specify the replacement text in the Replace with text box and then click Replace to replace the first occurrence of the text or Replace All to replace all occurrences.

HTML Tags tab

The HTML Tags tab allows you to specify a Find HTML tag and then choose a replacement action to define what needs to be replaced or changed in the tag. Choose the HTML tag you need to find by using the Find tag dropdown menu and then choose a replace action by using the Replace action dropdown menu. The Replace action dropdown menu has these options:

- **None:** Only finds the tag and doesn't perform any replace action
- **Replace tag and contents:** Shows a With text field where you can specify the replacement text that replaces the selected tag and its contents
- **Replace contents only:** Allows you to specify the replacement text that replaces only the contents of the tag
- **Add after start tag:** Allows you to specify the replacement text that's added after the start of the selected tag
- **Add after end tag:** Allows you to specify the replacement text that's added after the end of the selected tag
- **Add before start tag:** Allows you to specify the replacement text that's added before the start of the selected tag
- **Add before end tag:** Allows you to specify the replacement text that's added before the end of the selected tag
- **Remove tag and contents:** Removes the selected tag and contents
- **Remove tag:** Removes the tag only
- **Change tag:** Provides a To dropdown menu that allows you to choose a replacement tag for the selected tag
- **Set attribute value:** Shows an Attribute dropdown menu that allows you to choose the selected HTML tag's attribute and set a value for it
- **Remove attribute:** Allows you to choose an attribute for the tag that needs to be removed

Most of the settings in the Search options section of the dialog box are common across all tabs:

- **Find where:** Allows you set the search scope. You can choose to search in the current page, in pages selected in the Folder List task pane, in pages that are open, or all pages.

- **Display results in:** Allows you to choose the Find task pane where the results of the search are shown

- **Direction:** When searching in a page, you can choose the direction of the search.

- **Advanced:** Provides check boxes that allow you to set if the search should match the text case, find the whole word only, ignore white space differences, use regular expressions, or find text in a source code

Besides this, the Search options section also provides you with two buttons (placed in the bottom right) that allow you to open an existing query or save the query you create in the Find and Replace dialog box for later use.

 **SharePoint Designer saves the query you create in the Find and Replace dialog box by using an XML format in an FPQ file.**

Exploiting the HTML rules

The Find and Replace dialog box provides a cool feature to create matching criteria for your search for HTML tags inside the Web pages. All three tabs in the Find and Replace dialog box have an HTML Rules button. You can click this button to create HTML rules that help you drastically isolate your search. For example, you can find all `<a>` tags inside the Web site pages that have the `target` attribute value set to `blank` and then change the attribute to `_self` in a single operation.

To create a new rule, follow these steps:

1. **In the HTML Tags tab in the Find and Replace dialog box, choose the `<a>` tag from the Find Tag dropdown menu.**

2. **Click the HTML Rules button.** The HTML Rules dialog box, as shown in Figure 6.8, opens.

3. **Click New Rule to enable the New Rule dropdown menu at the bottom of the dialog box.**

4. **Choose the With Attribute menu option in the New Rule dropdown menu to enable another set of dropdown menus in the dialog box.**

5. **In the [any attribute] dropdown menu, choose the `target` attribute.** Keep the Equals option selected in the next dropdown menu.

6. **In the [any value] dropdown menu, choose `_blank`.**

7. **Click OK.**

FIGURE 6.8

The HTML Rules dialog box

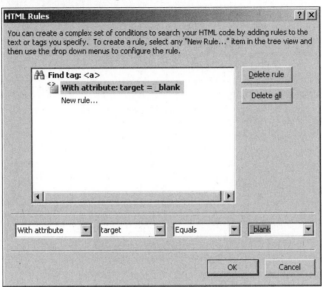

You just created an HTML rule that allows you to find all <a> tags that have the target attribute set to _blank. You can now use the Find and Replace dialog box to specify the replace actions.

Using regular expressions

Regular Expressions is a standard mechanism used by a lot of programs to help identify text strings in large amounts of text based on patterns. In simple terms, a regular expression is a format that describes a pattern of characters in text. For example, the regular expression ca. matches all three-letter words that have ca as prefix, such as cat, can, cap, etc.

The Find and Replace dialog box allows you to use these regular expressions to search for text or text patterns in Web pages and replace them with the needed text. If you click the right-pointing arrow next to the Find what text box, a menu appears showing you a number of commonly used regular expressions, as shown in Figure 6.9.

NOTE Regular Expressions is a complex but intuitive way to perform searches across Web content by using SharePoint Designer. You can combine the characters displayed in Figure 6.8 to make an advanced expression for comparison. For example, the [A-Za-z0-9] regular expression matches all alphanumeric characters.

FIGURE 6.9

The Regular Expressions menu in the Find and Replace dialog box

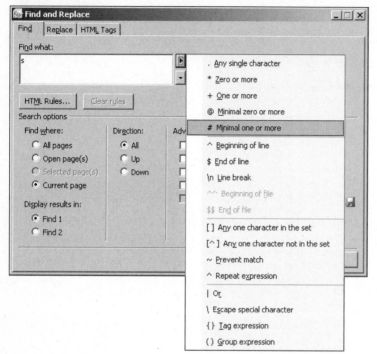

Using incremental searches

Incremental Search is another cool feature especially useful in the Code view. It allows you to search for code by just typing the search text and then jump from one occurrence to another. To use an incremental search, follow these steps:

1. **In the Code view, open the Web page where you want to perform an incremental search.**

2. **Press Ctrl+Alt+F to enable an incremental search.** The mouse pointer changes, and the status bar at the bottom of the SharePoint Designer window displays Incremental Search: text.

3. **Type some text that you want to search.** The Code view jumps to the text and then highlights it.

4. **Press Ctrl+Alt+F to jump to other occurrences of the search text in the Code view.** Also, you can press Ctrl+Alt+Shift+F to reverse the direction of the incremental search.

Working with the Quick Tag Selector

The Quick Tag Selector feature of SharePoint Designer allows you to quickly choose a tag and then highlight the content or code associated with the tag in the Design or Code view. On Web pages that have a lot of code, you can use the Quick Tag Selector to quickly identify the location of the code for a specific control in the Code view.

The Quick Tag Selector, as shown in Figure 6.10, is placed just above the page view of the Web page you're working on. It can be enabled or disabled by choosing View➪Quick Tag Selector.

FIGURE 6.10

The Quick Tag Selector

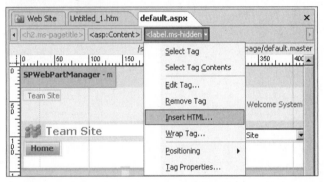

To use the Quick Tag Selector, simply place the cursor at the location of your choice in the Design view. The Quick Tag Selector shows you a breadcrumb trail–like view of the tags from the location where you placed the cursor to the first parent tag. For example, if you have nested tables in the body of the Web page and you place the cursor in a deeply nested cell, the Quick Tag Selector shows you a view of tags that identify the container table row and table tags until you reach the topmost parent tag. Just click the tag to highlight it in the Design or Code view.

If you hover over a tag in the Quick Tag Selector, an arrow on the right opens a dropdown menu. This dropdown menu has these options:

- **Select Tag:** Selects and highlights the tag in the Design or Code view
- **Select Tag Contents:** Selects the contents of the tag only
- **Edit Tag:** Opens the Quick Tag Editor, allowing you to make modifications to the tag
- **Remove Tag:** Removes the tag if it doesn't have associations with other tags
- **Insert HTML:** Allows you to insert HTML code inside the tag by using the Quick Tag Editor

- **Wrap Tag:** Wraps the tag with the tag you specify in the Quick Tag Editor
- **Positioning:** Allows you to choose the positioning of the tag
- **Tag Properties:** Takes you to the dialog box corresponding to the tag you selected. For example, clicking on the tag properties for the <body> tag opens the Page Properties dialog box.

Summary

In this chapter, I discussed the various features and tools available to you when working in the Code and Design views in SharePoint Designer. You also learned about Find and Replace, Regular Expressions, Incremental Search, and the Quick Tag Selector.

Chapter 7

Working with Graphics and Animation Components

IN THIS CHAPTER

Inserting pictures and symbols

Using the photo gallery Web component

Using advanced controls

Pictures, animation, and multimedia form one of the key components of a Web site; I don't really need to emphasize the importance of these components. Probably one of the first questions that you would ask of a product while designing Web sites is how easily can you work with graphics and animation. SharePoint Designer makes it a very simple task to work with pictures, create hyperlinks on pictures, and create photo albums on your Web sites. You can either quickly make modifications to pictures within SharePoint Designer or use it to open the picture in your favorite picture editor tool for editing. SharePoint Designer also allows you to add special controls, such as applets, plug-ins (including media players, Flash, and ActiveX controls), etc., on Web pages.

In this chapter, I take you through the features of SharePoint Designer related to working with pictures and graphics. I discuss how you can use SharePoint Designer to create hotspots on pictures as well as create photo albums and thumbnails.

Inserting Pictures and Symbols

Most of the menu and toolbar options related to pictures are disabled until you place the cursor on a Web page open in SharePoint Designer. Inserting and working with pictures is simple enough, and once your Web page is open, you just have to choose Insert ➪ Picture to pick a picture you want to insert on the page. You have the option of inserting a picture from a folder location on your computer where you saved it, from a scanner or camera, or from the pictures available in the Office clip art gallery.

NOTE Web pages in general are expected to load fast. Thus, it's recommended that you insert pictures of reasonable sizes on Web pages. This helps in loading the page faster. The file types suggested for the Internet are GIF, JPEG, and PNG.

For example, to add clip art to your Web site, follow these steps:

1. **Open the Web page you want to add a picture to, click your cursor where you want the picture to appear, and then choose Insert ➪ Picture ➪ Clip Art.** The Clip Art task pane opens. This task pane allows you to search for clip art and other media on your computer and on the Microsoft Office Web site.

2. **Type** Designer **in the Search for text field and then click Go.** If you're connected to the Internet, you might just find j0438675.wmf. Or choose a picture you like and then hover over it in the Clip Art task pane. You can also double-click the image. A menu button appears on the right side of the picture.

3. **Click this menu button and then click Insert.** You can also drag and drop the clip art onto the Web page. Notice the Preview/Properties option in this menu. As shown in Figure 7.1, this menu opens the Preview/Properties dialog box, which shows the name, the size and resolution, and the location of the picture.

FIGURE 7.1

The Preview/Properties dialog box

4. When you insert the picture on the Web page, the Accessibility Properties dialog box opens. You can use this dialog box to specify the alternate text for the picture. If you don't want this dialog box to appear every time you insert a picture, deselect the Show this prompt when inserting images check box.

NOTE Alternate text is used by screen readers and narrators to read out the description of the picture. Having an alternate text for pictures is one of the key requirements of common accessibility standards. Ensure that the text you type provides a short and clear description of the picture.

5. Click OK. The picture is then displayed on your Web page with the resolution indicated in the Preview/Properties dialog box.

Click the picture, and the Design view shows a picture border with holders that you can use to change the width and height of the picture. Also, notice that the picture is inserted as an <img> tag on the Web page. A smart tag is also displayed at a corner of the picture, as shown in Figure 7.2.

FIGURE 7.2

A smart tag for pictures

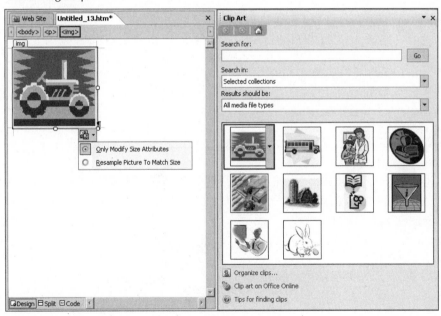

CAUTION To proportionally resize a picture, ensure that you hold Shift while dragging on a corner handle. If you drag the picture from another handle, you change the dimensions only for the side you grab.

TIP   **You can automatically change the dimensions of a picture by double-clicking the picture. The Picture Properties dialog box opens, and under the Appearance tab, you can change the height and width. Click the Keep aspect ratio check box to align the proportions.**

The smart tag has two options:

- **Only Modify Size Attributes:** This is the default option and signifies that only the width and height attributes of the picture are changed when you modify the picture.

- **Resample Picture to Match Size:** When you choose this option, the picture is resampled to fit the size, which means SharePoint Designer tries to refine the picture in its modified width and height.

When you save the Web page with the picture on it, you're shown the Save Embedded Files dialog box, which allows you to specify where you want to save the picture you inserted on the page. As shown in Figure 7.3, the Save Embedded Files dialog box allows you to rename the picture and specify the location where you want to save the file.

Besides allowing you to change the picture name and save location, the Save Embedded Files dialog box lets you to perform the following operations:

- **Set Action:** This option allows you to either save the picture within the Web site by clicking the Save File radio button or use the picture from its original location, such as a Web site on the Internet.

- **Picture File Type:** Discussed in the next section, this button allows you to change the file type of the picture.

FIGURE 7.3

The Save Embedded Files dialog box

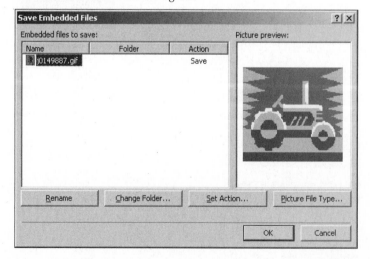

Setting picture properties

When you right-click on the picture you inserted on the Web page, a popup menu appears with a set of tools available for modifying the settings for the picture.

Reset Size

As the name suggests, you can use this option to reset the picture size back to the original size before modification. This option is only available in the menu if you've modified the size of the picture in the current Web page editing session. SharePoint Designer doesn't remember the original size of the picture after you save the page and close it.

Resample

This option can be used after you modify the size of the picture. Like the resample option in the smart tag for the picture, this option also resamples the picture after a change in size. Once used, this option isn't available until you modify the size of the picture again.

AutoThumbnail

The AutoThumbnail option allows you to automatically create a thumbnail of the picture on the Web page. Choosing the AutoThumbnail option tells SharePoint Designer to create a smaller thumbnail picture of the original picture.

As shown in Figure 7.4, the settings for how the thumbnail picture should be created can be specified by using the AutoThumbnail tab in the Page Editor Options dialog box.

You have the following options for configuring how SharePoint Designer generates the thumbnail for the picture you choose to create a thumbnail for:

- You can specify the width of the thumbnail. Thumbnails are square images, so the width you specify is used as the height of the thumbnail image.
- You can choose to have a border around the thumbnail image and specify the width of the border in pixels.
- The thumbnail picture can also be set to have a beveled edge.

Change Picture File Type

If you want to change the file type of the picture, you can use the Picture File Type dialog box to choose a file type that matches your needs. As shown in Figure 7.5, the Picture File Type dialog box gives you a brief description of the file type, its recommended usage, and allows you to specify the quality of the picture.

For GIF and JPEG file types, you have options to specify how the picture loads when viewed in a browser. You can enable interlacing for GIF images and progressive passes for JPEG files by using the Picture File Type dialog box.

FIGURE 7.4

The AutoThumbnail tab in the Page Editor Options dialog box

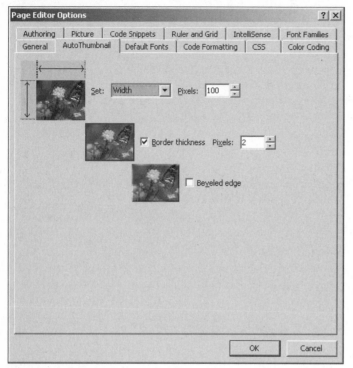

FIGURE 7.5

The Picture File Type dialog box

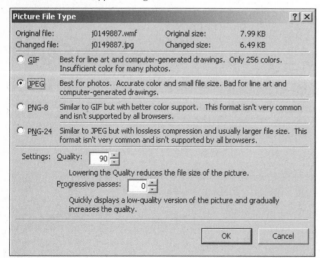

Picture Properties

As the name suggests, this dialog box can be used to change the general settings for the selected picture. As shown in Figure 7.6, the Picture Properties dialog box has the following tabs:

- **General:** Allows you to change the name of the picture and specify its alternate text. Clicking Edit opens the picture in the associated picture editing program installed on your machine. The Hyperlink section allows you to create hyperlinks on the picture. The Accessibility section can be used to specify alternate text and description for the image so it can be read by text reader programs.

- **Appearance:** Provides settings for positioning, margining, and resizing the picture. You can specify the border thickness as well as the picture's width and height.

FIGURE 7.6

The Picture Properties dialog box

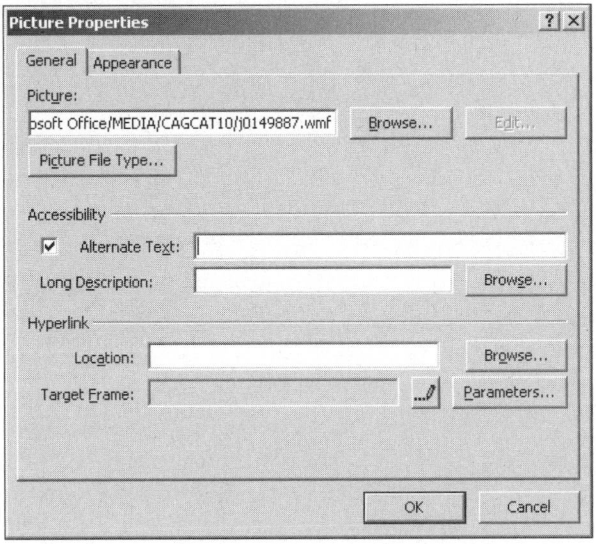

Creating hyperlinks on pictures

You can create a hyperlink on your picture by choosing either Picture Properties or Hyperlink from the popup menu when you right-click on a picture in the Design view.

The Hyperlink option opens the Insert Hyperlink dialog box, which you can use to create a hyperlink or bookmark. The more interesting exercise, however, is to create multiple hyperlinks at specific locations on a single picture.

SharePoint Designer provides the ability to create *hotspots* by using the Pictures toolbar. Hotspots are hyperlinks that are active on a specific area within a picture. So, a single picture can have multiple hyperlinks on it. To create hotspots on a picture, follow these steps:

1. **Choose View ⇨ Toolbars ⇨ Pictures to enable the Pictures toolbar and then drag it to the toolbar area in SharePoint Designer to dock it.**

2. **Open the Web page that has the picture on which you want to create hotspots.** Ensure you're working in the Design view.

3. **Hover over the buttons in the Pictures toolbar to find the Rectangular Hotspot button.** The mouse pointer changes to a Pencil icon.

4. **Using the mouse pointer, draw a rectangular box on a certain area of the picture where you want to create a hyperlink.** After the box is drawn, the Insert Hyperlink dialog box opens.

5. **Using the Insert Hyperlink dialog box, create a hyperlink for the hotspot.**

6. **Click OK.** Repeat these steps to create multiple hotspots in different areas of the picture.

7. **Save the page and then preview it in a browser.**

Now, when you hover over the picture, a number of hyperlinks are available. SharePoint Designer implements hotspots using the `<map>` and `<area>` tags. Here is a piece of HTML code for a Web page that has a picture with hotspots on it:

```
<map name="FPMap0" id="FPMap0">
<area href="http://spdexplorer:8009/button5.jpg" shape="rect"
    coords="146, 36, 293, 95" />
<area href="http://spdexplorer:8009/button6.jpg" shape="rect"
    coords="17, 131, 142, 185" />
<area href="http://spdexplorer:8009/Figure15.2.JPG" shape="rect"
    coords="185, 183, 262, 269" />
</map>
<img alt="" src="http://spdexplorer:8009/MPj04386750000[1].jpg"
    width="384" height="351" usemap="#FPMap0"/>
```

Notice the `<map>` tag containing the `<area>` tags that have been created for each hyperlink in the previous code. The `<map>` tag's ID is then used as a reference in the picture's `<img>` tag to enable the hotspot.

Exploiting the Pictures toolbar

The Pictures toolbar, as shown in Figure 7.7, allows a Web site designer to perform some basic operations on pictures that have been inserted on a Web page. As discussed in the previous section, you've already used the Pictures toolbar to create and manage hotspots on pictures. Besides creating hotspots, you can also perform the following operations:

FIGURE 7.7

The Pictures toolbar

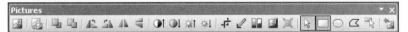

- **Insert Picture from File:** Opens the Picture dialog box to allow you to choose a picture to be inserted from a specific location
- **Auto Thumbnail:** Automatically creates a thumbnail for the selected picture
- **Bring Forward:** Changes the z-order of the picture to bring it to the top
- **Send Backward:** Reduces the z-order of the picture to take it to the bottom of other content on the page
- **Rotate Left 90°:** Rotates the picture to the left by 90 degrees
- **Rotate Right 90°:** Rotates the picture to the right by 90 degrees
- **Flip Horizontal:** Creates a horizontal mirror image of the picture
- **Flip Vertical:** Creates a vertical mirror image of the picture
- **More Contrast:** Increases the color contrast
- **Less Contrast:** Decreases the color contrast
- **More Brightness:** Increases the brightness
- **Less Brightness:** Reduces the brightness
- **Crop:** Allows you to crop a picture to desired dimensions. To crop a picture, click the Crop button on the Pictures toolbar. Use the box that appears on a picture to set the cropped dimensions. Click the Crop button again to implement the cropping.
- **Set Transparent Color:** For GIF picture file types, this option allows you to set the transparent color for the pictures. To use this option, you need to convert the picture to the GIF file type.
- **Color:** Allows you to change the look of a picture to grayscale or washout
- **Bevel:** Add beveled edges a picture
- **Resample:** Resamples a resized picture to improve quality
- **Select:** Selects a picture
- **Rectangular Hotspot:** Creates a rectangular hotspot
- **Circular Hotspot:** Creates a circular hotspot
- **Polygonal Hotspot:** Allows you to create a multisided hotspot
- **Highlight Hotspots:** Shows the hotspots that have been created on a picture
- **Restore:** Undoes the changes made to a picture in the current editing session

Using symbols

Sometimes, you might need to insert some special symbols on your Web pages that allow you to more accurately represent that data your Web pages are offering. Using the Symbol dialog box, as shown in Figure 7.8, you can insert a symbol you need.

To insert a symbol on a Web page, follow these steps:

1. Place the cursor at the location on the Web page where you want to insert a symbol.

2. Choose Insert ⇨ Symbol to open the Symbol dialog box.

3. Choose the font you want to use for the symbol by using the Font dropdown menu.

4. **Choose the symbol from the list of symbols in the dialog box or choose from the recently used symbols list.** The Character code for the symbol is displayed in Unicode encoding format. Specify the encoding that you want to use in the from dropdown menu.

5. **Click Insert to place the symbol at the cursor location on the Web page and then click Close to close the Insert dialog box.**

While the font formatting is applied to the symbol using in-page styles and basic symbols, such as ®, ©, etc., are inserted as is in the code of the Web page, certain subsets of symbols are inserted as numerical encodings, which are interpreted by a browser to display the actual symbol. For example, the smiley symbol is inserted in the code of the Web page as ☻.

FIGURE 7.8

The Symbol dialog box

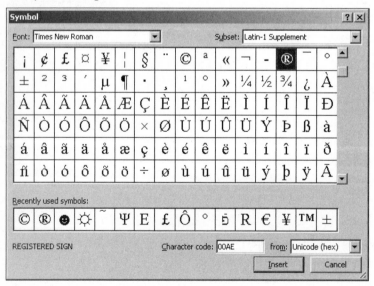

Using the Photo Gallery Web Component

The photo gallery Web component in SharePoint Designer is a simplified way to design galleries or albums for sharing pictures on Web sites. It offers a wizard-based approach to create photo galleries with captions and other features and provides four layouts that you can use to arrange pictures. To create a photo gallery by using SharePoint Designer, follow these steps:

1. **In the Design view, open the Web page where you want to insert a photo gallery.**

2. **Choose Insert ➪ Web Component to open the Insert Web Component dialog box.**

3. **Choose Photo Gallery in the list of components and then choose a layout option.** You can choose to insert a horizontal, montage, or vertical layout or you can insert a slide show of pictures.

4. **Click Finish.** The Photo Gallery Properties dialog box opens, as shown in Figure 7.9. You use this dialog box to choose pictures to be added to the gallery and change the chosen layout for the gallery.

FIGURE 7.9

The Photo Gallery Properties dialog box

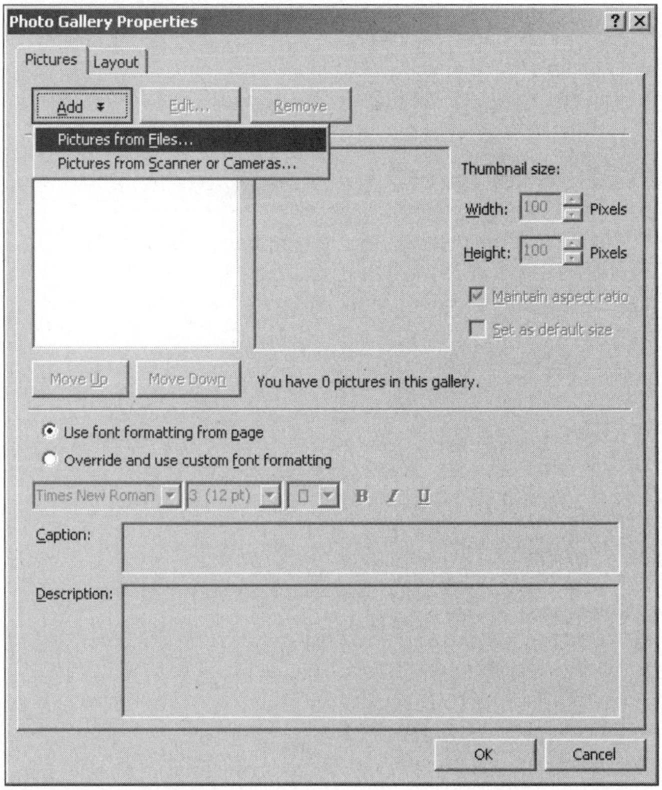

5. **Click the Add button to add pictures from a file location, a scanner, or a camera.** You can choose multiple images to be added to the gallery.

6. **After you select the images, click Open.** SharePoint Designer adds the pictures to the gallery. The Pictures tab in the Photo Gallery Properties dialog box shows the number of pictures inserted in the gallery. You can change the order of the pictures by clicking Move Up and Move Down.

7. **If you want to edit the pictures that you just added to the gallery, select a picture and then click the Edit button.** This opens the selected picture in the Edit dialog box, where you can resize, crop, or change the direction of the picture.

8. **Choose a picture in the list of pictures in the gallery.** Using the Thumbnail size options, specify the size of the thumbnail to be generated for the picture.

9. **Type the caption and description for the picture in the respective boxes.** You can also apply font formatting to the caption and description text by using the options provided.

10. **Click the Layout tab to change the layout of the photo gallery.** The Layout tab also provides a preview of the layout and allows you to specify the number of picture to be shown in a row.

11. **Click OK to allow SharePoint Designer to create the photo gallery component for you on the Web page.**

Like many of the legacy FrontPage components, the photo gallery component is shown in the Code view of the Web page as an HTML comment, which SharePoint Designer uses as a placeholder for rendering the component in the Design view:

```
<!--Webbot bot="PhotoAlbum" U-Include="photogallery/photo00031001/
    real.htm" clientside="" TAG="BODY" -->
```

However, if you open the same Web page in Notepad, the actual code that's used to implement the photo gallery Web component appears. Here is the sample code of the slide show photo gallery layout as viewed in Notepad by using the Open With⇨Notepad option in the SharePoint Designer Folder List task pane:

```
<!--Webbot bot="PhotoAlbum" U-Include="photogallery/photo00031001/
    real.htm" clientside="" TAG="BODY" startspan -->
<picture file-href="photogallery/photo00031001/real_p.htm" />
<picture file-href="photogallery/photo00031001/real_x.htm" />
<div align="center">
<center>
<layer visibility="hide">
<div style="display:none;" id="fpGalleryCaptions_5306">
<div></div><div></div></div>
<div style="display:none;" id="fpGalleryDescriptions_5306">
<div></div><div></div></div>
</layer>
```

```
<script language="javascript" src="photogallery/photo00031001/
    sldshow.js">
<!---->
</script>
<table border="0" cellspacing="0" cellpadding="5" width="700"
    dir="ltr">
<tr>
<td nowrap="" align="center">
<layer visibility="hide">
<img border="0" align="middle" src="photogallery/photo00031001/
    prevdis.gif" lowsrc="photogallery/photo00031001/prev.gif"
    id="fpGalleryLeftBtn_5306" onclick="JavaScript:fp_
    ScrollLeft(5306)" width="25" height="29" />
</layer>
<script language="JavaScript1.1">
<!--
        if (fp_ie4()) {
                document.write("<span align='center' style='width:23
    5;overflow:hidden' id='fpGalleryListCell_5306'>");
        }
        if (fp_ns6()) {
                document.getElementById("fpGalleryLeftBtn_5306").
    style.visibility="hidden"
        }
        -->
</script>
<a target="_self" href="Javascript:fp_ShowImg(document['fpphoto_2349'
    ],'430','567','5306',0);"><img hspace="10" vspace="5" border="0"
    src="photogallery/photo00031001/Figure15.2.JPG" id="fpphoto_2349"
    name="fpphoto_2349" lowsrc="Figure15.2.JPG" width="75"
    height="100" title="" align="absmiddle" /></a>
<a target="_self" href="Javascript:fp_ShowImg(document['fpphoto_3821'
    ],'17','16','5306',1);"><img hspace="10" vspace="5" border="0"
    src="photogallery/photo00031001/test.JPG" id="fpphoto_3821"
    name="fpphoto_3821" lowsrc="test.JPG" width="100" height="94"
    title="" align="absmiddle" /></a>
<span style="width:0;height:100;visibility:hidden">.</span>
<script language="JavaScript1.1">
<!--
        if (fp_ie4()) {
                document.write("</span>");
        }
        -->
</script>
<layer visibility="hide">
<img border="0" align="middle" src="photogallery/photo00031001/
    nextdis.gif" lowsrc="photogallery/photo00031001/next.gif"
    id="fpGalleryRightBtn_5306" onclick="JavaScript:fp_
    ScrollRight(5306)" width="25" height="29">
```

```
<script language="JavaScript1.1">
                    if (fp_ns6()) {
                                document.getElementById("fpGall
    eryRightBtn_5306").style.visibility="hidden"
                    }
            </script>
</img>
</layer>
<hr width="95%" size="1" color="#000000" />
</td>
</tr>
</table>
<img id="fpGalleryMainImg_5306" name="fpGalleryMainImg_5306"
    width="430" height="567" src="Figure15.2.JPG" title="" />
<layer visibility="hide">
<div id="fpGalleryCaptionCell_5306">
</div>
<div id="fpGalleryDescCell_5306">
</div>
</layer>
</center>
</div>
<!--Webbot bot="PhotoAlbum" i-checksum="3109" endspan -->
```

While you really don't need to understand this code, keep in mind that you shouldn't modify the code by using any other HTML editor or you might be at risk of losing the photo gallery Web component. Also highlighted are the files that form the backbone of the photo gallery component. These files may change depending on the layout that you chose when creating the gallery.

Exploring associated folders and files

After you insert the photo gallery component on the Web page, SharePoint Designer creates a `photogallery` folder to keep all associated files of the gallery together. Every gallery has a unique folder within this folder. These folders remain even after you delete the gallery from a Web page. Depending on the layout selected for the gallery, the following files are created when you insert a photo gallery on a Web page:

- `Real_p.htm`: Contains the tabular structure that defines the initial look and design of the Web page

- `Real_x.htm`: Contains references to the list of pictures added to the photo gallery component along with the properties (captions, descriptions, etc.) specified for the pictures

- `Real.htm`: Combines the `real_p.htm` and `real_x.htm` pages to form the actual layout of the photo gallery component

- `Sldshow.js`: This file has the JavaScript implementation of the slideshow layout of the photo gallery Web component

CAUTION The SharePoint Designer photo gallery component relies on a number of JavaScript files for creating the photo album of the selected pictures. If you have antivirus software installed on your machine that blocks JavaScript files, SharePoint Designer might fail while creating galleries.

Modifying the photo gallery properties

After the photo gallery is inserted on a Web page, you can simply right-click on the component and then choose Photo Gallery from the popup menu to open the Photo Gallery Properties dialog box. You can then modify the properties associated with the pictures inside the gallery by using the steps discussed in the previous sections.

Using Advanced Controls

SharePoint Designer's Insert Web Component dialog box allows you to insert a number of advanced controls that are commonly used by Web site designers. These include java applets, plug-ins, ActiveX controls, etc. In this section, I take you through the process of inserting such controls on Web pages by using SharePoint Designer.

Inserting Java applets and ActiveX controls

Applets are small applications that perform specific operations when inserted on a Web page. To insert a Java applet on your Web page, follow these steps:

1. In the Design view, open the Web page on which you want to insert an applet.

2. Choose Insert ⇨ Web Component to open the Insert Web Component dialog box and then click Advanced Controls.

3. In the Choose a control list, choose Java Applet and then click OK. The Java Applet Properties dialog box opens, as shown in Figure 7.10, where you can specify the source and settings for the applet you want to use.

4. Specify the Applet source (usually a `class` file) and Applet base URL in the text fields provided.

5. If the applet that you're using requires parameters to be passed to it, you can specify them in the Applet Parameters section in this dialog box.

6. Click OK to insert the applet on the Web page.

FIGURE 7.10

The Java Applet Properties dialog box

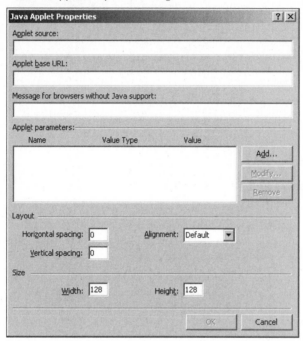

If you click the Code view tab after you insert the applet on the Web page, the Java Applet Properties dialog box merely becomes the interface to set attributes for the `<applet>` tag.

Similar to applets, ActiveX controls are predeveloped controls and applications that can be inserted on Web pages to provide specific functions. SharePoint Designer allows you to insert a number of Microsoft ActiveX controls usually available with the operating system. When you elect to insert an ActiveX control by using the Insert Web Component dialog box, you're provided with a list of ActiveX controls installed on the SharePoint Designer machine.

NOTE   **Both Applets and ActiveX controls aren't allowed to run in IE directly. When a user browses to a page that has an ActiveX control on it, he or she is prompted to confirm if he or she wants to allow the ActiveX control to run.**

ActiveX controls are inserted on Web pages by using the `<object>` tag. SharePoint Designer provides contextual Properties dialog boxes for ActiveX controls that allow you to modify the properties of the controls by using the user interface rather than having to set them in the Code view. After the control is inserted on a Web page, right-click on the control and then choose ActiveX Control Properties from the popup menu to modify the control properties.

Inserting Flash controls

Inserting Flash movies on a Web page by using SharePoint Designer can be a little tricky. However, if you understand the concept involved here, you might be able to subsequently insert Flash files in a quick manner. Follow these steps to insert a Flash movie on a Web page:

1. **Import the Flash file you want to use on your Web site.** You can do this by simply dragging and dropping the file from Windows Explorer to the SharePoint Designer Folder List task pane.

2. **Using the Insert Web Component dialog box, choose Advanced Controls ⇨ Plug-In and then click Finish.** This inserts a plug-in on the Web page and opens the Plug-in Properties dialog box.

3. **Type the name and location of the Flash file in the Data source dialog box.** Specify a text message to be shown for those browsers that don't support plug-ins.

4. **Save the Web page and then preview it in a browser.**

SharePoint Designer inserts the Flash movie by using the `<embed>` tag on the Web page. You can also use the `<object>` tag to play Flash movies on Web pages by using the following code:

```
<OBJECT classid="clsid:D27CDB6E-AE6D-11cf-96B8-444553540000"
codebase="http://download.macromedia.com/pub/shockwave/cabs/flash/
    swflash.cab#version=6,0,0,0">
<PARAM NAME=movie VALUE="flash.swf">
<EMBED src="flash.swf" TYPE="application/x-shockwave-flash"
    PLUGINSPAGE="http://www.macromedia.com/go/getflashplayer"></
    EMBED>
</OBJECT>
```

In the highlighted code, the value of the `classid` attribute is the `CLSID` (class identifier) of the Flash player ActiveX control.

Using MSN Web components

SharePoint Designer allows you to insert MSN components for creating and linking to maps, show stock quotes, and use MSN Search. These components are available in the Insert Web Component dialog box under MSN Mapping Components and MSN Components.

To insert an MSN map on your Web page by using the MSN mapping component provided by SharePoint Designer, follow these steps:

1. **In the list of Web components in the Insert Web Component dialog box, click MSN Mapping Components.**

2. **Choose Insert a map in the list of components and then click Finish.** The Insert a map Properties dialog box opens.

3. Use the Insert a map Properties dialog box to specify the address you want to insert a map of.

4. Click Next to preview the map, click Next, and then click Finish to insert the map on the Web page at the location of the cursor.

> **TIP** While inserting the MSN stock quote component on a Web page, ensure that you place the cursor outside the `<form>` tag in the page. This component inserts its own `<form>` tag and fails to get inserted inside an existing `<form>` tag.

Summary

Using SharePoint Designer to work with picture and animation can be quite fun, and you can quickly build a complex Web site without writing much code by hand. In this chapter, I discussed the SharePoint Designer picture and photo gallery features. I also talked about how you can insert advanced controls, such as applets, plug-ins, and other components, on Web pages.

Part III

Implementing Components and Controls

Chapter 8

Exploiting JavaScript and DHTML

IN THIS CHAPTER

Working with interactive buttons

Using SharePoint Designer behaviors

Using page transitions

Most of the Web sites on the Internet don't really have static content. Instead, the Web pages are mostly live with dynamics such as dropdown and popup menus, hover-over tabs and buttons, expanding and collapsing content, etc. While HTML is a great technology for developing static Web pages, if you combine it with a client-side scripting technology, such as JavaScript, you can really bring your Web pages to life. Using DHTML effects to enable and disable content on Web pages is recommended by many as a key strategy to structure and simplify access to key areas inside Web sites.

Dynamic effects on Web pages are driven by *events*. An event is an action that a user who browses to the Web page takes. For example, a user may move the mouse over a certain area or section of the Web page or click a certain HTML tag on the Web page. Most such user actions are categorized into events that can be associated with an HTML tag. When such an event happens, the Web site designer is given control on the operation that needs to be performed for that event. Most common events are `onmouseover`, `onmouseout`, `onclick`, `onkeydown`, `ondlbclick`, etc. Using a client-side script, a designer can program what operation should be performed when an event occurs.

SharePoint Designer carries forward one of the key features of dynamic Web page development from FrontPage 2003 called *behaviors*. Behaviors combined with layers offer limitless capabilities in creating dynamic effects on Web pages. In the back end, behaviors are mostly driven by JavaScript functions. However, SharePoint Designer hides the complexity of these functions from Web designers and offers an intuitive user interface to use JavaScript as a means to vitalize content on Web pages. The SharePoint Designer user doesn't really need to possess understanding of client-side scripting technologies and can just use the interface to use JavaScript for inserting dynamic effects on select HTML content.

In this chapter, I discuss how you can use the SharePoint Designer behaviors to create dynamic Web content. I take you through steps and exercises that help you develop an understanding about how to exploit behaviors in SharePoint Designer. Later in this chapter, I also talk about some legacy FrontPage DHTML effects that you might want to use on your Web sites.

But first, I begin by familiarizing you with one of the other cool features that SharePoint Designer inherited from FrontPage 2003. This feature, called interactive buttons, uses JavaScript at the back end to provide you with a set of buttons that become active when a user hovers over them. Interactive buttons were introduced in FrontPage 2003 and replaced the FrontPage hover buttons.

Working with Interactive Buttons

Inserting interactive buttons on Web pages is simple. You can follow these steps to create the interactive buttons of your choice on a Web page:

1. **In the Design view, open the Web page where you want to insert an interactive button.**

2. **Choose Insert ⇨ Interactive Button to open the Interactive Buttons dialog box, as shown in Figure 8.1.** This dialog box allows you to choose a format for the button and shows a quick preview of how the button will look on the Web page.

3. **In the Buttons list, choose the button you want to use, type the button text, and specify the URL to be associated with the button.**

4. **Click the Font tab.** Here, you can change the font of the text on the button and also specify the various colors that text should take when the mouse is over or moved off the button text.

5. **Click the Image tab.** Using this tab, you can specify certain properties of the image of the button that's created by SharePoint Designer. You can choose whether the hover and the clicked image should be created. The hover image is displayed when the mouse is hovered over the button, and the clicked image is displayed when the button is clicked.

6. **Click OK.** The button is inserted on the Web page.

7. **Save the Web page.** SharePoint Designer asks you to save the images associated with the interactive button. Save the images to the location of your choice.

When you preview the page in a browser, the button changes color when you move the mouse over it. When you click the button, the image changes again.

To understand what SharePoint Designer did internally for enabling the interactive buttons, open the Behaviors task pane from the Task Panes menu. After the Behaviors task pane opens, just click the newly inserted button. As shown in Figure 8.2, a number of events (onmousedown, onmouseout, onmouseover, and onmouseup) have been set for the <img> tag associated with the button.

FIGURE 8.1

The Interactive Buttons dialog box

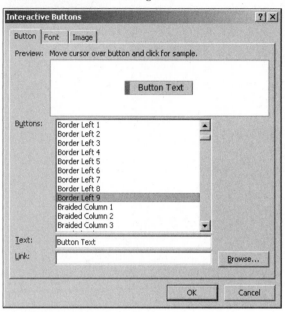

FIGURE 8.2

The Behaviors task pane for an interactive button

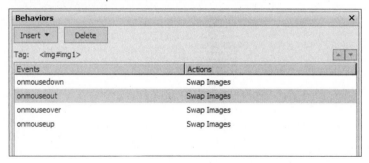

While I discuss these in more detail in the next section, the point to understand is that when you created the interactive button, SharePoint Designer first created three images and then created a set of JavaScript functions that swap the images based on the event that takes place. To successfully use the interactive button on a Web page, it's important that the images associated with the button are available. For example, when you publish a Web page that has an interactive button on it, you must ensure that the button images are also published.

Using SharePoint Designer Behaviors

Behaviors allow Web site designers to create DHTML effects and functionality on Web pages without having to write a lot of JavaScript code. SharePoint Designer has prewritten JavaScript actions that provide a large set of functions. In this section, I discuss these actions and show you how to use them for Web page development.

Understanding behaviors

Behaviors are basically predefined JavaScript functions that can be used with various DHTML events to obtain a specific functionality. Table 8.1 shows a list of behaviors available in SharePoint Designer.

TABLE 8.1

List of SharePoint Designer Behaviors

Behavior	Description
Call script	Allows you to use a JavaScript function that you want to use (in case you have a function you wrote)
Change property	Allows you to change the HTML properties and attributes of selected HTML tags and elements
Change property restore	Restores the HTML properties/attributes changed by the Change Property behavior
Check browser	Allows you to check the version of a browser being used and redirect to a URL based on that browser's version
Check plug-in	Allows you to check the plug-in type and redirect to a URL based on that type
Go to URL	Takes you to the specified URL
Jump menu	Allows you to create a dropdown menu with choices that take you to the associated URL
Jump menu go	After the Jump menu is used, allows you to go to a URL based on the selected index of the Jump menu
Open browser window	Opens the specified URL in a new browser window
Play sound	Allows you to specify a music file to be placed
Popup message	Displays a specified message
Preload images	Preloads the specified images at page load time
Set text	Allows you to set text for a frame, layer, browser status bar, or text field
Swap images	Allows you to change the display image of the `<img>` tag
Swap images restore	Restores the image swap

The basic process of implementing a behavior on an HTML element is as follows:

- Choose the HTML tag or element that you want to apply the behavior on in the currently open Web page.
- Choose the behavior that you want to use and then specify the settings for the behavior by using the associated dialog box.
- Choose the DHTML event on which the behavior should fire.

Working with the Behaviors task pane

The Behaviors task pane is the SharePoint Designer interface to create behaviors and associate them with HTML tags. As shown in Figure 8.3, the Behavior task pane is contextual — that is, only the behaviors associated with the current selection in the Web page are displayed in the task pane.

FIGURE 8.3

The Behaviors task pane

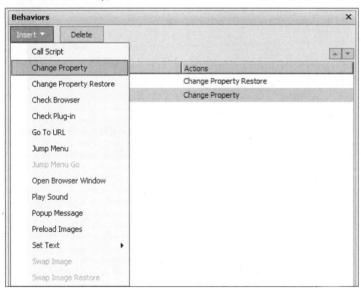

The Tag label indicates the selected tag for which the behaviors are being displayed. The list of the behaviors and the associated DHTML events applicable to the selected tag are displayed in the Behaviors list. You can insert new behaviors by using the Insert menu and delete existing ones by first selecting them from the list and then clicking Delete.

Inserting behaviors on HTML elements

To demonstrate how you can use SharePoint Designer behaviors to dynamically change HTML attributes, follow these steps:

1. **In the Design view, open your Web site and then create a new Web page.** Ensure that the Behaviors task pane is open.

2. **Choose Insert ➪ HTML ➪ Paragraph.** This inserts a <p> tag on the Web page, which is selected and shown in the Quick Tag Selector.

3. **Type some text inside the paragraph.** Ensure that the Behavior task pane shows the selected tag as a <p> tag. You see this in the Tag: label in the top section of the Behaviors task pane.

4. **In the Behaviors task pane, choose Insert ➪ Change Property.** The Change Property dialog box, as shown in Figure 8.4, opens.

FIGURE 8.4

The Change Property dialog box

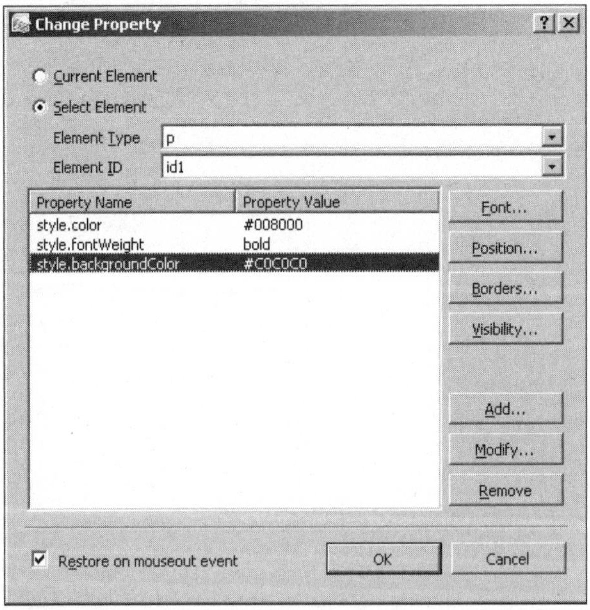

5. **Ensure that the Current Element radio button is selected and then click Font.**

6. **Choose Bold in the Font Style and then change the color to Green.**

7. **Click OK.** The selections made in the Font dialog box appear as styles in the Change Property dialog box.

8. Click Borders, click the Shading tab, choose Silver as the background color, and then click OK.

9. Click the **Restore on mouseout event** check box and then click OK. Two behaviors are then applied to the selected paragraph. The first behavior changes the look of the paragraph when the mouse is hovered over it, and the second behavior restores the original look of the paragraph when the mouse is moved away from it.

10. Save the page and then preview it in a browser.

You can use the behavior in a similar manner on other HTML tags and elements. In the next exercise, you use a combination of behaviors to show and hide content on a Web page.

Implementing dynamic effects by using behaviors

To begin this exercise, first create a new Web page using the following HTML code:

```html
<html xmlns="http://www.w3.org/1999/xhtml">

<head>
<meta http-equiv="Content-Language" content="en-us" />
<meta http-equiv="Content-Type" content="text/html;
    charset=windows-1252" />
<title>Untitled 10</title>
<style type="text/css">
.style1 {
    border: 2px solid #ffffff;
    background-color: #ffffff;
}
</style>
</head>

<body>

<table style="width: 100%" class="style1">
    <tr id="tr1">
        <td style="width: 305px">First Paragraph</td>
    </tr>
    <tr id="tr2">
        <td style="width: 305px">Second Paragraph</td>
    </tr>
</table>
<p id="p1" style="visibility:hidden">This is the text of the first
    paragraph.</p>
<p id="p2" style="visibility:hidden">This is the text of the second
    paragraph.</p>

</body>

</html>
```

The page simply contains a table with two rows and two columns. The first row, `tr1`, has the text First Paragraph in it, and the second row, `tr2`, has the text Second Paragraph. Later in the code, there are two paragraphs (`p1` and `p2`) with the `visibility:hidden` style applied to them.

The exercise is to use behaviors to show the `p1` paragraph when the mouse moves over the `tr1` row and show the `p2` paragraph when the mouse moves over the `tr2` row. To do this, follow these steps:

1. Ensure that `tr1` is selected in the Behaviors task pane and then choose Insert➪Change Property.

2. In the Change Property dialog box, click Select Element and then type p as the Element Type and `p1` as the Element ID.

3. Click Visibility and then click the Visible radio button. The resulting selection is shown in Figure 8.5.

FIGURE 8.5

Using behaviors to show and hide content

4. Click the Restore on mouseout event check box and then click OK.

5. Repeat the previous steps for the `tr2` row and the `p2` paragraph.

6. Save the page and then preview it in a browser.

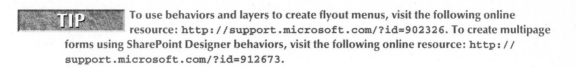 **TIP** To use behaviors and layers to create flyout menus, visit the following online resource: `http://support.microsoft.com/?id=902326`. To create multipage forms using SharePoint Designer behaviors, visit the following online resource: `http://support.microsoft.com/?id=912673`.

Using Page Transitions

Page Transition is a legacy feature carried forward from FrontPage versions that allows designers to create an effect of transition when a user browses from one page to another. Page transitions target four events: Site Enter, Site Exit, Page Enter, and Page Exit. As their names suggest, the transition associated with an event happens when the user enters or leaves a Web site or a Web page.

You can specify the page transitions settings by choosing Format ➪ Page Transition. As shown in Figure 8.6, the Page Transitions dialog box allows you to choose the event, the transition effect, and the duration within which the transition takes place.

FIGURE 8.6

The Page Transitions dialog box

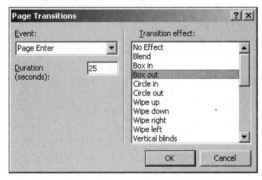

In the Code view of the Web page (after you apply a page transition effect to the Web page), a new Meta tag is added to the `<head>` section of the Web page HTML code. For example, the following code shows the Box out transition effect for 25 seconds when a user browses to this particular page:

```
<meta http-equiv="Page-Enter" content="revealTrans(Duration=25.0,Tran
    sition=1)" />
```

Summary

SharePoint Designer's behaviors and layers offer a lot of flexibility to Web site designers to allow them to create dynamic content using a no-code interface. You just need to know about the event for which you want to target the dynamic content, and SharePoint Designer allows you to make changes to the HTML based on your selection.

Chapter 9

Using FrontPage Legacy Components

IN THIS CHAPTER

Understanding the types of Web components

Inserting Web components

Creating forms

One of the most commonly used features of FrontPage is Web components, which provide prewritten functionality for use in Web sites. Web components, such as FrontPage forms, search forms, page hit counters, etc., offered with FrontPage have been quite popular and are used exceedingly on Web sites that support FPSE. The readiness and ease of usage of these Web components make them a choice for many Web site designers looking to quickly implement advanced Web site operations. SharePoint Designer inherits most of these Web components from FrontPage 2003 and allows Web site designers to use them on FPSE-based and, in some cases, SharePoint Web sites.

Each of these Web components provides an effortless interface that allows Web designers to set their properties and attributes. After a Web component is inserted on a Web page, a designer configures its properties by using the SharePoint Designer user interface and then saves the Web page. At runtime, based on the properties set for the Web component, a server-side code (usually implemented by FPSE or SharePoint) renders the HTML for the Web component to be displayed in a browser so that a Web site visitor can interface with the component. In this way, the Web component hides its code implementation from the Web designer, allowing him or her to simply make some settings for the component rather than having to think about coding the actual implementation of the functionality that the Web component offers.

To begin this chapter, I discuss how many of these Web components provide functionality that can now be obtained by using other advanced and more contemporary technologies, such as ASP.NET 2.0. Hence, I named these Web components here as FrontPage legacy components. If you're looking at developing new Web sites, my recommendation is to consider using ASP.NET 2.0 and other relatively new technologies to implement the features provided by these components. My intention in this chapter is to help you understand how to use Web components so that if you run into a Web site implementation that uses these Web components, you can use SharePoint Designer to maintain such Web sites effectively and develop suitable migration strategies.

This chapter discusses the FrontPage legacy components available in SharePoint Designer. These include components such as forms; search components; included content such as substitution, included pages, etc.; hit counters; and a table of contents, among others. I start by first broadly classifying these components based on the Web server requirements. Then, I introduce you to these Web components and show how you can insert and configure them on Web pages by using SharePoint Designer.

Understanding the Types of Web Components

SharePoint Designer, as in previous versions of FrontPage, installs many client components that provide support for authoring Web components. These client components facilitate insertion and setup of the Web components through SharePoint Designer. Web components available in SharePoint Designer can be of two types, depending on how they function after being configured on a Web page.

Author time Web components

Author time Web components require the services provided by FPSE only at the time they're being inserted and configured on a Web page. After they're set up on Web pages, they don't need FPSE to operate. This means that the Web pages that use these components can be placed on Web sites that don't have FPSE on them. The following is a list of some of the commonly used author time Web components:

- **Included Content:** Allows you to include content, such as pages, pictures, date, and time, on the Web pages
- **Link Bars:** Provides navigation features to Web sites by allowing you to create bars with links to various sections
- **FrontPage Themes:** Provides formatting and styling by using HTML and CSS
- **Photo Gallery Component:** Allows you to create picture galleries on Web pages
- **Table of Contents:** Allows you to compile a table of contents for your Web sites

 **NOTE**   While these components don't require FPSE, they still need to use the hidden metadata for functionality and maintenance.

Runtime Web components

Runtime Web components require the services provided by FPSE at the time they're configured on a Web page as well as at the time when a Web page is being browsed to. Runtime Web components don't work if the Web pages in which they're placed are published to a Web site that doesn't have FPSE properly configured for it. At runtime, these components use FPSE for performing their operations. The most commonly used runtime Web components include the following:

- **Hit Counter:** Keeps track of the number of page hits made to a Web page on which the component is inserted

- **FrontPage Form Handlers:** Provides features to create HTML forms that send data collected from a user to a file, e-mail address, etc. They also provide enhanced features, such as custom confirmation pages, save format, etc.

- **Search Component:** Allows you to enable content search on Web sites

- **File Upload Components:** Enables file upload by using form handlers

- **Confirmation Fields:** Allows you to create dynamic custom confirmation pages when using form handlers

Throughout the rest of this chapter, I show you how you can use SharePoint Designer to configure these Web components on Web pages.

Inserting Web Components

Most SharePoint Designer Web components are available in the Insert Web Component dialog box, which is accessible by choosing Insert ⇨ Web Component. You need to have a Web page active (open in the Design or Code view) in SharePoint Designer to be able to insert Web components.

NOTE If the Manage the Web site using hidden metadata check box in the Site Settings dialog box isn't selected for a Web site, most of the components in the Insert Web Components dialog box are thus disabled.

Creating hit counters

Hit counters are a very desirable feature, and the Hit Counter Web component provides an easy way to implement this functionality on a Web site. To insert a hit counter on a Web page of your Web site, follow these steps:

1. **Open the Web page where you want to insert the hit counter.**

2. **Choose Insert ⇨ Web Component to open the Insert Web Component dialog box.**

3. **In the Component type section, select Hit Counter.** In the Choose a counter style section, you can select the style of counter you want to use, as shown in Figure 9.1.

4. **Click Finish.** The Hit Counter Properties dialog box opens, as shown in Figure 9.2. Choose the style you want for your hit counter. You can also click the Reset counter to check box and then specify the initial value from which the counter should start counting. Clicking the Fixed number of digits check box allows you to specify the number of digits to be used in the hit counter.

5. **Click OK to complete the configuration of the hit counter for the Web page.**

FIGURE 9.1

Inserting a hit counter on a Web page

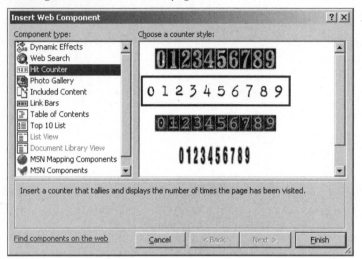

FIGURE 9.2

The Hit Counter Properties dialog box

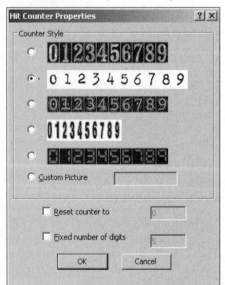

When you browse to the Web page that has the hit counter, the hit counter is incremented on every refresh of the Web page by using a hit counter image. The image that you choose is divided into 10 sections for each number and then the sections are swapped to show the increment in the hit count at runtime. As shown in Figure 9.3, the actual counter value is stored in a file with the extension .cnt in the _private folder for the Web site. You can change the value of the counter in this file to reset the counter.

FIGURE 9.3

Counter value for the Hit Counter Web component

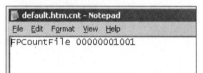

The design of the hit counter allows you to use a custom image for the hit counter. You can create an image of suitable dimensions by using your favorite graphics-creation program or picture editor program and then specify in the Hit Counter Properties dialog box that the hit counter should use the custom image.

Working with included content

As shown in Figure 9.4, when you select the Included Content component type in the Insert Web Component dialog box, you can make use of a number of options for including content on the active Web page. In this section, I take you through the components that assist in including content.

Comment

Selecting Comment in the Choose a type of content list allows you to insert an HTML comment on the Web page contents, which are visible in the Design view in SharePoint Designer. When you insert a comment in this way, the following code is written to the Code view of the Web page:

```
<!--webbot bot="PurpleText" PREVIEW="Insert image here" -->
```

SharePoint Designer provides the interface that allows you to change the value of the Preview attribute, which actually forms the comment that's displayed in the Design view. You can right-click on the comment component and then choose Comment Properties from the popup menu to change the preview text.

Date and Time

The Date and Time component provides a way to show when the page on which the component is inserted was last modified. As shown in Figure 9.5, when you insert a Date and Time component, you can choose whether you want to show the date when the page was last edited or when the page was last automatically updated.

FIGURE 9.4

Inserting included content Web components

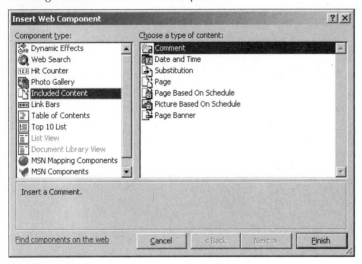

FIGURE 9.5

Date and Time component properties

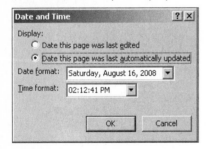

You can choose from a list of date and time formats by using the Date and Time dialog box. Depending on the format chosen, the following code is inserted on the Web page to enable the Date and Time component:

```
<!--webbot bot="Timestamp" S-Type="EDITED" S-Format="%A, %B %d, %Y
     %I:%M:%S %p" -->
```

When you preview the Web page in a browser, the Date and Time Web component displays the last modified date and time of the Web page. This information is picked up from the hidden metadata that's maintained for all pages inside the Web site that support hidden metadata.

NOTE If you try to put a Date and Time Web component on a Web page inside a Web site that doesn't support hidden metadata — for example, by cutting and pasting code — it won't work. This means that the dates and times in the Web component aren't refreshed.

Substitution

The Substitution Web component provides a way to centrally manage commonly displayed text on Web sites. For example, consider a situation where you need to specify some volatile information on a lot of pages inside a Web site. If you type this information on every page, a change would require you to go back and change the information on all the Web pages.

Instead, you can use a Substitution Web component in conjunction with a site parameter to display this information on all pages. Follow these steps:

1. **With your Web site that supports hidden metadata open in SharePoint Designer, choose Site ⇨ Site Settings.**

2. **Click the Parameters Tab, click Add to add a parameter name and value, as shown in Figure 9.6, and then click OK.**

FIGURE 9.6

Creating a new site parameter via the Site Settings dialog box

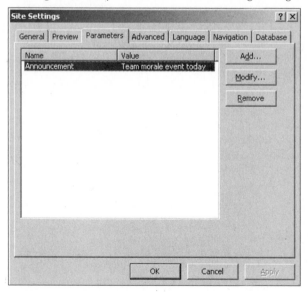

3. Choose Insert⇨Web Component to open the Insert Web Component dialog box and then select Substitution in the Included Content component type. This displays the Substitution Properties dialog box. The Substitute with dropdown menu shows the parameter created in step 2 as an available choice.

4. Select the site parameter and then click OK.

The value of the site parameter is inserted on the Web page, and the following code is inserted in the code of the Web page:

```
<!--webbot bot="Substitution" S-Variable="Announcement" -->
```

You can insert a Substitution Web component on all the Web pages where the value of the site parameter needs to be displayed. Whenever a change is required, all you need to do is change the site parameter by using the Site Settings dialog box, and the substitution components are automatically updated to show the new information.

Page

The Page Web component allows you to display the contents of a Web page inside another Web page. When you insert the Page Web component on a Web page, the user interface allows you to pick a Web page that needs to be included in the currently active Web page.

After you insert the page Web component, if you switch to the Code view of the Web page, the following code is inserted for the Web page:

```
<!--webbot bot="Include" U-Include="bottom.htm" TAG="BODY" -->
```

The Code view actually hides the fact that the actual code of the included Web page is included for the page on which the page component has been added. As shown in the following code, if you open the Web page by choosing Open With⇨Notepad, the code of the included page is actually present in the Web page:

```
<body>
<p> </p>
<!--webbot bot="Include" U-Include="bottom.htm" TAG="BODY" startspan
   -->
<p>Contents of bottom.htm</p>
<!--webbot bot="Include" i-checksum="18282" endspan -->
</body>
```

As shown in the previous code, the content of the included page exists with the webbot comments of the page Web component.

Page Based On Schedule

The Page Based On Schedule Web component allows you to configure the included page in such a manner that it's displayed only for a certain period of time.

For example, you can configure this Web component to show the included page only between certain dates. When the scheduled date and time passes, the included page isn't displayed on the parent page anymore. Optionally, as shown in Figure 9.7, you can configure another included page to display before and after the scheduled time.

FIGURE 9.7

Configuring an included page based on a schedule

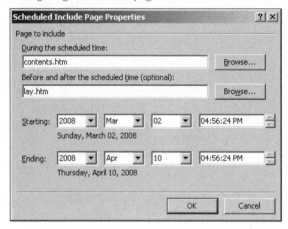

The following code is inserted on a Web page when you add the Page Based On Schedule Web component:

```
<!--webbot bot="ScheduledInclude" U-Include="contents.htm" U-Else-
    Include="lay.htm" D-Start-Date="02 Mar 2008 17:03:07" D-End-
    Date="10 Apr 2008 17:03:07" -->
```

NOTE   Because this Web component is an author time Web component, it's important to understand that the decision to make the switch is made at the time the component is inserted or the Web page is saved.

Picture Based On Schedule

The Picture Based On Schedule Web component allows you to insert a picture on a Web page and then schedule it to be displayed only during a certain time period. As shown in Figure 9.8, the Scheduled Picture Properties dialog box allows you to specify the picture and the alternate text to be used between the specified times. Optionally, you can specify to use a picture that's displayed before and after the specified time has passed.

FIGURE 9.8

Configuring a picture based on a schedule

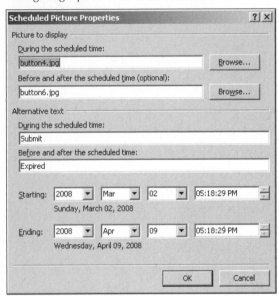

Page Banner

If the Web page that you're working on is part of a Web site's navigation structure, you can use the Page Banner Web component to display the title of the Web page. Using the Page Banner Properties dialog box, as shown in Figure 9.9, you can also specify whether the page banner should be displayed as a picture or just plain text. You can also modify the text to be displayed in the page banner.

FIGURE 9.9

The Page Banner Properties dialog box

Creating page categories and a table of contents

While creating Web pages in SharePoint Designer, you have the option to create Page Categories and then associate each newly created Web page with a specific category. Categorizing the Web pages in this manner is useful later in developing a table of contents for your Web site.

To create new page categories and then associate Web pages with them, follow these steps:

1. **Right-click on a Web page for a Web site in the Folder Lists task pane and then choose Page Properties from the popup menu.**

2. **Click the Workgroup tab.** As shown in Figure 9.10, the Workgroup tab can be used to associate the selected Web page with one or more categories. You can also add new categories by clicking Categories.

FIGURE 9.10

Associating a Web page with a page category

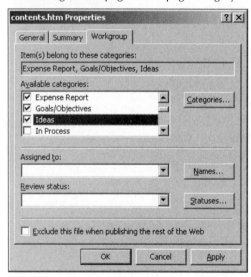

3. **Click Categories to open the Master Category List dialog box, type the name for your custom category, and then click Add.** The new category appears in the list of available categories.

4. **Choose the categories with which you want to associate the Web page.**

5. **Click OK to save the changes.**

After you categorize your Web pages in this manner, you can use the Table of Contents Web component to display a table of contents based on the page categories. When you insert a table of contents based on the page category by using the Insert Web Component dialog box, the Categories Properties dialog box, as shown in Figure 9.11, opens.

Choose the page categories you want to include by using the Choose categories to list files by section, specify the sorting order, choose whether to include date modified and comments added to the Web page, and then click OK. A categorized table of contents is created for you on the Web page. The table contains links that navigate the user to the corresponding Web page.

FIGURE 9.11

Selecting page categories to be used in the table of contents for the Web site

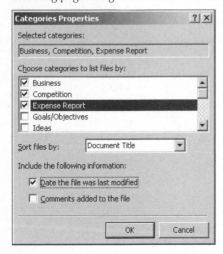

If you're not using page categories and just want to add a table of contents for your Web site, click the For This Web Site list option in the Table of Contents component type in the Insert Web Component dialog box. As shown in Figure 9.12, this displays the Table of Contents Properties dialog box, which allows you to specify the starting page for the table of contents.

CAUTION Clicking the Recompute table of contents when any other page is edited check box in the Table of Contents Properties dialog box makes SharePoint Designer recompute the table of contents every time any Web page inside the Web site is saved. Although negligible for small Web sites, it may take a long time to recompute the table of contents for large Web sites. Don't select this option on large Web sites. Instead, choose Site ⇨ Recalculate Hyperlinks to recompute the table of contents.

FIGURE 9.12

The Table of Contents Properties dialog box

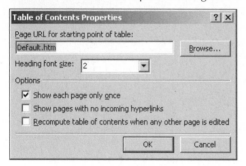

Implementing Web search

SharePoint Designer exposes the use of the search features available in Web sites that support FPSE. While FPSE handles the indexing and querying of the content of Web sites, SharePoint Designer allows Web designers to create search forms on Web pages (using the Search Form Web component), which act as the user interface for entering the search query.

The Web Search component type in the Insert Web Component dialog box has two options:

- **Current Web:** This option creates search forms on Web pages inside Web sites that have FPSE configured for them.

- **Full Text Search:** This option creates search forms on Web pages inside WSS v2 Web sites.

To insert a search form on a Web page inside an FPSE-enabled Web site, simply select the Current Web option in the Insert Web Component dialog box and then click Finish. The Search Form Properties dialog box shown opens, as shown in Figure 9.13, and can be used to configure some general settings for the search form.

The Search Form Properties dialog box allows you to customize the search form created by the Web Search component. You can specify the label for the search box and the captions for the Submit and Reset buttons. When you browse to a Web page containing the Web Search component, a search form is displayed, as shown in Figure 9.14.

When you type a query for a word to search in the Web site content, the search form redirects the request to the `_vti_bin/shtml.dll` file. This file is an FPSE file residing in the `_vti_bin` directory (created when you configure FPSE on a Web site) and processes the search query to return the results for display in a browser.

FIGURE 9.13

Configuring the search form properties

FIGURE 9.14

Using the search form on a Web page

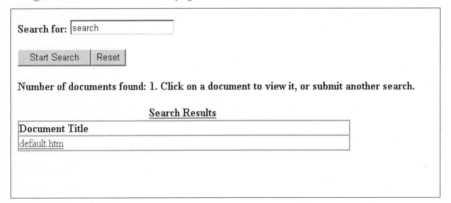

CAUTION If FPSE isn't properly configured or the Indexing service isn't running on the Web server hosting the Web site, the search fails to return results.

Using the Top 10 usage lists

The Top 10 List Web component allows you to display usage data made available by the usage analysis tools in FPSE and SharePoint sites on your Web pages.

 **CROSS-REF** For more on usage analysis for SharePoint and non-SharePoint Web sites, see Chapter 25.

As shown in Figure 9.15, the Insert Web Component dialog box allows you to choose from a number of usage lists. The data presented by the Web component is gathered by the FPSE or SharePoint components running on the Web server.

NOTE Top 10 lists are only updated when the component is inserted on a Web page or when a Web page containing the component is resaved.

FIGURE 9.15

The Top 10 Lists Web component options

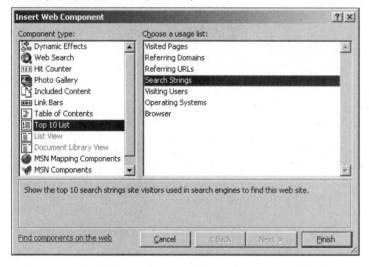

Creating Forms

The form components based on form handlers available with FPSE have been some of the most commonly used Web components of FrontPage 2003. They have also been inherited by SharePoint Designer, although the access points for configuring these forms have changed a little. FrontPage forms can be used to submit data to various types of files, to send to e-mail addresses, or to store it in databases. Web designers can use the SharePoint Designer interface to configure the forms, and the FPSE components implement the actual function of saving the data to the back-end file.

Because of the simplicity introduced by these form components to develop interactive forms for collecting data from users visiting the Web sites, these components have been a feature of choice for many Web site developers for a long time.

Using HTML form controls

The first step in creating a form by using SharePoint Designer is to collect data from a user to create the form. Most of the form controls that you might want to place in your form are available in the Form Controls section of the Toolbox task pane.

To create a simple form using the form controls in SharePoint Designer, follow these steps:

1. **Choose Task Panes ⇨ Toolbox to display the Toolbox task pane.**

2. **If the form control doesn't already exist on the Web page, using the Form Controls section, double-click Form to insert an HTML <form> tag inside the Web page.**

3. **Using the Form Controls section of the toolbar, add other form controls to the <form> tag to create a form.** Ensure that you also insert the Submit and Reset button controls on the form. A sample form is shown in Figure 9.16. An HTML table is used to format the form a little better.

4. **Save the Web page.**

FIGURE 9.16

Creating an HTML form using form controls

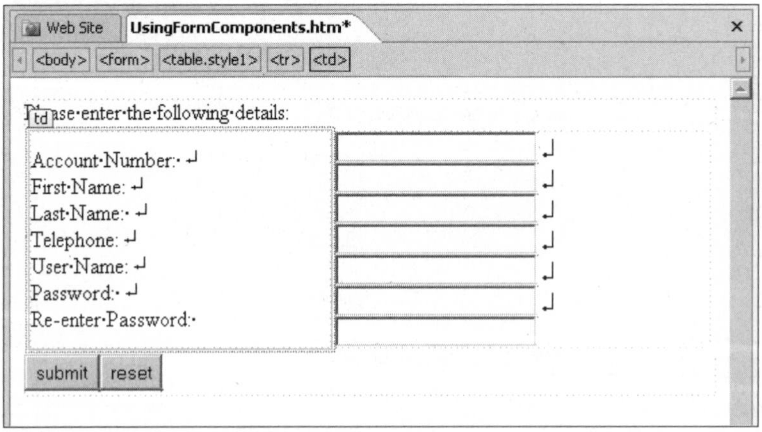

After you create the form structure, you have to choose how it performs the save operation. You can make these choices by configuring the form properties.

NOTE   Using the form handlers provided with FPSE to send data to files or e-mail addresses requires that the Web page where the form is inserted be an HTML/HTM Web page. If you use the form to send data to a database, the page is automatically saved as an ASP page.

Setting forms properties

You can right-click the HTML form on a Web page and then choose Form Properties from the popup menu to access the Form Properties dialog box. As shown in Figure 9.17, you can use the Form Properties dialog box to choose which method you want to use to save the form data.

Click Advanced to specify any hidden data that needs to be saved along with the form data. Based on the radio button selection you make in the Form Properties dialog box, the user interface available when you click Options changes.

FIGURE 9.17

The Form Properties dialog box

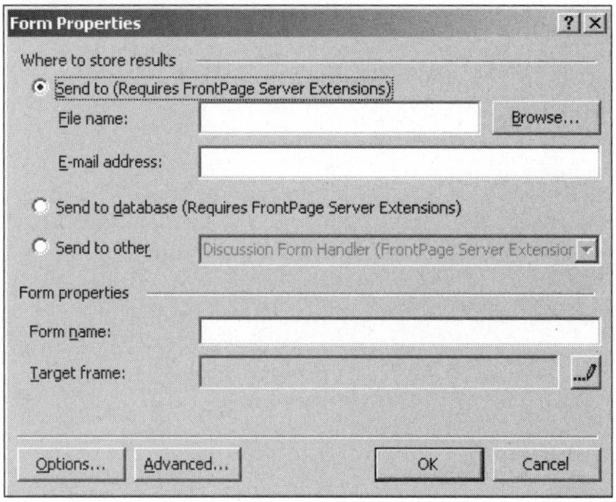

Sending to a file or an e-mail address

You can choose to send data submitted in the form to a file residing inside the Web site or to an e-mail address. Simply click Browse to choose the file where you want to save the data and then add an e-mail address in the E-mail address text field. As indicated in the Form Properties dialog box, you need to have FPSE configured on a Web site to use this feature.

NOTE   For security purposes, SharePoint Designer recommends that you save the files in the _private folder of your FPSE-based Web site. FPSE makes this folder secure by adding special permissions to it.

With this option selected in the Form Properties dialog box, clicking Options opens the Saving Results dialog box, as shown in Figure 9.18, where you can set more properties for the form.

The Saving Results dialog box provides the following tabs for setting form properties:

- **File Results:** Allows you to choose the file where the form data should be saved. You can also choose the format in which the form data should be saved in the file. Optionally, you can choose to send the form data to another file.

- **E-mail Results:** Allows you to specify the e-mail address where the form data should be sent to. Again, you can choose the format in which the form data should be sent and then type a custom Subject and Reply To line.

- **Confirmation Page:** Allows you to optionally specify a custom confirmation page that's displayed when the user submits the data by using the form

- **Saved Fields:** Allows you to choose from which form controls the data should be saved. Also, you can use this tab to optionally save the date and time when the form was submitted as well as additional fields, such as computer name, username, and browser type.

TIP If you're designing a custom confirmation page, you can use the Confirmation Fields control available in the Advanced Controls component type in the Insert Web Component dialog box to display the form data that the user provided to fill in the form on the confirmation page.

FIGURE 9.18

Configuring the form properties by using the Saving Results dialog box

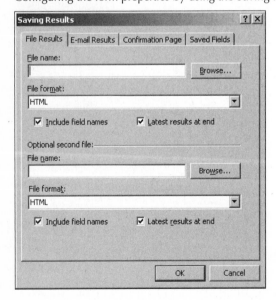

Sending to a database

Click the Send to database radio button in the Form Properties dialog box and then click Options to open the Options for Saving Results to Database dialog box. This dialog box allows you to create a database file (an .mdb file) with a table that holds the form data. When you click Create Database in this dialog box, SharePoint Designer automatically creates an Access database file with a table inside it to hold the data from the form. As shown in After you create the database, SharePoint Designer displays a message indicating that the database is stored in the fpdb folder inside the Web site, as shown in Figure 9.19.

Creating a new database file to store data from a form

Also, if you click Add Connection in the Options for Saving Results to Database dialog box, the Site Settings dialog box opens. The Database tab in this dialog box shows the newly created database connection that's used to establish the connection to the database file for storing the data. You can also click the Database tab to create custom connection strings to different database types. SharePoint Designer, like FrontPage 2003, generates ASP code in the background to enable the send results to database functionality. The database connection code is stored in a file named global.asa that's created during the process of creating a new database.

NOTE The Send to database feature in SharePoint Designer uses a lot of proprietary legacy ASP code. Given a choice, it's recommended that you use the new ASP.NET 2.0 data controls to create forms that save data in a database. These controls are discussed in Chapter 16.

After you create the database for storing the form data, click the Saved Fields tab in the Options for Saving Results to Database dialog box to match the columns in the database to the form controls. To summarize, follow these steps to send form data to a database:

1. **Right-click on the form and then choose Form Properties from the popup menu to open the Form Properties dialog box.**

2. **Click the Send to database radio button and then click Options to open the Saving Results to Database dialog box.**

3. **Click Create Database to let SharePoint Designer create an Access database for storing the form data.** After the database is created, the Database Connection to Use and Table to hold form results dropdown menus are automatically populated with the newly created database connection and newly created table in the database, respectively. You can also specify a custom confirmation and error page in the Database Results tab.

4. **Click the Saved Fields tab and then ensure that the form fields are correctly mapped to the corresponding database columns.** This is shown in Figure 9.20. If not, double-click the form field in the list and then use the Modify Field dialog box to match the form field to the database column. You can also add additional fields to be saved in the database by using the Additional Fields tab.

5. **Click OK.** If the Web page you started with is an HTM/HTML page, a request to change the extension of the Web page to ASP appears. This is important, as the Save Results to Database feature is implemented by using ASP.

6. **Save the Web page with an `.asp` extension.**

FIGURE 9.20

Mapping form fields to database fields

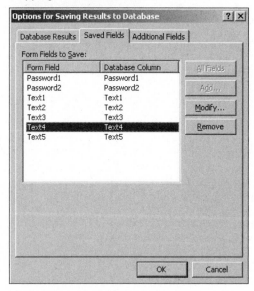

Sending to other

Clicking the Send to other radio button in the Form Properties dialog box allows you to send the form data to a custom CGI ASP script running on the Web server for processing. It also allows you to use the discussion and registration form handlers provided by FPSE.

In the next exercise, I show you how you can use the SharePoint Designer discussion form handler in conjunction with the Included Content's Page Web component to quickly create a discussion Web page inside a Web site. As a prerequisite to these steps, ensure that you have an HTML form created with the required form fields:

1. Right-click on the HTML form and then choose Form Properties from the popup menu to open the Form Properties dialog box.

2. Click the Send to other radio button and then choose Discussion Form Handler from the dropdown menu.

3. Click Options to open the Options for Discussion Form Handler dialog box.

4. In the Discussion tab, type the title for the discussion and the name of the folder to store all the discussion files.

NOTE The Directory box already has an underscore in it. Usually, the directories with the prefix _ are considered as directories containing files on which other functionality depends. Because the discussion form that you create in this exercise depends on the discussion folder, you might want to add an underscore prefix to it.

5. **Click the Date, Time, and User name check boxes.** The completed Discussion tab is shown in Figure 9.21.

FIGURE 9.21

The Options for Discussion Form Handler dialog box

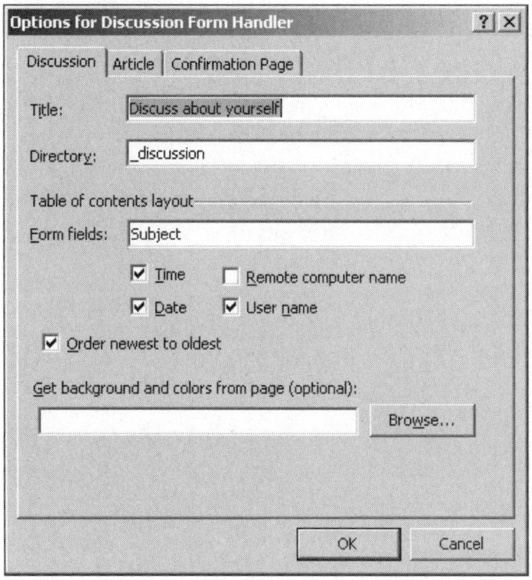

6. **Click OK and then save the Web page.** If you refresh the Folder List task pane, a new folder (_Directory Name) is created for storing the discussion files. This folder has a tocproto.htm file in it.

7. **Place the cursor below the form in the discussion form Web page.**

8. Choose Insert➪Web Component to display the Insert Web Component dialog box.

9. Select Included Content in the Component type section and then choose Page in the Choose a type of content list.

10. **Click Finish.** The Include Page Properties dialog box opens. Specify the location of the `tocproto.htm` file here.

11. **Click OK.**

12. Save the Web page and then preview it in a browser.

CAUTION   If you're working on a disk-based Web site, you need to publish the Web page to a server-based Web site that has FPSE configured for it.

When you submit the form, you're taken to the Form Confirmation page. When you go back to the form page and refresh (by pressing F5), a new article is shown at the location of the included page Web component. Clicking on the article takes you to a Web page inside the folder you created for storing the discussion files.

Validating forms

If you right-click on a form control inside your HTML form, the Form Field Properties menu option appears. Clicking on this menu takes you to the properties dialog box specific to the form control being worked on.

The Validate button in this dialog box provides an access point to the SharePoint Designer user interface to create validation constraints on the form fields. These constraints are implemented by SharePoint Designer as client-side scripts that are used to validate whether the user input matches a specific format. If the user input doesn't meet the required format, the form submission is cancelled. Figure 9.22 shows the validation dialog box specific to text form fields.

Depending on the constraint you choose in the Data Type dropdown menu, the rest of the validation options are enabled. For example, choosing Text as a data type in the Data type dropdown menu enables the Text Format group of options that allow you to further define the validation constraint for text format.

After the constraint is applied to a form field, the Code view just shows an HTML comment and hides the actual validation script that enables the constraint. For example, you should see the following code after applying a validation constraint to a text form field:

```
<!--webbot bot="Validation" S-Data-Type="Integer" S-Number-
    Separators="." B-Value-Required="TRUE" S-Validation-
    Constraint="Greater than" S-Validation-Value="9" -->
```

However, when you open the page in another text editor, such as Notepad, the actual script that implements the validation appears.

**NOTE**   SharePoint Designer hides the actual code for the script in the Code view to avoid unintentional tampering.

The Text Box Validation dialog box

Summary

FrontPage legacy components discussed in this chapter have been available for quite a while now, and you might run into many Web site implementations where these components are being heavily used. With the advent of many other Web technologies that make Web page development simpler, the future of these Web components is uncertain. In this chapter, I discussed many of the commonly used FrontPage components to familiarize you with them in case you run into a Web site implementation that uses these components. If you're working on a new Web project, it's recommended that you consider other technologies, such as ASP.NET 2.0, before implementing the functionality using these components.

Chapter 10

Working with ASP.NET Controls

A SP.NET 2.0 introduces a large number of server controls that can easily be used to implement most of the common Web site functions. The term server controls means that these controls hold ASP.NET code, which is actually processed on a Web server, and the resultant HTML code generated is then sent to a Web browser for display. Using these controls, Web designers can implement complicated scenarios on Web sites without having to manually write much code. Most of these controls can be worked with declaratively, which means you don't have to write a large amount of code to make use of these controls, and the purpose can be availed by setting properties or attributes for the controls in HTML at design time. This makes working with these controls very easy and significantly reduces the development time and overhead. ASP.NET 2.0 provides Web controls for many commonly needed Web site operations, such as data access, login screens, validation, navigation and menus, treeviews, etc.

SharePoint Designer provides the ability to make use of most of the ASP.NET 2.0 controls. Using a design interface similar to Visual Studio, Web designers can insert controls on ASP.NET Web pages and then exploit them by using control properties and attributes. SharePoint Designer allows you to work with the following set of control categories:

- **Standard Controls:** These are generic controls (including drop-down menus, list boxes, text fields, and buttons) that aid in designing Web site features, such as forms, views, wizards, etc.

- **Data Controls:** These are Web controls that allow you to declaratively develop applications for data access from a wide range of data sources, such as SQL Server, XML files, Access databases, etc.

- **Validation Controls:** This set of controls provides built-in validation capability for user input. These controls can be bound to other

IN THIS CHAPTER

Using standard controls

Implementing validation by using ASP.NET controls

Implementing navigation in ASP.NET Web sites

Working with login controls

Enhancing forms with ASP.NET controls

Exploring ASP.NET Web part controls

Web controls to constrain and verify user input, thereby providing security and protection to the back end that interfaces with the Web controls.

- **Navigation Controls:** These provide out-of-the-box functionality for developing site navigation, dropdown menus, and treeviews.

- **Login Controls:** These allow you to develop login screens for Web sites and helps implement an interface for custom authentication and secure access.

CROSS-REF For more on ASP.NET 2.0 data controls, see Chapter 16.

This chapter discusses using the SharePoint Designer designing interface to develop Web pages by using the ASP.NET 2.0 Web controls. You work with many of the ASP.NET 2.0 controls in the various exercises throughout this chapter and gain understanding about the properties, attributes, and usage of these Web controls.

ASP.NET pages need to be published to a Web server to run. The Web server is responsible for processing the code that ASP.NET pages carry. If you browse to an ASP.NET Web page directly from the file system path (for example, `C:\websitelocation`), you would see the actual code of a Web page in a browser. When you press F12 in SharePoint Designer to preview a Web page, SharePoint Designer invokes the ASP.NET Development Server for executing the Web page. The ASP.NET Development Server, which is installed when you install SharePoint Designer, is a lightweight Web server that assists designers who don't have a Web server machine to quickly preview the ASP.NET Web pages in a browser. As shown in Figure 10.1, when you work on a local Web site (residing on a file system location) and then preview an ASP.NET Web page in a browser by pressing F12 in SharePoint Designer, SharePoint Designer instantiates the ASP.NET Development Server.

FIGURE 10.1

The ASP.NET Development Server is invoked when previewing a disk-based ASP.NET Web page.

The local ASP.NET page is executed and rendered by the ASP.NET Development Server and then displayed in a browser. The ASP.NET Development Server isn't invoked when previewing the ASP. NET Web pages inside a server-based Web site. In that case, the Web page is requested from its Web server location itself.

If you click the ASP.NET Development Server button in the notification area of the taskbar, the ASP.NET Development Server dialog box opens, as shown in Figure 10.2.

FIGURE 10.2

The ASP.NET Development Server dialog box

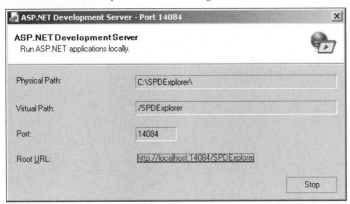

This dialog box displays the physical file system location of the Web site being rendered by using the ASP.NET Development Server. It also provides you with a Stop button that you can click to stop the ASP.NET Development Server. As shown in Figure 10.3, the Preview tab in the Site Settings dialog box (accessible by choosing Site ➪ Site Settings) allows you to specify whether you want to use the ASP.NET Development Server for previewing ASP.NET Web pages.

FIGURE 10.3

The Preview tab in the Site Settings dialog box

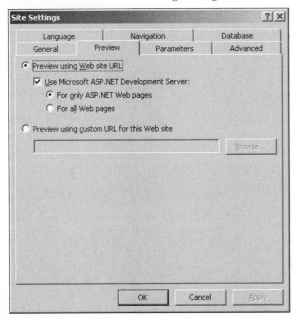

You can choose to use the ASP.NET Development Server for previewing only ASP.NET pages or all Web pages inside a Web site. The option to use the ASP.NET Development Server is grayed out when working on server-based Webs. SharePoint Designer indicates that you can only use the ASP.NET Development Server for disk-based Webs.

Using Standard Controls

The SharePoint Designer Toolbox task pane includes most of the standard ASP.NET 2.0 controls. You use the Toolbox task pane to insert controls on an ASP.NET Web page. You can either drag and drop the controls at the location of your choice on a Web page or insert the cursor at the required location on a Web page and double-click the control in the Toolbox task pane to insert it on a Web page. Figure 10.4 shows the standard controls available for use in the SharePoint Designer Toolbox task pane.

 NOTE While similar controls available in the Form Controls section of the Toolbox are HTML controls, these controls are different in that they're ASP.NET 2.0 controls.

FIGURE 10.4

Standard controls in the Toolbox task pane

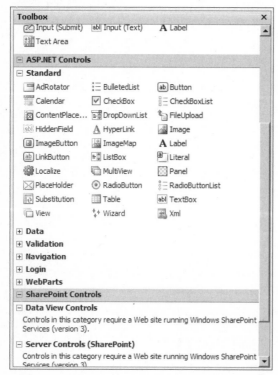

When you insert an ASP.NET control on an ASP.NET Web page, SharePoint Designer automatically places it in an HTML form that has the `runat="server"` attribute set.

```
<form id="form1" runat="server">
    <asp:MultiView runat="server" id="MultiView1">
    </asp:MultiView>
</form>
```

This means that the form controls are actually executed at the Web server where the Web site containing the Web page is being hosted. ASP.NET 2.0 controls expose a number of properties that can be used declaratively to set the control behavior at runtime. SharePoint Designer exploits this ability of ASP.NET controls to provide a user interface that can be used to modify these properties.

NOTE SharePoint Designer isn't really a very useful tool for manually writing code-behind files (files with extensions `.cs`, `.vb`, etc.) for ASP.NET Web pages. For more involved custom coding using ASP.NET programming languages, such as C# or VB.NET, you need a developer tool, such as Visual Studio.

When ASP.NET controls are inserted on a Web page, SharePoint Designer displays a control-specific Common Tasks menu in the Design view. As shown in Figure 10.5, the Common Tasks menu allows you to set the most common and important properties for the ASP.NET control.

FIGURE 10.5

The Common Tasks menu for the DropDownList ASP.NET control

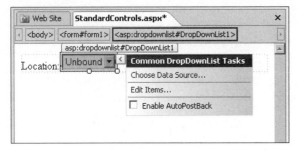

You can show or hide the Common Tasks menu for an ASP.NET control by using the small arrow button displayed in the top-right corner of the control in the Design view. The common operations available for ASP.NET controls in the Common Tasks menu include:

- **Choose Data Source:** Allows you to bind the ASP.NET control to a data source

CROSS-REF For more on data-bound controls, see Chapter 16.

- **Enable AutoPostBack:** Allows you to set the `AutoPostBack` property of an ASP.NET control

NOTE ASP.NET controls implement a mechanism that allows for the Web page to be posted back to the Web server for processing based on certain events in the control. Called as `AutoPostBack`, a property is available for certain controls, which, if set to `true`, sends the request to the server when an event happens in the control. For example, setting the `AutoPostBack` property for the DropDownList ASP.NET 2.0 control to `true` posts the ASP.NET Web page back to the server for processing whenever a user selects a different value in the DropDownList control.

- **Auto Format:** Allows you to choose from an out-of-the-box list of styling options for the ASP.NET control

- **Edit Templates:** For ASP.NET 2.0 controls that allow template-based editing, this menu option provides an access point to the user interface to change the templates associated with the control.

Working with the Tag Properties task pane

One of the more detailed panes for setting declarative properties for the ASP.NET 2.0 controls in SharePoint Designer is the Tag Properties task pane. As you already know, the Tag Properties task pane can be used to set properties and attributes for HTML form controls and tags. When you view Tag Properties for ASP.NET 2.0 controls, you make available a list of properties exposed for use by the control. The Tag Properties task pane provides a Visual Studio–like interface to Web designers for working with ASP.NET control properties. While you can use the IntelliSense feature in the Code view to set these properties, the table-like structure of the Tag Properties task pane lists the available properties and lets you set them without having to remember them. The Tag Properties task pane is especially useful for working with ASP.NET 2.0 controls, as it provides a tabular list of properties exposed by the control, and the designer can easily specify values for them. The Tag Properties task pane displays the properties in various categories, as shown in Figure 10.6.

You can enable the Tag Properties task pane by choosing Tasks ➪ Tag Properties or by right-clicking the ASP.NET 2.0 controls and then choosing Properties from the popup menu. When you select an ASP.NET control to show its properties in the Task Properties task pane, the top section of the Tag Properties task pane shows the HTML tag for the ASP.NET control. The top section also has the following buttons:

- **Show categorized list:** Sorts the properties in the task pane based on categories, such as accessibility, appearance, behavior, data, etc.

- **Show alphabetized list:** Sorts the properties in the task pane alphabetically

- **Show set properties on top:** Displays the properties that have been manually set at the top of the list or the category

FIGURE 10.6

FIGURE 10.6

The Tag Properties task pane for the DropDownList control

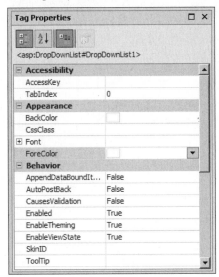

Besides categorizing the properties, the Tag Properties task pane also provides you with the option to expand or collapse property groups to attain more real state in the task pane. Many properties allow access points to the user interface that can be used to set them. For example, selecting the ForeColor property enables a dropdown menu that can be used to access the interface to choose a color to be set as a value for the property. The Items property on the DropDownList control has the ellipsis (…) button that allows you to access the user interface to create new list items in the control.

Working with standard controls

There are a number of commonly used controls in the Standard section of the Toolbox task pane. Many of these standard controls are pivotal in providing interface elements to ASP.NET forms. Controls such as Button, DropDownList, BulletedList, CheckBoxList, etc., are the primary controls that you use for designing server-side forms on ASP.NET 2.0 Web pages. Most of these standard controls can be bound to a source of data, such as a column in a table of a database, for displaying and using the data retrieved from it.

CROSS-REF For more on binding standard controls to data sources, see Chapter 16.

This section takes you through some exercises for using some of the controls available in the Toolbox task pane to familiarize you with the SharePoint Designer interface for declaratively working with ASP.NET controls.

Using the AdRotator control

The AdRotator control provides the ability to create banner ads on a Web page. The control is designed to shows images one after the other in a cyclic format. You can use the AdRotator control to create a banner on a Web page that switches images based on a frequency defined in an XML file. The XML file stores the configuration for the advertisements and is specified by the `AdvertisementFile` property of the control. A sample `AdvertisementFile` is displayed in the following code:

```xml
<Advertisements>
 <Ad>
      <ImageUrl>images/Image16.jpg</ImageUrl>
      <NavigateUrl>http://spdexplorer:8009/Page16.htm</NavigateUrl>
      <Impressions>16</Impressions>
 </Ad>
 <Ad>
      <ImageUrl>images/Image21.jpg</ImageUrl>
      <NavigateUrl>http://spdexplorer:8009/Page21.htm</NavigateUrl>
      <Impressions>21</Impressions>
 </Ad>
</Advertisements>
```

In the previous XML structure, the <Ad> element is repeated for every advertisement that you want to schedule in the AdRotator control. The `ImageUrl` element specifies the image to be displayed for the advertisement, and the `NavigateUrl` can be used to set the URL the user is taken to when the image is clicked on. `Impressions` allows you to define the frequency of the image in the banner. This means that the higher the value of the `Impressions` element for an image, the more it's shown. As shown in Figure 10.7, the elements of the advertisement XML file are actually properties of the AdRotator control.

Ensure that you have a valid XML file created by using the previous structure for use in the AdRotator control. To set up and use the AdRotator control, follow these steps:

1. **Insert the AdRotator control on an ASP.NET Web page by using the Toolbox task pane.**

2. **Right-click on the AdRotator control in the Design view and then choose Properties from the popup menu.** The Tag Properties dialog box opens, with the properties of the AdRotator control shown.

3. **Select the `AdvertisementFile` property and then click the ellipsis (...) button.** The Select XML File dialog box opens, which you can use to specify the XML file to be used by the AdRotator control.

4. **Choose the XML file you want to use for the AdRotator control.**

5. **Save the Web page and then preview it in a browser.**

Whenever you refresh the Web page in a browser, the image displayed in the banner changes. How often the image is displayed is defined by how high the value of the `Impressions` property is for the Advertisement.

FIGURE 10.7

Properties for the AdRotator control in the Tag Properties task pane

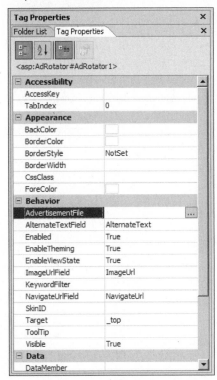

Using the ImageMap control

The ImageMap control allows you to create images with hotspots on them. As you already know, hotspots are areas or regions on an image that have hyperlinks on them. You can choose whether a user clicks on the hotspot region to navigate to another URL or incurs a postback. To create hotspots on an image by using the ImageMap control in SharePoint Designer, follow these steps:

1. Using the Toolbox task pane, double-click the ImageMap control to insert it on a Web page.

2. Right-click on the ImageMap control inserted on the Web page and then click the Tag Properties menu option to open the Tag Properties task pane.

3. In the Appearance category of the ImageMap control properties, select the ImageUrl property and then click the ellipsis (...) button. The Select Image dialog box opens.

4. Using the Select Image dialog box, select the image that you want to use for the image map.

5. **Click OK.** Now that you have selected the image, you can create hotspots on the image.

6. **Select the HotSpots collection by using the Tag Properties task pane and then click the ellipsis (...) button.** The HotSpot Collection Editor dialog box, as shown in Figure 10.8, opens. The Add button has an arrow indicating that it's a dropdown menu.

7. **Click the arrow to show three types of hotspots: CircleHotSpot, RectangleHotSpot, and PolygonHotSpot.** Based on the type of hotspot you select, the list of properties in the Properties list in the HotSpot Collection Editor dialog box changes.

8. **Choose CircleHotSpot to add a circular hotspot to the collection.** The Properties list is filled with the properties that you can set for this hotspot.

9. **Specify the Radius, X, and Y properties for this hotspot.** You can also specify the `AlternateText` property, which is displayed when you hover over the hotspot.

FIGURE 10.8
_____

The HotSpot Collection Editor dialog box

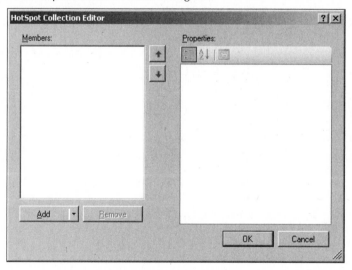

10. **Change the `HotSpotMode` property to Navigate.** The following modes are available for the hotspot:

   ▪ **NotSet:** Indicates that the hotspot has not been set

   ▪ **PostBack:** Specifies that clicking on the hotspot should postback the Web page for processing

   ▪ **Navigate:** Indicates that clicking on the hotspot should navigate to the URL specified in the `NavigateUrl` property

11. Click the ellipsis (...) button in the `NavigateUrl` property, and using the Select URL dialog box, choose the URL that a browser should navigate to when a site visitor clicks the hotspot. The complete hotspot settings are shown in Figure 10.9.

12. Repeat the previous steps to create multiple hotspots by using the HotSpot Collection Editor dialog box.

13. Save the Web page and then preview it in a browser.

When you hover over the image containing the hotspots, the mouse pointer changes, and you can click the specific portion to navigate or postback. Also, if you have set the `AlternateText` property for a hotspot, a screen tip appears when you hover over that hotspot.

FIGURE 10.9

Creating a circular hotspot by using the HotSpot Collection Editor dialog box

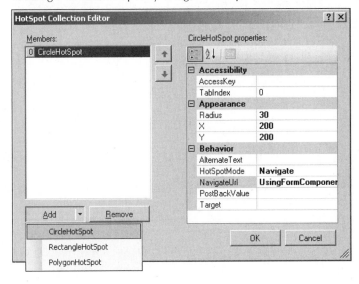

Using the Wizard control

The Wizard control is a very interesting tool in ASP.NET 2.0 and allows you to create screens or multiple views for collection data from users. The control provides for implementing a step-based approach for developing user forms and surveys. Rather than having a single large form, the components of the form can be divided into steps (called WizardSteps). The user can go back and forth from one step to another while filling out the form without losing any data already filled in.

> **NOTE** It's important to note that while the Wizard control allows you to design the user interface for a seemingly multipage input form, it doesn't provide the implementation for actually saving the user data. The developer must implement the logic for saving the data collected to a data source.

In the next exercise, you use the Wizard control to create a multipage survey form's user interface. Follow these steps:

1. **Using the Toolbox task pane, double-click the Wizard control to insert it on a Web page in the Design view.** This inserts the Wizard control on the Web page and displays the Common Wizard Tasks menu, as shown in Figure 10.10. By default, two steps have been created for you in the Wizard control.

FIGURE 10.10

Inserting a Wizard control on an ASP.NET Web page

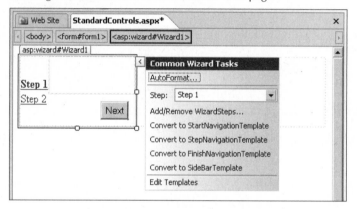

2. **Click the Add/Remove WizardSteps link in the Common Wizard Tasks menu to open the WizardStep Collection Editor dialog box.** Use this dialog box to create new steps in the wizard, as shown in Figure 10.11. The StepType property in the Behavior category in the Step 2 properties list determines the buttons that are displayed in the step:

   ▪ **Start:** The step having this StepType displays a Next button.

   ▪ **Step:** The step having this StepType displays the Next and Previous buttons.

   ▪ **Finish:** The step having this StepType displays a Finish button.

   ▪ **Complete:** The step having this StepType displays no navigation buttons and hides the navigation bar (called the SideBar) on the left if it's displayed.

   ▪ **Auto:** If selected, one of the previous StepTypes is chosen for the step based on where the step is in the list of steps. For example, the first step is set to use the Start StepType.

3. **Click Add to add new steps to the Wizard control.** As shown in Figure 10.12, each step can correspond to a page in the survey form. You can use the Title property to name the steps.

FIGURE 10.11

Creating new steps in the Wizard control by using the WizardStep Collection Editor
dialog box

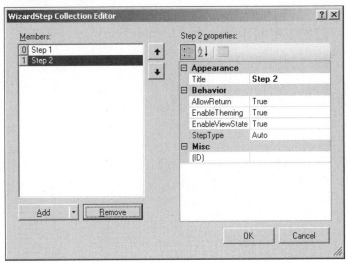

FIGURE 10.12

Corresponding steps to pages in the survey form

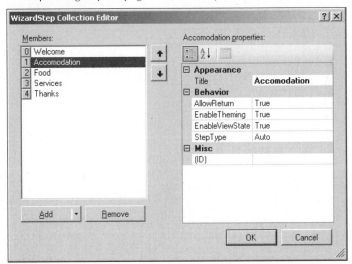

4. **Click OK after you add the steps.**

5. **Click the arrow in the top-right corner of the control in the Design view to open the Common Wizard Tasks menu.**

6. **Click the AutoFormat link to open the AutoFormat dialog box.**

7. **Choose the format you want to apply to the Wizard control and then click Apply.**

8. **Click OK.** In the Design view, the wizard with the steps is created. If you preview the Web page in a browser, the Wizard control lets you move from one step to another by using the navigation buttons: Start, Previous, Next, and Finish.

Using the Design view, you can now insert other controls to complete your survey form. Place the cursor in the main area of the wizard and then add the controls for user input, as shown in Figure 10.13.

After you finish creating one step of the wizard, you can click the link for the next step in the Design view to add controls and build the next step. When your wizard is complete and you preview the Web page in a browser, when you move between steps, the values that you filled in for the controls in each step are preserved.

FIGURE 10.13

Adding other form controls to a step in the Wizard control

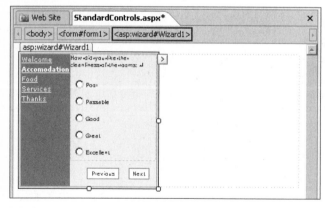

Understanding Expressions

A common property found in most ASP.NET 2.0 controls is Expressions. Displayed in the Data section in the Tag Properties task pane for ASP.NET 2.0 controls, the `Expressions` property is a mechanism to bind properties of an ASP.NET control with settings defined in the application configuration file; that is, the `web.config` file of the ASP.NET Web application.

> **NOTE** The `web.config` file is an XML configuration file stored in the root of the ASP.NET Web application. This file is used to store general settings for the Web application, such as connection strings, authorization settings, application settings, etc.

You can create a `web.config` file for your ASP.NET Web site in SharePoint Designer. Follow these steps:

1. Choose File ⇨ New to open the New dialog box.
2. Select Web Configuration in the ASP.NET section of the Page tab, as shown in Figure 10.14.

FIGURE 10.14

Creating a `web.config` file in SharePoint Designer

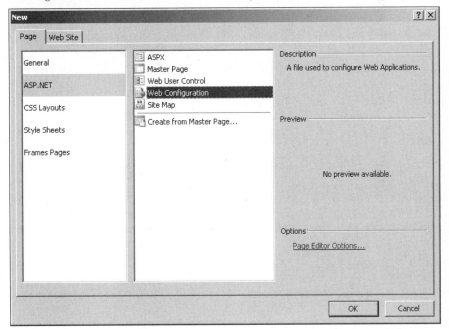

3. Click OK. SharePoint Designer creates a `web.config` file for a Web site, with some sections by default. The following code is written by SharePoint Designer by default for the `web.config` file it creates:

```
<?xml version="1.0"?>

<!--
    A full list of settings and comments can be found in
```

```
       machine.config.comments usually located in
       \Windows\Microsoft.Net\Framework\v2.x\Config
-->
<configuration xmlns="http://schemas.microsoft.com/.
   NetConfiguration/v2.0">
   <appSettings/>
   <connectionStrings/>
   <system.web>

       <!--
           Set compilation debug="true" to insert debugging
           symbols into the compiled page. Because this
           affects performance, set this value to true only
           during development.
       -->
       <compilation debug="false"/>

       <!--
           The <authentication> section enables configuration
           of the security authentication mode used by
           ASP.NET to identify an incoming user.
       -->
       <authentication mode="Windows"/>

       <!--
           The <customErrors> section enables configuration
           of what to do if/when an unhandled error occurs
           during the execution of a request. Specifically,
           it enables developers to configure html error pages
           to be displayed in place of a error stack trace.

       <customErrors mode="RemoteOnly" defaultRedirect="GenericEr
   rorPage.htm">
           <error statusCode="403" redirect="NoAccess.htm"/>
           <error statusCode="404" redirect="FileNotFound.htm"/>
       </customErrors>
       -->
   </system.web>
</configuration>
```

The highlighted <appSettings/> and <connectionStrings/> section of the web.config file can be used to store some general settings and connection strings that can be referenced later in any ASP.NET Web page inside the Web site associated with the web.config file.

The Expressions property is used to bind the properties on an ASP.NET control to settings defined in these sections of the web.config file. For example, you can define a general connection string for a database in the web.config file and then use the Expressions property of the ASP.NET control to bind the connection string to a property of the control. The following exercise illustrates this. Here, you define an application setting in the web.config file of the Web site and then bind it to a property of an ASP.NET control by using Expressions. Follow these steps:

1. Create a web.config file for your Web site by using SharePoint Designer.

2. Open the web.config file in the Code view and then look for the <appSettings/> code.

3. Replace the <appSettings/> code with the following code:

```
<appSettings>
    <add key="category" value="hotels"/>
</appSettings>
```

You have just added an application setting named "category" in the application settings section of the web.config file.

4. Save the web.config file in the root folder of your Web site.

5. Open a Web page in SharePoint Designer and then insert a Label ASP.NET control by using the Toolbox task pane.

6. Using the Tag Properties task pane for the Label control, select the Expressions property.

7. Click the ellipsis (...) button to open the Expressions dialog box for the Label control, as shown in Figure 10.15.

FIGURE 10.15

The Expressions dialog box

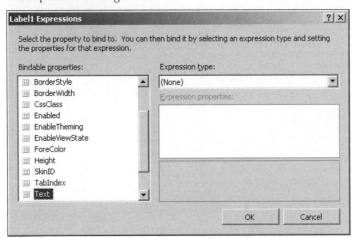

8. In the Bindable properties list, select the Text property.

9. Select AppSettings in the Expressions type dropdown menu.

10. In the Expression properties list, select the category application setting as the value for `AppSettings`, as shown in Figure 10.16. That category is the `AppSettings` that you defined in step 3. If you add more `AppSettings` in the web.config file, they're all listed here.

11. Click OK. The value of the category `AppSetting` is substituted as the value for the Text property of the label control. Similarly, you can use the `web.config AppSetting` in multiple controls. When you need to make a change to the `AppSettings`, you just need to change the `web.config` file, and the changes are applied to all the controls bound by using `Expressions`.

The `Expressions` property is especially useful in binding the connection strings stored in the `web.config` file with the ASP.NET controls spread across a Web site. This way, you can keep the connection strings at a single location and then reuse them.

CROSS-REF   For more on connection strings, see Chapter 15.

FIGURE 10.16

Binding control properties by using the Expressions dialog box

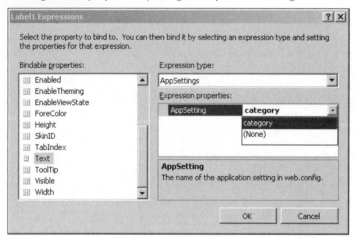

Editing ASP.NET control templates

While most of the ASP.NET 2.0 controls provide styling capabilities by using properties and styles that you can access in SharePoint Designer via the Tag Properties task pane, some ASP.NET 2.0 controls offer granular control on the layout of the control at runtime by allowing you to modify the control's look by using predefined templates. Templates essentially don't provide for changing the style or appearance of the control but allow you to add elements and controls to specific portions of the ASP.NET control.

Templates can be used to hold HTML and ASP.NET server controls. When the control exposing the template is rendered at runtime, the default HTML for the control is replaced with the contents of the template. For example, if you want to change the navigation buttons in a particular step in the Wizard control to LinkButton controls, you can do so by changing the templates associated with various WizardSteps. The following exercise takes you through the steps to change the Next button in the first step of the Wizard control to an ImageButton control. Follow these steps:

1. **Using the Wizard control, create a wizard with two steps so that clicking the Next button in the first step takes you to the second step.**

2. **In the Common Wizard Control Tasks menu, click the Edit Templates link, as shown in Figure 10.17.** In the Wizard control, the Next button that appears in the step with the StepType property set to Start is templated by using the StartNavigationTemplate.

3. **Click the Edit Templates link to switch the Common Wizard Control Tasks menu to the Template Editing Mode and then choose StartNavigationTemplate from the Display dropdown menu, as shown in Figure 10.18.**

4. **Place the cursor in the StartNavigationTemplate and then double-click the ImageButton control in the Toolbox task pane to insert an ImageButton control in the template area.**

5. **Using the Tag Properties task pane, set the ImageUrl property of the ImageButton control to the image you want to use for the button.**

FIGURE 10.17

Editing the templates for the Wizard control

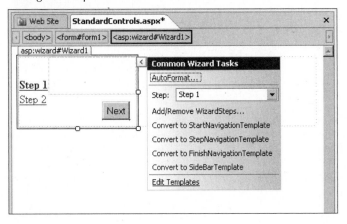

FIGURE 10.18

FIGURE 10.18

Switching to the Template Editing mode in the Common Control Tasks menu

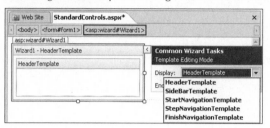

6. Type MoveNext in the value column on the CommandName property for the ImageButton control in the Tag Properties task pane, as shown in Figure 10.19.

7. **Click the End Template Editing link.** The Next button is replaced with the ImageButton control.

8. Save the Web page and then preview it in a browser.

FIGURE 10.19

Setting the StartNavigationTemplate for the Wizard control

When you click the ImageButton control in the first step, it takes you to the next step in the wizard. You can change the other templates for the wizard in a similar manner to customize the layout of your Wizard control.

NOTE While using templates, it's important to set the CommandName property of the controls you place in the templates. For example, if you want to customize the left navigation bar by using the SideBarTemplate of the Wizard control, keep in mind that the navigation bar is built up of a DataList control (having the CommandName=SideBarList), which has a Button control (with the CommandName=SideBarButton) in its ItemTemplate template. To customize, you have to place a custom DataList control in the SideBarTemplate, which has a Button control in its ItemTemplate template.

Implementing Validation by using ASP.NET Controls

ASP.NET 2.0 provides a number of Web controls that can be used to declaratively validate user input on other ASP.NET controls. Simply put, associating a control with a validation control enables you to perform a specific sort of validation operation on the input that's made to the control. The Validation section of the Toolbox task pane lists the ASP.NET 2.0 validation controls. The validation controls are capable of performing both client-side validation (if the browser supports scripting) and server-side validation.

> **NOTE** For increased security and suppressing malicious validation, the validation controls are designed to always perform server-side validation even if the client-side validation has already been performed.

Understanding ASP.NET validation controls

As discussed earlier, the process of validating user input to ASP.NET controls using validation controls is by associating the validation control with the ASP.NET control. This is usually done by setting the `ControlToValidate` property of the validation control. ASP.NET 2.0 makes the following validation controls available:

- **CompareValidator:** This control is used to either compare the value of a control to a static value or compare the values of two controls on the Web page. You can also specify the operator for the comparison.

- **CustomValidator:** Allows you to write a custom piece of code that can be used to validate user input to a control

- **RangeValidator:** Can be used to find out if the user input to a control matches within a particular range of values

- **RegularExpressionValidator:** Allows you to find out if the user input matches a pattern of characters defined by a regular expression syntax

- **RequiredFieldValidator:** Allows you to constrain a user from typing empty values in the associated control

- **ValidationSummary:** Sums up the validation errors of all the validation controls on the page in a single summary

The `CauseValidation` property of a control triggers the validation to be performed on the Web page. For example, submitting a form containing validation controls associated with the form controls by using an ASP.NET button control with the `CauseValidation` property set to `true` causes the validation to occur during the postback.

Using validation controls

The following exercise takes you through the steps you need to take to implement validation on a number of form controls on form submit. You mandate user input on the controls by using the RequiredFieldValidator control, compare the inputs using a CompareValidator control, and display the error messages using a ValidationSummary control. Follow these steps:

1. **Open an ASP.NET Web page in the Design view and then create a form with three ASP.NET TextBox controls and a Button control.** Change the `Text` property of the Button control to Submit and then ensure that the `CauseValidation` property of this control is set to `true`. The sample form is shown in Figure 10.20.

FIGURE 10.20

A sample form with three TextBox controls and a Button control

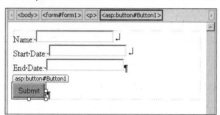

2. **Using the Validation section of the Toolbox task pane, insert a ValidationSummary control below the Button control inserted in step 1.**

3. **Insert three RequiredFieldValidator controls and a CompareValidator control at the bottom of the form.**

4. **Select the first RequiredFieldValidator control and then set its `ControlToValidate` property to the first TextBox control.**

5. **Set the `ControlToValidate` property of the other two RequiredFieldValidator controls to the corresponding TextBox controls.**

6. **Set the `ErrorMessage` property for all the RequiredFieldValidator controls appropriately.** These should be the messages that display when user input isn't a match.

7. **Select the CompareValidator control and then set its `ControlToValidate` and `ControlToCompare` properties to the appropriate TextBox controls (Start Date and End Date, respectively, for this exercise).**

8. **Set the `Operator` property of the CompareValidator control to `Less Than` and the `Type` property to `Date`. Also, set the `ErrorMessage` property of this control appropriately, as shown in Figure 10.21.**

9. **Save the Web page and then preview it in a browser.**

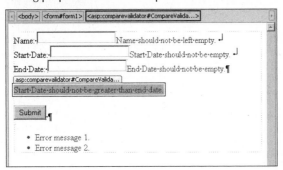

FIGURE 10.21

Setting properties for the CompareValidator control

If you submit the form without filling in the text fields, the RequiredFieldValidator catches this and reports an error. Also, if the Start Date is greater than the End Date, the CompareValidator reports an error. The ValidationSummary control displays the summary of the errors.

Implementing Navigation in ASP.NET Web Sites

While ASP.NET 2.0 provides a number of controls to implement site navigation, almost all of them depend on a sitemap. A sitemap is simply an XML file (called web.sitemap) that stores the navigational information about the site in a structured format. The ASP.NET navigation controls use this XML file as a source of data to display the information contained in different graphical manners.

Creating sitemaps

SharePoint Designer provides a template file that allows you to start building a web.sitemap file for your Web site. To create a web.sitemap file, choose File ➪ New to display the New dialog box. In the ASP.NET section of the Page tab is the Site Map option. The default sitemap file that SharePoint Designer creates has the following code:

```
<?xml version="1.0" encoding="utf-8" ?>
<siteMap xmlns="http://schemas.microsoft.com/AspNet/SiteMap-File-1.0" >
    <siteMapNode url="" title="" description="">
        <siteMapNode url="" title="" description="" />
        <siteMapNode url="" title="" description="" />
    </siteMapNode>
</siteMap>
```

The sitemap XML file needs the `<siteMap>` element as the root element for the XML structure. Within the `<siteMap>` element, there needs to be at least one `<siteMapNode>` element that describes the name, relative URL, and description of the link in the site navigation. Then, you have a `</siteMapNode>` that helps define the nested navigation links. The following code is a sample XML for the web.sitemap file:

```
<?xml version="1.0" encoding="utf-8" ?>
<siteMap xmlns="http://schemas.microsoft.com/AspNet/SiteMap-File-1.0" >
    <siteMapNode url="~/default.htm" title="Home"  description="Home
    Page">
        <siteMapNode url="~/InsertingWebComponents.htm" title="Web
    Components"  description="Inserting web components on web pages" />
        <siteMapNode url="~/StandardControls.aspx" title="Standard
    Controls"  description="Inserting standard controls" />
    </siteMapNode>
</siteMap>
```

The ASP.NET 2.0 controls can now use this web.sitemap file to display the stored navigation. SharePoint Designer makes available the Menu, TreeView, and SiteMapPath controls for use on Web pages.

Using ASP.NET navigation controls

In the next exercise, you use the TreeView control to display the navigation structure defined in the web.sitemap file for the Web site. To enable the ASP.NET 2.0 controls on a Web page, you need to follow these steps:

1. Create a web.sitemap file for your Web site.

2. **Using the Data section of the Toolbox task pane, insert a SiteMapDataSource control on a Web page where you want to insert a navigation control.** This control acts as a data source and helps the navigation control retrieve data from the web.sitemap file for display.

3. **Insert the TreeView control on the Web page.** The Common TreeView Tasks menu is displayed in the Design view, as shown in Figure 10.22.

4. **Using the Choose Data Source dropdown menu, select the SiteMapDataSource control you inserted on the Web page in step 2.**

5. **Click the AutoFormat link to open the AutoFormat dialog box and then choose a style for the TreeView control.** There are a number of interesting formats to choose from in the AutoFormat dialog box for the TreeView control. You can format the tree to look like a file structure, help file, mailbox, etc.

6. **Save the Web page and then preview it in a browser.**

FIGURE 10.22

Choosing the data source for the TreeView control

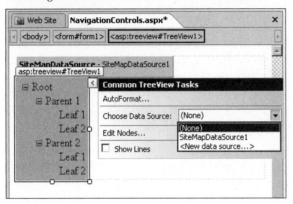

Similarly, other navigation controls can also be bound to the SiteMapDataSource control to display navigation stored in the `web.sitemap` file. It's recommended to place the navigation control on a master page so that all the attached Web pages can inherit it.

 **For more on master pages in ASP.NET 2.0, see Chapter 13.**

Working with Login Controls

The ASP.NET 2.0 login controls allow Web designers to quickly develop template-based login interfaces on Web pages for creating, updating, and deleting users as well as authenticating and authorizing users. This form of authentication is called Form-Based Authentication and requires additional setup for membership services, role provides, etc., in the `web.config` file and a database to store the usernames and passwords. SharePoint Designer provides the following ASP.NET 2.0 login controls:

- **ChangePassword:** Allows you to create an interface for changing user passwords for a Web site. The control verifies the old password provided as user input before changing the password.

- **CreateUserWizard:** This control is derived from the Wizard control and allows you to create a step approach for providing an interface for creating new users on a Web site.

- **Login:** This allows you to create a user interface on a Web page that logs a user into the Web site.

- **LoginName:** Displays the currently logged-on user's name on the Web page. The control doesn't display anything if you're logged on anonymously.

- **LoginStatus:** This control determines whether a user is logged on to a Web site. If it finds a user logged on, it displays a link to log out. Otherwise, it offers the user a link to log in that redirects to a page containing the Login control.

- **LoginView:** This control determines the login status of a user and, based on his or her authentication status, displays different content to the user. For example, this control can be used to display different content to a user based on whether he or she is logged in or not.

- **PasswordRecovery:** Includes the implementation of the user interface for recovering passwords after confirming the user identity. It also combines the facility to change the passwords.

> **NOTE** All the Login controls use the ASP.NET membership provider/service defined in the `web.config` file for the Web application for performing their operations. Developers are responsible for appropriately configuring the application configuration settings for the membership service before these controls can actually be actively used on a Web site. Implementing the membership service also includes creating a back-end database that's used to store user information.

Enhancing Forms with ASP.NET Controls

By now, you have created the user interface for a number of forms by using both HTML and ASP.NET controls. It's very important for you to review Chapters 15–18 to be able to implement the complete form functionality because most forms are intended to collect data from users and then save it to a back-end data source for review, analysis and investigation, retrieval, etc.

Forms are a pivotal piece of Web site implementation. As a result, most of the ASP.NET 2.0 controls concentrate on making form development easier and more declarative. Still, with so many controls available, it's important to pick the right ones based on your requirements. Here are some considerations that you might find useful when developing form Web pages via SharePoint Designer:

- Forms tend to become large when and as more information is required to be collected from users. It's a good practice to page such large forms into multiple steps. This helps reduce user frustration in scrolling down Web pages while filling in forms. You can use the Wizard control to implement a multipage form quite effortlessly.

- There are various formats and styles in which users may perceive date and time. Therefore, it's a bad idea to have users fill out the dates in a text field. It's recommended that you use the Calendar control instead. Still, if the form design mandates that you use simpler controls, such as Textbox, ensure that you validate it properly by, for example, using the RegularExpressionValidator control. While the ASP.NET controls are pretty robust in this area, to ensure protection from malicious user input and avert attacks, ensure that you properly validate user input before submission to the back-end data source.

Wherever applicable, you should use predefined or data-bound Dropdown controls or Listbox controls to facilitate user input in the forms. Users like to make a choice from a list of options rather than having to type in the values. Besides, this automatically reduces the chances of malicious user input.

Exploring ASP.NET Web Part Controls

The Toolbox task pane in SharePoint Designer hosts another set of ASP.Net 2.0 controls called Web part controls. These are generic controls that can be used to host custom Web part controls and server controls developed programmatically. The primary hosting controls offered in ASP.NET 2.0 for Web parts are:

- **WebPartZone:** This control acts as a placeholder control and hosts other server Web part controls and ASP.NET 2.0 controls.

- **CatalogZone:** A catalog is basically a list of Web part controls. The CatalogZone allows developers to create a list of Web parts that can be used to insert them on Web pages dynamically at browse time.

- **EditorZone:** This control acts as a host for a number of editor Web parts, such as AppearanceEditorPart, BehaviorEditorPart, LayoutEditorPart, and PropertyGridEditorPart. The editor Web parts can be used to design the editing interface of the Web part properties, which are displayed to the end user at browse time.

- **ConnectionZone:** The ASP.NET 2.0 ConnectionZone Web part allows developers to enable connections between Web parts at browse time. This means that end users visiting the Web sites can connect two or more Web parts together and then transfer data from one Web part to another.

Web part controls are different from other ASP.NET controls in that ASP.NET 2.0 provides the infrastructure to dynamically add, remove, and modify properties of Web part controls directly in a browser. This means that developers can use these controls to program Web site interfaces in such a way that the end user visiting a Web site can add or remove Web parts from a list of predefined Web part controls. This way, developers can offer enhanced control of the Web site interface to Web site users.

SharePoint extensively uses these Web part controls as well as controls inherited from these controls to implement its Web part functionality. ASP.NET 2.0 also forms the basis for the ability to add Web parts dynamically to Web pages at browse time, creating Web part connections, editing Web part properties, etc.

Summary

Although SharePoint Designer can't be used to write code-behind files for writing custom code, it provides Web designers with a visual experience to work with ASP.NET 2.0 controls and declaratively set properties without having to write any code. The Toolbox task pane in SharePoint Designer allows you to insert and configure standard, data, navigation, login, and validation controls on ASP.NET Web pages. It provides Web designers with a property grid-like interface for modifying properties for these ASP.NET controls. It can be used to work with ASP.NET 2.0 expressions, layout control templates, and implement styles and formatting. SharePoint Designer also installs a lightweight ASP.NET development server that it uses for enabling ASP.NET Web page previewing on disk-based Web sites.

Chapter 11

Using SharePoint Web Parts and Controls

Earlier in this book, I introduced some basic concepts about SharePoint sites. I talked about the interface and layout of a SharePoint site as well as how to create SharePoint sites, site collections, and Web pages. I showed how you can use SharePoint Designer to create Web pages for SharePoint sites. You were also given a quick overview of what a SharePoint Web part is. Now that you have been exposed to SharePoint Designer for creating non-SharePoint content, I want to revisit SharePoint to offer more details about the components of a SharePoint site and how they interact with SharePoint Designer.

In this chapter, I introduce you to some key concepts about SharePoint that readily apply when you work with SharePoint Designer on SharePoint sites. I discuss concepts such as ghosting and un-ghosting of SharePoint content, take you through the user interface provided by SharePoint and SharePoint Designer for working with SharePoint Web parts and controls, and mention the commonly used SharePoint Web parts and controls. I familiarize you with SharePoint Web part galleries and discuss how you can add Web parts to these galleries for use in SharePoint sites. You also become familiar with the concept of Web part zones and how you can use SharePoint Designer to insert Web part zones on custom pages to facilitate easier interaction with Web parts on SharePoint sites.

To start, you must know that every SharePoint site or site collection is based on a site definition. At creation, based on the site template chosen for the site, SharePoint reads the site definition files from its file system location and uses it to define the look and feel, features, and functionality that are applied and made available for the site being created. As with most SharePoint files, you can create new site definitions or modify existing ones to define how the site should behave and what features should be made available to it. Site definitions are installed on the machine running SharePoint at installation time and are stored at `C:\Program Files\Common Files\Microsoft Shared\Web Server Extensions\12\TEMPLATE\SiteTemplates`. In fact, the `TEMPLATE` folder hosts most of the SharePoint definition files, templates, layouts, CSS and JavaScript files, themes, etc.

Every SharePoint Web application has virtual directories created in it that point to various folders in the `TEMPLATE` folder. For example, the `layouts` virtual directory created at Web application creation points to the `C:\Program Files\Common Files\Microsoft Shared\Web Server Extensions\12\TEMPLATE\LAYOUTS` folder and hosts most of the SharePoint settings for Web pages, master pages, JavaScript files, images, etc.

When a SharePoint Web page is requested for display in a browser, SharePoint combines the file system copy of the Web page and the data retrieved from the SharePoint databases to show the final Web page to the user. The file system copy may be common to multiple SharePoint pages. This ghosted approach used for displaying Web pages is the default behavior followed by SharePoint to render all pages inside the Web site. However, this approach changes after the Web page has been modified and saved by SharePoint Designer.

After you modify a Web page using SharePoint Designer, the Web page becomes completely stored in the SharePoint database. The process that un-ghosts the Web page is important for SharePoint Designer to be able to make persistent changes and allow for remote authoring of the Web pages. When the Web page is un-ghosted, the file system copy is no longer used, and the page is directly retrieved from the database for display.

While previous versions of SharePoint didn't allow for an option to re-ghost the Web pages so that they fall back to the default behavior, WSS v3 and MOSS sites allow you to re-ghost the Web pages by using a process called Reset to Site Definition. When you edit and save a SharePoint Web page, such as `default.aspx`, in SharePoint Designer, a warning pops up, as shown in Figure 11.1.

FIGURE 11.1

Un-ghosting Web pages by using SharePoint Designer

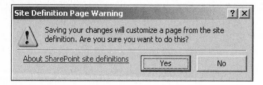

After you click Yes in the Site Definition Page Warning dialog box, a blue icon appears next to the modified page in the SharePoint Designer Folder List task pane, as shown in Figure 11.2. If you hover over the Web page in the Folder List task pane, a screen tip shows that the page has been customized.

FIGURE 11.2

The Folder List task pane displays a blue icon next to a modified Web page.

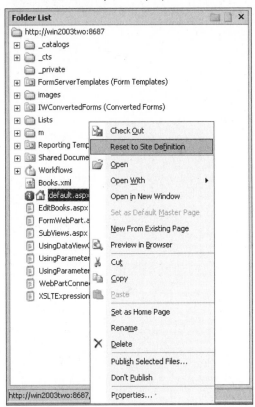

When you right-click in the Web page, the popup menu shows a Reset to Site Definition option. This allows you to reset the Web page back to the default SharePoint behavior of ghosting by using the site definition files.

CAUTION **Resetting a Web page back to site definition means that you lose all customizations that you made to the Web page via SharePoint Designer. SharePoint falls back to the default ghosting behavior.**

If you have a large number of SharePoint Web pages that have been customized by using SharePoint Designer, you can use the master Reset to site definition link on the SharePoint Site Settings Web page, as shown in Figure 11.3.

Clicking on the link opens the `layouts/reghost.aspx` Web page, which allows you to either specify a URL of the Web page that you want to re-ghost or reset all pages in the site-to-site definition.

Web pages created from scratch by using SharePoint Designer are always stored in the SharePoint database and can't be ghosted. So, you won't find the Reset to site definition link on such Web pages.

FIGURE 11.3

Use the Reset to site definition link on the Site Settings Web page to reset all customized pages to the default site definition.

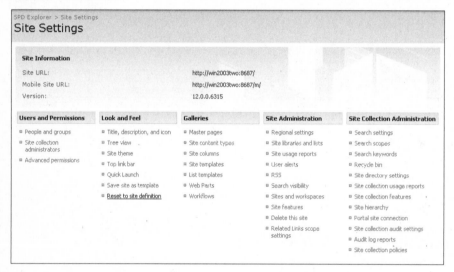

Understanding SharePoint Web Parts

SharePoint Web parts are mostly just special types of Web controls that provide a specific set of features and abilities for a SharePoint site. For example, the Image Web part allows you to display pictures on a SharePoint Web site. By default, SharePoint provides a large number of Web parts that are either used by the sites themselves or can be inserted on the Web pages by using the SharePoint interface. Before discussing more about Web parts, I want to briefly talk about the various galleries that are available in SharePoint sites.

If you go to the Site Settings page of a SharePoint site by choosing Site Actions ➪ Site Settings ➪ Modify All Site Settings, there are a number of galleries in the section called Galleries. These galleries are basically libraries that hold special types of documents and files. You can expect to see the following galleries on a SharePoint site:

- **Master pages:** This gallery holds the default master pages and page layouts that are available for a SharePoint site. Page layouts are available only for MOSS Web sites.

- **Site content types:** This holds the default and user-created site content types available for use on a Web site.

- **Site columns:** Holds the default and user-created site columns available for use on a Web site. Think of site columns as independent site-level columns that can be added to a list or content types.

- **Site templates:** SharePoint allows you to save a site as template that can later be used to create a new site. The Site template gallery allows you to upload site template files for use in SharePoint.

- **List templates:** Similar to site templates, lists can be stored as templates for reuse. The List template holds the list templates for a site.

- **Web Parts:** The Web parts gallery contains the Web parts that have been activated for a SharePoint site. There's a list of `.dwp` or `.Webpart` files in this gallery. To be able to use a Web part on a SharePoint site, you need to add the Web part to the Web part gallery.

- **Workflows:** Shows the list of workflows activated for a site.

As shown in Figure 11.4, if you open a SharePoint site in SharePoint Designer and then expand the `_catalogs` folder by using the Folder List task pane, a number of libraries appear in SharePoint Designer.

While you use the master page gallery listed here for working with SharePoint master pages and page layouts in SharePoint Designer, other galleries aren't used in SharePoint Designer.

Web parts, like most other applications, need to be deployed on a SharePoint server before they can be used on a Web site. Once they're properly deployed, the Web parts are available for upload to a Web part gallery. As shown in Figure 11.5, Web parts that are properly deployed on a SharePoint server are available for addition to the Web part gallery in the New Web Parts page.

You can access the New Web Parts page by clicking the New action button in the Web Part Gallery. Just select the Web parts you want to include in your Web part gallery and then click Populate Gallery. From here on, the Web part is available for use for a Web site.

FIGURE 11.4

The SharePoint galleries in SharePoint Designer

FIGURE 11.5

The New Web Parts page in Site Settings

Inserting Web Parts and Web Part Zones

You insert Web parts on Web pages by using the Add Web Part Web dialog box, which is available in the Edit mode of a SharePoint Web page. To open a Web page in Edit mode, choose Site Actions ⇨ Edit Page in the SharePoint Web page. By default, SharePoint Web pages contain Web part zones that allow management of Web parts by using the SharePoint user interface. Each Web part zone has the Add Web Part bar at the top, which allows users to access the Add Web Part dialog box for adding Web parts to the zone. Figure 11.6 shows two Web part zones — Left and Right — that have two Web parts each. The Left zone has the Announcements and Calendar Web parts, and the Right zone has the Image and Links Web parts.

FIGURE 11.6

Examples of Web part zones on a SharePoint Web page

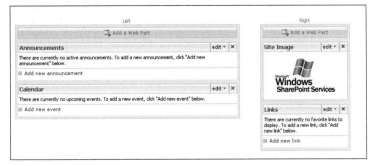

To add a Web part to a zone, simply click the Add Web Part bar to open the Add Web Part dialog box, which shows the list of available Web parts. Simply select the Web parts that you want to insert in a zone and then click Add. The selected Web parts are added to the applicable zone.

Notice the Advanced Web Part gallery and options link at the bottom on the Add Web Part dialog box. As shown in Figure 11.7, clicking on this link opens the Add Web Parts pane on the right side of the Web page.

You can use this pane to add Web parts to the zone selected by using the Add to dropdown menu at the bottom of the pane.

Using the Web Parts task pane

In SharePoint Designer, open a Web page in a SharePoint site and then choose Task Panes ⇨ Web Parts. The Web Parts task pane, as shown in Figure 11.8, opens.

FIGURE 11.7

The Add Web Parts pane for a SharePoint Web site

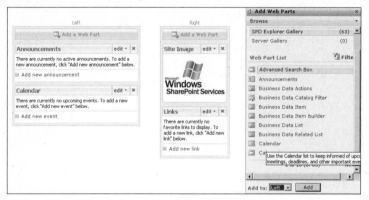

FIGURE 11.8

You can insert Web parts by using the Web Parts task pane.

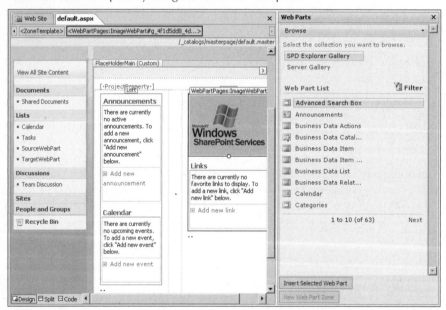

The Web Parts task pane shows that both SharePoint and SharePoint Designer have similar user interfaces for inserting Web parts. As in the case of the SharePoint user interface, simply click the Web part you want to insert on a Web page and then click Insert Selected Web Part at the bottom of the task pane.

You can also access the Web Parts task pane by choosing Insert ⇨ SharePoint Controls ⇨ Web Part. This menu also allows you to insert a new Web Part Zone on the Web page. Because you can't have a zone inside a zone, the Web Part Zone menu option is grayed out until you place the cursor outside an existing Web part zone.

Commonly used SharePoint Web parts

In this section, I single out some of the interesting Web parts that are very commonly used by site designers for SharePoint sites. While there are a number of specific Web parts providing functionality for Outlook, Business data, Dashboard, Search, etc., available in SharePoint and viewable from the Add Web Part dialog box, the following Web parts allow for generic display of data and Web pages:

- **Content Editor:** This Web part provides users with a rich text editor that can be used to create content with detailed formatting and graphics. You can also type HTML content for display by using this Web part.

- **Current User Filter:** This Web part, along with other ones in the Filter category, allows users to filter data in a target Web part by using Web part connections. This Web part provides the information of the currently logged-on user as a value to the connected Web part.

- **Page Viewer:** Allows you to specify a URL for a Web page to be displayed inside a Web part. The Web page could either be a SharePoint Web page internal to the site or a Web page on an external site.

- **RSS Viewer:** Allows you to connect to and view an RSS feed either on a SharePoint or external site

- **XML:** Allows you to display XML data transformed by using an XSL style on the SharePoint site. You can either type XML data and XSL style by using the Web part properties or specify an XML file to be used as a data source and an XSL file to transform the date for display by using the Web part.

Besides the out-of-the-box SharePoint Web parts, a large number of custom Web parts are available. SharePoint exposes a robust object model that allows Web developers to develop and deploy custom Web parts to facilitate special requirements and functions.

Modifying Web part properties

SharePoint allows users to modify the Web part properties in a browser. If you have the proper SharePoint permissions, you can just click the arrow on the right corner of the Web part to change the Web part properties. As shown in Figure 11.9, you have the following menu options:

- **Minimize:** Allows you to minimize the Web part

- **Close:** Allows you to close the Web part on the page. This means that while the Web part still exists on the Web page, it's not rendered.

■ **Delete:** Available only when the page is in Edit mode, this option allows you to delete a Web part from a Web page.

■ **Modify Shared Web Part:** Opens the Web Part Properties pane, which allows you to modify the properties for the Web part

■ **Connections:** Available when the page is in Edit mode, this option allows you to create Web part connections.

FIGURE 11.9

Editing Web part properties for the SharePoint site interface

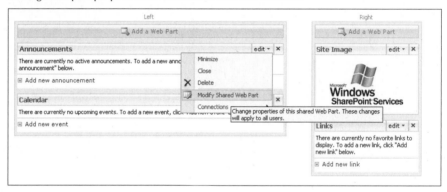

CROSS-REF For more on Web part connections, see Chapter 18.

As previously mentioned, clicking the Modify Shared Web Part menu option opens the Properties pane on the right side of the Web page. As shown in Figure 11.10, besides having some specific Web part properties, the Properties pane shows properties that are generic to all Web parts.

The SharePoint Designer interface to modify a Web part's properties is exactly similar to the SharePoint site user interface. To modify properties of a Web part by using SharePoint Designer, simply right-click on the Web part and then choose Web Part Properties from the popup menu. A Web Part Properties pane very similar to the one available in the SharePoint site interface opens.

If you believe that a Web part on your SharePoint Web page is causing problems in successfully rendering a page in a browser, a good troubleshooting mechanism is to browse to the Web page with the contents query string enabled. To do this, just type **?contents=1** at the end of the Web page URL in the browser address bar. A Web part maintenance Web page, as shown in Figure 11.11, is displayed and allows you to delete problematic Web parts from a Web page, thereby salvaging the Web page for display.

The problematic Web parts might show with the text Error in the column Open on Page?. You can also use this page to close or delete selected Web parts from the associated Web page.

FIGURE 11.10

The Properties pane for modifying Web part properties in a browser

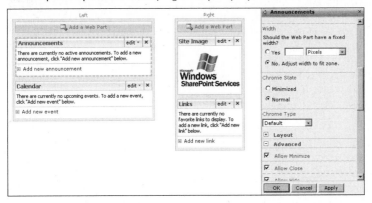

FIGURE 11.11

The Web Part Page Maintenance page for troubleshooting Web part rendering issues

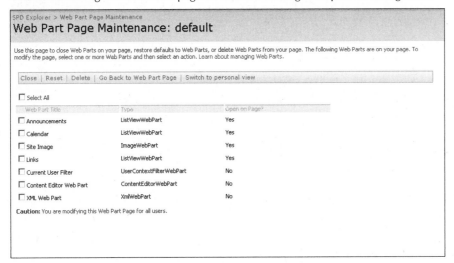

Exploiting SharePoint Controls

SharePoint Web sites use a number of Web controls on out-of-the-box Web pages. These controls, unlike Web parts, can't be directly inserted on the Web pages by using the SharePoint site user interface. SharePoint Designer provides many of these server controls in the Toolbox task pane for use on Web pages inside SharePoint sites. This section introduces you to the server controls available for use on SharePoint sites.

Working with SharePoint server controls

If you choose Insert ➪ SharePoint Controls ➪ More SharePoint Controls, you're taken to the SharePoint Controls section in the Toolbox task pane, as shown in Figure 11.12. There are four types of controls available: Data View Controls, Server Controls, Page Fields, and Content Fields.

While you may question the usability of many of the SharePoint server controls listed in the SharePoint controls section of the Toolbox task pane, you can use some of these controls in really intuitive ways. For example, just by inserting the CSSLink server control on a new Web page, you can associate it with the default CSS file being used for a SharePoint Web site.

FIGURE 11.12

SharePoint Controls in the Toolbox task pane

To use the SharePoint server control AspMenu to gain data from the PortalSiteMapDataSource, follow these steps:

1. **Create a new Web page in your SharePoint Web site and then open it in the Design view.**

2. **Using the SharePoint Controls section in the Toolbox task pane, insert the PortalSiteMapDataSource and the AspMenu controls on the Web page.**

3. **Select the AspMenu control on the Web page, and using the Tag Properties task pane, locate the `DataSourceID` property.**

4. **In the Tag Properties task pane, select the ID of the `PortalSiteMapDataSource` as a value for the `DataSourceID` property of the AspMenu control.**

5. **Save the Web page and then preview it in a browser.** The AspMenu displays the navigation structure of the SharePoint site.

Using page fields

You can use the Page and Content fields only if you're working with Page Layouts in a SharePoint site based on the Publishing site template. The Publishing site template is available only with MOSS installations of SharePoint.

CROSS-REF For more on master pages and page layouts, see Chapter 13.

While working with page layouts in SharePoint Designer, you can insert page and content fields on the page layouts from the Toolbar task pane, as shown in Figure 11.13. The page fields display the columns defined in the content type associated with the page layout. If you have defined any custom columns in the content type associated with the page layout, those also appear in the Toolbox task pane.

NOTE Content Types, introduced in WSS v3 and MOSS, define the nature and behavior of the content that can be stored in items. For example, the Document content type allows for creation of items that can store documents and related metadata. If you have multiple content types associated with a SharePoint list, you can create items based on these content types and then store them in a SharePoint list.

When these page fields are inserted in the page layout, they can be used on the publishing pages created by using the page layouts.

Using content fields

Content fields, like page fields, are columns that are defined in the content type associated with the page layout being modified in SharePoint Designer. While designing the page layout, SharePoint Designer allows you to insert these content fields at the location of choice. As in the case of page fields, the content fields, once inserted in a page layout, are available for use in the publishing pages created based on the page layouts for a SharePoint site.

FIGURE 11.13

Page and Content Fields in the Toolbar task pane

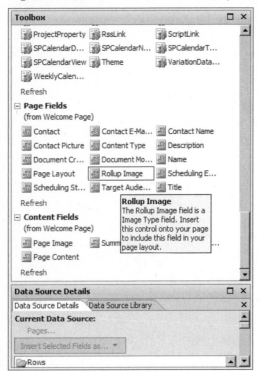

Summary

In this chapter, you learned how to insert Web parts and Web part zones on SharePoint Web pages. You also learned how to insert and use SharePoint controls available in SharePoint Designer.

Web parts provide the user interface used to perform operations on a SharePoint site. They act as placeholders on the Web page and interact with the internal data sources to present information to users. For example, the ListViewWebPart provides the interface to view items in a list.

Most of the Web part configuration can be performed by using the SharePoint site user interface itself. However, SharePoint Designer provides an interface similar to SharePoint for inserting Web parts and working with Web part properties. It does so to avoid randomization for site designers. Thus, they don't need to switch from the design surface to insert and modify Web parts.

Part IV

Designing Web Sites

Chapter 12

Exploiting Cascading Style Sheets and Themes

IN THIS CHAPTER

Introducing Cascading Style Sheets

Working with styles

Creating and using CSS layouts

Using CSS reporting features

C ascading Style Sheets (CSS) is a World Wide Web Consortium (W3C) standardized design mechanism for implementing formatting, fonts, and positioning on elements in Web pages. CSS has been available for quite a while now, and the current version, CSS 2.1, along with inheriting most of the features of previous versions, fixes some problems and provides enhanced capabilities for presenting Web pages.

CSS provides a segregated approach to apply formatting and present structured documents, such as HTML Web pages, XML documents, etc., for display in a browser. In simple terms, instead of applying a font directly to an HTML element on a Web page, you create a style by using CSS that can live either on the Web page itself or in a separate file in your Web site. At render time, a browser applies the styles specified in the CSS file to the HTML elements for display to the user.

By segregating the style implementation from the document, designers can enhance their productivity and output. For example, instead of having to apply the same formatting on every Web page inside a Web site, a Web designer can separate the formatting into a separate CSS file and then link this file to the Web pages for reference.

Now, whenever a change needs to be made to the formatting, the designer needs to modify only the CSS file. The change automatically trickles down to all the Web pages linked to the CSS file. The CSS file discussed previously is called a *style sheet*. The reference to the style sheet on the Web pages is called a *style sheet link*.

SharePoint Designer provides a rich user interface to create, modify, and apply style sheets to Web pages on SharePoint and non-SharePoint sites. It also offers mechanisms to run reports that allow you to check the CSS implementation and determine usage of CSS elements on the Web pages. This chapter discusses how you can use SharePoint Designer's CSS tools to implement style sheets on your Web sites.

I start by discussing the structure and composition of CSS styles and then explain the use of CSS-related task panes and toolbars in SharePoint Designer for creating style sheets. As you may know, SharePoint sites implement extensive CSS-based formatting. Later in this chapter, I also familiarize you with SharePoint CSS implementation and introduce you to the important SharePoint CSS styles. This should help you build on your understanding of how you can brand SharePoint sites by using CSS.

Introducing Cascading Style Sheets

CSS styles define the formatting for the elements they apply to. In HTML, for example, every tag is an element, and you can use styles to modify the way the tag looks and behaves. As previously mentioned, styles provide a centralized framework for implementing formatting on a large number of pages.

For example, if you want to have all tables in your Web site formatted in a similar manner, you can create a style for the table, and whenever you create a table for your Web site, you can associate that style with the table. That way, all tables inside your Web site use the same style. Now, whenever you want to change the formatting applied to the tables, you just need to modify the style. By virtue of the style association with the tables, the formatting is automatically picked up by all tables. In this manner, styles help you maintain uniformity in your Web sites and thus reduce design hours.

Understanding CSS classes and rules

Before detailing CSS implementation by using SharePoint Designer, I want to quickly touch upon some of the CSS basics and familiarize you with a couple of important concepts in CSS terminology.

CSS rules

To understand how CSS applies to Web pages, follow these steps to create a simple style and then associate it with an element on a HTML page:

1. **Using SharePoint Designer, create a new HTML Web page inside your Web site and then open it in the Design view.**

2. **Choose Insert ⇨ HTML ⇨ Span to insert a `<span>` tag on the Web page.**

3. **Type some text inside the `<span>` tag.** In this exercise, apply formatting to the text in the `<span>` tag by using a simple style.

4. **Choose Format ⇨ CSS Styles ⇨ Apply Styles to open the Apply Styles task pane, as shown in Figure 12.1.**

5. **Click the New Style link in the Apply Styles task pane to open the New Style dialog box, as shown in Figure 12.2.** Use this dialog box to create a new style.

6. **In the Selector dropdown menu, select the `<span>` tag.** Keep the Current page option in the Define in dropdown menu.

FIGURE 12.1

Creating a simple style in SharePoint Designer

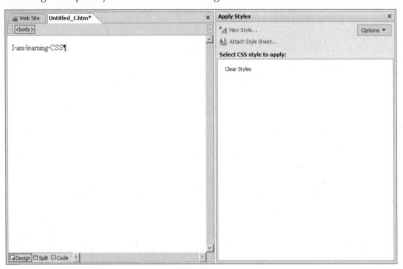

FIGURE 12.2

The New Style dialog box

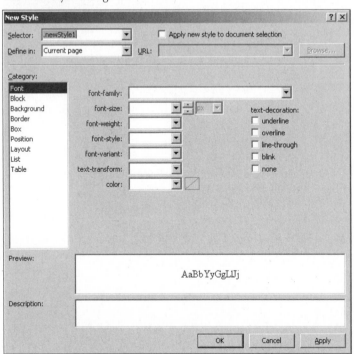

7. **In the Font category, specify the font-size, font-weight, and color.** The configured style is shown in Figure 12.3. The preview and description of the style are displayed at the bottom of the dialog box.

8. **Click OK.** The newly created style has been applied to the <span> tag, and the text shows as formatted in the Design view in SharePoint Designer.

If you switch to the Code view of the Web page, the following code appears inside the HEAD tags. This code defines the style that has been implemented on this Web page by using steps in the previous exercise:

```
<style type="text/css">
   span
   {
         color: #C0C0C0;
         font-weight: bolder;
         font-size: medium;
   }
   </style>
```

What you see is a CSS rule that defines the behavior for the <span> tag on this Web page. A CSS rule has two parts: a *selector* that associates the rule to an element on the Web page and a *declaration* that defines the formatting aspects that the rule carries. In this code, you created a CSS rule with the span selector and a number of declarations. A declaration, in turn, has two portions: a property and a value. For example, in this code, the color property has been given the value #C0C0C0.

By the virtue of this CSS rule, all the <span> tags on the Web page have the formatting specified in the declarations in the rule. As shown in the following example, CSS allows you to group selectors so that multiple selectors can be associated with the same declarations:

```
span, p, tr
   {
         color: #C0C0C0;
         font-weight: bolder;
         font-size: medium;
   }
```

Besides associating the CSS rule to the tags or elements by name, as shown in this code, you can also associate the style by using the id attribute. For example, the following CSS rule applies to all tags that have the id attribute set to the value right_col.

```
#right_col
   {
         width: 200px;
         position: absolute;
         top: 0px;
         right: 0px;
   }
```

FIGURE 12.3

An example of a style created by using the New Style dialog box

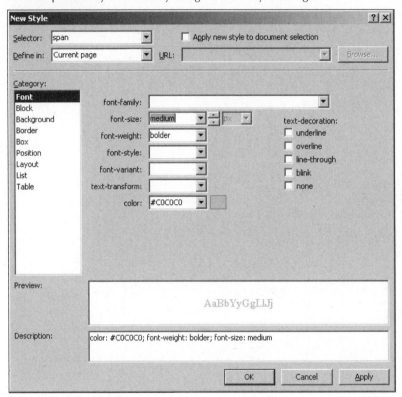

CSS shorthand properties

While the previous examples showed how you can create a declaration by using a `property:value` pair, CSS allows you to combine a number of similar properties into a shorthand property, thereby allowing you to define your formatting more concisely.

Shorthand properties let you declare many similar properties in a single declaration. For example, you can combine multiple font properties and then declare them in a single shorthand property:

```
span
    {
            font: #C0C0C0 bolder medium;
    }
```

CSS classes

The next exercise takes you through a set of steps to discuss another important CSS concept called CSS classes:

1. **Open a Web page in the Design view, and using the Apply Styles task pane, click the New Style link to open the New Style dialog box.**

2. **In the Selector dropdown menu, type** .myclass. Keep the Current page option in the Define in dropdown menu.

3. **In the Font category, specify a font-size, font-weight, and color.** This is illustrated in Figure 12.4.

4. **Click OK and then click the Code view tab.**

FIGURE 12.4

Creating a new CSS class by using the New Style dialog box

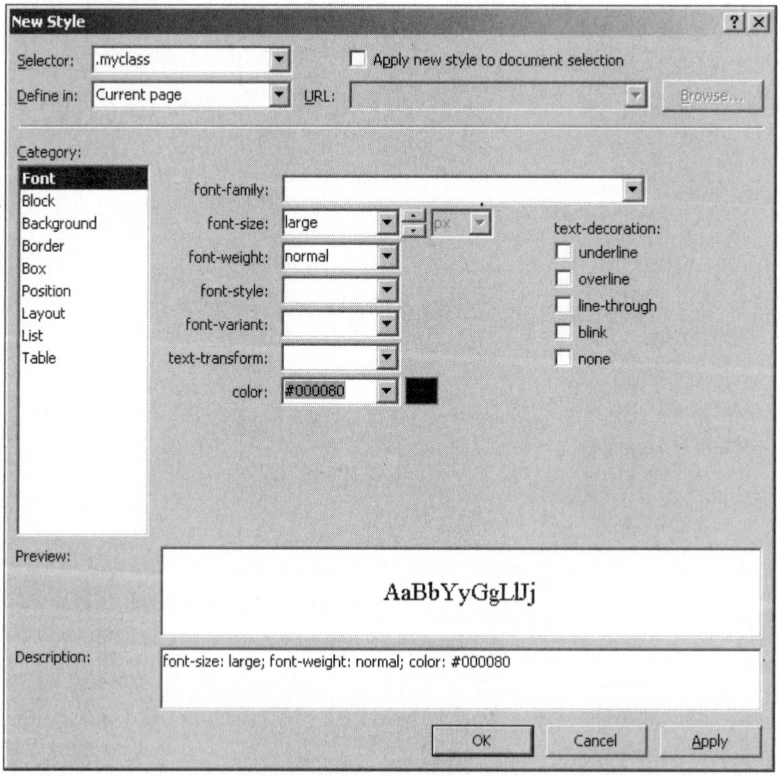

Using the previous steps, you created the following code in the `<style>` tag of your Web page:

```
.myclass
    {
        font-size: large;
        font-weight: normal;
        color: #000080;
    }
```

As shown in this code, the selector is now a custom name that you specified in the New Style dialog box. This custom name, called a CSS class, unlike the CSS rule, isn't associated with an element on the Web page by default. However, using the `class` attribute of the element, you can associate the class with the element. For example, the following code associates the above CSS class with the `<span>` tag:

```
<span class="myclass">I am learning CSS</span>
```

By providing the ability to create classes, CSS allows you to classify chosen elements to have formatting different than the one specified in a CSS rule. By virtue of the CSS class being associated with the `<span>` tag, the CSS rule specified by the `span` selector in the previous exercise is overridden.

Understanding CSS implementation hierarchy

Before discussing CSS hierarchy, I want to mention that you can apply CSS styles on a Web page in three ways:

- **In-line styles:** These styles refer to the formatting that you can apply directly to an element, such as an HTML tag as an attribute value. All HTML tags have a `style` attribute that can be used to specify declarations for the tag. As shown in the following example, the style is applied directly in-line with the HTML tag:

```
<span style="font-size:medium; font-weight:bolder; color:gray">I am
    learning CSS</span>
```

- **In-page styles:** These styles refer to the declarations that you make in a common `<style>` tag for the entire Web page. The `<style>` tag is usually placed in the `<head>` section of the Web page:

```
<style type="text/css">
    span {color: #C0C0C0;
        font-weight: bolder;
        font-size: medium;
    }
    .myclass {
        font-size: large;
        font-weight: normal;
        color: #000080;
    }
    </style>
```

■ **External styles:** These style declarations refer to the most styles that are defined in a separate style sheet document (with the extension `.css`). The CSS document is then linked to the Web page by using a style sheet link:

```
<link rel="stylesheet" type="text/css" href="myCSS.css" />
```

One important concept to understand regarding CSS is that multiple styles are cascaded to form a single style set before the styles are applied to the elements on associated Web pages. That means that if you add in-line, in-page, and external styles to your Web page, when a browser interprets the CSS for implementation, it combines all these styles to form a master style set for the elements before application.

NOTE The rule for precedence for CSS style implementation is that whichever style is closest to the element wins. This means that the styles defined in-line with the element always take precedence over the in-page or external styles. For example, if you specify the same font property by using both in-line and in-page styles, the value of the property for the in-line style is applied to the element.

Working with Styles

SharePoint Designer provides you with a new, intuitive user interface to create, modify, and apply CSS on Web pages. The new interface includes a number of task panes that can be used to authoritatively implement advanced style sheets on Web sites. In this section, I help you understand how to use SharePoint Designer to apply and manage styles for your Web sites. While the New Dialog box allows you to choose from a list of CSS templates on which to base your CSS files, I show you how you can create styles in new style sheets from scratch.

However, before discussing the SharePoint Designer interface to create and modify styles, I want to take you through some general settings for CSS in SharePoint Designer. The Page Editor Options dialog box, available by choosing Tools ➪ Page Editor Options, allows you to set some specifics that you want SharePoint Designer to follow while working with CSS on Web sites.

As shown in Figure 12.5, the Authoring tab in the Page Editor Options dialog box allows you to set the CSS schema that SharePoint Designer should follow when providing you with suggestions related to CSS properties and attributes in the Code view. While SharePoint Designer chose the CSS 2.1 schema, you might want to set this to the preferred schema for your Web site's CSS implementation.

As shown in Figure 12.6, the CSS tab in the Page Editor Options dialog box allows you to specify defaults for how styles should be applied for various property categories. For example, by default, the Page properties on the `<body>` tag are set to CSS (inline styles). This means that the page properties are applied by default as in-line styles inside the `<body>` tag.

FIGURE 12.5

Choose CSS schema by using the Page Editing Options dialog box.

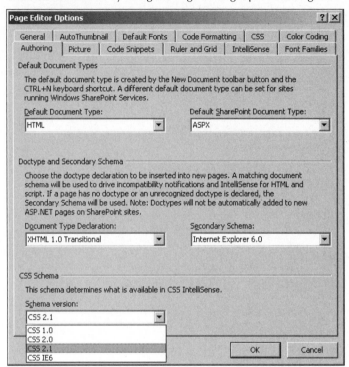

So, if you right-click in a Web page and then choose Page Properties from the popup menu to open the Page Properties dialog box and make changes in the Formatting tab, the changes are implemented by using in-line styles in the <body> tag of the Web page:

```
<body style="background-color: #FF00FF">
```

However, if you want to change this behavior of SharePoint Designer, you can do so by using the CSS tab in the Page Editor Options dialog box. This allows you to have flexibility for how the CSS styles should be generated by SharePoint Designer user interface tools.

FIGURE 12.6

Selecting style applications by using the Page Editor Options dialog box

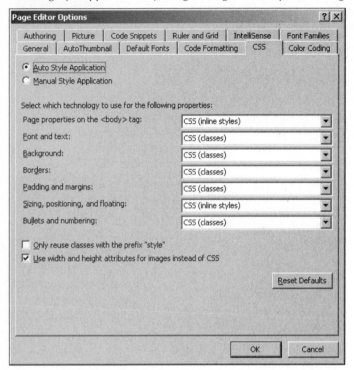

Creating, modifying, and deleting styles

The three main access points to the SharePoint Designer user interface for working with styles are the Apply Styles, Manage Styles, and CSS Properties task panes. Available through the Task Panes menu, these panes combine most of the SharePoint Designer features to work with styles. Besides these task panes, you can also use the Styles and Styles Application toolbars for implementing styles on Web pages. Figure 12.7 shows the SharePoint Designer interface for working with style sheets.

On the right are the Manage Styles and Apply Styles task panes, which are used to create and manage styles on Web pages. The CSS Properties task pane on the left provides a Visual Studio–like interface to modify CSS declarations.

Creating styles

You create new styles in SharePoint Designer by using the New Style dialog box. The New Style dialog box is accessible by using the Apply Styles and Manage Styles task panes, choosing Format ➪ New Style, or clicking the New Style button on the Style toolbar.

FIGURE 12.7

The various style task panes in SharePoint Designer

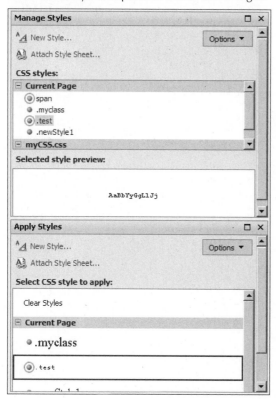

As shown in Figure 12.8, key specifics of the New Style dialog box include:

- **Selector:** Allows you to choose the tag you want to use as the selector for the CSS rule. Alternatively, you can type the name of the CSS class you want to create. Remember that a CSS class syntactically begins with a dot. Or you could choose the in-line style option if you want to create an in-line style. The Apply new style to document selection check box is used to indicate whether you want to apply the newly created style to the selected element or content in the document.

- **Define in:** Allows you to choose whether you want to create the new style in the currently opened document, a new style sheet, or an existing style sheet. When you select the Existing style sheet option in this dropdown menu, the URL text field is highlighted and allows you to specify the location of the CSS file.

- **Category:** This section provides a graphical list of available CSS properties, which are categorized into various areas of formatting. The categories for which the properties have been set are highlighted in bold.

- **Preview:** This section shows you a short preview of how the style appears when implemented on the content.

- **Description:** This box specifies the actual code of the style that you created with the New Style dialog box. As you proceed with the creation of the style, this box is updated to show the code for the style.

FIGURE 12.8

The New Style dialog box

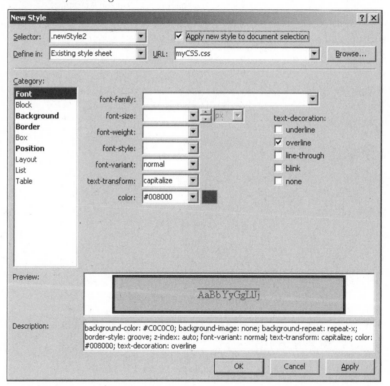

To create a new CSS class in a new style sheet and then apply it to the selection in a Web page, follow these steps:

1. **Open a Web page in the Design view and then select the content on which you want to apply the newly created style.**

2. **Choose Format ➪ New Style to open the New Style dialog box.**

3. **In the Selector dropdown menu, type the name of the CSS class you want to create.** Ensure that the Apply new style to document selection check box is selected.

4. In the Define in dropdown menu, choose New Stylesheet.

5. Using the Category list, choose the CSS properties that you want to use for the style and then set the values for these properties.

6. Review the style in the Preview box before clicking OK.

7. Click Yes when the message shown in Figure 12.9 appears.

The newly created style is applied to the selection you made in step 1 of the previous exercise. Also, a new CSS file is created, which holds the definition of the new style. You should save this file and the Web page.

If you review the code of the Web page, the style sheet link is automatically added to your Web page to attach the newly created style sheet to the Web page:

```
<link rel="stylesheet" type="text/css" href="myCSS.css" />
```

FIGURE 12.9

Attaching a style sheet to the document

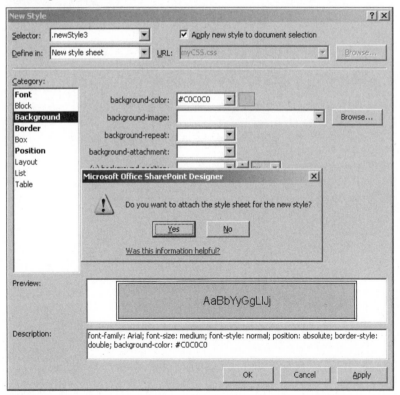

Modifying styles

You can view and modify the styles associated with the content of your Web page or CSS by using the Manage Styles, Apply Styles, and CSS Properties task panes. When you select the content on the Web page where the style has been applied, the CSS Properties task pane highlights in blue the properties of the style associated with the selection.

Also, as shown in Figure 12.10, the Manage Styles and Apply Styles task panes show and highlight the style applied to the selection.

To modify a style using these panes, simply right-click on a style and then choose Modify Style from the popup menu. The Modify Style dialog box opens, allowing you to change the properties associated with the style. The user interface for the Modify Style dialog box is similar to the New Style dialog box.

FIGURE 12.10

Modifying styles by using SharePoint Designer

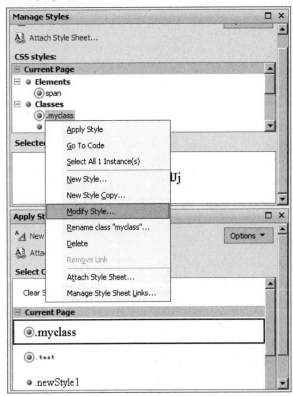

Deleting styles

You can delete a style by using the Manage Styles and Apply Styles task panes simply by right-clicking on a style and then choosing Delete from the popup menu, as shown in Figure 12.11.

When you confirm that you want to delete a style, the style is removed from the location (for example, a style sheet) where it was defined. After deleting a style, you need to save the file where the style was stored. SharePoint Designer automatically opens the associated file so that you can save it.

Using the Apply Styles task pane

In this section, I use the SharePoint core style sheet called `core.css` to illustrate the use of the Apply Styles task pane.

FIGURE 12.11

Deleting styles by using SharePoint Designer

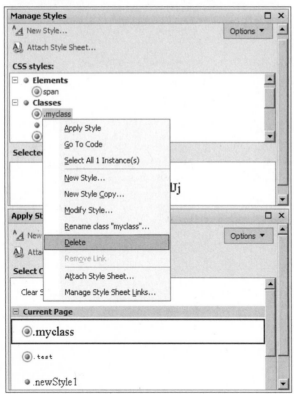

NOTE   While there are a number of style sheets that help you completely implement formatting and styles for SharePoint Web sites, the `core.css` stores most of the styles that define the look and feel of SharePoint Web pages.

To view the styles applied to a SharePoint Web page, open the Web page in SharePoint Designer. When you open the Apply Styles task pane, a number of styles appear in the Select CSS style to apply list, as shown in Figure 12.12.

The Apply Styles task pane lists the CSS styles that are applied to the Web page that's active in SharePoint Designer. The CSS styles from the style sheets attached to the active Web page are listed along with the styles that have been applied in-line or in-page. The Apply Styles task pane also shows a preview of the style in the Select CSS style to apply list. If you hover over a style, the code for the style is displayed in a screen tip.

The Apply Styles user interface uses the following icons to differentiate among the various styles:

- **Green Dot:** Indicates that the style is a CSS class either defined in-line on the Web page or in a separate style sheet

- **Encircled Green Dot:** Indicates that the style is a CSS class being used on the current page

- **Blue Dot:** Indicates that the style is a CSS rule either defined in-line on the Web page or in a separate style sheet

- **Encircled Blue Dot:** Indicates that the style is a CSS rule being used in the current page

- **Red Dot:** Indicates that the style is a CSS rule, which matches using the `id` attribute of a tag

- **Encircled Red Dot:** Indicates that the style is a CSS rule based on matching `id` and is being used in the current page

NOTE   Depending on the number of in-page style tags on a Web page, the Current Page header repeats in the Apply Styles task pane list of styles. For example, as shown in Figure 12.13, the currently opened Web page has two style tags. This becomes more understandable when you collapse the headers in the list. Because the `core.css` is the main style sheet file for SharePoint Web sites, you almost always see styles from this file listed in the Apply Styles task pane when working with SharePoint Web pages.

The Options dropdown menu in the top-right corner of the Apply Styles task pane allows you to categorize the styles being shown in the Select CSS style to apply list in the following ways:

- **Categorize By Order:** Selected by default, categorizes the styles in the order they're encountered in the associated file

- **Categorize By Type:** Categorizes the styles based on the type. For example, with this option selected, the CSS classes are grouped together.

- **Show All Styles:** Selected by default, shows all the styles that are available either in-line, in-page, or in an external style sheet linked to the Web page active in SharePoint Designer

- **Show Styles Used In Current Page:** Shows styles that are being used on the current page only. Selecting this option ensures that you only see the encircled green or blue styles in the list.

- **Show Style Used On Selection:** Shows the styles being used on the currently selected item in the active Web page

- **Preview Background Color:** Allows you to change the background color used when showing the style in the Select CSS style to apply list

FIGURE 12.12

The Apply Styles task pane showing the styles in the `core.css` style sheet

FIGURE 12.13

The collapsed view of the list of styles in the Apply Styles task pane

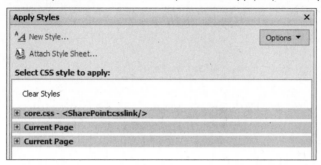

The Select CSS style to apply list shows the Clear Styles option at the top of the list. This option can be used to clear the styles from the selection made in the currently active Web page.

When you right-click on a style that shows up in the Select CSS style to apply list, a popup menu appears with the following options:

- **Apply Style:** Applies the style to the selection made in the document

- **Go to Code:** Takes you to the location on the Web page or the style sheet where the style is defined

- **Select All Instances:** Highlights all instances where the style is being used on the currently active Web page

- **New Style:** Allows you to create a new style by using the New Style dialog box

- **New Style Copy:** Allows you to create a new style based on the selected style

- **Modify Style:** Allows you to modify the style by using the Modify Style dialog box

- **Rename Class:** Allows you to change the name of the CSS class

- **Delete:** Deletes the CSS style

- **Remove Link:** Enabled when the header in the Select CSS style to apply list is right-clicked on, this option allows you to remove the link to the style sheet from the document.

- **Attach Stylesheet:** Allows you to attach a style sheet to the active Web page by using the Attach Stylesheet dialog box

- **Manage Stylesheet Links:** If you have multiple style sheets associated with the active document, you can use this option to manage style sheet links.

- **Remove Class:** Removes the CSS class from the selection in the active Web page

- **Remove ID:** Removes the CSS IDs from the selection in the active Web page

- **Remove Inline Style:** Removes in-line styles from the selection in the active Web page

The Apply Styles task pane also allows you to attach new style sheets to the currently active document by using the Attach Style Sheet link. As shown in Figure 12.14, the Attach Style Sheet dialog box that opens when you click the Attach Style Sheet link allows you to specify the URL of the external style sheet.

FIGURE 12.14

The Attach Style Sheet dialog box

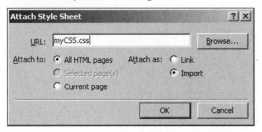

You can choose if you want to add the style sheet link only to the current page, selected pages, or all HTML pages inside a Web site. If you choose to attach as a link, a style sheet link is inserted into the Web page. Choosing to import the style sheet copies all the styles from the style sheet into the Web page as in-page styles.

Using the CSS Properties task pane

The CSS Properties task pane is useful primarily if you're used to working with a Visual Studio–like interface for setting properties. This task pane shows a contextual view of the properties associated with the selection made in the active Web page. When you make a selection on a Web page in the Design or Code view, the CSS Properties task pane shows the associated properties in a categorized manner. By default, the properties that have been set by using styles are displayed on top of the list of properties in a given category.

One of the really cool features of the CSS Properties task pane is that it shows a hierarchical view of the CSS rules implementation on the current selection on a Web page. As illustrated in Figure 12.15, the Applied Rules section in the CSS Properties task pane shows the CSS implementation on the HTML tags from the topmost to the currently selected tag.

As you can see, the topmost `<body>` tag matches two CSS rules: body, form, and body. The next child tag, `<form>`, only matches one CSS rule body: form. This hierarchy continues until you reach the container of the currently selected tag.

If you hover over a CSS rule, a screen tip shows the code associated with that CSS rule. When you right-click on a rule, a popup menu very similar to the Select CSS style to apply list opens, allowing you to create and modify styles. Also, on the top-right corner of the CSS Properties task pane, the link to the style sheet where the CSS rule has been defined is shown.

FIGURE 12.15

The applied rules in the CSS Properties task pane

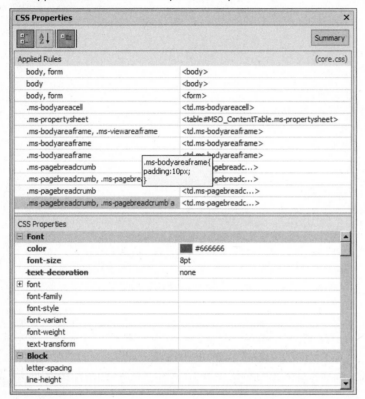

Working in the Manage Styles task pane

While the Apply Styles task pane is oriented toward Web pages where the styles need to be applied and shows the styles that are active on an HTML selection, the Manage Styles task pane allows you to work on the CSS styles directly. When you open a CSS by using SharePoint Designer, the Manage Styles task pane lists all the CSS rules and classes defined in the style sheet. Similarly, opening a Web page in SharePoint Designer allows the Manage Styles task pane to list in-line, in-page, and external styles associated with a Web page.

Figure 12.16 shows the Manage Styles task pane for a SharePoint Web page. Like the Apply Styles task pane, the user interface represents the CSS rules, elements, and classes by using the same indicators. For example, the styles that are being used on the Web page are encircled.

However, while the Apply Styles task pane mostly showed CSS classes, the Manage Styles task pane allows you to also work with CSS rules and elements. You can simply select the CSS style in the code of the Web page or the CSS file, and the style is highlighted in the Manage Styles task pane.

Then, you can use the task pane to modify the style by using the familiar tools for styles creation and modification. As in the case of the Apply Styles task pane, the Manage Styles task pane also shows a quick preview of the style by using the Preview pane at the bottom of the task pane.

FIGURE 12.16

The Manage Styles task pane

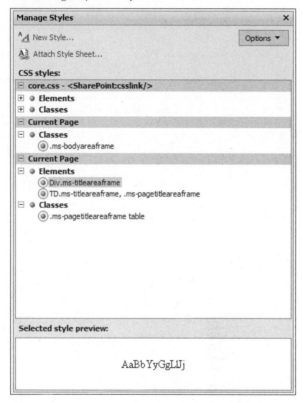

Creating and Using CSS Layouts

CSS layouts is a mechanism of laying out Web pages by using formatting applied via CSS. When you create a CSS layout, you're basically creating a CSS and then applying a style sheet to a Web page for layout formatting. So, instead of using a table to lay out your Web page, for example, you can choose to create a layout based on a CSS. By default, SharePoint Designer provides a number of templates for creating CSS layouts. These are available in the New dialog box in the CSS Layouts section.

To create a new Web page using CSS layouts, follow these steps:

1. **Choose File ➪ New to open the New dialog box and then click the CSS Layouts section in the Page tab, as shown in Figure 12.17.**

2. **Choose the layout that best suits the layout of the page you want to create.**

3. **Click OK.** SharePoint Designer creates a Web page and a CSS for you. By default, the CSS is linked to the newly created Web page. By default, the page just has some `<div>` tags with `id` attributes that match CSS rules. But when you type some text in the `<div>` tags, the layout formatting applied by using the CSS layout takes affect, and the content is placed according to the CSS formatting defined in the rules, as shown in Figure 12.18.

FIGURE 12.17

Creating CSS layouts by using the default templates provided with SharePoint Designer

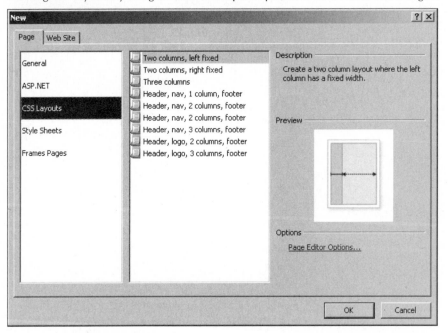

The CSS rules in this case are being matched by using the `id` attribute of the tags. As mentioned previously in this chapter, the CSS rule created in such a manner applies to all tags that have a matching `id` attribute. Because you would usually want to keep the `id` attributes unique for the tags, this method of applying rules ensures that the CSS rules only apply when the `id` matches.

The next step is to modify the CSS rules to apply the formatting you want to add to the CSS layout. You can easily do this by modifying the CSS style by either using the Apply Styles or Modify Styles task panes. For example, if you want the page header to have a background color, simply modify the #header CSS rule by using the Modify Style menu option in the Apply Styles task pane and then specify the background color in the background category.

FIGURE 12.18

The Split view of a page created by using a CSS layout

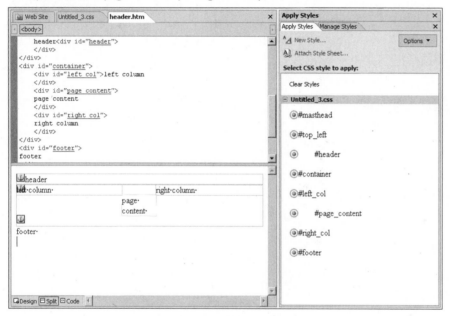

Using CSS Reporting Features

SharePoint Designer provides a set of reporting tools for CSS that are pretty useful for checking the CSS implementation of a Web site and then comparing it with the Web standards for errors, problems, mismatches, or usage. You can run reports on selected pages or across an entire Web site and then determine whether the CSS styles are being used efficiently. CSS Errors and CSS Usage are the two main CSS-related reports that you can run on your Web site:

- **CSS Errors:** Allows you to find CSS styles that exist but aren't being used, CSS classes that are associated with elements but haven't been defined, and mismatched cases when associating styles with elements

- **CSS Usage:** Allows you to determine usage of the various CSS rules and classes

To run the CSS reports, choose Tools ⇨ CSS Reports to open the CSS Reports dialog box, as shown in Figure 12.19. The Errors tab allows you run reports to check for CSS errors, and the Usage tab allows you to run reports on usages of various CSS classes and rules. To run a CSS Error report across an entire Web site, follow these steps:

1. **In the CSS Reports dialog box, click the All Pages radio button and then click the appropriate check boxes for the issues you want to identify in the CSS implementation.**

2. **Click Check.** This opens the CSS Reports task pane, as shown in Figure 12.20. You use the CSS Reports task pane to view the errors encountered in the CSS implementation on the selected Web pages.

3. **After you identify the CSS issue and then qualify it as a valid problem, you can right-click on the error in the Reports task pane to navigate to the Web page and then take corrective measures to fix the issue.**

FIGURE 12.19

Running CSS reports on a Web site by using SharePoint Designer

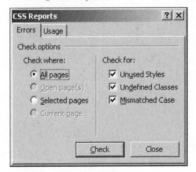

FIGURE 12.20

Using the CSS Reports task pane to find CSS errors

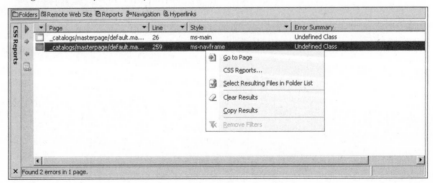

You can also access the CSS Reports dialog box by clicking the Play button in the CSS Reports task pane. If you run the CSS usage reports on an entire Web site, you should see an output similar to the one shown in Figure 12.21.

SharePoint Designer lists the CSS classes and rules that have been applied to the selected pages, indicates the location where the CSS style has been defined, and denotes the line number where the CSS style association exists on a Web page. You can use this report to quickly jump to the CSS style you want to modify in a CSS implementation on a large Web site.

NOTE   **When you run CSS reports on SharePoint sites with the All Pages radio button selected, the report actually runs only on the selected pages. This has been designed to avoid introducing an overhead on the SharePoint site if multiple users run CSS reports simultaneously.**

FIGURE 12.21

Running CSS Usage reports for a Web page

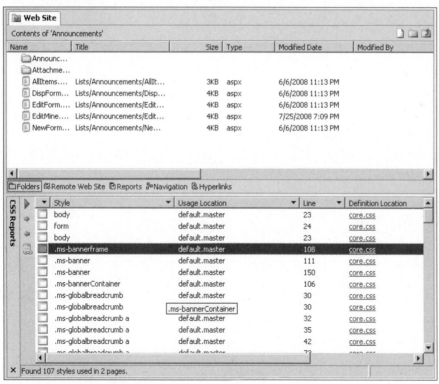

Summary

CSS is one of the primary tools for Web designers to implement standardized styling across Web sites, helping to reduce redundancy and improve productivity. This chapter discussed some concepts about CSS to familiarize you with the CSS terminology. Then, I showed you how you can use the SharePoint Designer user interface to create and manage styles on Web pages. I took you through a number of exercises to familiarize you with the Apply Styles, Manage Styles, and CSS Properties task panes. You also learned about creating a CSS layout and using the CSS reporting features.

Chapter 13

Implementing Master Pages and Page Layouts

Designing Web sites entails that you consider a number of techniques to ensure uniformity and consistency in the formatting and branding of the Web pages. It's important to ascertain that users browsing through the Web pages of a Web site feel a sense of standardization while navigating between various Web pages. You might not want to have Web pages inside a Web site presenting content in a manner that's totally oblivious of the presentation style of the entire Web site. For example, you may want to always have the navigation links and bars at the same location on the Web pages of the Web site so that when the user navigates around pages, he or she doesn't feel confused.

IN THIS CHAPTER

Working with dynamic Web templates

Implementing master pages

Managing page layouts

While CSS is a key technology that helps you maintain a consistent look and feel for your Web site, it applies mostly to styling, fonts, and formatting. SharePoint Designer allows you to make use of a number of other technologies, such as dynamic Web templates (DWTs), master pages, and page layouts to help you maintain a standard branding and layout across all the Web pages.

Although the implementation of the aforementioned technologies might be different, the concept behind them is similar. You mostly follow these steps to create Web site content by using these technologies:

- You create a template Web page that suits the requirements of your Web site's design. In this template page, you define a uniform blueprint that's implemented for the entire Web site or a set of pages inside the Web site. Usually, this is the time when you decide where to place common elements, such as branding images, navigation components and link bars, headers and footers, etc.

- After you place the common elements, you create unique areas in the template page to hold content that's unique to the Web pages based on the template.

- You then create new Web pages based on the template page. These Web pages inherit the common elements of the template page and allow editing of the unique areas only.

While designing Web pages in this fashion, the concept described previously is enforced by the editing tool, which in this context is SharePoint Designer. SharePoint Designer allows you to create template pages by using dynamic Web templates (DWTs), master pages, and page layouts. You can define the design, formatting, and common elements on the template pages by using the available tools. Then, you can either create new Web pages based on the template pages or attach the template pages to existing Web pages.

After attaching the Web page to the template page, it inherits the formatting and layout of the template page. The Design view in SharePoint Designer doesn't allow you to modify the common elements that the Web page inherits from the template page. You can only make modifications to the unique areas you defined in the template page. This ensures that all the common elements from the template page are and stay enforced on the attached Web pages.

To modify the common elements, you need to modify the template page. When you save the template page after modifications, the attached Web pages are automatically updated to inherit the modifications. So, rather than having to make modifications to every page, you modify only one template page and then the changes are applied to all attached Web pages. In this way, this concept reduces redundancy and provides you with an efficient way to maintain your Web pages.

Working with Dynamic Web Templates

Dynamic Web templates (DWTs) is an HTML-based SharePoint Designer feature that allows you to create templates and then use them on Web pages of your Web site. As mentioned earlier, you design the template in a DWT template file (having the extension .dwt) and then place unique areas called editable regions at the required locations in the template file. After you create the template file, you can either create new pages based on it or attach it to existing pages.

NOTE   To be able to use DWTs on your Web site, you need to enable the use of hidden metadata. You can do this by clicking the Manage the Web site using hidden metadata check box in the General tab of the Site Settings dialog box. To open this dialog box, choose Site ➪ Site Settings.

Creating and attaching dynamic Web templates

In this section, I take you through the steps to create a dynamic Web template and then add editable regions to it. Then, I show you how you can create new pages based on this template:

1. **Open your Web site in SharePoint Designer and then choose Site ⇨ Site Settings to open the Site Settings dialog box.** Ensure that the Manage the Web site using hidden metadata check box is selected.

2. **Choose View ⇨ Toolbars ⇨ Dynamic Web Template to enable the Dynamic Web Template toolbar.** This toolbar comes in handy while creating DWTs.

3. **Choose File ⇨ New to open the New dialog box, and in the Page tab, under the General section, select Dynamic Web Template and then click OK.** This creates a new Web page with the extension .dwt and opens it in the Design view.

4. **Using the SharePoint Designer tools and features, design the DWT to suit your requirements.** As shown in Figure 13.1, for illustration purposes, I created a simple Web page design by using tables. The next step is to insert editable regions in this DWT. Editable regions are the unique areas that are editable on the Web pages attached to the DWT.

FIGURE 13.1

Designing a Dynamic Web Template

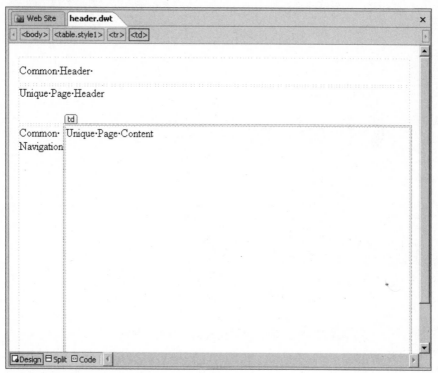

5. **Place the cursor at the location on the DWT where you want to add an editable region, right-click on the DWT in the Design view, and then choose Manage Editable Regions from the popup menu.** The Editable Regions dialog box, as shown in Figure 13.2, opens. By default, there are two editable regions, doctitle and body, that are placed by SharePoint Designer on the DWT. The doctitle editable region facilitates editing the title of the Web page attached to the DWT.

6. **To add a new region, type a name for it in the Region name text field and then click Add.** As shown in Figure 13.3, in the DWT in the background, the editable region is inserted at the location where the cursor was located.

FIGURE 13.2

The Editable Regions dialog box

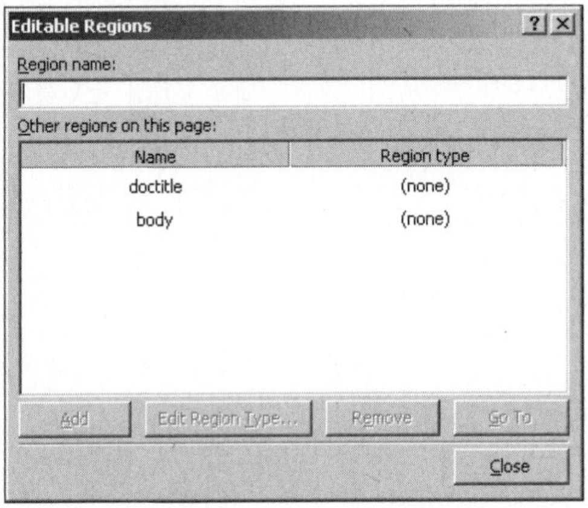

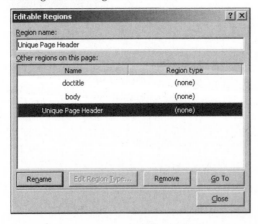

FIGURE 13.3

Adding editable regions on DWTs

7. **Click Close.** Place the cursor at the location on the DWT where you want to add another editable region and then open the Editable Regions dialog box again. Then, add another editable region, as shown in Figure 13.4. Repeat these steps to add more editable regions to the DWT.

Multiple editable regions inserted on a DWT

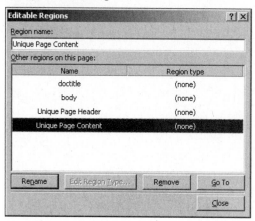

8. **Save the DWT by pressing CTRL+S or choosing File ⇨ Save.** The DWTs need to be saved with the extension .dwt.

Now that you have created a DWT for your Web site, you can use it to create new Web pages. To create new Web pages based on an existing DWT, follow these steps:

1. **Choose File ⇨ New ⇨ Create From Dynamic Web Template.** The Attach Dynamic Web Template dialog box opens, allowing you to choose the DWT that you want to use for the new Web page.

2. **Select the DWT and then click Open.** SharePoint Designer creates a new Web page and then attaches the selected DWT to the Web page. Once finished, SharePoint Designer shows an update message, as shown in Figure 13.5. This message box indicates that SharePoint Designer has attached and updated the new Web page with the selected DWT.

3. **Click Close and then save the newly created Web page.** When you open this page in the Design view, you're only able to edit the Web page within the editable regions that you previously defined in the DWT. Editing the rest of the Web page is prohibited in the Design view. This is illustrated in Figure 13.6.

FIGURE 13.5

Creating a new Web page based on a DWT

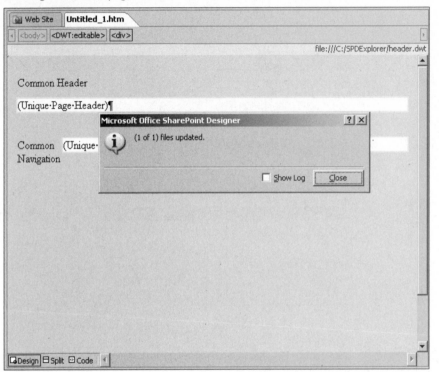

If you open the Web page in the Code view, all the code from the DWT actually exists in the attached Web page. However, the code from the DWT is highlighted. If you try to modify the highlighted code, you receive an update message, as shown in Figure 13.7.

As indicated in the message, the changes that you make to the noneditable code from the DWT are discarded when the DWT is modified and saved. However, you're provided with an option to detach the Web page from the DWT.

 **NOTE**   Modifying the content of the editable regions in the DWT doesn't really make much sense because you would always modify them in the attached Web pages.

FIGURE 13.6

Editing a Web page attached to a DWT

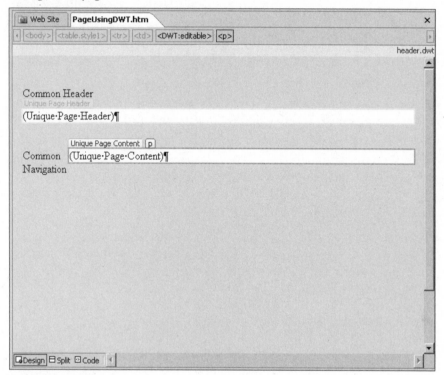

FIGURE 13.7

Modifying the code from the DWT in the Code view of the attached Web page

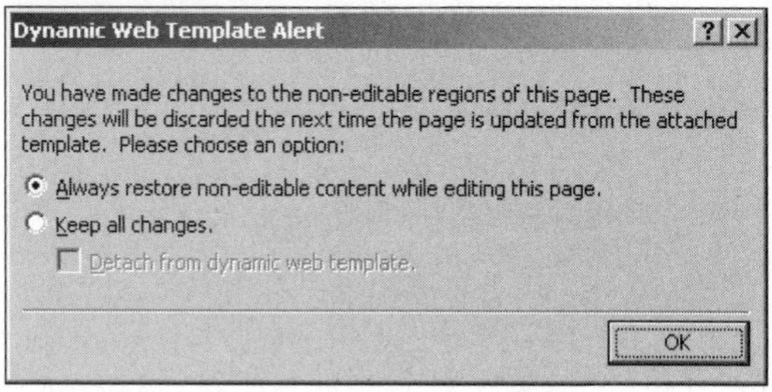

Choosing Format ⇨ Dynamic Web Template allows you to pick from a number of DWT-related actions you can perform on a Web page:

- **Attach Dynamic Web Template:** Opens the Attach Dynamic Web Template dialog box, which allows you to attach a DWT to the active Web page

- **Detach from Dynamic Web Template:** Detaches the DWT from the Web page. The content of the DWT still remains on the Web page. However, the content is now all editable.

- **Open Attached Dynamic Web Template:** Opens the DWT attached to the Web page

- **Update Selected Page:** When the active Web page in SharePoint Designer is a DWT, this option updates the selected page with the modifications made to the DWT.

- **Update All Pages:** Regardless of the selection, this updates all pages attached to the active DWT.

- **Update Attached Pages:** Updates all the Web pages that are attached to the DWT

- **Manage Editable Regions:** Opens the Editable Regions dialog box, which you can use to add and modify editable regions on the DWT

The Dynamic Web Template toolbar allows you to view all the editable regions associated with the selected DWT and provides another access point to the Editable Regions dialog box. It also has a Template Region Labels button, which can be used to toggle the display of the editable region names in the Design view of the Web page.

Managing editable regions

While the Editable Regions dialog box can be used to perform the usual job of adding, modifying, and removing editable regions on a DWT, it also hosts one feature that allows you to control and channelize designers working on SharePoint sites. Combined with the Contributor Settings feature available in SharePoint Designer for SharePoint sites, the Editable Regions dialog box can be used to define control on the type of modifications that are allowed in an editable region.

CROSS-REF   **For more on the Contributor Settings feature, see Chapter 24.**

Using the Contributor Settings feature in SharePoint Designer, you can create region types and define what authoring actions and features are allowed in the region type. For example, you can define a region type that doesn't allow inserting images.

Using the Editable Regions dialog box, you can associate a region with a region type. When you add an editable region to a DWT inside a SharePoint site, you have the option to choose from a number of region types. If Contributor Settings are enabled for a SharePoint Web site, a number of regions are available by default. As shown in Figure 13.8, you can associate an editable region with one of the available region types.

After the association is made, the editable region is controlled by the settings of the associated region type. If the region type is configured to disallow use of a certain SharePoint Designer feature, the editable region doesn't allow the designer to perform that operation in SharePoint Designer.

FIGURE 13.8

Associating regions with region types

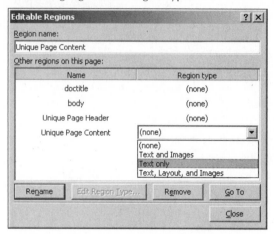

Implementing Master Pages

Master pages is an ASP.NET 2.0 feature for implementing template-based Web site design. Like a DWT, you design a master page in SharePoint Designer that holds the common elements for your Web pages, identifies the locations you want to keep unique, and inserts unique areas at those locations on the master pages. Then, you can either create new Web pages based on the master page or attach the master page to existing Web pages.

Although the process that you follow to create and attach master pages in SharePoint Designer is similar to DWTs, the internal implementation of master pages is very different from that of DWTs. The major difference is that while the content of a DWT is copied over to the attached Web page, a master page is displayed with the unique content of the attached Web page at runtime when a Web page is rendered for display in a browser.

However, the concept described in the beginning of this chapter still holds true. The unique areas in a master page are defined by using ASP.NET 2.0 controls called content placeholders. So, on a master page that you design by using SharePoint Designer, you place content placeholder controls at the locations where you want to bring unique content from the attached Web page. If the attached Web page has unique content that needs to be displayed at the location of the content placeholder controls present in the master page, you have to place ASP.NET content controls on the Web page and then associate them with the target content placeholder controls.

In summary, a master page has a number of ASP.NET content placeholder controls, and the attached Web page can have ASP.NET content controls associated with the content placeholder controls placed on a master page.

Managing content regions and placeholders

To understand the concept of content placeholders and content controls better, the following exercise takes you through the process of creating a master page by using SharePoint Designer and then creating a new page based on that master page:

1. **Open your Web site in SharePoint Designer and then choose File ⇨ New to open the New dialog box.**

2. **Choose Master Page in the General section of the Page tab in the New dialog box, and using the programming language dropdown menu, choose the language you want to use for the master page.**

3. **Click OK.** This creates a master page (with the file extension `.master`) and then opens it in the Design view in SharePoint Designer.

4. **Design the master page according to your requirements.**

5. **Place the cursor at the location where you want to insert a content placeholder, right-click on the master page, and then choose Manage Microsoft ASP.NET Content Regions from the popup menu.** As in the case of DWTs, there are two content regions placed on the master page by default. The head content region allows you to modify the `<head>` section.

6. **Type a name for the content region and then click Add.** As shown in Figure 13.9, an ASP.NET content placeholder control is placed at the location of the cursor.

7. **Click Close and then save the master page at the location of your choice inside the Web site.**

FIGURE 13.9

Inserting content regions on a master page by using SharePoint Designer

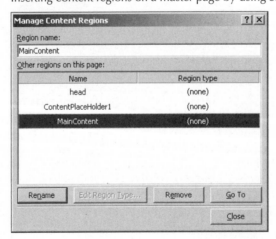

You have just created a master page with a content region (an ASP.NET content placeholder control) on it. If you switch to the Code view of the master page, the following code appears for the content region you just inserted:

```
<asp:ContentPlaceHolder runat="Server" id="MainContent">
    <p>(MainContent)</p>
</asp:ContentPlaceHolder>
```

Notice the `id` attribute of the content placeholder control. This `id` is used to match the ASP.NET control on the Web page attached to the master page.

NOTE Notice the dummy content `<p>(MainContent)</p>` placed in the content placeholder control. This content facilitates the display of the control in the Design view. If the content placeholder control doesn't have this dummy content, it might not be easily locatable in the Design view in the attached Web pages. This is particularly true for Web pages created by using SharePoint Designer's master pages. When creating Web pages based on SharePoint master pages, ensure that the master page has some dummy content in the PlaceHolderMain content placeholder control. This facilitates the display of the control in the attached page's Design view.

Now that you've created a master page, follow these steps to create a new Web page based on the master page:

1. **Choose File ➪ New ➪ Create from Master Page.** The Select a Master Page dialog box, as shown in Figure 13.10, opens.

FIGURE 13.10

Creating a Web page based on a master page

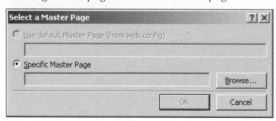

2. **Click the Specific Master Page radio button and then click Browse to locate the master page you want to use to create the new Web page.**

3. **Click OK.** A new Web page is created for you. If you go to the Code view of the Web page, the following code appears:

```
<%@ Page masterpagefile="MyMaster.master" language="C#" title="Header
    Goes here" %>
```

Unlike a Web page attached to a DWT, a Web page attached to a master page doesn't have the content of the master page. The Page directive shown in the previous code defines the location of the master page file at runtime when the page is rendered for display.

If you switch to the Design view of the attached Web page, the name and location of the master page file attached to the Web page are displayed in the top-right section. As shown in Figure 13.11, to add unique content to the Web page, click the arrow toward the right of the content region and then choose Create Custom Content from the popup menu.

Creating custom content on the attached Web page

After you click the Create Custom Content link, the content region on the Web page becomes editable, and you can use the SharePoint Designer tools to place content in the region. If you switch back to the Code view of the Web page, the following code appears:

```
<asp:Content id="Content1" runat="server" contentplaceholderid="MainC
   ontent">
   <p>(MainContent)</p>
</asp:Content>
```

This is the ASP.NET content control that holds the unique content of the Web page. The value of the contentplaceholderid attribute of this control is the same as the id attribute of the content placeholder control placed in the master page. This way, the content control in the attached Web page is associated with the content placeholder control in the master page.

> **NOTE** It's not necessary for the attached Web page to have a content control associated with a master page content placeholder control. However, if the Web page has a content control, the `contentplaceholderid` of which can't be matched to a content placeholder control on the attached master page, an update message, as shown in Figure 13.12, appears in the Design view.

FIGURE 13.12

A master page error due to mismatched content regions

Master Page error

The page has one or more <asp:Content> controls that do not correspond with <asp:ContentPlaceHolder> controls in the Master Page.

Attach a different Master Page, or change the mapping of the content regions, or correct the problem in Code View:

- MainContentx

The message shows the list of problematic content controls. You can click the change the mappings of the content regions link to match the content control to an appropriate existing content placeholder control in the attached master page.

Attaching master pages to Web pages

Like the DWTs, choosing Format ⇨ Master Pages also offers a number of menu options for performing master page–related operations on Web pages:

- **Attach Master Page:** Opens the Select a Master Page dialog box, which allows you to choose a master page that you want to attach to a Web page

- **Detach from Master Page:** Detaches the master page from the Web page. The content of the master page is placed directly on the Web page, and the ASP.NET content controls are removed.

- **Open Attached Master Page:** Opens the attached master page in SharePoint Designer

- **Manage Content Regions:** Opens the Manage Content Regions dialog box for the active master page, which allows you to add, modify, or remove content placeholders on the master page

> **NOTE** You can't attach DWTs to master pages or Web pages that have master pages attached to them. Also, you can't attach master pages to DWTs and Web pages that have DWTs attached to them.

By default, SharePoint Web sites have out-of-the-box master pages associated with their Web pages. These master pages are stored in the Master Page Gallery of SharePoint sites, which is accessible by using the Site Settings Web page. In SharePoint Designer, you can view the master pages of a SharePoint site by expanding _catalogs ⇨ masterpage (Master Page Gallery) in the Folder List task pane, as shown in Figure 13.13.

FIGURE 13.13

Viewing SharePoint master pages in SharePoint Designer

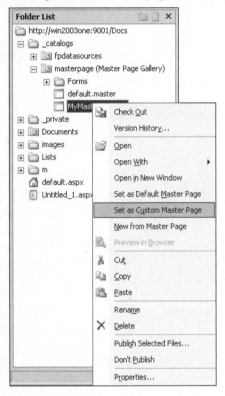

SharePoint sites have two categories of master pages:

- **Site Master Page:** This master page applies to all the publishing pages of the SharePoint site. In SharePoint Designer, this is called the Custom Master Page.

- **System Master Page:** Called the Default Master Page, this master page applies to all forms and view pages of the SharePoint Web site.

To set a master page to be the SharePoint site's site or system master page, simply right-click on the master page in the Folder List task pane in SharePoint Designer and then choose the associated master page setting from the popup menu.

CAUTION While designing master pages for SharePoint Web sites, keep in mind that SharePoint Web pages by default have a content-to-content placeholder control matching system (based on the default SharePoint master pages). Before you associate your custom master page to be the SharePoint site's site or system master page, ensure that you maintain the content placeholders as expected by the SharePoint Web pages. Otherwise, you run into errors when rendering the SharePoint Web pages attached to your custom master page.

TIP   The Site Settings pages of a SharePoint site use the `application.master` master page residing in the `_layouts` virtual directory of the Web site.

Understanding nested master pages

Master pages can be nested, which means that you can attach a master page to another master page and then attach the child master page to your Web pages. This feature provides you the ability to further refine the layout implementation on your Web pages.

The application of nested master pages is no different than directly attaching master pages to Web pages. It's just that now you attach a parent master page to a child master page; the parent and child master pages have the content-to-content placeholder mappings. While attaching a master page to another master page, the existing content of the child master page has to be mapped to a single content placeholder on the parent master page.

NOTE   You can only attach one master page to another master page or Web page in SharePoint Designer.

As shown in Figure 13.14, the Match Content Regions dialog box opens when you attached a master page to another master page (or a master page to a Web page that already has content on it).

Using this dialog box, you specify which content placeholder on the parent master page the existing content of the child master page (or the attached Web page) should be matched with. After you choose the content placeholder on the parent master page, a content control is placed on the child master page (or the attached Web page), with the `contentplaceholderid` matching the `id` attribute of the content placeholder control on the parent master page.

FIGURE 13.14

The Match Content Regions dialog box

Match Content Regions		? X

Content regions in the current page and Master Page do not match. Match regions in the current page to regions in the Master Page.

Current Page: `file:///C:/SPDExplorer/MyMaster.master`

Master Page: `file:///C:/SPDExplorer/HeadMaster.master`

Current Page	Master Page	Modify
(Body)	ContentPlaceHolder1	

	OK	Skip Current Page	Cancel

Managing Page Layouts

MOSS introduces a feature called page layouts with the Publishing site template. Page layouts, in essence, are a set of layout pages from which SharePoint site authors can use to create new pages. Like master pages, the page layouts are also stored in the Master Page Gallery of a SharePoint site based on the Publishing site template. As shown in Figure 13.15, you can view the default page layouts available in the Master Page Gallery.

FIGURE 13.15

The Master Page Gallery of a SharePoint site based on the Publishing site template

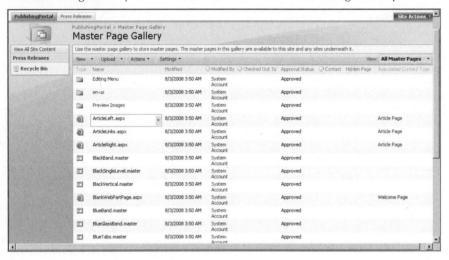

Every page layout is associated with a page layout content type, which defines the columns/fields that can be used to hold metadata associated with a page created by using the page layout. The Site Content Type Gallery, as shown in Figure 13.16, can be used to view the default page layout content types and also create new custom page layout content types based on existing content types.

NOTE Content Types, introduced in WSS v3 and MOSS, define the nature and behavior of the content that can be stored in items. For example, the Document content type allows for creation of items that can store documents and related metadata. If you have multiple content types associated with a list, you can create items based on these content types and then store them in the list.

This section describes how you can use the page layout feature available in SharePoint publishing Web sites to create Web pages from the SharePoint site interface. Then, I take you through the steps to create custom page layouts by using SharePoint Designer.

FIGURE 13.16

Page Layout Content Types in the Site Content Type Gallery

Link to a Document	Document	PublishingPortal
Master Page	Document	PublishingPortal
Picture	Document	PublishingPortal
Web Part Page	Basic Page	PublishingPortal
Folder Content Types		
Discussion	Folder	PublishingPortal
Folder	Item	PublishingPortal
List Content Types		
Announcement	Item	PublishingPortal
Contact	Item	PublishingPortal
Far East Contact	Item	PublishingPortal
Issue	Item	PublishingPortal
Item	System	PublishingPortal
Link	Item	PublishingPortal
Message	Item	PublishingPortal
Task	Item	PublishingPortal
Page Layout Content Types		
Article Page	Page	PublishingPortal
Redirect Page	Page	PublishingPortal
Welcome Page	Page	PublishingPortal
Publishing Content Types		
Page	System Page	PublishingPortal
Page Layout	System Page Layout	PublishingPortal
Publishing Master Page	System Master Page	PublishingPortal
Special Content Types		
Unknown Document Type	Document	PublishingPortal

Understanding SharePoint publishing pages

Publishing pages are SharePoint Web pages that are created based on a page layout. SharePoint users with appropriate permissions can create publishing pages either by using the default page layouts available in SharePoint or the custom page layouts created with SharePoint Designer. To create a publishing page in a SharePoint site based on the Publishing site template, follow these steps:

1. **Browse to the SharePoint site based on the Publishing site template.**

2. **Choose Site Actions ⇨ Create Page to go to the Create Page Web page in the SharePoint site.** This is shown in Figure 13.17.

3. **Type a title for your publishing page, choose the page layout to be used for creating the publishing page, and then click Create.** As shown in Figure 13.18, this creates a publishing page and opens it in the Edit mode in the SharePoint Web site. Based on the layout of the page layout, fields are displayed on the publishing page for modification. For example, Figure 13.18 shows the Title, Page Content, and Rollup Image fields available for modification on the publishing page.

NOTE These fields are actually columns that are defined in the content type associated with the page layout used to create the publishing page.

4. **When you finish modifying the fields available in the publishing page, you can save the publishing page, start approval workflows, check-in, or perform other operations on the publishing page by using the Page, Workflow, and Tools action menus available in the top-left section of the SharePoint page interface.**

By default, the publishing pages are stored in the Pages library of the SharePoint site. You can use this library to view various properties of the publishing pages, such as approval status, check-in/check-out status, workflow status, etc. To access this library, choose Site Actions ⇨ View All Site Content and then click the Pages library.

FIGURE 13.17

Creating a publishing page in a SharePoint site

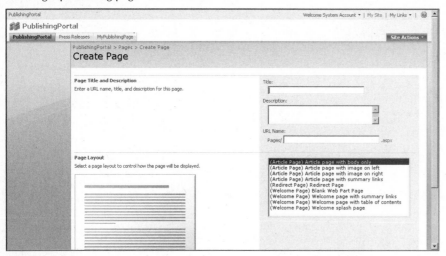

FIGURE 13.18

The publishing page in a SharePoint Web site

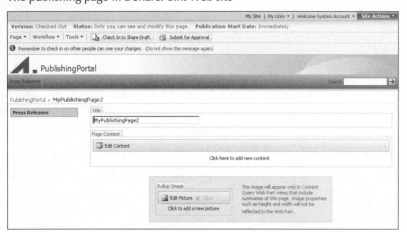

Creating and editing page layouts

SharePoint Designer allows you to create custom page layouts that SharePoint users can later use to create publishing Web pages in the SharePoint site interface. You can either create new page layouts or modify the existing page layouts by using SharePoint Designer.

> **NOTE** You can't directly modify a publishing page in SharePoint Designer. If you try to do so, SharePoint Designer displays the message shown in Figure 13.19, allowing you to either edit the publishing page in a browser or open the page layout associated with the publishing page in SharePoint Designer for editing.

FIGURE 13.19

The available options for editing a publishing page in SharePoint Designer

You can follow these steps to create a new page layout by using SharePoint Designer:

1. **Open your SharePoint site based on the Publishing site template in SharePoint Designer.**

2. **Choose File ➪ New to open the New dialog box.** Notice the SharePoint Publishing category in the SharePoint Content tab, as shown in Figure 13.20.

3. **Click Page Layout.** In the Options section, the Content Type Group dropdown menu lists the various page layout content groups defined for the SharePoint site. By default, here you should see the Page Layout Content Types and Publishing Content Types groups.

4. **Based on the selection made in the Content Type Group dropdown menu, the associated page layout content types are displayed in the Content Type Name dropdown menu.** Choose the page layout content type you want to use for your page layout.

5. **Type the URL name and title of the page layout and then click OK.**

The new page layout created by using the previous steps uses the custom master page (site master page) defined for the SharePoint Web site. Once the page layout is created, you can use the SharePoint Designer tools and features to modify the page layout just like any other Web page with a master page attached to it.

> **NOTE** The SharePoint Designer user interface can't be used to change the custom master page for a specific page layout. The page layouts always inherit the master page settings from the site level.

FIGURE 13.20

Creating a page layout by using the New dialog box

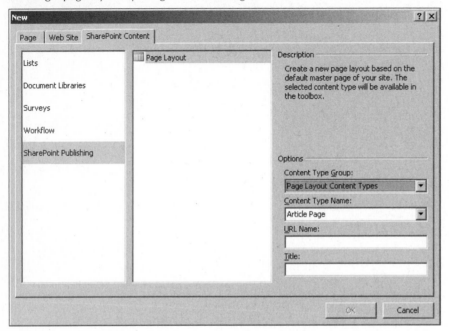

Summary

In this chapter, I discussed the abilities of SharePoint Designer to create Web site layout designing elements. You learned how to create and use DWTs, master pages, and page layouts. While DWTs and master pages can be used on non-SharePoint sites, the page layouts feature is only available with SharePoint sites that are based on the Publishing site template.

Chapter 14

Using Navigational Controls and Components

While designing your Web site, it's very important to consider how users might move from one part of the Web site to another with the least amount of confusion. Web sites tend to grow exponentially, which makes it even more essential to ensure that the content exposed is well-structured so that users don't waste a lot of time looking in the wrong places for the information they need. Although one of the major components that helps reduce this ambiguity is Web Site Search, having an intelligently developed navigation structure can save visitors to your Web site a lot of frustration and time loss while browsing for specific content.

SharePoint Designer has a number of tools and components that can be used to quickly develop a strong navigation structure for a Web site. While it inherits many of the navigation components from FrontPage 2003, SharePoint Designer also allows Web site developers to use the ASP.NET navigation controls to develop navigation components. For SharePoint sites, SharePoint Designer offers the capability to use the SharePoint navigational elements, controls, and Web parts to design and interconnect Web pages.

This chapter discusses the components that you can use in SharePoint Designer to develop navigation structures for Web sites. I begin by talking about non-SharePoint FrontPage author time components, such as link bars and bars based on navigation structure. I take you through the steps to create navigation structures by using the SharePoint Designer navigation panes and then create navigation bars based on these structures. Later in this chapter, I talk about how you can use ASP.NET navigation components and controls to design Web site navigation by using SharePoint Designer.

IN THIS CHAPTER

Designing navigation for non-SharePoint Sites

Understanding SharePoint navigation elements

Working with navigation controls

Finally, I discuss how you can use the capabilities offered in SharePoint sites to create navigation controls. I take you through the built-in features that SharePoint has for navigation, and I discuss the SharePoint launch bar and navigation settings. Then, I show you how you can use SharePoint Designer to exploit SharePoint link bars, navigation, and breadcrumb controls to implement a customized Web site navigation framework.

Designing Navigation for Non-SharePoint Sites

For non-SharePoint sites, the navigation structure has to be built from scratch, unlike SharePoint sites where you already might have a number of controls to work with. Here again, based on whether you're working with a Web site that allows hidden metadata, you can use SharePoint Designer tools in a number of ways to create your Web site's navigation.

CROSS-REF   **For more on hidden metadata, see Chapter 1.**

Using the Navigation pane

The SharePoint Designer Navigation pane is the key interface that you use to design a Web site's structure in a very simple manner. After the structure is ready, you can have a number of components available in SharePoint Designer make use of the structure you created in the Navigation pane to display navigation links on Web pages.

NOTE   **The Navigation pane can only be used with Web sites that have hidden metadata allowed for use. The structure of the Web site you create in the Navigation pane is stored in the `structure.cnf` file in the hidden `_vti_pvt` folder of the Web site.**

When working with the Navigation pane, you have two options:

- Add existing Web pages to the Navigation pane to form a structure.
- Use the Navigation pane to form a structure with new Web pages and then later design those pages.

Whichever way you choose, creating the navigation structure is half the part of implementing your Web site navigation. The other half is to insert navigation controls on Web pages that use the structure you created in the Navigation pane.

To create a structure for your Web site by using the Navigation pane, follow these steps:

1. **Open your Web site in SharePoint Designer, and in the Web Site pane, click the Navigation button at the bottom of the screen.** The Navigation pane opens.

2. **Using the Folder List task pane, simply drag and drop Web pages into the Navigation pane to form a treelike structure.** Or you can choose an existing Web page by right-clicking on the parent page in the Navigation pane and then choosing Add Existing Page from the popup menu. The concept to understand while creating the navigation structure is that each node (or page) in the structure is a landing point (or href) for a hyperlink.

3. **If you want to add new pages to the navigation structure instead of existing ones, simply choose the parent node by clicking on it and then choosing New ⇨ Page.** A child page is created under the selected page. As your navigation tree becomes bigger, you can expand or collapse the tree structure by clicking on a + or - sign, as shown in Figure 14.1. This allows you to quickly reach a particular node in the navigation structure and add some real estate in the Navigation pane.

By default, the home page of your Web site is listed as the top page of the navigation structure. If you want the top page to be some other page, you can start the navigation structure by creating a new top page by right-clicking on the empty space in the Navigation pane and then choosing New ⇨ Top Page from the popup menu. From then on, you can use the approach detailed previously to add new or existing pages to the navigation structure.

FIGURE 14.1

The navigation structure for a Web site by using new pages

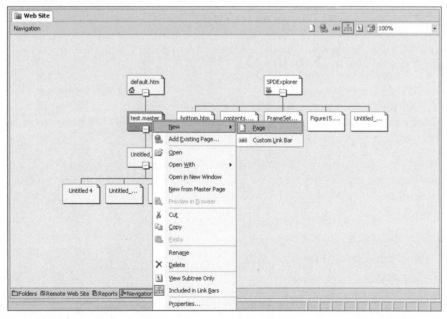

As indicated before, the navigation structure of the Web site is stored in the `structure.cnf` file in the `_vti_pvt` folder of the Web site. Here's a sample `structure.cnf` file from the previous steps:

```
3.0.0.507
1009
1000,default.htm,0,default.htm,0,1215813469,1
vti_globalpage:BW|true
1008,toppage1.htm,0,Top Page 1,0,1215815741,1
vti_globalpage:BW|true
1002,Untitled_3.aspx,0,Untitled 3,1000,1215814347,0
1003,Untitled_2.aspx,0,Untitled 2,1000,1215814347,0
1005,Untitled_1.htm,0,Untitled 1,1000,1215815255,0
1004,Untitled_3.htm,0,Untitled 3,1003,1215814347,0
1006,Untitled_4.htm,0,Untitled 4,1003,1215815255,0
1007,Untitled_5.htm,0,Untitled 5,1006,1215815255,0
```

As evident in this script, the structure is maintained in a sort of a parent-child relationship of pages in this file. In this code example, pages marked 1002, 1003, and 1005 are child pages of the page marked 1000. Similarly, pages marked 1004 and 1006 are child pages of the page marked 1003. The page marked 1008 is another global top-level page, just like the page marked 1000 (signified by `vti_globalpage:BW|true`). The number 1009 at the top is the counter number to be used for the next page that's added to the Navigation pane.

CAUTION Deleting the `structure.cnf` file causes the navigation structure to be lost and in turn causes failure in any of the components that depend on the navigation structure of the Web site. The only way to bring back the navigation in such a case is to restore the `structure.cnf` file from a previous backup.

If you right-click on the empty space in the Navigation page and then choose New ⇨ Custom Link Bar from the popup menu, you have the option to create a linear single-level set of Web pages. These link bars serve as a source for link bar Web components that SharePoint Designer lets you insert on Web pages.

After you create the navigation structure for your Web site, the next step to expose this navigation structure to your users is to use the navigation Web components provided by SharePoint Designer. SharePoint Designer has the following main Web components that make use of the navigation structure:

- Bar with custom links
- Bar with Next and Back links
- Bar based on navigation structure

Depending on your design, you can choose from any of these link bars for your Web pages.

Working with link bars

To insert a link bar on your Web page, follow these steps:

1. Open the Web page where you want to insert the link bar.
2. Choose Insert ➪ Web Components to open the Insert Web Component dialog box.
3. Choose Link Bars in the left pane, choose Bar with custom links in the right pane, and then click Next.
4. Choose a style for your link bar and then click Next.
5. Choose whether you want to place the link bar horizontally or vertically and then click Finish. The Link Bar Properties dialog box opens, with the Create a New Link Bar dialog box highlighted.
6. Type a name for the new link bar and then click OK.
7. In the General tab of the Link Bar Properties dialog box, as shown in Figure 14.2, click Add link to add new links to the link bar. You can arrange the link order by clicking Move up and Move down.
8. Click the Home Page and Parent Page check boxes if you want to add the links to the default home page of the Web site and the parent of the Web page.
9. Click the Style tab to change the theme for the link bar.
10. Click OK to insert the link bar on the Web page.

FIGURE 14.2

The Link Bar Properties dialog box

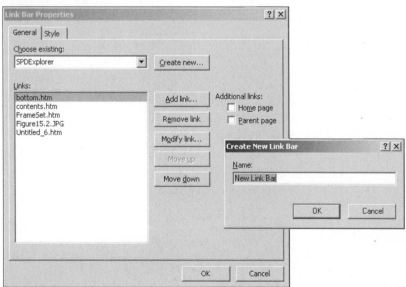

> **NOTE** After you insert a link bar on the Web page by using the previous method, a new custom link bar is added to the navigation structure of the Web site and can be seen in the Navigation pane. Any custom link bars that you create directly in the Navigation pane appear in the dropdown menu in the General tab of the Link Bar Properties dialog box for insertion as link bars on Web pages.

When you view the code of the Web page after the link bar is inserted, the link bar is inserted as the following comment:

```
<!--Webbot bot="Navigation" S-Type="sequence"
    S-Orientation="horizontal" S-Rendering="graphics" S-Theme="blends
    0110" B-Include-Home="FALSE" B-Include-Up="FALSE"
    U-Page="sid:1003" -->
```

Like many author time SharePoint Designer Web components, this is actually a placeholder for the HTML code associated with the link bar. The actual HTML code is not shown in the Code view to prevent unintended editing of the link bar code. If you want to view the actual code of the link bar that's interpreted by a browser, you need to open the Web page in Notepad (by right-clicking the Web page in the Folder List task pane and then choosing Open With ⇨ Notepad from the popup menu). The following is sample HTML code for the link bar:

```
<!--Webbot bot="Navigation" S-Type="sequence"
    S-Orientation="horizontal" S-Rendering="graphics" S-Theme="blends
    0110" B-Include-Home="FALSE" B-Include-Up="FALSE"
    U-Page="sid:1003" startspan --><script language="JavaScript"><!--
MSFPhover =
    (((navigator.appName == "Netscape") &&
    (parseInt(navigator.appVersion) >= 3 )) ||
    ((navigator.appName == "Microsoft Internet Explorer") &&
    (parseInt(navigator.appVersion) >= 4 )));
function MSFPpreload(img)
{
    var a=new Image(); a.src=img; return a;
}
// --></script><script language="JavaScript"><!--
if(MSFPhover) { MSFPnav1n=MSFPpreload("_derived/bottom.htm_cmp_
    blends110_hbtn.gif"); MSFPnav1h=MSFPpreload("_derived/bottom.htm_
    cmp_blends110_hbtn_a.gif"); }
// --></script><a href="bottom.htm" language="JavaScript"
    onmouseover="if(MSFPhover) document['MSFPnav1'].src=MSFPnav1h.
    src" onmouseout="if(MSFPhover) document['MSFPnav1'].
    src=MSFPnav1n.src"><img src="_derived/bottom.htm_cmp_blends110_
    hbtn.gif" width="140" height="60" border="0" alt="bottom.htm"
    align="middle" name="MSFPnav1"></a><!--Webbot bot="Navigation"
    i-checksum="42331" endspan -->
```

As shown here, the actual code that implements the link bar is rather complicated and uses a number of JavaScript functions. To avoid confusion for Web developers, this code is hidden from the Code view.

Using bars based on the navigation structure

Link bars don't really use the navigation structure of the Web site that you create in the Navigation pane. Instead, they just use the `structure.cnf` file to store their own link data. As a matter of fact, the link bars can even have hyperlinks pointed to external sites.

On the other hand, the Web component called Bar based on navigation structure, as its name suggests, is the one that allows you to place a set of hyperlinks on the Web page that exposes the site's navigation structure you created in the Navigation pane. To insert a Bar based on navigation structure on a Web page, follow these steps:

1. **Open a Web page in SharePoint Designer and then choose Insert ⇨ Web Component.** The Insert Web Component dialog box opens.
2. **Click Link Bars, choose Bar based on navigation structure in the right pane, and then click Next.**
3. **Choose a style for the navigation bar and then click Next.**
4. **Choose an orientation (horizontal or vertical) for the navigation bar and then click Finish.** The Link Bar Properties dialog box opens, as shown in Figure 14.3.

FIGURE 14.3

The Link Bar Properties dialog box for Bar based on navigation structure

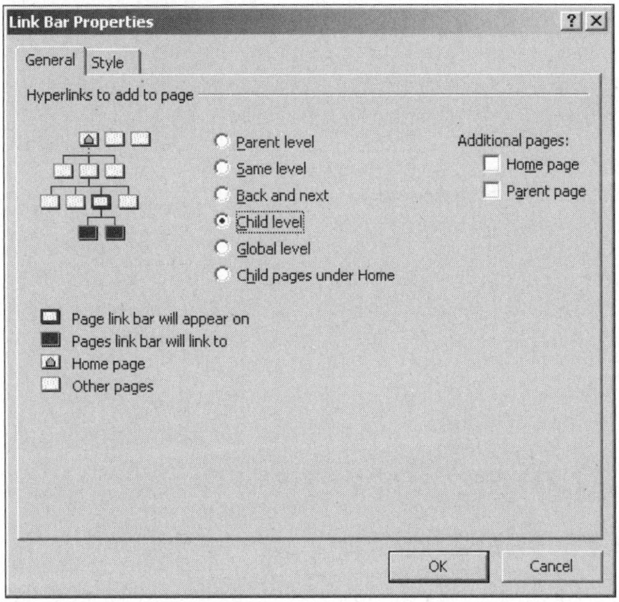

5. In the Link Bar Properties dialog box, you have a choice of a number of radio buttons to specify how the links appear on the link bar:

-   **Parent level:** The bar shows the links to all the pages in the parent level of the page where it's inserted.

-   **Same level:** The bar shows the links to all the pages that are in the same level as the page where it's inserted.

-   **Back and next:** The bar has Back and Next links that take you to the pages that are in the same level as the page where it's inserted.

-   **Child level:** The bar shows the links to all the pages in the child level of the page where it's inserted.

-   **Global level:** The bar shows all the top-level pages in the navigation structure.

-   **Child pages under home:** The bar shows all the child pages under the home page of the Web site.

6. **Click the Home page and the Parent page check boxes as required.** Click OK to insert the bar on the Web page.

If the page where you inserted the navigation bar is not part of the navigation structure of the Web site, you're shown the following message:

```
[Add this page to the Navigation view to display hyperlinks here]
```

After you add the Web page to the structure, the navigation bar shows the links (with the chosen style applied) based on the selection of radio buttons made in the Link Bar Properties dialog box. Like a custom link bar, the code of a Bar based on navigation structure is also hidden from the Code view. You can open the Web page in Notepad to view the actual code.

> **TIP** By using Notepad to see the actual code of the link bars, you can insert them on Web pages where SharePoint Designer would not support direct use of link bars, such as ASP.NET master pages.

Also, it's important to understand that link bars are author time components. This means that they don't need FPSE to be installed on the Web server to run properly. As long as you have the hidden metadata of the Web site, you should be able to get the link bar to work in a non-SharePoint, non-FPSE environment.

Understanding SharePoint Navigation Elements

SharePoint out of the box offers a number of controls that facilitate navigation across the Web site. Features such as Quick Launch bars, global navigation menus and tab controls, breadcrumb Web parts, etc., provide Web site designers with a number of ways to allow users to access content located across a Web site. The home page of a SharePoint Web site, as shown in Figure 14.4, has navigation controls and Web parts scattered all over the default Web page.

The Quick Launch bar is on the left pane, the site breadcrumb control is just above the content area, and the top navigation bar is just under the title of the Web page. Later in this chapter, I discuss how you can use these controls to your advantage while designing Web pages for SharePoint sites. Right now, though, I discuss the SharePoint interface for managing the navigation settings.

FIGURE 14.4

A SharePoint Web site using the Collaboration site template (available with MOSS)

Working with the Quick Launch bar

Whenever you create a new list, document library, or other forms of containers in SharePoint Designer, you have the option to add it to the Quick Launch bar. This bar is situated by default in many site templates on the left pane of the Web pages. Later in this section, the Quick Launch bar is implemented by using a set of controls (namely `<asp:SiteMapDataSource>` and `<SharePoint:AspMenu>`), which are at your disposal in SharePoint Designer to use on other Web pages or SharePoint Web part pages.

On WSS v3 sites, the Quick Launch bar and the Top Link bar can be edited in SharePoint Designer in a manner similar to the non-SharePoint navigation structure by using the Navigation pane. If you open a WSS v3 site and switch to the Navigation pane, the Quick Launch bar and the Top Link bar are shown there as the custom link bars. You can use the navigation pane to add new pages to the Quick Launch bars. Also, the WSS v3 site settings provide you with the Quick Launch bar and Top Link bar links under the Look and Feel section, as shown in Figure 14.5. Here, you can add or remove links from these bars.

To add new links to the Quick Launch bar, follow these steps:

1. Click the Quick Launch link in the Look and Feel section of the Site Settings page in the WSS v3 site.

2. In the Quick Launch Web page, click New Heading, type the URL and description of the link, and then click OK.

3. Click New Link, type the URL and description of the new link, and then specify the heading created in step 2.

 **NOTE** The Quick Launch bar and Top Link bar links aren't available in Site Settings for Office SharePoint Server 2007 templates, such as Collaboration and Publishing.

FIGURE 14.5

The Look and Feel section in the WSS v3 site by using the Team Site template

Exploring SharePoint site navigation settings

For Office SharePoint Server 2007–specific templates, such as Collaboration and Publishing, the SharePoint navigation settings are editable to a certain extent by using the SharePoint user interface accessible to users with appropriate permissions under Site Actions ➪ Site Settings ➪ Modify Navigation. As shown in Figure 14.6, the Site Navigation Settings page allows you to specify whether to include subsites and pages in the site navigation and provides an interface to add new headings and links to the site navigation.

FIGURE 14.6

The Site Navigation Settings page on a site based on the Collaboration template

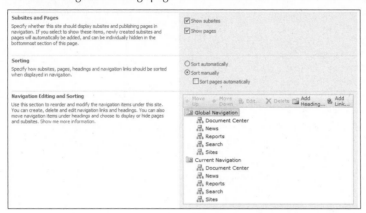

The settings that you make for this Web page apply to the tabbed top navigation menu that shows on the SharePoint Web pages just below the title of the Web site.

Working with Navigation Controls

In this section, I talk about a number of ASP.NET and SharePoint navigation controls that can be inserted on Web pages by using SharePoint Designer. SharePoint uses these navigation controls by default for its Quick Launch bar, top navigation menu, breadcrumb menus, etc. I start by helping you understand the nature of these navigation controls by showing you how they have been implemented on SharePoint sites. Later, you can use this understanding to create navigation menus on new Web pages.

Understanding navigation sources

To develop understanding about how SharePoint navigation controls are used in SharePoint sites, follow these steps:

1. **Open a SharePoint site that uses the Team Site template.** Open the `default.aspx` page for this site in the Split view.

2. **In the Design view, hover over the top navigation menu on the `default.aspx` Web page.** The `PlaceHolderHorizontalNav` content region is highlighted and shows the Common Tasks arrow.

3. **Click the arrow to open the Common Content Tasks menu and then click Create Custom Content.** The content region for editing on the `default.aspx` Web page opens.

4. **Click the top navigation menu in the** `PlaceHolderHorizontalNav` **content region.** The following code is highlighted in the Code view:

```
<SharePoint:AspMenu
      ID="TopNavigationMenu"
      Runat="server"
      DataSourceID="topSiteMap"
      EnableViewState="false"
      AccessKey="<%$Resources:wss,navigation_accesskey%>"
      Orientation="Horizontal"
      StaticDisplayLevels="2"
      MaximumDynamicDisplayLevels="1"
      DynamicHorizontalOffset="0"
      StaticPopoutImageUrl="/_layouts/images/menudark.gif"
      StaticPopoutImageTextFormatString=""
      DynamicHoverStyle-BackColor="#CBE3F0"
      SkipLinkText=""
      StaticSubMenuIndent="0"
      CssClass="ms-topNavContainer">
        <StaticMenuStyle/>
        <StaticMenuItemStyle CssClass="ms-topnav"
   ItemSpacing="0px"/>
        <StaticSelectedStyle CssClass="ms-topnavselected" />
        <StaticHoverStyle CssClass="ms-topNavHover" />
        <DynamicMenuStyle BackColor="#F2F3F4" BorderColor="#A7B4CE"
BorderWidth="1px"/>
        <DynamicMenuItemStyle CssClass="ms-topNavFlyOuts"/>
        <DynamicHoverStyle CssClass="ms-topNavFlyOutsHover"/>
        <DynamicSelectedStyle CssClass="ms-topNavFlyOutsSelected"/>
      </SharePoint:AspMenu>
```

In the HTML code of the `<SharePoint:AspMenu>`, notice the highlighted properties `DataSourceID` and the `StaticDisplayLevels`. The `DataSourceID` attribute specifies the data source that's being used for the navigation control.

5. **Scroll a little below this code in the Code view of the** `default.aspx` **page to find the following code:**

```
<asp:SiteMapDataSource
              ShowStartingNode="False"
              SiteMapProvider="SPNavigationProvider"
              id="topSiteMap"
              runat="server"
              StartingNodeUrl="sid:1002"/>
```

This is the code of the data source control being used by the `<SharePoint:AspMenu>` navigation control. The `id` attribute of the `<asp:SiteMapDataSource>` control is the same as the `DataSourceID` property specified in the `<SharePoint:AspMenu>` navigation control.

To summarize, the `<SharePoint:AspMenu>` navigation control shows the data provided by the `<asp:SiteMapDataSource>` data source control to generate the top navigation menu on the SharePoint Web page. While the navigation control being used here is SharePoint-specific, the `<asp:SiteMapDataSource>` data source control is a generic ASP.NET data control. You can use this data source control with other navigation controls, such as `<asp:Menu>` and `<asp:TreeView>`.

It's important to notice the `SiteMapProvider` property of the `<asp:SiteMapDataSource>` data source control. The value that you specify for this property determines the data that's passed on to the navigation control for display. Depending on the version of SharePoint you're working with, the `SiteMapProvider` property can have various values. For example, WSS v3 has the `SPNavigationProvider`, `SPSiteMapProvider`, `SPContentMapProvider`, and `SPXmlContentMapProvider` providers available for use out of the box.

In the next exercise, you use the understanding gained from the previous discussion to implement navigation on a new ASP.NET Web page in a SharePoint site.

Binding to ASP.NET data and navigation controls

The `<asp:SiteMapDataSource>` data source control is available for inserting on Web pages by using the Toolbox task pane in SharePoint Designer. To create navigation using this data source control on a new Web page in a SharePoint site, follow these steps:

1. **Choose File ⇨ New to create a new ASPX page in the SharePoint site you're working with.**

2. **In the Toolbox task pane, double-click the SiteMapDataSource control in the list of data controls under ASP.NET controls.** This inserts the data control on the Web page.

3. **Click the SiteMapDataSource control that you just inserted on the Web page.** The Tag Properties task pane shows you the properties of the control in a grid view.

4. **Type** SPSiteMapProvider **as a value for the** `SiteMapProvider` **attribute of the control.** Leave the rest of the properties as default.

5. **Using the Toolbox task pane, insert the Menu control from the Navigation controls under ASP.NET controls.** By default, when the control is inserted on the Web page, SharePoint Designer opens the Common Menu Tasks dropdown menu.

6. **In the Common Menu Tasks menu, click the Choose Data Source dropdown menu. Choose the ID of the SiteMapDataSource control inserted into the Web page in the previous steps.**

7. **Click the Auto Format link to open the Auto Format dialog box, choose the Professional scheme from the list of schemes, click Apply, and then click OK.**

8. **Save the Web page and then preview it in a browser.**

You now have a navigation bar that shows the list of sites inside the site where the Web page exists. Try changing the value of the `SiteMapProvider` to `SPNavigationProvider` and then notice the difference in the way the links in the menu appear.

> **NOTE**　The Design view doesn't refresh the page view when you change the value of the
> `SiteMapProvider`. To refresh the view, you have to close and reopen the Web
> page in SharePoint Designer.

You can also use the SiteMapPath navigation control to display a breadcrumb navigation control on the Web page using these steps:

1. Using the Toolbox task pane, insert the SiteMapPath navigation control on your ASPX Web page.

2. Choose the control in the Design view to see the list of control properties in the Tag Properties dialog box.

3. Type SPNavigationProvider as the value for the `SiteMapProvider` property.

4. Type 0 for the value of the `ParentLevelsDisplayed` property.

5. In the Styles category, use the `CurrentNodeStyle` property to apply formatting to the active node of the navigation control.

Exploiting SharePoint navigation controls

SharePoint exposes a number of custom controls that a Web designer can exploit for achieving the desired functionality without having to write too much code. However, the skill that you need is to find out the controls that you want to use by looking at the code of the Web page in SharePoint Designer and then exploit that code in another implementation on your Web site.

The following steps show how you can identify such controls and then use them specifically for your purpose. Two such controls specific to navigation for SharePoint sites are `<SharePoint:SP HierarchyDataSourceControl>` and `<Sharepoint:SPTreeView>`. While SharePoint Designer doesn't directly expose these controls for use, it doesn't prevent you from using them in the Code view of the Web page (although it might have some issues rendering them properly).

1. Using your Site Actions menu of your SharePoint site, click Create to open the Create Web page.

2. In the Web Pages section, click Web Part Page to create a new Web part page.

3. In the New Web Part Page Web page, type the name of the new Web part page, choose a page layout for this page, specify a document library where the page should be saved, and then click Create.

4. Open this SharePoint site in SharePoint Designer.

5. Using the Folder List task pane, navigate to the document library where you saved this page and then open it in SharePoint Designer.

6. Click the Code view tab of the Web page and then locate the `PlaceHolderMain` content region.

7. Within this content region, just after the closing table tag, add the following code:

```
<SharePoint:SPHierarchyDataSourceControl runat="server"
    id="TreeViewDataSource1" RootContextObject="Web" IncludeDiscussio
    nFolders="true"/>
<Sharepoint:SPTreeView id="WebTreeView1" runat="server"
    ShowLines="True" DataSourceId="TreeViewDataSource1"/>
```

8. Save the page and then preview it in a browser.

The control renders to show the list of document libraries and other content of the Web site. The treeview controls discussed here are placed just below the Quick Launch bar on the SharePoint Web page and become enabled for viewing on the Web page only when allowed by using the Tree View Web page in the Look and Feel section of the Site Settings page.

> **NOTE** Although SharePoint Designer might not be able to render the `SPTreeView` control properly in the Design view, the control should work in the Code view without issues. Any content that's newly added to the site is appended to the list shown by this control.

Summary

SharePoint Designer inherits the navigation structure components and link bars from FrontPage 2003. You can use these components on sites that allow hidden metadata. WSS v3 sites also allow for use of these navigation components. In this chapter, I discussed the SharePoint Designer navigation tools for SharePoint and non-SharePoint sites.

You also learned how you can use the Navigation pane to design structures. I discussed the internals of the navigation structure and its storage. I explained the Quick Launch bar and site navigation as well as how you use the SharePoint site settings pages to modify the navigation for Web sites.

Finally, I took you through some exercises to help you develop an understanding about how to use SharePoint and ASP.NET navigation controls on a Web site.

Part V

Driving with Data

Chapter 15

Managing Data Sources

I t's the nature and functionality of Web sites to provide information and present data in an easily understandable, intuitive, and attractive manner. Data is a record of information about something that needs to be stored for analysis or retrieval at a later point in time.

The standard storage mechanisms that current database technologies use for storing data don't keep it in a format that's easily comprehensible. You may find enormous tables containing millions of rows of data or large XML documents that may be even more difficult to read. The reasons are obvious: Storing data requires space (such as hard drives, magnetic tapes, etc.), and the cost of data storage increases as you use more space. Inherently, the success of software designed to store data lies in its ability to squeeze data as much as possible to use less hardware and, at the same time, quickly uncompress it for timely retrieval.

Such compression leaves data in sort of an encapsulated format that makes business decisions, analysis, and reporting difficult. The ability of a Web site to display data in an attractive way, thereby easing these operations, decides its success.

Understanding Data Sources

SharePoint Designer provides an easy interface for Web site designers to use standard Web technologies, such as ASP.NET 2.0, to connect to data sources and retrieve, format, and display data on Web pages. The functionality is driven by intuitive GUI (Graphical User Interface)–based wizards, and although you might need some understanding of ASP.NET, you most likely won't need to write a single line of code to be able to complete a standard data-driven Web site.

The basic steps involved in working with data are usually the same no matter what technology you choose. You do the following every time you work with a data source:

- **Use a data source control to connect to a source of data.** The source of data is usually a database for an MS-Access database file, an SQL Server database instance, or an XML file. In more complicated scenarios, you might be connecting to a server-side script or a Web service. The data source control uses a *connection string* to connect to the source of data. A connection string is a string of text that specifies information about connecting to a specific data source.

- **Using a data display control, connect to the data source control you set up to display the data.** You can modify, transform, or lay out (or any other term you like to use) data to make it look inviting. Usually, this is where you use your imagination and design skills to convert a row or table of data into what your end users would relish working with. Remember, developing a Web site is more art than science.

The data display control usually provides an interface to manipulate the data. However, it's mostly the job of the data source control to perform the manipulation of data on the actual data source.

One brilliant shift that SharePoint Designer now makes in contrast to its predecessors is that it doesn't use any proprietary approaches to provide database functionality to its users. The Database Results and Database Interface wizards (available in FrontPage), although powerful tools of their time, wrote a lot of proprietary code for working with databases. This code wasn't easily understood and added a layer of complexity for Web site designers. Who remembers deleting those files inside the _fpclass folder, thinking of them as nonessential, and thus causing havoc on Web sites?

NOTE   Although you can still edit your existing database results pages created in FrontPage 2003 by using SharePoint Designer, you can't directly add new database results pages to your Web sites. The entry point for the Database Results and Database Interface wizards isn't directly available in the SharePoint Designer user interface.

With SharePoint Designer, you can work directly with standard ASP.NET data controls to retrieve and display data on Web pages. The design surface provides a no-code interface to work with these controls to set up Web pages that display data. Behind the scenes, SharePoint Designer writes ASP.NET code to implement the functions for data retrieval. Advanced users can then switch to the Code view to modify or alter the code and further advance the functionality provided by the wizards.

Although SharePoint Designer is primarily focused on developing data-driven Web pages for SharePoint Web sites, it could very easily be used to work with data sources on non-SharePoint sites. This chapter discusses both SharePoint- and non-SharePoint-related data source options available in SharePoint Designer. I also help you understand how to use the Data Source Library task pane to create connections to data sources for later use by the available data source controls.

The three main pieces of any data-driven Web site were mentioned earlier in this chapter. The following section covers them in more detail. Figure 15.1 shows the relationship between the sources of data, data source controls, and data display controls.

FIGURE 15.1

FIGURE 15.1

View data sources, data source controls, and data display controls.

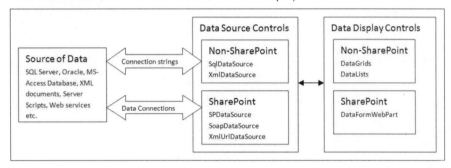

Available data sources

Depending on the Web site you're working with in SharePoint Designer, the list of available data sources might change. Here are the standard non-SharePoint data sources:

- **Database applications:** These include most commonly deployed database technologies, such as SQL Server, Oracle, MS-Access, or other sources that support ODBC/OLEDB connections.

- **XML documents:** You can make connections to the XML files that exist in the realms of the Web site in which you're working. SharePoint Designer allows you to import into your Web site any XML files that you want to use as data sources.

Besides these, SharePoint sites also expose the following data sources:

- SharePoint lists
- SharePoint libraries
- Server-side scripts
- XML Web services
- Business data catalogs from SharePoint sites
- Linked data sources

SharePoint sites only support OLEDB connections to data sources. This means that you can't specify ODBC connection strings for connection to data sources.

Data source controls

Most of the non-SharePoint data source controls that you can use in SharePoint Designer are ASP. NET 2.0–based. .NET Framework 2.0 needs to be installed on the computer to make these controls available in SharePoint Designer. These include the following:

- AccessDataSource
- SQLDataSource
- XMLDataSource
- SiteMapDataSource

These controls are accessible from the Toolbox task pane in SharePoint Designer. Don't worry if you find these controls baffling. They're discussed in much more detail with examples and scenarios in later chapters.

SharePoint sites expose special data source controls (for example, SPDataSource, SoapDataSource, etc.) to connect to SharePoint or non-SharePoint-related data sources (although you can still use standard ASP.NET data source controls in SharePoint sites, too). As discussed in later chapters, these data source controls aren't directly available in the SharePoint Designer user interface but are inserted behind the scenes as the result of working with the available data sources.

Data display controls

Like the data source controls, SharePoint Designer allows for the use of standard ASP.NET 2.0 data display controls. Most of the ASP.NET 2.0 controls that SharePoint Designer makes available can be bound to a data source control to display and work with data that the data source control offers.

For SharePoint sites, SharePoint Designer exposes a more powerful and robust XSLT-based (Extensible Stylesheet Language Transformations) data display control called DataFormWebPart. Chapter 17 is devoted to discussing this versatile tool.

Using the Data Source Library Task Pane

To utilize the available data sources, SharePoint Designer offers a single easy-to-use interface condensed into a single task pane called the Data Source Library. You can gain access to the Data Source Library task pane by choosing Data View ➪ Manage Data Sources in SharePoint Designer.

Another related task pane is the Data Source Details task pane that's used to work with the data exposed by a data source. Depending on which type of Web site you're working with, the Data Source Library interface changes to show or hide the available data sources.

For example, Figure 15.2 shows the Data Source Library task pane for a simple file system based on an FPSE-extended Web site.

However, if you have a SharePoint site open in SharePoint Designer, the Data Source Library has a larger number of data sources you could work with, as shown in Figure 15.3.

FIGURE 15.2

The Data Source Library for non-SharePoint sites

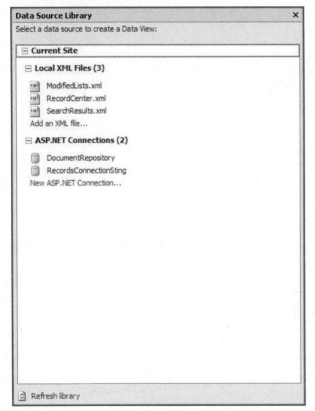

FIGURE 15.3

The Data Source Library for SharePoint sites

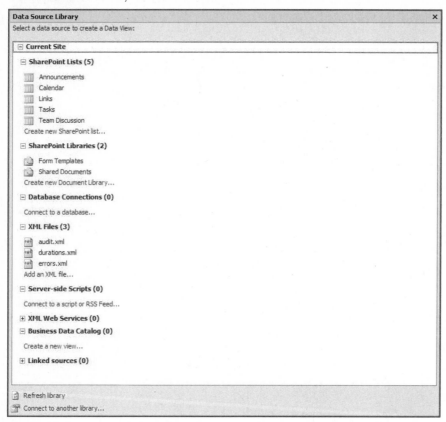

Working with Non-SharePoint Data Sources

When working with data sources in non-SharePoint Web sites, the following options are available in the Data Source Library task pane:

- Local XML files
- ASP.NET connections

The treeview appearance of the Data Source Library task pane allows for collapsing data sources in case the list of available data sources becomes long (which might become the case during extensive Web site development).

Local XML files

The Data Source Library is intelligent enough to list the existing XML files inside your Web site for you to use. As its name suggests, these XML files need to reside inside the Web site content location. If you want to use an XML file as the source of data for your Web site, you can do so by following these steps:

1. **Click the Add an XML file link in the Data Source Library task pane**. The Data Source Properties dialog box, as shown in Figure 15.4, opens, allowing you to choose the location of the XML you want to use.

 The Data Source Properties dialog box changes its user interface depending on the type of data source you're working with.

FIGURE 15.4

The Data Source Properties dialog box for XML files

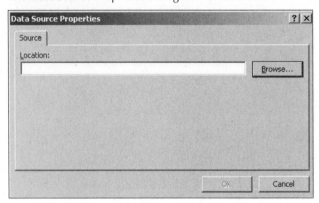

2. **Click Browse to open the Open dialog box and then navigate to the location where your XML file exists.**

3. **Select the XML file and then click Open.** Every time you select an XML file by using this process, SharePoint Designer asks if you want to import the XML file into the Web site content location. Because you need to have the XML file inside your Web site for use, the obvious answer is yes.

4. **Click ok when you receive the message box "To use <FileLocation/FileName> as a data source, you must import it into your Web site. Would you like to import the file now?"** This opens the Import dialog box, which allows you to select the location/ folder where the XML file should reside inside your Web site.

5. **Choose the desired location for the XML file and then click OK.** Apart from the XML file being imported into your Web site, SharePoint Designer also updates the Data Source Library task pane to show you the newly imported XML file along with the existing ones.

The only way now to delete the XML file from the Data Source Library is to remove it from the Web site. Click the Refresh Library link in the Data Source Library task pane to refresh the library after you delete the XML file.

6. **Hover over the newly added XML file, and SharePoint Designer displays a screen tip to show you the location of the XML file inside your Web site.** A dropdown menu to use the data source also appears.

7. **Click the newly added XML file.** A dropdown menu appears on the right.

> **NOTE** This dropdown menu is standard for the Data Source Library task pane and is available for all data sources. The available menu options change depending on the data source you choose from the task pane.

8. **Choose Show Data from the dropdown menu to open the Data Source Details task pane.** Here, you can see a preview of the data exposed by the XML file.

9. **Switch back to the Data Source Library task pane, open the dropdown menu again, and then choose Properties.** The Data Source Properties dialog box opens, which displays information about the XML file that you're working with.

> **CAUTION** If the XML file that you're working with is invalid, the Data Source Details task pane fails to display a preview of the data. You must ensure that the XML file is valid before it can be used. The Data Source Details task pane tries to provide you with a message indicating the problem that happened when trying to show the data from the XML file for troubleshooting purposes.

ASP.NET connections

The ASP.NET connections section in the Data Source Library task pane provides you with a no-code interface to start connecting to a number of data sources, such as SQL Server, Oracle, MS-Access, and other OLEDB/ODBC sources. What you can essentially make using the ASP.NET connections are *connections strings* that your data source controls can use later to connect to data sources.

Connection strings are important because they provide the underlying mechanism that enables you to work with data sources. The most basic ASP.NET connection string has at least the following components:

- The name of the data source to which you're connecting; for example, an SQL server database name

- The object in the database to which you want to make the connection; for example, a table name

- Information about the authentication mechanism to use; for example, a username and password

- The name of the data provider to use for making the connection

> **NOTE** The Web site www.connectionstrings.com shows examples of connection strings that could be used to connect to various data sources.

SharePoint Designer by default saves connection strings for non-SharePoint sites in the configuration section of the `web.config` file of your Web site (or ASP.NET Web application, as many developers like to call it). Whenever you create a connection string by using the Data Source Library task pane or other mechanisms, the connection string is placed in the `web.config` file, as shown in Figure 15.5, at the root folder of your Web site/Web application. If the `web.config` file doesn't exist in the root folder, SharePoint Designer creates one for you to use.

FIGURE 15.5

The Code view of a `web.config` file that's created when SharePoint Designer is used to create an ASP. NET connection

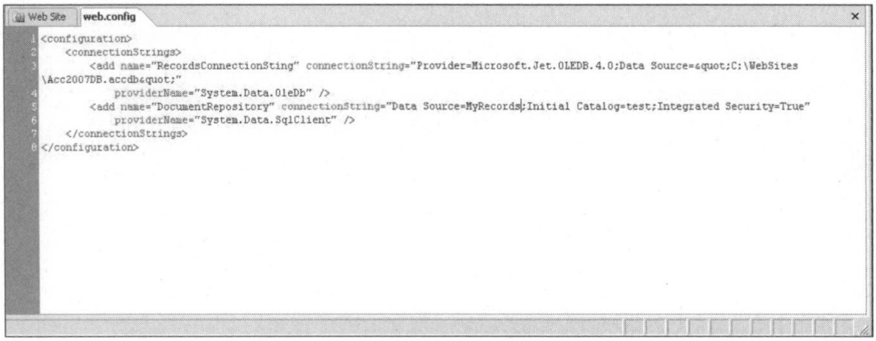

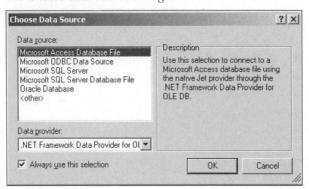

To create a new ASP.NET connection string, click the New ASP.NET Connection link in the Data Source Library. The Choose Data Source dialog box, as shown in Figure 15.6, opens. This is where you choose the data source to which you want to connect. The next set of dialog boxes changes depending on the selection you make here.

FIGURE 15.6

The Choose Data Source dialog box

Depending on the selection you make in the data source list, an appropriate set of data provider lists is made available in the data provider dropdown menu. Table 15.1 lists the available ASP.NET data provider options.

TABLE 15.1

Available Data Providers

Data Provider Name	Usage
.NET Framework Data Provider for ODBC	For connecting to various ODBC data sources or User or System Data Source Names
.NET Framework Data Provider for OLEDB	For connections to MS-Access database files or SQL Server 7.0 to SQL Server 2005 databases
.NET Framework Data Provider for SQL Server	Connections to SQL Server 2000–2005 database and attaching SQL Server database files
.NET Framework Data Provider for Oracle	Connecting to Oracle databases

To create an ASP.NET connection to an MS-Access Database and thereby understand the user interface and the resulting connection string, follow these steps:

1. **Click the New ASP.NET Connection link in the Data Source Library task pane.** The Choose Data Source dialog box opens.

2. **In the Data Source list, select the Microsoft Access Database file option.** The only option for Data Provider is .NET Framework Data Provider for OLEDB.

3. **Click OK.** The Connection Properties dialog box opens. This dialog box is specifically tailored for working with MS-Access database files.

NOTE   The interface of the Connection Properties dialog box changes depending on your selection of a data source, thus facilitating the creation of a corresponding connection string. The Data Source box shows your choice of data source. Clicking Change takes you back to the Choose Data Source dialog box to let you change your selection.

4. **Click Browse to open the Select Microsoft Database file dialog box.** Here, you can browse to the location where your MS-Access database resides.

5. **Select the database file and then click Open.** If your database file is protected with a username and password, type the username and password in the text fields provided.

6. **Click Advanced.** The Advanced Properties dialog box opens, allowing you to manually select or change the properties for the connection string. The steps you have followed until now have already filled in some properties, such as Data Provider, UserID, File Name, etc. The available properties also change based on the data source you chose.

7. **Click Test Connection to test whether the connection to the data source would succeed based on the information you provided in the Connection Properties dialog box.**

NOTE Depending on the data source you're working with, you might run into a number of problems while connecting to the data source. You're shown an appropriate message indicating the error SharePoint Designer received while trying to establish the connection to the data source by using the connection string.

8. Click OK to save your connection string to the Web site's `web.config` file.

The first thing you see when you finish creating the connection string is that the new connection is displayed in the Data Source Library task pane. If you want to change the properties of the connection, just click the connection, and a dropdown menu appears on the right. Choose Properties from this dropdown menu, and SharePoint Designer takes you back to the Connection Properties dialog box, where you can make the changes you desire. Or you can choose Delete to delete the connection and start over.

You should now be able to use this ASP.NET connection string inside a Data Source Control to connect to and work with the data provided by the data source.

CROSS-REF For more on ASP.NET data controls, see Chapter 16.

Right now, I take you through the steps for creating an ODBC connection to an MS-Access 2007 database file by using Data Source Names (DSN) through SharePoint Designer.

NOTE DSNs are an ODBC mechanism to locate and connect to data sources. There can be two types of DSNs: File or Machine. The machine data sources are machine-specific; that is, they can only be used on the machine where they're created. If you're authoring directly on your Web server, you can first create a machine data source on the Web server and then access it in SharePoint Designer for creating the connection string by using the Use user or system data source name dropdown menu.

Although SharePoint Designer provides for an interface for creating DSNs, you can also create them by choosing Start ➪ Administrative Tools ➪ Data Sources (ODBC). On Windows XP and Vista, you can access Administrative Tools by choosing Start ➪ Control Panel ➪ Administrative Tools.

For this exercise, it's assumed that you're authoring directly on your Web server and that the MS-Access 2007 database file resides inside the root content location of your Web site. Follow these steps:

1. **Click the New ASP.NET Connection link in the Data Source Library task pane.** The Choose Data Source dialog box opens.

2. **In the Choose Data Source dialog box, select Microsoft ODBC Data Source as the data source and then click OK.** The Connection Properties dialog box opens, which is customized for making connections to ODBC data sources.

3. **In the Connection Properties dialog box, select Use connection string and then click Build.** The Select Data Source dialog box opens.

4. **In the Select Data Source dialog box, click the Machine Data Source tab and then click New.** The Create New Data Source dialog box opens.

5. **In the Create New Data Source dialog box, select System Data Source (Applies to this machine only) and then click Next.**

6. **Select Microsoft Access Driver [*.mdb, *.accdb], click Next, and then click Finish.** The ODBC Microsoft Access Setup dialog box opens. You use this dialog box to specify the location of the MS-Access 2007 database file that you want to use for your ODBC connection.

7. **Type the name and description of the DSN by using the Data Source Name and Description text fields, respectively.**

8. **Inside Database section, click Select to open the Select Database dialog box.**

9. **Specify the location of your MS-Access 2007 database file and then click OK twice.** You should now see the newly created DSN in the list of Machine Data Sources.

10. **Select the newly created DSN and then click OK.** A Login dialog box opens that allows you to specify a username and password to use for the connection if required.

11. **Type the username and password if required (or leave them blank) and then click OK to return to the Connection Properties dialog box.**

12. **Click Test Connection to test your connection string and then click OK.** If the test succeeds, you're displayed the message "Test connection succeeded." In case of failure, an appropriate message indicating the cause of the failure is displayed.

13. **In the New Connection dialog box, type a name for your newly created connection and then click OK.**

You can now open the web.config file inside the root folder of your Web site to see the newly added connection string in the configuration section:

```
<configuration>
      <connectionStrings>
          <add name="ConnectionString1" connectionString="Dsn=MyAcc
essDSN;dbq=C:\WEBSITES\Acc2007DB.accdb;driverid=25;fil=MS Access;
maxbuffersize=2048;pagetimeout=5;uid=admin" providerName="System.
Data.Odbc" />
      </connectionStrings>
      </configuration>
```

Notice the providerName and connectionString attributes. These change depending on the type of data source that you choose and the settings you make in the Choose Data Source and Connection Properties dialog boxes.

While working with MS-Access databases is fun, most of the enterprise-level Web applications leverage the capabilities of a more robust and scalable database solution — for example, SQL Server or Oracle databases.

However, you can manage connections to these data sources as easily as you manage one for an MS-Access database file inside SharePoint Designer. The Connection Properties dialog box, where you make connections to SQL server databases, as shown in Figure 15.7, is very simple and requires only a few basic user inputs.

The Server Name dropdown menu provides a list of available SQL Server instances that could be found on the network to which your Web server machine is connected (if you're authoring directly to the Web server by using SharePoint Designer). You can either select one or type the name of the SQL Server instance that you want to use.

After you select the SQL Server, the Select or enter the database name dropdown menu inside the Connect to a database section is enabled and allows you to either select or type the name of the database to which you want to connect by using the connection. Or you can attach an SQL Server database file (*.mdf) to the SQL Server instance you selected earlier.

FIGURE 15.7

The Connection Properties dialog box for Microsoft SQL Server

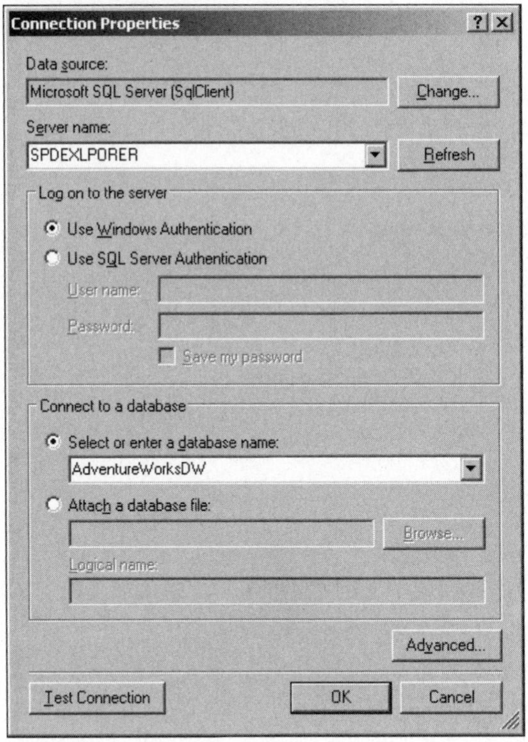

NOTE   The Log on to the server section is important here, as it allows you to choose what authentication mechanism you want to use to connect to the SQL Server instance. SQL Server supports either Windows Authentication or both Windows and SQL Server authentication. Based on how SQL Server is configured, you have to decide whether to use Windows Authentication or SQL Server Authentication. SQL Server Authentication (also known as Mixed Authentication) isn't as secure as Windows Authentication, and many database administrators endeavor to keep their servers set up for Windows Authentication.

Again, by clicking Test Connection, you can test if you can connect to the SQL Server instance successfully. If SharePoint Designer fails to connect to SQL Server due to a configuration issue, it displays a message indicating the probable cause of failure.

Exploring SharePoint Data Sources

The focus now shifts to understanding the functions of SharePoint Designer when working with SharePoint sites. As discussed earlier in this chapter, the SharePoint Designer interface is primarily designed to provide easy access to all the data sources exposed by SharePoint. Also, as discussed previously, there are a large number of data sources that you can use when working with SharePoint sites.

NOTE   Unless specified, a SharePoint site in this section refers to both MOSS and WSS v3 sites. There are some SharePoint Designer features that are MOSS-specific and are noted when encountered.

Configuring data retrieval services

SharePoint implements a mechanism that allows data source controls to interact with a large number of data sources by using Simple Object Access Protocol (SOAP) and XML Web services. These services are called data retrieval services and are installed with SharePoint. You can control some functions of the data retrieval services by using the Operation section of the SharePoint Central Administration Web site. To access these settings, open the SharePoint Central Administration Web site by choosing Start ➪ Administrative Tools ➪ SharePoint 3.0 Central Administration on a SharePoint Web server and then choose Operations ➪ Data Retrieval Service. This takes you to a Web page containing the settings for the data retrieval services, as shown in Figure 15.8.

While the default settings work for most SharePoint Designer operations, you might want to consider changing the following settings depending on your Web application:

- **Update Support:** To enable support for update queries when working with data sources in SharePoint Designer, click the Enable update query support check box.

- **Data Source Time-out:** This setting controls the duration after which the data retrieval service times out if it doesn't hear back from the data source it's trying to connect to. If you're trying to connect to a data source — for example, a Web service that takes a long time to respond — you might want to increase this setting. The time-out value is specified in seconds.

FIGURE 15.8

The Data Retrieval Settings page in the SharePoint Central Administration

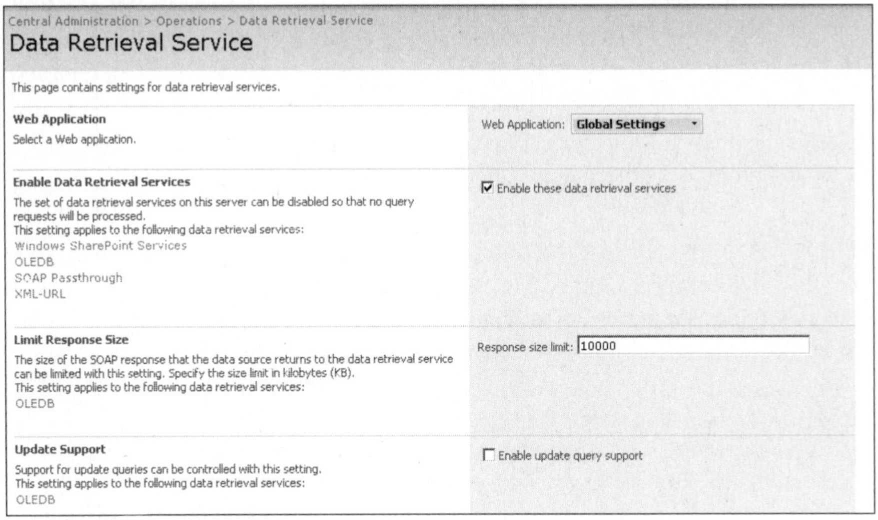

These properties can also be controlled using the `stsadm` command-line tool for SharePoint.

Creating SharePoint connection files

Unlike non-SharePoint sites, where the connection strings are stored in a `web.config` file inside the root content location of the Web site, connections to data sources in SharePoint sites are stored in a special document library that's hidden in the SharePoint user interface. This document library, called FPDataSources, is primarily used to store connections that have been created in SharePoint Designer. Unlike other document libraries you create in SharePoint, this document library doesn't have any views because, essentially, you don't need them.

The system of connections is also very different when compared to non-SharePoint sites. Rather than having connection strings, the FPDataSources library hosts XML files that each represents a single connection created with the Data Source Library task pane. To understand this better, I take you through the steps for creating a connection by using the Data Source Library task pane.

Connecting to XML Web services

For this exercise, you establish a connection to an XML Web service that SharePoint installs called `alerts.asmx` (SharePoint uses this Web service for its alerts functionality). Also, it's assumed that you're working with a SharePoint site that uses the Team Site template. Follow these steps:

1. Open a SharePoint site in SharePoint Designer.
2. Choose Data View ⇨ Manage Data Sources to open the Data Source Library task pane.

3. **Under the XML Web Services section, click Connect to a web service.** The Data Source Properties dialog box, as shown in Figure 15.9, opens. You can use this dialog box to specify settings for the connection to the `alerts.asmx` XML Web service.

4. **In the Data Source Properties dialog box, click the General tab.**

5. **In the Name text field, type a name for this connection, and in the Description text field, type a description for this connection.**

6. **Click the Login tab and then select the authentication mechanism that applies to your SharePoint site.** If you want to connect anonymously, click the Don't attempt to authenticate radio button.

7. **Click the Source tab.** This is where you specify the settings for the XML Web service to which you want to connect.

8. **In the Service description location text field, type the location of the** `alerts.asmx` **Web service.** This is usually `http://servername/_vti_bin/alerts.asmx`.

9. **Click Connect Now to let SharePoint Designer establish a connection to the Web service.** If your SharePoint site is configured correctly and you have access to the `alerts.asmx` Web service, SharePoint Designer automatically populates the Select Connection Info section.

10. **Leave the defaults for the Port and Operations text fields and then click OK.** The GetAlerts operation (also called Web method) doesn't require any parameters. For Web methods that have required or optional parameters, the Parameters (* required) list shows all the available parameters and allows you to set values for these parameters. The first thing you see is that the newly created connection is listed under the XML Web services section inside the Data Source Library. If you click the connection, a dropdown menu appears that now has many more options, which are discussed later in this chapter.

11. **Click Show Data to see the preview of the data exposed by the connection in the Data Source Details task pane.**

You can now look at the actual connection file that you created in this process. Using the Folder List task pane, expand the _catalogs folder. You see the FPDataSources document library, among others. Inside this FPDataSources library is an XML file corresponding to the connection that you just created. Double-click the file to open it in the Code view. As shown in Figure 15.10, this XML file is a connection file in the Universal Data Connection (UDC) format.

FIGURE 15.9

The Data Source Properties dialog box for connecting to XML Web services

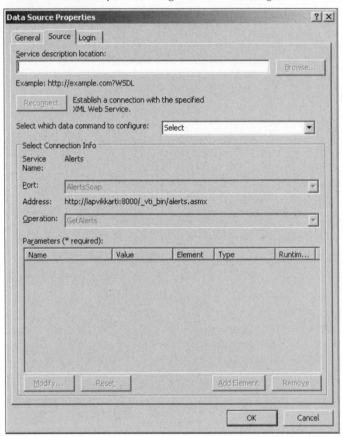

If you look closely, you see that all the settings for the connection that you chose in the Data Source Properties dialog box in the previous steps — for example, name, description, URL of the XML Web service, etc. — are saved in this XML file by using a format that can be understood by the SharePoint Data Retrieval Web Services.

FIGURE 15.10

A sample Universal Data Connection (UDC) connection file

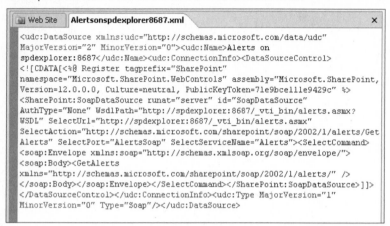

The interesting one to look at is the following excerpt from the code of the UDC connection file, which includes the name of the Web service, port, and Web method you used to define your connection:

```
<SharePoint:SoapDataSource runat="server" id="SoapDataSource"
    AuthType="None" WsdlPath="http://servername/_vti_bin/alerts.
    asmx?WSDL" SelectUrl="http://servername/_vti_bin/alerts.asmx"
    SelectAction="http://schemas.microsoft.com/sharepoint/
    soap/2002/1/alerts/GetAlerts" SelectPort="AlertsSoap" SelectServi
    ceName="Alerts"><SelectCommand><soap:Envelope xmlns:soap="http://
    schemas.xmlsoap.org/soap/envelope/"><soap:Body><GetAlerts
    xmlns="http://schemas.microsoft.com/sharepoint/soap/2002/1/
    alerts/" /></soap:Body></soap:Envelope></SelectCommand></
    SharePoint:SoapDataSource>
```

Understanding the nature of UDC files is important because if the SharePoint Designer user interface misbehaves for a particular data source, you can directly modify the XML UDC file to achieve the desired results.

CAUTION   You may notice later when you work with other data sources in the Data Source Library that usernames and passwords being used to access a data source may also be stored in these connection files. However, these credentials are viewable only by Web site authors. Obviously, the data source administrators want to make sure that you access the data source by using a common username and password. This ensures that multiple authors can't see each others credentials while working in SharePoint Designer.

If you right-click on the FPDataSources library and then choose Properties from the popup menu, you can see the properties for this library in the Document Library Properties dialog box. Click the Settings tab to see that the Hide from browsers check box is selected. If you deselect this check box, this document library appears in the list of document libraries in the SharePoint user interface. However, because this document library doesn't have any views, you're taken to the settings page for the document library.

Inside the Data Source Library, clicking the data connection displays an actions dropdown menu that allows you to work with the data connection you just created. As shown in Figure 15.11, the dropdown menu has the following menu options:

- **Show Data:** Like non-SharePoint sites, for data connections in SharePoint sites, this menu option takes you to the Data Source Details task pane, where you can see a preview of the data from the data connection and then create views and forms depending on the data connection you're working with.

- **Insert Data Source Control:** If you have an active Web page open in SharePoint Designer, this menu option allows you to add a data source control to the Web page. The data source control that you choose depends on the type of data connection. A SoapDataSource data source control is used for an XML Web service data connection, while an SPDataSource data source control is used for a SharePoint list or document library. I discuss these controls in later chapters.

- **Link to another Data Source:** This menu option provides a way to link this data source to another by using Linked Data Sources, as discussed later in this chapter.

- **Copy and Modify:** This menu option allows you to copy the existing data connection and modify properties for it. It opens the Data Source Properties dialog box corresponding to the data connection and allows setting properties for a copy of it.

- **Move to:** If you're connected to a Data Source Library on another SharePoint site by using the Connect to another library link at the bottom of the Data Source Library task pane, you can use this menu option to move the data connection to the other Data Source Library.

- **Save As:** This option allows you to save the XML data connection file associated with the connection to a location of your choice.

- **Mail Recipient (as Attachment):** This allows you to send the XML data connection file to someone — for example, a fellow author — via e-mail.

- **Remove:** This allows you to delete the data connection.

- **Properties:** This displays the Data Source Properties dialog box for modifying the properties of the existing data connection.

FIGURE 15.11

The Data Source Library dropdown actions menu

Connecting to databases

Now that you understand the underlying concepts behind data connections for SharePoint-based data sources, you can work with some of them. Start by creating a connection for the most commonly used data source, Databases. As with any other data source, you can create a connection to a database by using the Data Source Library task pane. Follow these steps:

1. **Click the Connect to a database link in the Data Source Library.** This displays a Data Source Properties dialog box that's now redesigned for a Database connection.

2. **Click the General tab to set the name and description of the data connection.**

3. **Click the Source tab and then click Configure Database Connection.** The Configure Database Connection dialog box, as shown in Figure 15.12, opens.

4. **In the Server Name text field, type the name of the database server to which you want to connect.** As mentioned earlier in this chapter, SharePoint only supports OLEDB connections.

5. **Depending on the database you want to connect to, select the appropriate provider name.** For SQL Server, for example, you can use the Microsoft .NET Framework Data Provider for SQL Server.

6. **Type the username and password to successfully authenticate to the database.**

CAUTION Due to some security implications, database connections for SharePoint sites don't allow use of Windows Authentication. The option to select Windows Authentication isn't available in the user interface. Internally, the use of Windows Authentication is detected if a connection string has Integrated Security or Trusted Connection strings specified it in. If you create such a connection string by selecting the Use custom connection string option, it's rejected by SharePoint.

7. **Click Next.** The message "The selected authentication option saves the username and password as clear text in the data connection. Other authors of this web site can access this information." appears. As indicated previously, the username and password are stored as text in the UDC data connection file.

8. **Click OK.** SharePoint Designer tries to establish a connection with the database you specified. If this succeeds, you proceed to the next step; otherwise, an error message indicating the cause of the failure appears. If the connection to the database is established, the Configure Database Connection dialog box, as shown in Figure 15.13, opens, with the interface enabled for you to select the object (for example, table, view, etc.) to which you want to connect.

FIGURE 15.12

The Configure Database Connection dialog box

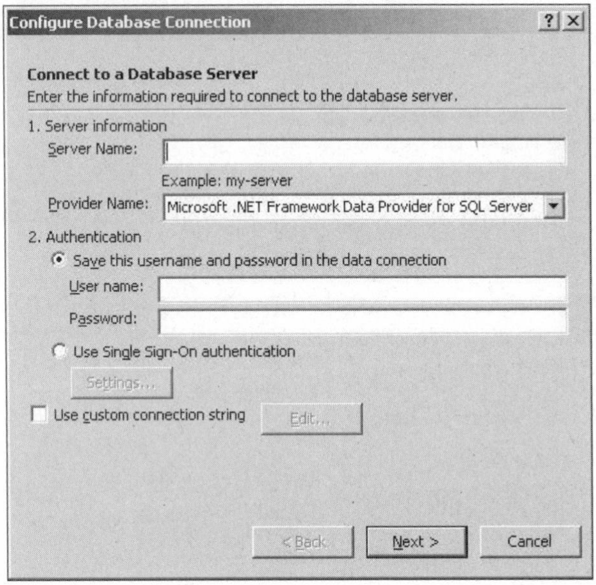

NOTE You can use an HTTP network tracing tool, such as Fiddler, to determine the response received from the server when SharePoint Designer tries to establish a connection to the database. If there's a failure, Fiddler shows you an HTTP 500 error (red in color) with a body having a SOAP message indicating the error response from SharePoint.

FIGURE 15.13

The Configure Database Connection dialog box with the list of databases and objects

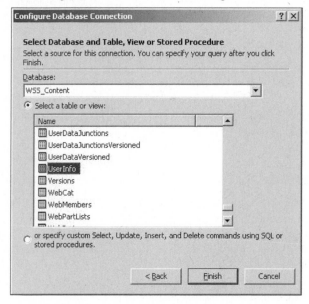

9. **In the Database dropdown menu, choose the name of the database the connection is for.** Selecting the database retrieves the list of tables and views in the Select a table or view list.

10. **Using the Select a table or view list, select the table or view you want to use for this data connection.**

TIP You can use the "or specify custom Select, Update, Insert, and Delete command by using SQL or stored procedures." option to specify your own SQL statement or use stored procedures inside the database. This option takes you to the Edit Custom SQL Commands dialog box, which has the Edit Command button that can be used to add custom SQL statements, store procedures, and specify parameter sources (for example, `from Query String`, `Cookies`, `Form`, etc.) and their default values.

11. **Click Finish.** This takes you back to the Data Source Properties dialog box, as shown in Figure 15.14, where you see options for selecting fields, sorting, and filtering in the Query section. The Query section allows you to further extend the query for the data connection that you have been creating in this exercise.

NOTE The Filter and Sort buttons in the Query Section provide filtering and sorting capabilities using the Filter Criteria and Sort dialog boxes right at the data connection level. I discuss the interface for these dialog boxes in more detail in Chapter 17.

12. **Click Fields to display the Displayed Fields dialog box.**

13. **If you want to remove any fields from the connection, select them in the Displayed Fields list and then click Remove.** If you try to remove any primary key fields from the list, a message warns you that the field chosen for removal is a primary field. Although you can remove a primary key field, you might want to consider keeping it because it might be useful for establishing relationships between data sources. Also, you can click Move Up and Move Down to change the order in which the fields appear.

14. **Click OK twice to complete the data connection.** The newly created database connection appears in the Data Source Library, and the associated XML data connection file appears in the FPDataSources library.

15. **Click the database connection and then click Show Data to see the preview of the data exposed by the database connection in the Data Source Details task pane.** If you open the XML data connection file in the FPDataSources dialog box, you see your UDC connection. The following excerpt of code is from the connection file:

```
<asp:SqlDataSource id="SqlDataSource1" runat="server" __
designer:commandsync="true" ProviderName="System.Data.
SqlClient" ConnectionString="Data Source=sqlDataBase;User
ID=username;Password=P@ssw0rd;Initial Catalog=WSS_Content;"
SelectCommand="SELECT [tp_SiteID], [tp_ID], [tp_DomainGroup],
[tp_GUID], [tp_SystemID], [tp_Deleted], [tp_
ExternalTokenLastUpdated], [tp_Locale], [tp_CalendarType], [tp_
AdjustHijriDays], [tp_TimeZone], [tp_Time24], [tp_
AltCalendarType], [tp_CalendarViewOptions], [tp_WorkDays], [tp_
WorkDayStartHour], [tp_WorkDayEndHour] FROM [UserInfo] " />
```

FIGURE 15.14

The Data Source Properties dialog box of a finished database connection

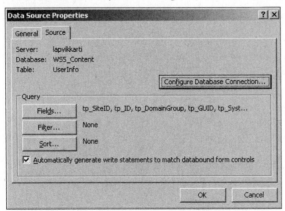

The ASP.NET `SqlDataSource` with the `ProviderName`, `ConnectionString`, and `SelectCommand` attributes are set here for the database connection. If you set any filtering or sorting by using the Query Section in the Data Source Properties dialog box, you see it take effect in the `SelectCommand` (as a `WHERE` clause or an `ORDER BY` clause, respectively).

One important thing to notice in the Configure Database Connection dialog box is the Use Single Sign-On authentication option. SSO (Single Sign-On) is a SharePoint mechanism that provides for Web sites users to authenticate only once and then receive access to all resources associated with the Web site without being prompted again.

Using SharePoint administration tools, your SharePoint administrator can create an SSO application with a username and password. You use this application name, username, and password in SharePoint Designer to authenticate to SharePoint and create database connections. The Settings button in the Configure Database Connection dialog box allows you to specify these SSO settings in SharePoint Designer.

 SSO is only available as an option in SharePoint Designer if you have the Enterprise features enabled for SharePoint, and it requires some SharePoint server configuration.

Given that you can't use Windows Authentication to create database connections in SharePoint sites by using SharePoint Designer, SSO becomes the most secure authentication mechanism that SharePoint offers to connect to databases.

Other data sources that need mention here are the server-side scripts, Business Data Catalogs, and linked data sources.

Connecting to server-side scripts

You can use this data connection type to connect to either a server-side script, such as an ASPX page exposing information using an HTTP POST, or a Really Simple Syndication (RSS) feed.

The Data Source Library offers the use of the SharePoint XmlUrlDataSource through the Connect to a script or RSS Feed option. To understand this better, you can use this option to connect to an RSS feed of your SharePoint site's Announcements list, assuming that you're using a Team Site template for this exercise. Follow these steps:

1. Determine the URL for the RSS feed of your Announcements list.
2. Browse to your SharePoint site and then click Lists in the Quick Launch bar.
3. In the All Site Content page, click the Announcements list.
4. Click the Actions menu and then click View RSS Feed to display the list feed URL in the browser.
5. Using the address bar, copy the URL for the RSS feed — for example, `http://servername/sites/myteamsite/_layouts/listfeed.aspx?List=%7BED687BBE%2DAD68%2D40B4%2D83C4%2D51683BBBBE39%7D`.

6. Open the site in SharePoint Designer, and using the Data Source Library task pane, click Connect to a script or RSS Feed.

7. Click the General tab to specify the name and description of the data connection.

8. Click the Source tab, and because you're going to retrieve the RSS data, select HTTP Get in the HTTP method dropdown menu. The HTTP Post option can be used here to send POST requests to server-side scripts (with parameters if required).

9. Copy the RSS Feed URL in the Enter the URL to the server-side script text field and then click OK.

From the FPDataSources library in the Folder List task pane, open the newly created XML data connection to the RSS feed. The following code appears for the data connection:

```
<SharePoint:XmlUrlDataSource runat="server" id="XmlUrlDataSource"
    AuthType="None" HttpMethod="GET" selectcommand="http://servername/
    sites/myteamsite/_layouts/listfeed.aspx"><SelectParameters><asp:P
    arameter Name="List" __designer:runtime="yes"
    DefaultValue="{ED687BBE-AD68-40B4-83C4-51683BBBBE39}" /></
    SelectParameters></SharePoint:XmlUrlDataSource>
```

As indicated earlier, the SharePoint XmlUrlDataSource data source is used here to set up the data connection. The selectcommand parameter specifies the RSS feed's URL, and the DefaultValue parameter specifies the Globally Unique Identifier (GUID) of the list that corresponds to the RSS feed.

The Data Source Properties dialog box provides you with the interface to specify any parameters that you might need to pass to a server script or RSS feed. The user interface is simple: Click Add to open the Parameter dialog box and then specify the name and default value for the parameter. Select the "The value of this parameter can be set via Web Part Connection" option if you need to set the value of the parameter by using a Web part connection.

 For more on Web Part Connection, see Chapter 18.

Connecting to Business Data Catalogs

Business Data Catalog (BDC) is a great feature offered by MOSS 2007 that allows for a no-code technique to present data from a range of back-end databases as well as Line of Business (LOB) applications and services. It provides a mechanism to show data from such applications into SharePoint lists and Web parts.

BDCs are only available as an option for use in the Data Source Library task pane if a Shared Services Provider (SSP) is configured for the SharePoint server you're using. BDC functionality is exposed in SharePoint through SSPs. Because SSP is an Office Server feature, you can't use BDCs on a WSS-only SharePoint site.

Although your SharePoint administrator would be responsible for most of the BDC configuration and setup on the SharePoint server, you need to be familiar with the following terms for using SharePoint Designer against BDC data sources:

■ **Application:** A computer application that runs in an enterprise environment and provides key business purposes to the organization. An application is added to the BDC by using the SharePoint SSP interface and an application definition file that describes the connection strings, authentication mechanisms, and other information needed to connect to the application.

■ **Entity:** The list of objects provided by the application. Commonly used entities could be objects such as products, orders, etc.

To create a connection to a BDC, follow these steps:

1. **Click Create a new view inside Business Data Catalogs in the Data Source Library task pane.** The Data Source Properties dialog box for BDC data connections opens.

2. **Click the General tab and then type the name and description for the data connection.**

3. **Click the Source tab.** The Select an application dropdown menu shows the list of available applications. Choose the one you want to use for the view.

4. **Based on the application you selected, the entities are displayed in the Select an entity dropdown menu.** Select the entity you want to use for your view.

5. **Click the Filter button in the Query section to specify any filter criteria for this view.**

6. **Click OK.** Use the Show Data menu option to preview the data from the BDC.

Connecting to linked data sources

Linked data sources provide a mechanism to link two or more existing data sources to aggregate the data provided by them in a consolidated view of data. They can be very useful when you want to display data from multiple data sources in a single view.

You can link any of the data sources available to use in the Data Source Library. You can even link two linked data sources to combine their data into a single view. Follow these steps:

1. **To link two data sources, either click one of them in the Data Source Library and then click Link to another Data Source or simply click Create a new Linked Source.** The Data Source Properties dialog box opens. If you selected the first method, you see that one data source already exists in the Component source properties list.

2. **Click the General tab to set the name and description of the data connection.**

3. **Click the Source tab and then click Configure Linked Source.** The Link Data Sources Wizard, as shown in Figure 15.15, opens.

4. **Click Add to select and add the data sources you want to link and then click Next.**

5. **If you want to sort, group, or filter on the resulting dataset as one long list option, click the Merge the contents of the data sources radio button.** This option simply merges the data from the chosen data sources into a single large list irrespective of any field or column matches.

6. **To display the data in a parent-child subview appearance, click the Join the contents of the data sources by using the Data Source Details to insert data views and joined subviews radio button.** This option allows for selecting fields or columns that contain matching data to join the data sources based on a relationship. The Link Data Sources Wizard shows you an interface for selecting columns containing matching data and choosing the displayed fields.

7. **Click Finish and then click OK to complete the creation of the linked data source.**

FIGURE 15.15

The Link Data Sources Wizard

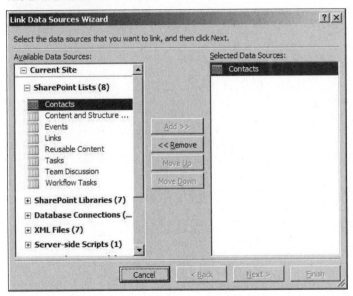

NOTE One of the primary reasons for creating linked data sources is to be able to create subviews and joined subviews. Linked or aggregate data sources can only be used to create views (read only) of data. SharePoint Designer currently doesn't support form (read/write) capabilities for linked data sources. I discuss creating these views in Chapter 17.

Connecting to other data source libraries

One really cool feature that the Data Source Library task pane offers for SharePoint sites is the ability to connect to and use data connections in data source libraries from other SharePoint sites. Follow these steps:

1. **Click the Connect to another library link in the Data Source Library task pane to connect to other SharePoint sites.** The Manage Library dialog box opens.

2. **Click Add to open the Collection Properties dialog box.**

3. **Type a Display name for this data source library and the location of the site (in the format** `http://servername/sitename`**) whose data source library you want to connect to.**

4. **Click OK twice to exit the Manage Library dialog box.** The Data Source Library from the other site is listed in the Data Source Library task pane.

You can now perform all the Data Source Library operations, such as showing data, creating linked data sources, etc., on these available data connections in a single interface.

The expand/collapse signs (+/- signs next to the Display name of the data source library) become handy because the list of available data source libraries increases in the Data Source Library task pane.

CAUTION   It's highly recommended that you use this feature for working with sites within the same site collection. Although you should be able to connect to and work with other SharePoint site collections or Web applications, you might notice a number of problems while doing so.

Working with the Data Source Details Task Pane

After you create your data connection by using the Data Source Library task pane, you normally switch to the Data Source Details task pane, as shown in Figure 15.16, to work with the data provided by the connection.

The easiest way to open the Data Source Details task pane corresponding to a data connection is to click it and then click the Show Data menu option.

NOTE   If SharePoint Designer encounters an error while trying to display data from a previous data connection, it won't be able to refresh the Data Source Details task pane until it determines the data to display for the current data connection. The Stop icon in the standard toolbar is lit during this time.

The current data source you're working with is shown in the Current Data Source section at the top of the Data Source Details task pane.

In the following list, the data (with values) from the data source is displayed. If there are multiple items, you can view them by using the left and right arrows in the top-right corner in the list. You can hide the data values by deselecting the Show data values check box, which gives you a little more real estate to work within the list if you have a large number of fields and columns displayed. The Related Data Sources menu shows the list of related data sources and allows for linking the shown data source to others.

FIGURE 15.16

The Data Source Details task pane

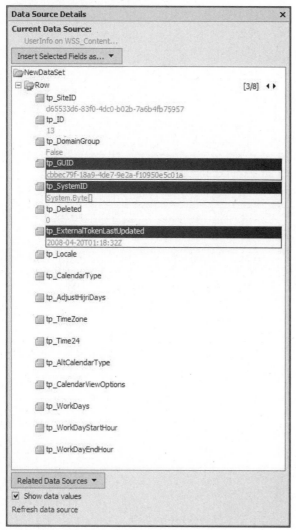

If you have an active Web page open in SharePoint Designer, the Insert Selected Fields As menu is enabled and allows you to insert a view or form on the Web page. The following options are available depending on the data source with which you're working:

- Single Item View
- Multiple Item View
- Single Item Form
- Multiple Item Form
- New Item Form
- Subview
- Joined Subview

I discuss each of these in more detail in Chapter 17.

Finding Data Sources

In case you're connected to a number of data source libraries from different SharePoint sites, it might be difficult for you to find a data source connection by using the Data Source Library task pane. To facilitate this, SharePoint Designer provides a Find Data Source task pane, as shown in Figure 15.17.

The Find Data Source task pane allows you to search data sources in all the data source libraries that you have added to the Data Source Library task pane. Simply type the full name (or the part of it you remember) of the SharePoint list, library, or data connection and then click Search Now.

The Search Results list displays the list of data sources that SharePoint Designer finds. Clicking on the data connection displays a dropdown action menu, which is similar to the one available through the Data Source Library task pane, that you can use to work with the connection.

FIGURE 15.17

The Find Data Source task pane

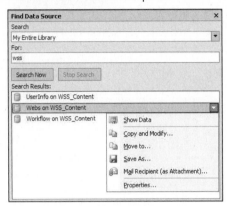

Summary

This chapter focused primarily on creating and managing data sources for non-SharePoint and SharePoint sites. You learned how to use the SharePoint Designer interface to create connection strings in non-SharePoint sites and UDC data connections in SharePoint sites.

While it gave you a background on exploiting data sources available for non-SharePoint and SharePoint sites, it also set the pace for the later chapters where I discuss how to use data from these data sources to develop interactive, data-based Web pages.

Chapter 16

Using ASP.NET Data Controls

IN THIS CHAPTER

Working with data source controls

Displaying data with ASP.NET data controls

Using ASP.NET controls with SharePoint data sources

Now that you're familiar with using SharePoint Designer's Data Source Library task pane to create database connections to data sources, the next step toward creating dynamic data-driven Web pages is to place the data exposed by these data sources on the Web pages and then to format the data as per your requirements. SharePoint Designer allows Web designers to use ASP.NET 2.0 data source and data display controls to work with the data exposed by data connections. Using a simple Visual Studio–like interface, you can insert ASP.NET 2.0 data controls, bind them together to retrieve data, and then show that data on Web pages. This chapter takes you through a number of ASP.NET data controls available in SharePoint Designer. You can use these controls to display and format data on Web pages.

Like other ASP.NET controls discussed before, it's important to understand that SharePoint Designer merely provides a user interface to work with the data controls, set their properties, and bind them with each other. Each ASP. NET data control has an HTML representation that defines the control and the properties and attributes that it exposes.

Internally, SharePoint Designer writes the HTML code that facilitates the ASP.NET rendering of these controls at browse time. SharePoint Designer doesn't provide for a mechanism to write ASP.NET code-behind files. It's just that some of these ASP.NET controls are so powerful that you don't really need to write any code-behind files to use them for displaying data and changing the formatting and appearance on the Web pages.

NOTE ASP.NET code-behind files written in .NET languages, such as C# and VB.NET, provide a mechanism to program the functionality of Web pages and the controls inserted on them.

Before you begin, here's a quick recap on the steps that are involved in working with data in ASP. NET 2.0:

- Create an ASP.NET connection string that defines the mechanism to be used to connect to a data source. You do this in SharePoint Designer by using the Data Source Library as discussed in the previous chapter.

- Use an ASP.NET data source control to define how the data is retrieved and what operations are performed on the data source. The SharePoint Designer Toolbox task pane exposes a number of data source controls for a variety of data sources.

- Bind the ASP.NET data source control to a data display control to format the appearance of data that's being exposed by the data source control. ASP.NET data display controls are also available in SharePoint Designer by using the Toolbox task pane.

Working with Data Source Controls

ASP.NET 2.0 provides new data source controls that expose data from a number of data sources to data display controls on Web pages. Data source controls aren't actually shown on the Web pages at browse time and are back-end providers of data to data display controls. But they're very powerful and provide you with capabilities to perform a lot of data retrieval and manipulation operations, such as inserting, updating, deleting, sorting, and filtering, without having to write any code.

By default, the following data source controls are provided by ASP.NET 2.0:

- **SQLDataSource:** Allows for connection to an ADO.NET SQL database provider, such as SQL Server, OLEDB, ODBC, Oracle, etc. The properties exposed by this data source control allow you to specify queries to the back-end database, which are then stored directly on the Web page code.

- **ObjectDataSource:** Not available in SharePoint Designer, this data source control is aimed at three-tier architecture for data retrieval, where the business logic for querying data is implemented separately rather than having it directly in the Web page code (as in the case of SQLDataSource).

- **XMLDataSource:** Allows you to expose data from XML files

- **AccessDataSource:** Derived from the SQLDataSource, this control provides properties that allow you to specify the MS-Access database filename directly while creating the data source control.

- **SiteMapDataSource:** Allows you to retrieve data from the ASP.NET site navigation hierarchy and then bind it to data display controls for navigation

This section takes you through a number of exercises to help you understand how data source controls are configured by using SharePoint Designer. I focus on non-SharePoint data sources first; later, the same concepts can be applied when working on SharePoint sites.

Using ASP.NET connections

After you create your ASP.NET connections by using the Data Source Library task pane, you can use them in your data source controls. The most commonly used data source control is the SQLDataSource control because of its capabilities to connect to a large number of back-end database servers. The next exercise walks you through the steps needed to set up the SQLDataSource to use an ASP.NET connection string. It's assumed that you already have an ASP.NET connection string to a SQL database created with the Data Source Library task pane. You can set the SQLDataSource control properties to retrieve a set of records from a table in a database by following these steps:

1. **Create a new ASPX page inside your Web site by using the New dialog box and then open it in the Design view.**

2. **Choose Task Panes ⇨ Toolbox to open the Toolbox task pane.**

3. **In the Toolbox task pane, expand the Data section in the ASP.NET controls to view the list of available data controls, as shown in Figure 16.1.**

FIGURE 16.1

The list of available data controls in SharePoint Designer

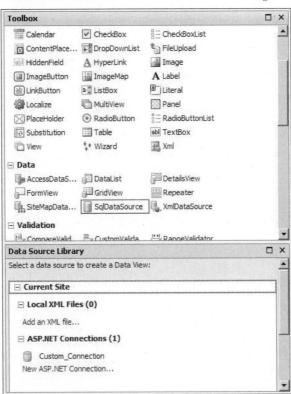

---

4. **Ensure that the cursor is placed in the Design view and then double-click the SQLDataSource control to insert it on the Web page.** Alternatively, you can drag and drop the control from the Toolbox task pane to the Web page. As shown in Figure 16.2, when the control is inserted on the page, the Common SqlDataSource Tasks menu appears in the Design view. You can use the small arrow on the SQLDataSource control to show and hide the Common SqlDataSource Tasks menu.

FIGURE 16.2

The Common SqlDataSource Tasks menu

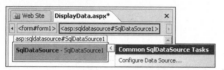

5. **Click the Configure Data Source link in the Common SqlDataSource Tasks menu to open the Configure Data Source dialog box, as shown in Figure 16.3.**

FIGURE 16.3

The Configure Data Source dialog box

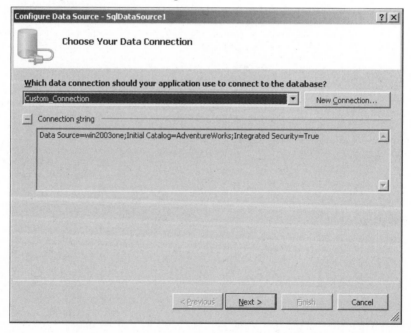

6. **From the dropdown menu in the Data Source Library task pane, choose the ASP. NET connection you created.** You can also click New Connection to quickly create a new ASP.NET connection. If you want to view the connection string in the ASP.NET connection, click the plus (+) sign next to Connection string.

7. **Click Next.** This takes you to the Configure the Select Statement screen in the Configure Data Source dialog box. As shown in Figure 16.4, you can use this screen to either specify a custom SQL statement or choose a table or view in the database exposed by the ASP. NET connection.

8. **For this exercise, choose a table from the Name dropdown menu.** This shows the column names in the table.

9. **Choose the columns you want to retrieve for display by using the Columns list.**

10. **Click the Return only unique rows check box to show only distinct records.** The SQL SELECT statement is shown in the SELECT statement box at the bottom of the Configure Data Source dialog box.

11. **Click Next.** The Test Query screen in the Configure Data Source dialog box opens. You can quickly test the select query by clicking the Test Query button. If the query succeeds, you see the list of records that the SQLDataSource retrieves from the table.

12. **Click Finish to complete the configuration of the SQLDataSource control.**

FIGURE 16.4

The Configure the Select Statement screen

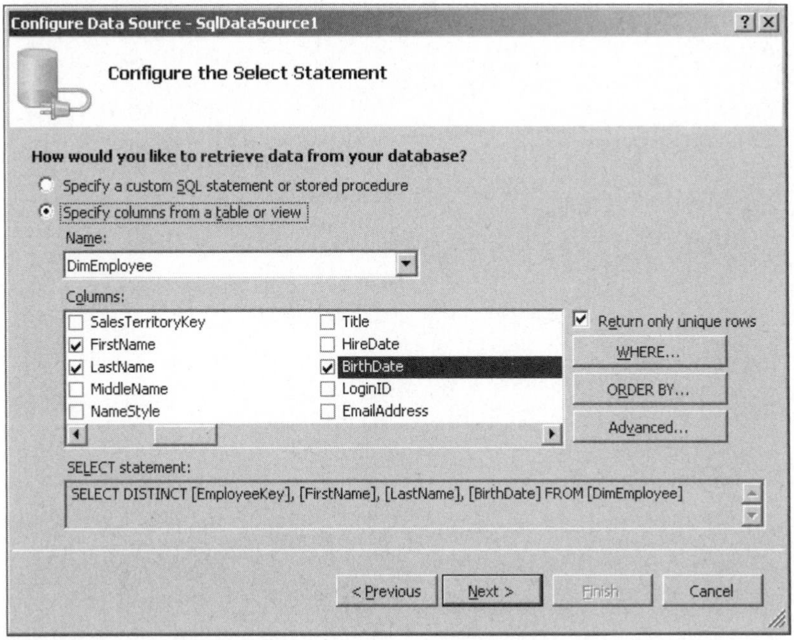

After you insert the control on the Web page, click the Code view tab in SharePoint Designer to view the code that was inserted and configured using the previous steps. The following is a sample code for the SQLDataSource configured to retrieve a set of records by using a SELECT statement:

```
<asp:SqlDataSource runat="server" id="SqlDataSource1"
    ConnectionString="<%$ ConnectionStrings:Custom_Connection %>"
    SelectCommand="SELECT DISTINCT [EmployeeKey], [FirstName],
    [LastName], [BirthDate] FROM [DimEmployee]">
    </asp:SqlDataSource>
```

SharePoint Designer automatically gives the control a unique ID. The previous steps set the ConnectionString and the SelectCommand properties of the SQLDataSource control.

Setting data source control properties

As shown in Figure 16.5, you can use the Tag Properties task pane to view and modify the properties of the data control using a Visual Studio–like interface.

For example, if you want to use a provider name other than the one specified in the ASP.NET connection that the SQLDataSource is using, you can change the ProviderName property by using the Tag Properties task pane. As shown in Figure 16.6, the properties of the controls that have been manually set are displayed in blue.

FIGURE 16.5

The Tag Properties task pane for the SQLDataSource control

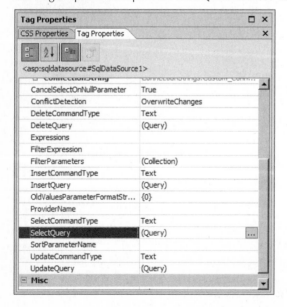

FIGURE 16.6

Changing control properties in the Tag Properties task pane

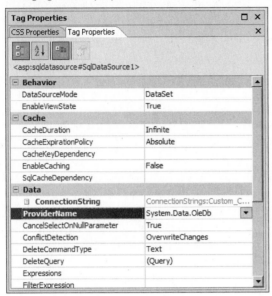

After you change the property by using the Tag Properties task pane, a new property in the HTML code for the control appears in the Web page:

```
<asp:SqlDataSource runat="server" id="SqlDataSource1"
    ConnectionString="<%$ ConnectionStrings:Custom_Connection %>"
    SelectCommand="SELECT DISTINCT [EmployeeKey], [FirstName],
    [LastName], [BirthDate] FROM [DimEmployee]" ProviderName="System.
    Data.OleDb">
    </asp:SqlDataSource>
```

While this code is a simple SELECT statement retrieving a number of columns from a table, you can use the SharePoint Designer interface of the SQLDataSource control to create advanced queries. In the next exercise, you create an advanced query for data retrieval that receives inputs via a query string to filter records from a table in a database. Follow these steps:

> **NOTE** A query string is a mechanism offered in HTTP to pass information in a name-value pair format in the URL to a Web server to facilitate logical processing. For example, in the URL www.servername.com/default.aspx?ID=1&Format=string, the query string is the portion of the URL after the question mark and has two name-value pairs (ID=1 and Format=string) separated by an ampersand.

1. Create an ASPX page, open it in the Design view, and then use the Toolbox task pane to insert the SQLDataSource control on the Web page.

2. Click Configure Data Source in the Common SqlDataSource Tasks to open the Configure Data Source dialog box.

3. Specify the ASP.NET connection and then click Next.

4. Choose the table from which you want to get the records and the columns that need to be shown in the results.

5. **Click Where to open the Add WHERE Clause dialog box.** You use this dialog box to specify the parameters that you want to use to filter the records returned. Additionally, as the criteria that you're filtering the records on are received from a query string, you set those parameters by using this dialog box. As shown in Figure 16.7, the Add WHERE Clause dialog box allows you to choose the columns that become part of your filter criteria.

6. Using the Column dropdown menu, choose the column that's part of your filter criteria.

7. **Specify the operator you want to use for the comparison by using the Operation dropdown menu.** Depending on the field type, the number of operators that can be used changes. For example, you can't use the CONTAINS operator for columns of field type Number.

8. **In the Source dropdown menu, choose QueryString as the source from where the value for the comparison is received.** You can receive values for comparison from controls, cookies, forms, profiles, and sessions. When you choose Query String, the Parameter Properties section, as shown in Figure 16.8, opens, allowing you to type the name and default value for the QueryString parameter.

9. **Type the name of the parameter in the QueryString field text field and then specify a default value in the Default value text field.** The dialog box builds the SQL expression and the value with the inputs you type.

10. **Click Add to complete the creation of the expression of comparison by using inputs from the Query String.**

11. **Repeat the previous steps to create multiple expressions by using a query string as source.** Once done, the Add WHERE Clause dialog box should look like the one in Figure 16.9.

12. Click OK to complete the creation of the SELECT statement and then click Next.

13. **Click Test Query.** A Parameter Values Editor dialog box opens, allowing you to change the values you want to use for the filtering of records. The parameters have the default values specified when the dialog box opens.

14. **Specify the values for the filtering and then click OK.** If the query succeeds, you see the filtered results in the Test Query screen.

15. Click Finish to complete the configuration of the SQLDataSource control.

FIGURE 16.7

The Add WHERE Clause dialog box

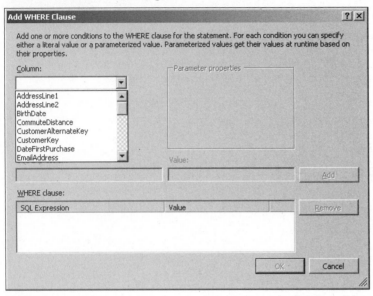

FIGURE 16.8

Specifying `QueryString` parameters in the Add WHERE Clause dialog box

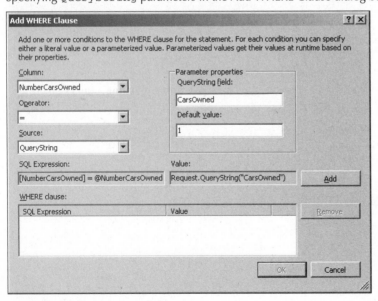

To view the changes that were made to the SQLDataSource control's code using the previous steps, click the Code view tab. Here's a sample code:

```
<asp:SqlDataSource runat="server" id="SqlDataSource1"
    ConnectionString="<%$ ConnectionStrings:Custom_Connection %>"
    SelectCommand="SELECT DISTINCT [CustomerKey], [Title],
    [FirstName], [LastName], [BirthDate], [Gender], [EmailAddress]
    FROM [DimCustomer] WHERE ((([NumberCarsOwned] = @NumberCarsOwned)
    AND ([TotalChildren] = @TotalChildren) AND ([Gender] = @
    Gender))">
        <SelectParameters>
                <asp:querystringparameter
    QueryStringField="CarsOwned" DefaultValue="1"
    Name="NumberCarsOwned" Type="Byte" />
                <asp:querystringparameter
    QueryStringField="Children" DefaultValue="2" Name="TotalChildren"
    Type="Byte" />
                <asp:querystringparameter QueryStringField="Gender"
    DefaultValue="M" Name="Gender" Type="String" />
        </SelectParameters>
</asp:SqlDataSource>
```

FIGURE 16.9

SQL expressions built by using the Add WHERE Clause dialog box

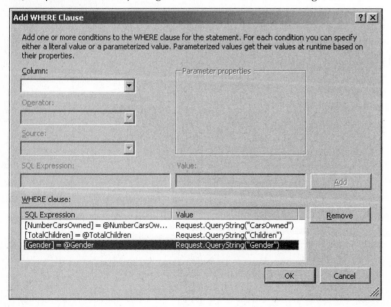

As highlighted in the previous code, you now have a WHERE clause on the SELECT statement, which specifies how the records from the table should be filtered. Because we're receiving the values for filtering from query strings, the asp:querystringparameter tag inside the SelectParameters tag specifies the name of the query string variable, the default value, and the field type.

If you want to change the parameters associated with the filter criteria, you can either edit the SQLDataSource control by using the Configure Data Source dialog box or you can use the Tag Properties task pane to quickly jump to the Command and Parameter Editor dialog box.

Editing commands and parameters

As shown in Figure 16.10, the Command and Parameter Editor dialog box allows you to modify the SQL command and associated parameters. You can open this dialog box by clicking on the ellipsis next to the query properties (for example, SelectQuery, InsertQuery, etc.) of the SQLDataSource control in the Tag Properties dialog box.

FIGURE 16.10

The Command and Parameter Editor dialog box

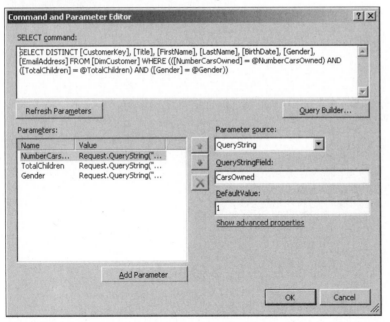

Besides adding, removing, and modifying the parameters, you also get an advanced view similar to the Tag Properties task pane for changing the advanced properties associated with a parameter. In this view, the properties that have already been set are displayed in bold.

In the next exercise, you specify the SQLDataSource control's properties to enable inserting, updating, and deleting operations on a table inside a database. Follow these steps:

1. **Insert an SQLDataSource control on a Web page by using the Toolbox task pane and then open the Configure Data Source dialog box.**

2. **Specify the ASP.NET connection and then choose the table inside the database and columns to be used on the SELECT statement.** Based on the understanding from the previous steps, you can also create an advanced WHERE clause for the SELECT statement. Also, notice the Order button on the Configure the Select Statement screen. You can use this button to specify ordering of the records to three levels via the interface.

3. **Click Advanced to open the Advanced SQL Generation Options dialog box.** As shown in Figure 16.11, you can use this dialog box to allow automatic generation of the INSERT, UPDATE, and DELETE commands for your SQLDataSource control. As indicated in the interface, you must have a primary key defined in your table to be able to make use of this option.

4. **Click the Generate INSERT, UPDATE, and DELETE statements as well as the Use optimistic concurrency check boxes and then click OK.**

5. **Click Next and then Finish to complete the configuration of the SQLDataSource data control.**

FIGURE 16.11

The Advanced SQL Generation Options dialog box

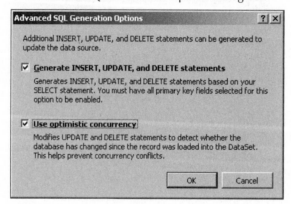

As shown in the following code, the interface has automatically generated the INSERT, UPDATE, and DELETE commands for your table:

```
<asp:SqlDataSource runat="server" id="SqlDataSource1"
    DeleteCommand="DELETE FROM [DimCustomer] WHERE [CustomerKey] = @
    original_CustomerKey AND [FirstName] = @original_FirstName AND
    [LastName] = @original_LastName AND [BirthDate] = @original_
    BirthDate AND [Title] = @original_Title AND [EmailAddress] = @
    original_EmailAddress" InsertCommand="INSERT INTO [DimCustomer]
    ([FirstName], [LastName], [BirthDate], [Title], [EmailAddress])
    VALUES (@FirstName, @LastName, @BirthDate, @Title, @
    EmailAddress)" UpdateCommand="UPDATE [DimCustomer] SET
    [FirstName] = @FirstName, [LastName] = @LastName, [BirthDate] = @
    BirthDate, [Title] = @Title, [EmailAddress] = @EmailAddress WHERE
    [CustomerKey] = @original_CustomerKey AND [FirstName] = @original_
    FirstName AND [LastName] = @original_LastName AND [BirthDate] = @
    original_BirthDate AND [Title] = @original_Title AND
    [EmailAddress] = @original_EmailAddress" OldValuesParameterFormat
    String="original_{0}" ConflictDetection="CompareAllValues"
    ConnectionString="<%$ ConnectionStrings:Custom_Connection %>"
    SelectCommand="SELECT [CustomerKey], [FirstName], [LastName],
    [BirthDate], [Title], [EmailAddress] FROM [DimCustomer]">
        <DeleteParameters>
            <asp:parameter Name="original_CustomerKey"
    Type="Int32" />
            <asp:parameter Name="original_FirstName"
    Type="String" />
            <asp:parameter Name="original_LastName"
    Type="String" />
            <asp:parameter Name="original_BirthDate"
    Type="DateTime" />
            <asp:parameter Name="original_Title" Type="String"
    />
            <asp:parameter Name="original_EmailAddress"
    Type="String" />
        </DeleteParameters>
        <UpdateParameters>
            <asp:parameter Name="FirstName" Type="String" />
            <asp:parameter Name="LastName" Type="String" />
            <asp:parameter Name="BirthDate" Type="DateTime" />
            <asp:parameter Name="Title" Type="String" />
            <asp:parameter Name="EmailAddress" Type="String" />
            <asp:parameter Name="original_CustomerKey"
    Type="Int32" />
            <asp:parameter Name="original_FirstName"
    Type="String" />
            <asp:parameter Name="original_LastName"
    Type="String" />
```

```
                    <asp:parameter Name="original_BirthDate"
        Type="DateTime" />
                    <asp:parameter Name="original_Title" Type="String"
        />
                    <asp:parameter Name="original_EmailAddress"
        Type="String" />
            </UpdateParameters>
            <InsertParameters>
                    <asp:parameter Name="FirstName" Type="String" />
                    <asp:parameter Name="LastName" Type="String" />
                    <asp:parameter Name="BirthDate" Type="DateTime" />
                    <asp:parameter Name="Title" Type="String" />
                    <asp:parameter Name="EmailAddress" Type="String" />
            </InsertParameters>
        </asp:SqlDataSource>
```

A number of parameters are automatically generated to facilitate the insert, update, and delete operations. Also, the `ConflictDetection` property was set as a result of clicking the Use optimistic concurrency check box to ensure that the DataSet on which the `INSERT`, `UPDATE`, and `DELETE` commands run reflect the most current state of the data inside the database. Now you can use the Command and Parameter Editor dialog box to modify the `INSERT`, `UPDATE`, and `DELETE` queries.

> **CAUTION** The automatic creation of the manipulation statements, such as `INSERT`, `UPDATE`, and `DELETE`, might not essentially work in complex scenarios where you have multiple tables linked to each other using relationships. In such cases, you should write your own statements to ensure proper operation and database consistency.

Another data source control that might generate interest is the XMLDataSource control. As mentioned earlier, the XMLDataSource control is useful for interfacing with XML files as back-end data sources. To configure an XMLDataSource in SharePoint Designer, follow these steps:

1. **Using the Toolbox task pane, insert the XMLDataSource control on a Web page.**

2. **Click Configure Data Source in the Common XMLDataSource Tasks menu to open the Configure Data Source dialog box for the XMLDataSource.** As shown in Figure 16.12, you can use this dialog box to specify properties for the XMLDataSource control.

3. **In the Data File text field, type the name of the XML file to be used as the data source.** You can also optionally specify a transform file to transform the structure of your XML file and an XPATH file to filter the XML file and return only a subset of the data exposed.

4. **Click OK to finish the configuration of the XMLDataSource control.**

FIGURE 16.12

Specifying properties for the XMLDataSource control

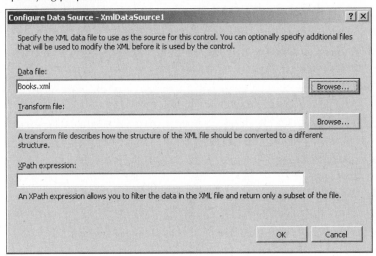

Once the properties are set, you can bind the control with the available data display controls to display the data exposed in the XML file on Web pages. The XMLDataSource is particularly useful in displaying the hierarchy of nodes inside an XML file by using the ASP.NET TreeView and Menu controls.

Displaying Data with ASP.NET Data Controls

The third and final step toward showing data on an ASP.NET Web page by using data controls is about binding the data source control to a data display control. Data display controls are responsible for showing the data that's exposed by the data source controls. At browse time, these controls are rendered on Web pages to provide the interface for displaying data.

Most of the ASP.NET 2.0 controls can be bound to data source controls. However, ASP.NET 2.0 offers special controls for displaying data from data sources in a tabular or grid format. This section discusses how you can bind the data source controls you configured earlier to display and format data on Web pages.

Binding with data source controls

As mentioned earlier, most of the ASP.NET 2.0 controls can be bound to data source controls to display data on the Web pages. For example, you can use the following steps in SharePoint Designer to bind an ASP.NET `DropDownList` control to the SQLDataSource data control:

1. Insert an SQLDataSource control on your ASPX page and then configure it to use a `SELECT` statement to return a number of records from a table in your database.

2. Using the Toolbox task pane, insert a DropDownList control on your Web page. The Common DropDownList Tasks menu appears in the Design view.

3. Click Choose Data Source to open the Data Source Configuration Wizard, as shown in Figure 16.13. Here, you specify the column that you want to display in the dropdown menu.

4. In the Select a data source dropdown menu, select the ID of the SQLDataSource you configured earlier.

5. Choose the data fields (or data columns in the table) to be used for the display of the values of the items in the DropDownList control.

6. Click OK, save the Web page, and then press F12 to preview it in a browser.

The values of the data column that you chose in step 5 are displayed in the dropdown menu on the Web page. As mentioned earlier, the ASP.NET Development Server is invoked every time you preview an ASP.NET Web page to facilitate rendering of the controls on Web pages.

So, you've just completed the steps to bring the data from a back-end database to a Web page in SharePoint Designer without handwriting a single line of code. If you open the Code view of the Web page you just created, the HTML code of the DropDownList control appears:

```
<asp:DropDownList runat="server" id="DropDownList1"
    DataTextField="FirstName" DataSourceID="SqlDataSource1"
    DataValueField="CustomerKey">
    </asp:DropDownList>
```

The Data Source Configuration Wizard has allowed you to set the `DataTextField`, `DataSourceID`, and `DataValueField` for the `asp:DropDownList` control. You can also use the Tag Properties task pane to specify these properties.

Using ASP.NET data display controls

While the `DropDownList` control is useful, you might want to display the data from the data source control in a tabular or grid format. SharePoint Designer provides a number of ASP.NET 2.0 controls that can be used to display and work with data on a Web page.

FIGURE 16.13

The Data Source Configuration Wizard

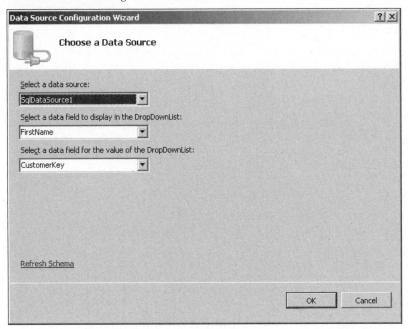

Using the DataList control

The DataList control can be used to display a view of data in a repeating fashion and optionally edit and delete the records. In the following exercise, you use the ASP.NET 2.0 DataList control to display data from the SQLDataSource on the Web page. Follow these steps:

1. **As in the previous exercise, insert an SQLDataSource control on your ASPX page and then configure it to use a SELECT statement to return a number of records from a table in your database.**

2. **Using the Toolbox task pane, insert a DataList control on your Web page.** The Common DataList Tasks menu appears in the Design view.

3. **Using the Choose Data Source dropdown menu, specify the SQLDataSource control you want to bind the DataList to.**

4. **Save the Web page and then press F12 to browse to it.** You should see the data from your table on the Web page now. However, as shown in Figure 16.14, the data displayed isn't that compelling to look at. You can use SharePoint Designer to quickly format the data to look better.

FIGURE 16.14

A preview of the unformatted DataList control

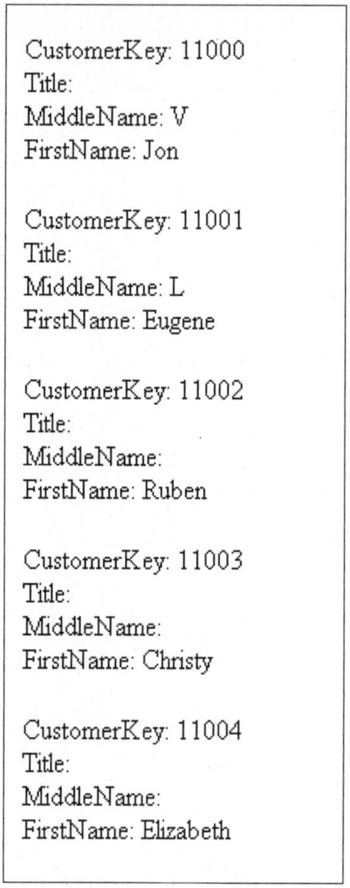

CustomerKey: 11000
Title:
MiddleName: V
FirstName: Jon

CustomerKey: 11001
Title:
MiddleName: L
FirstName: Eugene

CustomerKey: 11002
Title:
MiddleName:
FirstName: Ruben

CustomerKey: 11003
Title:
MiddleName:
FirstName: Christy

CustomerKey: 11004
Title:
MiddleName:
FirstName: Elizabeth

5. **Open the Common DataList Tasks menu and then click the AutoFormat link.** The AutoFormat dialog box, as shown in Figure 16.15, opens. This dialog box provides some predefined formats for the DataList control and shows a preview of the formatting.

6. **Pick a scheme that you like and then click OK, save the Web page, and then preview the page in a browser.** As shown in Figure 16.16, the DataList looks a little better now.

The AutoFormat dialog box

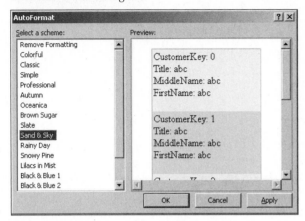

FIGURE 16.16

A preview of the formatted DataList control

CustomerKey: 11000
Title:
MiddleName: V
FirstName: Jon

CustomerKey: 11001
Title:
MiddleName: L
FirstName: Eugene

CustomerKey: 11002
Title:
MiddleName:
FirstName: Ruben

CustomerKey: 11003
Title:
MiddleName:
FirstName: Christy

CustomerKey: 11004
Title:
MiddleName:
FirstName: Elizabeth

If you view the code of the DataList in the Code view, SharePoint Designer has automatically applied some formatting styles and tags to the DataList. These properties are highlighted in blue in the Tag Properties task pane for the DataList control:

```
<asp:DataList runat="server" id="DataList1"
    DataKeyField="CustomerKey" DataSourceID="SqlDataSource1"
    BorderColor="Tan" CellPadding="2" BackColor="LightGoldenrodYellow
    " BorderWidth="1px" ForeColor="Black">
        <FooterStyle BackColor="Tan" />
        <AlternatingItemStyle BackColor="PaleGoldenrod" />
        <SelectedItemStyle BackColor="DarkSlateBlue"
ForeColor="GhostWhite" />
        <HeaderStyle BackColor="Tan" Font-Bold="True" />
        <ItemTemplate>
                CustomerKey:
                <asp:Label Text='<%# Eval("CustomerKey") %>'
runat="server" id="CustomerKeyLabel" />
                <br />
                Title:
                <asp:Label Text='<%# Eval("Title") %>'
runat="server" id="TitleLabel" />
                <br />
                MiddleName:
                <asp:Label Text='<%# Eval("MiddleName") %>'
runat="server" id="MiddleNameLabel" />
                <br />
                FirstName:
                <asp:Label Text='<%# Eval("FirstName") %>'
runat="server" id="FirstNameLabel" />
                <br />
                <br />
        </ItemTemplate>
</asp:DataList>
```

Alternatively, you can use the Property Builder dialog box available through the Property Builder link in the Common DataList Tasks menu to modify the formatting of the DataList control. As shown in Figure 16.17, you can use the Property Builder dialog box to specify format settings for the DataList header, footer, items, and separators.

> **NOTE** Although the AutoFormat option is available for most of the data display controls, you might not find the Property Builder dialog box for some controls depending on the nature of the control and the properties it exposes.

Using the Property Builder dialog box for the DataList control, you can set the formatting and style properties for this control without having to know firsthand the purpose of the property. The interface is fairly simple to use: Simply select the object to which you want to apply formatting and then use the controls provided in the Appearance section to specify values for the properties.

FIGURE 16.17

The Property Builder dialog box

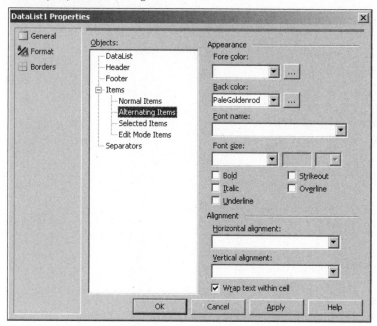

Using the GridView control

All ASP.NET 2.0 controls have characteristics and features that differentiate them from each other. For example, the DataList control in SharePoint Designer doesn't allow paging of rows, while the GridView control does. Based on the functionality required, you can choose which control you want to use. In the next exercise, you use the GridView control to display the data from the same SQLDataSource used earlier to see the difference in the appearance of the controls:

1. **Using the Toolbox task pane, insert a GridView control on your Web page.**

2. **Use the Common GridView Tasks menu to specify the SQLDataSource control you want to bind the DataGrid control to.**

3. **Click the AutoFormat link, choose a format scheme of your choice, and then click OK.**

4. **Click the Enable Paging and Enable Sorting check boxes.**

5. **Save the Web page and then preview it in a browser.** As shown in Figure 16.18, the GridView controls display the data in a more compact and navigable manner.

You can navigate more easily between pages of data by using the links at the bottom on the GridView. The Columns headers also allow you to sort the data by clicking on them. You can specify the properties of the GridView by using the Tag Properties task pane. For example, as shown in Figure 16.19, if you want to change the location of the paging links from bottom to top, you can use the Tag Properties task pane to change the `Position` property in the Paging section to Top.

FIGURE 16.18

A preview of the GridView control on a Web page

CustomerKey	Title	MiddleName	FirstName
25205			John
27840		A	John
28589		M	John
28946		C	John
11254		W	Johnathan
12291		E	Johnathan
12768		J	Johnathan
13626		D	Johnathan
14097			Johnathan
17723			Johnathan

1 2 3 4 5 6 7

FIGURE 16.19

Changing properties of the GridView control by using the Tag Properties task pane

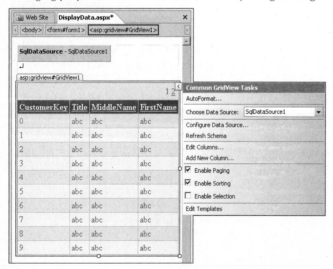

The GridView also allows for updating and deleting data, provided that the data source control it's bound to has properly written UPDATE and DELETE statements. After you bind the GridView to such a data source control, the Enable Editing and Enable Deleting check boxes become available in the Common GridView Tasks menu. You can click these check boxes to enable the links for updating and deleting records in the GridView.

Using the DetailsView Control

While the GridView control allows for editing and deleting data, the DetailsView control allows for inserting new rows of data into a table in the database. In the next exercise, you use the DetailsView control in combination with the GridView control to create a Web page that can be used to insert and update rows of data in a table in a database:

> **NOTE** While configuring the data source controls in this exercise, ensure that you specify proper INSERT and UPDATE commands. If you're using a single table without relationships, you can have the SQLDataSource control auto-generate these commands by using the Advanced SQL generation options.

1. **Use the New dialog box to create a new ASPX page and then open it in SharePoint Designer.**

2. **Insert a table with one row and two columns on the Web page.** The first column in this table is used to insert the GridView control and the second one for the DetailsView control.

3. **Place the cursor inside the first column of the table and then insert a GridView control by using the Toolbox task pane.** The GridView has the ID GridView1 because it's the first GridView on the Web page.

4. **In the Common GridView Tasks menu, choose New Data Source from the Choose Data Source dropdown menu.** The Data Source Configuration Wizard, as shown in Figure 16.20, opens.

5. **Click Database in the Data Source Configuration Wizard, type GridViewDataSource in the Specify an ID for the data source text field, and then click OK to open the Configure Data Source dialog box.**

6. **Specify the ASP.NET connection to your database and then click Next.**

7. **Choose the table you want to use for this exercise, select the columns for display, click the Return only unique rows check box, click Next, and then click Finish.** As shown in Figure 16.21, this process creates an SQLDataSource control with ID GridViewDataSource and binds it with the GridView control.

8. **In the Common GridView Tasks menu, click the Enable Paging, Enable Sorting, and Enable Selection check boxes.**

9. **Click the AutoFormat link in the Common GridView Tasks menu.** Using the AutoFormat dialog box, choose the schema to format the GridView.

10. **Place the cursor in the second column of the table created in step 2.**

11. **Using the Toolbox task pane, insert a DetailsView control on the Web page.**

FIGURE 16.20

The Data Source Configuration Wizard

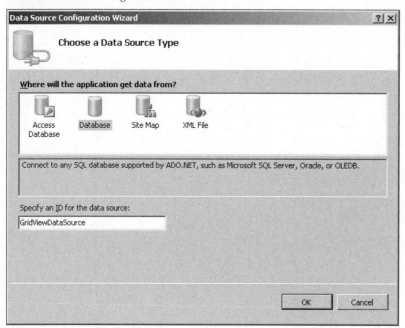

FIGURE 16.21

The SQLDataSource control bound to the GridView control

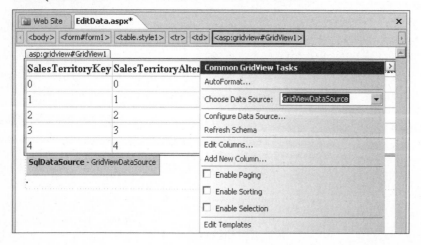

12. **In the Common DetailsView Tasks menu, select New Data Source in the Choose Data Source dialog box.** The Data Source Configuration Wizard opens.

13. **Choose Database in the Data Source Configuration Wizard, type DetailsViewDataSource in the Specify an ID for the data source text field, and then click OK to open the Configure Data Source dialog box.**

14. **Again, specify the ASP.NET connection to your database and then click Next.**

15. **Choose the same table you used for the GridViewDataSource and then select all the columns for display.**

16. **Click the WHERE button to open the Add WHERE Clause dialog box.** Use this dialog box to specify a WHERE condition that filters the data in the DetailsViewDataSource control based on the selected item in the GridView control.

17. **Specify the unique column in the chosen table by using the Column box.** Ensure that the Operator box shows the equal (=) operator.

18. **Select Control from the Source dropdown menu.** This shows the Parameter Properties section in the Add WHERE Clause dialog box.

19. **In the Control ID dropdown menu, specify the ID of the GridView control inserted earlier.** The resulting screen is shown in Figure 16.22.

20. **Click Add to add the WHERE clause and then click OK.**

FIGURE 16.22

Creating a filter parameter by using the Control source

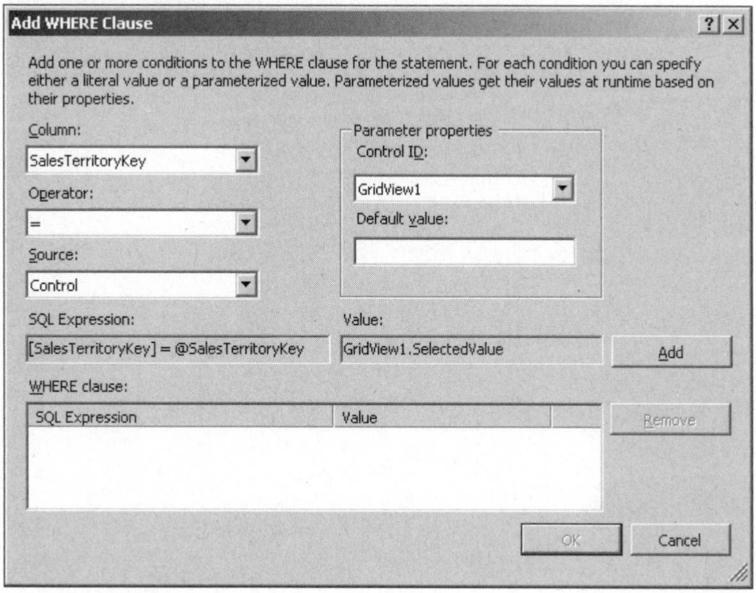

21. Click Advanced to open the Advanced SQL Generation Options dialog box and then click the Generate INSERT, UPDATE and DELETE statements and Use optimistic concurrency check boxes.

22. Click OK, Next, and then Finish to complete the configuration of the **DetailsViewDataSource**. As shown in Figure 16.23, the DetailsView control is now bound to the DetailsViewDataSource control.

23. Click the Enable Inserting and Enable Editing check boxes in the Common DetailsView Tasks menu.

24. Click the AutoFormat link to choose a formatting scheme for the DetailsView control.

25. Save the Web page and then preview it in a browser.

FIGURE 16.23

The Common DetailsView Tasks after binding to an SQLDataSource control that supports data manipulation

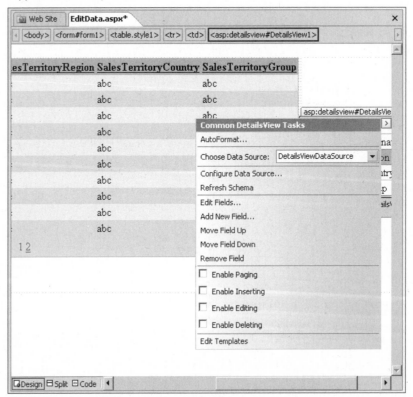

As shown in Figure 16.24, when you click the Select link on the GridView, the DetailsView shows the corresponding item and allows you to edit it. The DetailsView also provides a New link to add a new record to the table.

The resulting Web page after linking the GridView and DetailsView controls

Formatting the display of data

While the AutoFormat dialog box provides you with many attractive templates and schemes to choose from, you might still want to change the look of the data display controls to better suit your design requirements.

Most of the control properties for the data display controls related to formatting and appearance are combined in the Appearance and Styles categories of the Tag Properties task pane. You can use these properties to modify the formatting of the controls. For example, the `AlternateRowStyle` property collection in the `GridView` control provides a set of properties that allows you to change the formatting of the alternate rows in the GridView.

Using ASP.NET Controls with SharePoint Data Sources

Because SharePoint (WSS v3 and MOSS) is based on ASP.NET 2.0, you can also use the generic ASP.NET 2.0 data display controls with SharePoint data sources. When you open a SharePoint Web site in SharePoint Designer, the Data Source Library task pane shows all the available lists, libraries, and other data sources associated with the Web site. If you right-click on a data source in the Data Source Library task pane, an option to insert a data source control for the data source appears. You can bind this data source control with a generic ASP.NET data control to display data on a Web page.

In the following exercise, I show you how you can use the ASP.NET GridView control to display data from a SharePoint list. Follow these steps:

1. **Using the SharePoint interface, create a new Announcements list on your Web site and then add several items to this list.**

2. **Open the SharePoint site in SharePoint Designer and then enable the Data Source Library task pane.**

3. **Use the New dialog box to create a new ASPX page and then place the cursor in the Design view.**

4. **In the Data Source Library, expand SharePoint Lists, right-click on the newly created Announcements list, and then choose Insert Data Source Control from the popup menu.** An SPDataSource control is inserted on the Web page.

5. **Using the Toolbar task pane, insert a GridView control on the Web page.**

6. **Using the Common GridView Tasks menu, select the SPDataSource control from the Choose Data Source dropdown menu.**

7. **Save the Web page and then preview it in a browser.**

This approach provides an alternative means to display data from SharePoint data sources on Web pages. Because inserting and updating data is obfuscated in SharePoint sites, you can't use this approach to manipulate SharePoint list data. SharePoint Designer provides you with a robust data display control called DataFormWebPart to perform these operations on SharePoint data sources.

 **For more on the DataFormWebPart, see Chapter 17.**

Summary

This chapter primarily focused on familiarizing you with using ASP.NET data controls in SharePoint Designer. As you work with ASP.NET 2.0 controls, you can learn more about new properties and methods to exploit these controls.

In this chapter, you configured ASP.NET 2.0 data source controls by using the SharePoint Designer interface. Then, you learned how to bind the ASP.NET data display controls to the data source controls and display data on Web pages. You also learned about formatting the data controls by using the SharePoint Designer interface.

Chapter 17

Working with the Data Form Web Part

The Data Form Web Part qualifies as one of the most powerful and extensible SharePoint Web parts. Available with WSS v3 and MOSS sites, the Data Form Web Part extends the capabilities of its predecessor — the Data View Web Part available with WSS v2 and SPS 2003 sites — by providing features for inserting, editing, and deleting data stored in SharePoint data sources in addition to displaying and formatting data. In other words, while the Data View Web Part is only capable of providing a way to create views of data stored in SharePoint data sources, the Data Form Web Part allows for creating both views for displaying data and forms for inserting and manipulating data from SharePoint data sources. You can use the Data Form Web Part with almost all available SharePoint data sources. These include all SharePoint lists and libraries, business data catalogs, database connections, XML files, etc.

The Data Form Web Part expands the data-displaying capabilities of the Data View Web Part by providing the creation of single- and multiple-item views, subviews, and joined subviews of data. Subviews and joined subviews allow Web designers to aggregate data from various data sources into a single view, thereby enhancing data analysis and review abilities. Like its predecessor, the Data Form Web Part allows parameter-based filtering, sorting, and grouping of SharePoint data. You can also make use of advanced formatting for showing and hiding content as well as applying styles for changing data appearance and layout.

The Data Form Web Part allows creation of single- and multiple-item forms as well as new item forms for inserting, updating, and deleting data stored in SharePoint data sources. Along with this, the Data Form Web Part can also be used to create customized new item, edit item, and display item forms for list and document libraries.

This chapter discusses the internals of the Data Form Web Part and how you can use this wonderful Web part to work with data sources on SharePoint Web sites. I also take you through a number of exercises that help you develop your understanding about using the Data Form Web Part in a number of scenarios.

Unlike other Web parts provided by SharePoint sites, you can't use the SharePoint user interface to insert and configure the Data Form Web Part. Instead, you use SharePoint Designer to work with the Data Form Web Part. SharePoint Designer offers a simple, wizard-driven approach to insert the Data Form Web Part on Web pages. SharePoint Designer also provides a number of task panes and dialog boxes to specify settings for manipulating and formatting data being fed to the Data Form Web Part by SharePoint data sources.

Understanding the Basics of the Data Form Web Part

To understand the internals of the Data Form Web Part, follow these steps to insert a simple view of data by using the Data Form Web Part. Then, I help analyze the key components that make the Data Form Web Part work:

1. **Open a WSS v3 site in SharePoint Designer by using the Open Site dialog box to specify the location of the Web site.** Alternatively, you can open the WSS v3 site in Internet Explorer and then choose File ➪ Edit with SharePoint Designer to open the site in SharePoint Designer.

2. **Choose File ➪ New ➪ Create from Master Page to open the Select a Master Page dialog box, click the Default Master Page radio button, and then click OK.** This creates a new Web page with the default master page of the SharePoint site attached to it.

3. **Open the newly created Web page in the Design view and then hover over the body area of the Web page to locate the PlaceHolderMain content region.** As shown in Figure 17.1, clicking the arrow in this region opens the Common Content Tasks menu.

4. **Click the Create Custom Content link in the Common Content Tasks menu to open the PlaceHolderMain content region for editing.**

5. **Choose Data View ➪ Manage Data Sources to open the Data Source Library task pane.**

6. **Expand the SharePoint Lists section, click any of the default lists, and then click Show Data.** The Data Source Details task pane opens.

7. **Ensure that some columns of the list are selected and then choose Insert Selected Fields as ➪ Multiple Item View.** The DataFormWebPart is inserted on the Web page.

With the Data Form Web Part selected in the Design view, if you click the Code view tab, a large chunk of highlighted code forms the HTML code for the Data Form Web Part. There are four major components of the Data Form Web Part: `DataSources`, `ParameterBindings`, `DataFields`, and `XSL`.

FIGURE 17.1

Finding the PlaceHolderMain content region in the Web page associated with the master page

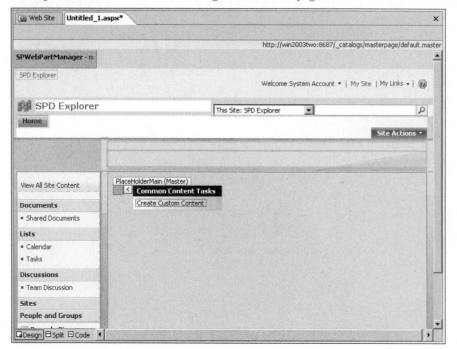

DataSources

The <DataSources> tag inside the DataFormWebPart specifies the data source control that the DataFormWebPart uses for interfacing with the SharePoint data source. As represented by the following code, the data source control used by the DataFormWebPart for SharePoint lists is the SharePoint:SPDataSource:

```
<DataSources>
        <SharePoint:SPDataSource runat="server"
DataSourceMode="List" UseInternalName="true"
selectcommand="&lt;View&gt;&lt;/View&gt;" id="Announcements1">
<SelectParameters><WebPartPages:DataFormParameter Name="ListID"
ParameterKey="ListID" PropertyName="ParameterValues"
DefaultValue="3B310B2C-F7C0-4BD9-82AA-92C6F302F15D"/></ SelectPar
ameters><DeleteParameters><WebPartPages: DataFormParameter
Name="ListID" ParameterKey="ListID" PropertyName="ParameterValues"
DefaultValue="3B310B2C-F7C0-4BD9-82AA-92C6F302F15D"/></
SeleteParameters><UpdateParameters><WebPartPages:
DataFormParameter Name="ListID" ParameterKey="ListID"
```

```
PropertyName="ParameterValues" DefaultValue="3B310B2C-F7C0-4BD9-82AA-
92C6F302F15D"/></ UpdateParameters><InsertParameters><WebPartPages:
DataFormParameter Name="ListID" ParameterKey="ListID" PropertyName=
"ParameterValues" DefaultValue="3B310B2C-F7C0-4BD9-82AA-
92C6F302F15D"/></InsertParameters></SharePoint:SPDataSource>
</DataSources>
```

The DataSourceMode property specifies the scope of the data source and the selectcommand provides the Collaborative Application Markup Language (CAML) query to retrieve data from the SharePoint
list. The <SelectParameters>, <DeleteParameters>, <UpdateParameters>, and
<InsertParameters> tags provide the select, delete, update, and insert parameters when required.

ParameterBindings

This section of the DataFormWebPart code specifies how parameters in the DataFormWebPart should be
bound to the various sources of data. As shown in the following code, the Name attribute specifies the
name of the parameter and the Location attribute indicates the source of data for the parameter:

```
<ParameterBindings>
        <ParameterBinding Name="ListID" Location="None"
DefaultValue="3B310B2C-F7C0-4BD9-82AA-92C6F302F15D"/>
        <ParameterBinding Name="dvt_apos" Location="Postback;Connection"
/>
        <ParameterBinding Name="UserID" Location="CAMLVariable" DefaultV
alue="CurrentUserName"/>
        <ParameterBinding Name="Today" Location="CAMLVariable"
DefaultValue="CurrentDate"/>
</ParameterBindings>
```

SharePoint provides the following values for the Location attribute:

- **PostBack:** Indicates that the value of the parameter is sustained between page refreshes
- **Connection:** Indicates that the source of data for the parameter could be from another
  Web part
- **Query String:** Indicates that the value of the parameter can come from a query string
- **CAMLVariable:** Indicates that the source of data for the parameter could be a CAML variable
  specified in the SharePoint code
- **SSOTicket:** Indicates that the source of data for the parameter could form an SSO connection

DataFields

The DataFields section of the DataFormWebPart code specifies the fields of data available for use inside
the DataFormWebPart. Here is an excerpt of the code from the previous exercise:

```
<datafields>@ID,ID;@ContentType,Content Type;@Title,Title;@
    Modified,Modified;@Created,Created;@Author,Created By;@Editor,Modified
```

```
By;@_UIVersionString,Version;@Attachments,Attachments;@File_
x0020_Type,File Type;@FileLeafRef,Name (for use in forms);@
FileDirRef,Path;@FSObjType,Item Type;@_HasCopyDestinations,Has
Copy Destinations;@_CopySource,Copy Source;@ContentTypeId,Content
Type ID;@_ModerationStatus,Approval Status;@_UIVersion,UI
Version;@Created_x0020_Date,Created;@FileRef,URL Path;@
Body,Body;@Expires,Expires;</datafields>
```

As indicated in this code, the <datafields> tag lists all the available columns with their internal and actual names. The internal names are used later in the XSL section.

XSL

The <XSL> property encapsulates the display functionality of the DataFormWebPart. The most elegant feature of the Data Form Web Part is that it uses Extensible Stylesheet Language (XSL) transformations to transform XML data received from the data source control discussed previously for display purposes. Most of the SharePoint Designer user interface for the Data Form Web Part is concentrated on providing abilities to modify this XSL code to implement advanced filtering, sorting, grouping, paging, formatting, and styling. If you're XSL-savvy, you can only imagine the amount of control the Data Form Web Part provides to work with the data from SharePoint data sources.

Highlighted in the following code are some of the important pieces to understand the XSL implementation of the Data Form Web Part. Each XSL template performs some transformation and then calls another template to proceed with the transformation. For example, the dvt_1 calls the dvt_1.body, which in turn calls the dvt_1.rowview.

```
<XSL>
<xsl:stylesheet xmlns:x="http://www.w3.org/2001/XMLSchema"
    xmlns:d="http://schemas.microsoft.com/sharepoint/dsp"
    version="1.0" exclude-result-prefixes="xsl msxsl ddwrt"
    xmlns:ddwrt="http://schemas.microsoft.com/WebParts/v2/DataView/
    runtime" xmlns:asp="http://schemas.microsoft.com/ASPNET/20"
    xmlns:__designer="http://schemas.microsoft.com/WebParts/v2/
    DataView/designer" xmlns:xsl="http://www.w3.org/1999/XSL/
    Transform" xmlns:msxsl="urn:schemas-microsoft-com:xslt"
    xmlns:SharePoint="Microsoft.SharePoint.WebControls" xmlns:ddwrt2=
    "urn:frontpage:internal">
<xsl:output method="html" indent="no"/>
<xsl:decimal-format NaN=""/>
<xsl:param name="dvt_apos">&apos;</xsl:param>
<xsl:variable name="dvt_1_automode">0</xsl:variable>
<xsl:template match="/">
        <xsl:call-template name="dvt_1"/>
</xsl:template>
<xsl:template name="dvt_1">
        <xsl:variable name="dvt_StyleName">Table</xsl:variable>
```

```
    <xsl:variable name="Rows" select="/dsQueryResponse/Rows/
Row"/>
    <table border="0" width="100%" cellpadding="2"
cellspacing="0">
        <tr valign="top">
            <xsl:if test="$dvt_1_automode = '1'"
ddwrt:cf_ignore="1">
                <th class="ms-vh" width="1%"
nowrap="nowrap"></th>
            </xsl:if>
            <th class="ms-vh" nowrap="nowrap">ID</th>
            <th class="ms-vh" nowrap="nowrap">Content
Type</th>
            <th class="ms-vh" nowrap="nowrap">Title</th>
            <th class="ms-vh" nowrap="nowrap">Modified</
th>
            <th class="ms-vh" nowrap="nowrap">Created</
th>
        </tr>
        <xsl:call-template name="dvt_1.body">
            <xsl:with-param name="Rows" select="$Rows"/>
        </xsl:call-template>
    </table>
</xsl:template>
<xsl:template name="dvt_1.body">
    <xsl:param name="Rows"/>
    <xsl:for-each select="$Rows">
        <xsl:call-template name="dvt_1.rowview"/>
    </xsl:for-each>
</xsl:template>
<xsl:template name="dvt_1.rowview">
    <tr>
        <xsl:if test="position() mod 2 = 1">
            <xsl:attribute name="class">ms-alternating</
xsl:attribute>
        </xsl:if>
        <xsl:if test="$dvt_1_automode = '1'" ddwrt:cf_
ignore="1">
            <td class="ms-vb" width="1%" nowrap="nowrap">
                <span ddwrt:amkeyfield="ID" ddwrt:amke
yvalue="ddwrt:EscapeDelims(string(@ID))" ddwrt:ammode="view"></
span>
            </td>
        </xsl:if>
        <td class="ms-vb">
            <xsl:value-of select="format-number(@ID,
'#,##0.#;-#,##0.#')"/>
        </td>
        <td class="ms-vb">
```

```
                        <xsl:value-of select="@ContentType"/>
                </td>
                <td class="ms-vb">
                        <xsl:value-of select="@Title"/>
                </td>
                <td class="ms-vb">
                        <xsl:value-of select="ddwrt:FormatDate(string
    (@Modified), 1033, 5)"/>
                </td>
                <td class="ms-vb">
                        <xsl:value-of select="ddwrt:FormatDate(string
    (@Created), 1033, 5)"/>
                </td>
        </tr>
    </xsl:template>
</xsl:stylesheet>
</XSL>
```

New XSL templates are added to this code when and as more formatting options are selected by using the user interface. Don't be let down if you're not comfortable with using XSLT, as the SharePoint Designer interface provides straightforward abilities to modify this XSL transformation without having in-depth understanding of XSLT and XPath expressions. This chapter familiarizes you with the SharePoint Designer user interface for manipulating the XSL code of the DataFormWebPart and thereby implementing formatting on data exposed by SharePoint data sources.

> **NOTE** When you insert a DataFormWebPart as a view of data, it's called the Data View. When you insert it as a form, it's called a Data Form. In both cases, the Web part is the same; just the rendering mode changes based on the XSL applied.

Using the Data Form Web Part

The SharePoint Designer user interface for working with the Data Form Web Part is mostly spread across three task panes: the Data Source Library, Data Source Details, and Conditional Formatting. The Data View top menu also provides the access points to most of the user interface for working with the Data Form Web Part.

> **CROSS-REF** For more on the Data Source Library task pane, see Chapter 15.

Creating views of data

Inserting views of data on Web pages for SharePoint data sources is made quite simple by the SharePoint Designer user interface. You use the Data Source Details task pane to insert views on SharePoint Web pages.

Inserting data views

Following are the common steps that apply to all data sources for inserting views:

1. **In the Data Source Library, click the data source you want to create a view of.** A menu of action items for that data source opens.

2. **Click the Show Data menu option to open the Data Source Details task pane.** The Data Source Details task pane shows the data associated with the selected data source and is the playground for inserting the Data Form Web Part as a view or a form. The representation of data in the Data Source Details task pane is mostly hierarchical. By default, you should see the first row of data from the data source with all the available columns. As shown in Figure 17.2, you can navigate between rows by using the arrows next to the top repeating node.

FIGURE 17.2

Navigating between rows of data in the Data Source Details task pane

3. **You can select multiple columns for inserting as a view or form by holding Ctrl and then clicking on the columns.** Alternatively, you can select multiple consecutive columns by clicking the first column, holding Shift, and then clicking the last column.

4. **Click the Insert Selected Fields as button in the Data Source Details task pane to open a list of menu options that allow you to insert the selected columns as a view or a form.** Alternatively, as shown in Figure 17.3, you can insert a view of data by right-clicking the repeating node and then choosing the specified layout from the popup menu.

NOTE The menu options in the Insert Selected Fields as button are contextual. That is, depending on the nature of the data source, you might not see some of these menu options. For example, you can't insert forms for linked data sources. So, the menu options for inserting forms aren't enabled when working with linked data sources.

5. **Choose the way you want to insert the DataFormWebPart by choosing a menu option from the Insert Selected Fields as menu.** The DataFormWebPart is inserted on the Web page at the location where the cursor is placed.

FIGURE 17.3

Inserting a formatted view of data by using the menu option for the repeating node

As shown in Figure 17.4, when you insert the DataFormWebPart on the Web page by using the previous steps, the Common Data View Tasks menu appears in the Design view. This menu forms one of the access points to modify the properties of the DataFormWebPart. You can show or hide the menu by clicking on the small arrow at the top-right corner of the DataFormWebPart.

New for the Data Form Web Part is the ability to insert subviews and joined subviews of related data sources. If you have multiple data sources related to each other, such as two tables in a database having a master-detail relationship, you can quickly insert an aggregated view of data by using the Data Form Web Part. Combined with some DHTML effects by using Behaviors in SharePoint Designer, you can enhance the Data Form Web Part to create a dynamic view of data.

 A master-detail relationship implies that for every row in the master table, there are a number of related rows in the details table.

FIGURE 17.4

The Common Data View Tasks menu

Common Data View Tasks

Filter:

Sort and Group:

Paging:

Edit Columns...

Change Layout...

Data View Preview: Default

☐ Show with sample data

Conditional Formatting...

Web Part Connections...

Parameters...

Refresh Data View

Data View Properties...

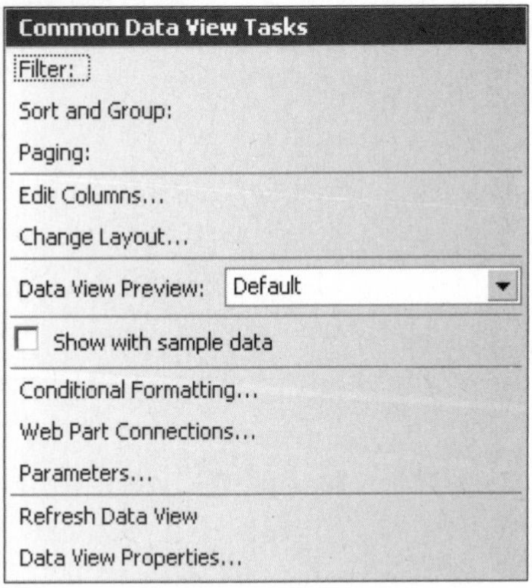

Creating subviews

The following exercise shows how you can display a combined view of data from a linked data source by using the Data Form Web Part. As a prerequisite, you need to create a linked data source by using the Data Source Library task pane, which joins two tables in a database that have a master-detail relationship.

1. Open your Web page in SharePoint Designer and then place the cursor at the location where you want to insert the DataFormWebPart as a view.

2. **Click Linked Data Source in the Data Source Library task pane and then click Show Data to open the Data Source Details, which shows the associated data from the linked data source.** As shown in Figure 17.5, you should see the combined view of data from your linked data source. In this example, the master table is shown at the top in the hierarchy, while the details table is shown at the bottom. Both the tables have arrows that allow for navigation between rows in the Data Source Details task pane,

3. **As shown in Figure 17.6, select the columns you want to display from the master table and then choose Insert Selected Fields as ⇨ Single Item View.** A single-item view of the columns selected is inserted, with paging of rows enabled by default. After you insert the view, the HTML code for the view is formatted by using `<table>` tags.

FIGURE 17.5

A linked data source opened in the Data Source Details task pane

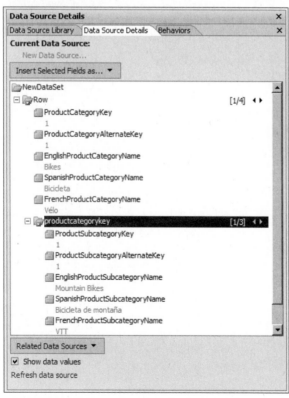

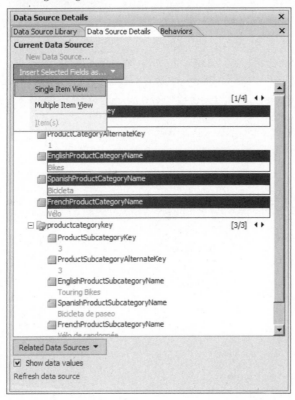

FIGURE 17.6

Inserting a single-item view from the Data Source Details task pane

4. Place the cursor inside the view you inserted in step 3.

5. **Using the Quick Tag Selector, locate and click the top `<tr>` tag inside the table inserted for the view.** The tag and its content are highlighted in the Design view.

6. **Right-click on the highlighted content and then choose Modify ⇨ Split Cells.** This step is illustrated in Figure 17.7. Clicking on the Split Cells menu option opens the Split Cells dialog box.

7. **Using the Split Cells dialog box, split the selected cell into two columns.** Place the cursor inside the newly created column.

8. **As illustrated in Figure 17.8, select the columns you want to insert as a subview and then choose Insert Selected Fields as ➪ Subview.** A multiple-item subview of the selected columns is inserted inside the existing view.

9. **Save the Web page and then preview it in a browser.** Figure 17.9 shows the completed result of these steps. You can move between the rows of the master table by using the paging links. This automatically changes the association in the subview to reflect the related data.

While this view looks compelling, you can further enhance it by implementing dynamic effects by using Behaviors in SharePoint Designer.

FIGURE 17.7

Splitting the HTML table row for inserting a subview

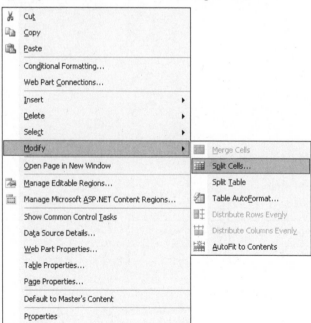

FIGURE 17.8

Inserting a subview inside the main view of data

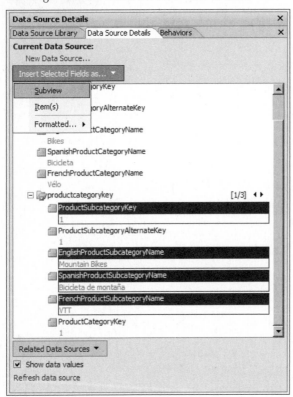

FIGURE 17.9

A master-detail view created by using the DataFormWebPart subview feature

		ProductSubcategoryKey	EnglishProductSubcategoryName	SpanishProductSubcategoryName	FrenchProductSubcategoryName
		18	Bib-Shorts	Culote corto	Cuissards avec bretelles
		19	Caps	Gorra	Casquette
ProductCategoryKey:	3	20	Gloves	Guantes	Gants
EnglishProductCategoryName:	Clothing	21	Jerseys	Jersey	Maillot
SpanishProductCategoryName:	Prenda	22	Shorts	Pantalones cortos	Cuissards
FrenchProductCategoryName:	Vêtements	23	Socks	Calcetines	Chaussettes
		24	Tights	Mallas	Collants
		25	Vests	Camiseta	Veste

Creating dynamic data views

The next exercise takes you through the steps to create a dynamic view of related data by using the Data Form Web Part as well as Behaviors and Layers. To be able to comfortably move around, ensure that the Behaviors and Layers task panes are enabled in the SharePoint Designer interface. The idea is to create a view of the master table in such a way that when you hover over the rows of the master table, the corresponding records from the details table are shown dynamically:

1. **Insert a multiple-item view of rows from the master table by using the Data Source Details task pane.**

2. **Place the cursor in the second column of any row of the table that's inserted in step 1 and then choose Insert ⇨ HTML ⇨ Layer.** This is shown in Figure 17.10. Because the XSL templates applied to the data view are recursive, one layer is inserted in each row of the data view. The cursor is placed by default in one of the layers.

FIGURE 17.10

Inserting layers in the rows of a data view

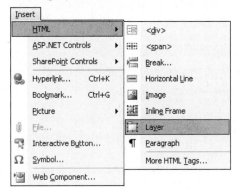

3. **As shown in Figure 17.11, use the Data Source Details task pane to insert a subview of details table inside the layers.** Again, due to the recursive nature of the XSL applied to the view, a corresponding subview is inserted in each layer, cluttering the Design view with a number of multiple-item subviews.

4. **Switch to the Layers task pane, right-click on any layer listed in the task pane, and then choose Set Visibility:Hidden from the popup menu.** The default setting for all layers changes to Hidden.

5. **Select the `<tr>` tag associated with a table row of the master table data view inserted in step 1.** This is important because selecting the wrong `<tr>` tag might cause the functionality to be impaired.

FIGURE 17.11

Inserting a subview inside a layer in the Data view

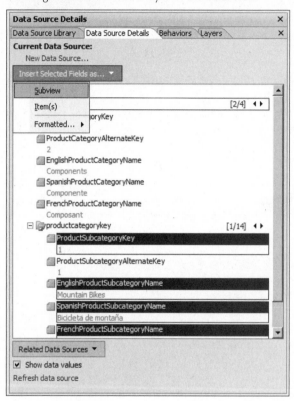

6. Switch to the Behaviors task pane and then choose Insert ⇨ Change Property to open the Change Property dialog box, as shown in Figure 17.12.

7. Click the Select Element radio button and then choose div in the Element Type dropdown menu and the ID of any layer in the Element ID dropdown menu.

8. Click the Visibility button, click the Visible radio button, click OK, and then click the Restore on mouseout event check box.

9. **Click OK, save the Web page, and then preview it in a browser.** As shown in Figure 17.13, you now have a dynamic view in which when you hover over a row in the main view, a subview appears with the corresponding records from the related table.

SharePoint Designer provides a no-code user experience for working with the DataFormWebPart. Later in this chapter, I discuss the advanced formatting of data displayed by data views by using the SharePoint Designer user interface.

FIGURE 17.12

Associating a behavior with a table row in the view for the master table

FIGURE 17.13

A dynamic master-detail view by using DHTML effects

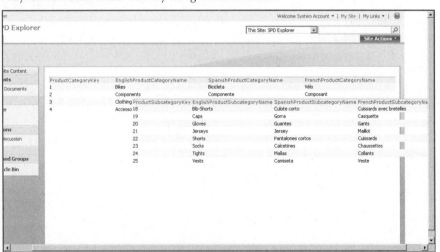

Working with data forms

The Data Form Web Part enables you to create Web pages with forms that allow users to add and modify data stored in SharePoint data sources. Using the Data Source Details task pane, you can insert single-item, multiple-item, and new item forms. The following exercise takes you through the steps to create a complete interface of inserting, editing, and deleting data within a SharePoint data source by using the Data Form Web Part:

1. Open the Web page where you want to insert the DataFormWebPart for interfacing with your data source.

2. Click the data source in the Data Source Library task pane and then click Show Data to display the Data Source Details task pane.

3. Select the columns you want to use for the data form and then choose Insert Selected Items as ⇨ Single Item Form. The DataFormWebPart is inserted on the Web page and shows the Common Data View Tasks menu.

4. Click the Data View Properties link in the Common Data View Tasks menu to open the Data View Properties dialog box.

5. Click the Editing tab and then click all the check boxes, as shown in Figure 17.14.

6. Save the Web page and then preview it in a browser.

FIGURE 17.14

Enabling inserting and editing for data forms by using the Data View Properties dialog box

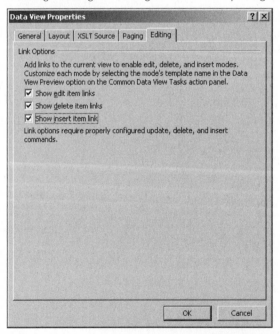

You now have all the capabilities to interface with the data source in a single control. By default, the Data Form Web Part shows the first row of data in the data source. Clicking the Edit link allows you to change the selected item. Clicking the Delete link allows you to delete the item, and clicking the Insert link allows you to add new items to the data source.

CAUTION   If you use the Data Form Web Part to add, modify, or delete data from a data source in a manner that might result in inconsistencies in the data source, you might receive errors. The data source might not allow the Data Form Web Part to perform the incorrect operation to avoid problems. For example, if you use the Data Form Web Part to delete a row of data in a master table that has related records in the corresponding details table, the database server might disallow the operation.

Creating custom list forms

Out-of-the-box SharePoint lists and libraries have a set of item forms that allow for creating new items as well as displaying and modifying existing items. For each content type associated with a list or library, you can have a set of item forms. These item forms facilitate item creation and modification for the associated content type.

NOTE   Content Types, introduced in WSS v3 and MOSS, define the nature and behavior of the content that can be stored in items. For example, the Document content type allows for creation of items that can store documents and related metadata. If you have multiple content types associated with a list, you can create items based on these content types and then store them in the list.

As shown in Figure 17.15, the item forms reside on Web pages that are stored within a list or library. These Web pages form the supporting files for a list or library.

Supporting files are used whenever you're working in the SharePoint user interface to create, modify, or display items. For example, the `NewForm.aspx` file is used to create a new item in the SharePoint list. By default, supporting files are created at the time of creation of the list or library by using templates provided by SharePoint sites. So, essentially, the look and feel of these pages are pretty standard across lists and libraries. The item forms on the supporting files are implemented by using the List Form Web Part offered by SharePoint. While you can make some modifications to the appearance of the List Form Web Part, it's still not as extensible as the Data Form Web Part.

Using SharePoint Designer, you can create customized supporting files by using the powerful capabilities of the Data Form Web Part and then change the supporting file associations to make the lists and libraries start using the files you created. This section discusses the recommended practices to create and associate customized supporting files with SharePoint lists and libraries.

CAUTION   Before you begin, it's very important to know that you should never delete the existing ListFormWebPart or the default supporting files associated with a list or library. While SharePoint Designer doesn't disallow you from deleting these files or the ListFormWebPart, this operation can lead to a complete loss of the editing capabilities for the list, which is recoverable only by either re-creating the list or restoring it from backups.

FIGURE 17.15

Supporting files for Announcement lists

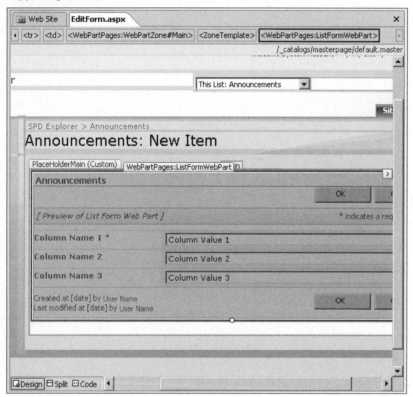

Follow these steps to create a customized supporting file by using SharePoint Designer. In this exercise, you create a custom edit form Web page and associate it with your list:

1. Open your SharePoint site in SharePoint Designer and then open the Folder List task pane.

2. Expand the Lists folder and the list you want to create a custom edit item form Web page for.

3. Select the existing EditForm.aspx and then press Ctrl+C (copy) and Ctrl+V (paste) to create a copy of the EditForm.aspx at the same location.

4. Rename the copy of the EditForm.aspx to CustomEditForm.aspx and then open it in the Design view. The default ListFormWebPart exists on CustomEditForm.aspx.

5. Right-click on the ListFormWebPart and then choose Web Part Properties from the popup menu to open the property editor for the Web part.

6. **Expand the Layout section and then click the Close the Web Part and Hidden check boxes, as shown in Figure 17.16.**

7. **Click OK.** The ListFormWebPart is now grayed out. If you save the Web page and browse to it now, the ListFormWebPart isn't shown on the Web page.

8. **Place the cursor at the bottom of the closed ListFormWebPart and then choose Insert ⇨ SharePoint Controls ⇨ Custom List Form.** The List or Document Library Form dialog box, as shown in Figure 17.17, opens.

9. **Select the list and content type associated with the list for which you want to create the custom edit item form, click the Edit item form radio button, and then click OK.** A DataFormWebPart is inserted on the Web page. The XSL of this DataFormWebPart has been created to match the look of the default ListFormWebPart. However, you're free to use SharePoint Designer to modify the appearance of the DataFormWebPart to suit your requirements.

FIGURE 17.16

Hiding the existing ListFormWebPart

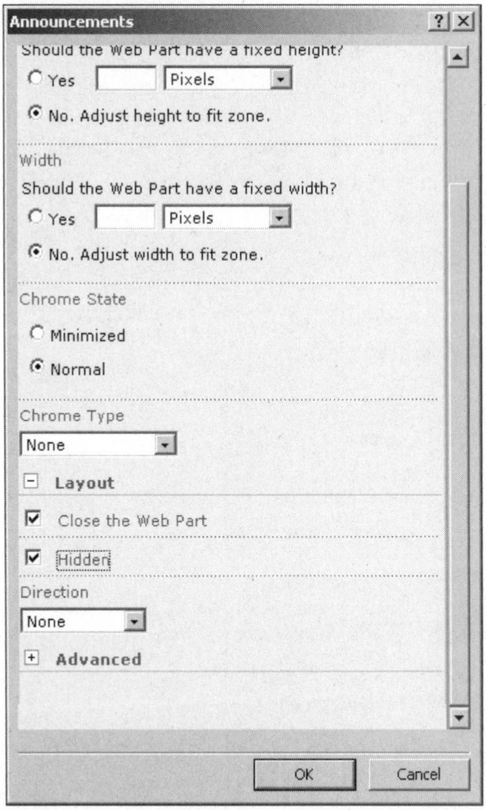

The List or Document Library Form dialog box

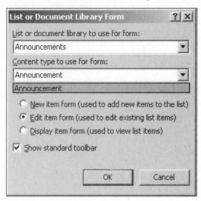

10. Save the `CustomEditForm.aspx` **Web page.**

11. **In the Folder List task pane, right-click on the list you're working with and then choose Properties from the popup menu.** The List Properties dialog box opens.

12. **Click the Supporting Files tab in this dialog box.** As shown in Figure 17.18, the Supporting Files tab allows you change the item forms for a particular list content type. Ensure that the content type for which you want to change the edit item form is selected in the Content type specific forms dropdown menu.

Changing supporting files by using the List Properties dialog box

13. Click Browse next to the Edit item form text field, choose `CustomEditForm.aspx`, and then click OK.

> **NOTE** Although the folder content type is listed as a choice in the Content type specific forms dropdown menu, it can't be really used in SharePoint Designer for changing the item form associations. Ensure that you select this content type while changing supporting file associations.

14. Click Apply and then OK in the List Properties dialog box to change the supporting file association.

Now, when you try to edit an item based on the content type for which you changed the edit item form, the new `CustomEditItem.aspx` is displayed for use. As mentioned earlier, you can modify the look and feel of the Data Form Web Part in SharePoint Designer and implement customized branding and formatting to your item form pages just like any other Web page inside a SharePoint site.

Using data view controls

The SharePoint Controls section in the Toolbox task pane hosts a number of controls especially for use in the Data Form Web Part. While the Data Form Web Part uses these controls internally for many operations, you can use the Toolbox task pane to insert and configure these controls manually for specific operations.

For example, while filling a new item form, you might want to have your user choose from a list of existing values (a lookup) rather than having to type them manually. In such a case, you can replace the default text fields with a Data View `DropDownList` control and configure it to show the values from a data source. The following exercise shows how you can accomplish this by using the Data View controls:

1. **On a SharePoint site, create a new Web page and then insert a new item form for a data source, such as an XML file, by using the New Item Form menu option in the Data Source details task pane.** The Data Form Web Part uses the text box controls by default for columns.

2. **Delete the text box for the column that you want to create a lookup for.**

3. **Switch to the Data Source Library task pane and then click the data source from where the values of the lookup should be retrieved.**

4. **Click the Insert Data Source Control menu option to insert a data source control for this data source on the Web page.**

5. **Using the Toolbox task pane, double-click the Data View DropDownList control to insert it at the location of the cursor.** As shown in Figure 17.19, the Common DVDropDownList Tasks menu opens in the Design view.

6. **Click the Data Fields link in the Common DVDropDownList Tasks menu to open the Change Data Bindings dialog box.**

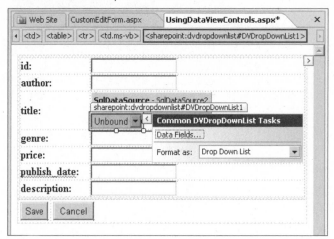

FIGURE 17.19

The Common DVDropDownList Tasks menu

7. In the Select a field to save values to dropdown menu, select the column for which you want to use the lookup for, choose the data source inserted in step 4, and then specify the data fields to be used for display text and the value of the lookup.

8. Click OK, save the Web page, and then preview it in a browser.

Rather than having to manually type the value of the column, the user can pick it from a lookup. You can use the similar approach to work with other Data View controls provided in the Toolbox task pane.

One interesting data view control that I want to mention is the Form Action Button (and Form Action Hyperlink). When you insert a data form on the Web page, the action buttons (such as Save, Cancel, Edit, etc.) that are inserted actually have form actions associated with them. If you right-click the Save button and then choose Form Actions from the popup menu, in the Form Actions dialog box that opens, the chosen action for the Save button is Commit. This is shown in Figure 17.20.

The Actions List shows the available actions that you can associate with the buttons. The following actions are available to you when working with Data View Form Actions buttons. Note that you can have multiple form actions associated with a form action button:

- **Commit:** Updates the data from the form inside the associated data source
- **Refresh:** Removes the changes made to the data inside the forms and refills it with the data from the data source
- **Cancel:** Cancels the changes that were made to the data
- **Navigate to source:** Takes the user to the page that's specified by the query string variable `Source`
- **Navigate to page:** Takes the user to the page specified. When you choose this option, the Settings button becomes enabled in the Form Actions dialog box, allowing you to specify the target page.
- **Custom Action:** Allows you to start a workflow when the form action button is clicked. The Settings button in the Form Actions dialog box takes you to the SharePoint Designer's Workflow Designer interface.

CROSS-REF For more on creating workflows, see Chapter 20.

FIGURE 17.20

The Form Actions dialog box

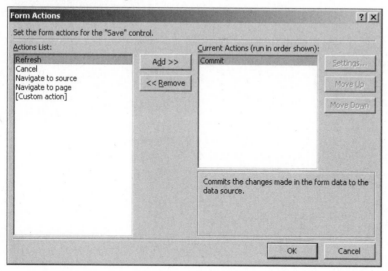

Using the Common Data View Control Tasks

Now that you understand how to use the SharePoint Designer interface to insert a Data Form Web Part as a data view and a data form, I take you through some enhanced XSL formatting features that are available for Data Form Web Parts.

As mentioned earlier, the Data Form Web Part is made very powerful by the fact that it supports formatting via XSL transformations. Most of the filtering, sorting, grouping, formatting, etc., for the Data Form Web Part is implemented by using XSLT. However, you don't need to be an XSLT expert to work with the Data Form Web Part in SharePoint Designer because the functionality is exposed by using a simple user interface that writes XSL for you behind the scenes.

Bring up the Common Data View Tasks menu for a Data Form Web Part to see the options to enhance the Data Form Web Part functions. While I discuss filtering, sorting, and grouping, I want to quickly mention the following options for data view display and preview:

- **Edit Columns:** Opens a dialog box that allows you to choose the columns that need to be displayed in the view. You can add, remove, and change the order of the columns to be displayed.

- **Data View Preview:** You can use this menu option to specify how the preview of data view should appear in the Design view of SharePoint Designer. You can choose to hide all filters or limit the number of rows when showing the data view in the Design view.

- **Show with sample data:** Provides a way to avoid performance overhead by displaying the data view by using sample data rather than the original data from the data source

- **Refresh Data View:** Allows you to refresh the data view by requesting the data from the data source again

Choosing the Data View Properties menu option takes you to the Data View Properties dialog box, as shown in Figure 17.21. This dialog box allows you to make some general settings related to enabling filtering, sorting, and grouping toolbars; specifying settings for paging; and choosing layouts for the Data Form Web Part.

FIGURE 17.21

The General tab for the Data View Properties dialog box

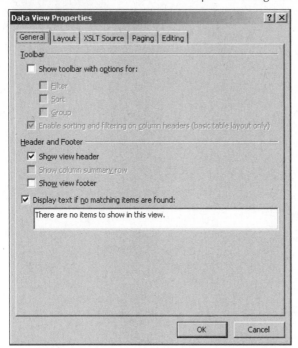

The General tab allows you to enable the following abilities for the Data Form Web Part:

- **Toolbar:** The options in this section allow to you enable a filtering, sorting, and grouping toolbar for your data view. Alternatively, you can click the Enable sorting and filtering on column headers check box to enable sorting and filtering on the column headers. Figure 17.22 shows what the column headers look like when sorting and filtering is enabled on them.

FIGURE 17.22

Sorting and filtering column headers

- **Header and Footer:** The Header and Footer section allows you to show header, footer, and column summary rows for the data view table. For example, you can click the Show column summary row check box if you need to create a row of totals at the bottom of a data view.

- **No Matching Item text:** Clicking the Display text if no matching items are found check box allows you to set the text that should be displayed on the data view if no matching records are found in the data source.

The Layout tab in the Data View Properties dialog box allows you to choose from a list of styles and the layout that needs to be applied to the data view. When you select a layout, a short description of the layout style is displayed at the bottom in the dialog box. If you want to transform the data being shown in the Data Form Web Part by using a custom XSL code, you can click the XSLT Source tab to specify the location of the XSLT source file. This option is useful when you want to share your custom XSLT with other designers.

Implementing filtering, sorting, and grouping

The SharePoint Designer user interface allows you to perform advanced filtering, sorting, and grouping on the rows that are presented by using the Data Form Web Part. Internally, SharePoint Designer implements these operations by using XSLT and XPATH expressions, which are stored in the <XSL> section of the Data Form Web Part code.

Appling XSLT filters

If you want to filter the rows of data shown in the data view based on a certain criteria, you can implement filtering by using the Common Data View Tasks menu in the Design view. The next exercise shows you how to use the Filter Criteria dialog box to create filters for your data view. Follow these steps:

1. Create a new ASPX page in your SharePoint Web site by using SharePoint Designer.

2. Using the Data Source Library task pane, insert a data view of a data source on the Web page.

3. Click the Filter menu option in the Common Data View Tasks menu to open the Filter Criteria dialog box, as shown in Figure 17.23.

4. Click the **Click here to add a new clause** link to enable the interface for inserting new filter criteria.

5. In the Field Name column, click the dropdown menu, choose the field that you want to base the filter on, and then select the operator in the dropdown menu for the Comparison column.

6. Using the dropdown menu for the Value column, type a value for matching the criteria of the filter.

 Notice the Create new parameter options in the dropdown menu. Later in this section, you use these to create advanced filtering clauses.

FIGURE 17.23

The Filter Criteria dialog box

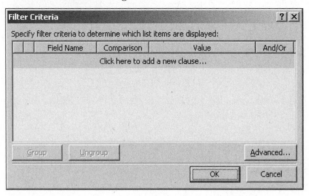

7. **Using the And/Or column, specify how you want to combine the filter clauses.** For example, the AND operator matches all rows that match multiple clauses, while the OR operation matches either.

8. **Repeat steps 3 to 6 to create multiple filter clauses.** To remove a filter clause, simply right-click on it and then click Remove from the popup menu. Figure 17.24 shows the Filter Criteria dialog box with multiple clauses applied.

9. **To group multiple clauses in the Filter Criteria dialog box, hold Shift, select the filter clauses you want to group, and then click Group.**

10. **Click OK to implement the filter clauses you specified in the previous steps to the data view.** The Design view now shows the filtered data view. Save the Web page and then browse to it to preview the data view in a browser.

FIGURE 17.24

Multiple filter clauses in the Filter Criteria dialog box

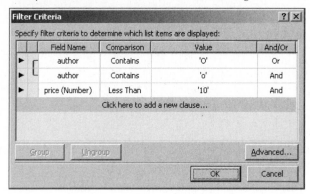

After you apply a filter criterion to a data view, the Filter menu option in the Common Data View Tasks menu shows the portion of the filter that fits in the menu. You can modify the filter by clicking the Filter menu option.

If you click the Code view tab, the filter has been implemented as an XPath expression in the XSL section of the Data Form Web Part code:

```
<xsl:variable name="Rows" select="/catalog/book[ (
    contains(normalize-space(author), 'O') or contains(normalize-
    space(author), 'o') ) and number(price) &lt; '10']"/>
```

You can also view this advanced filter expression by clicking the Advanced button in the Filter Criteria dialog box to open the Advanced Condition dialog box, as shown in Figure 17.25.

Later in this section, I discuss creating Advanced XSLT expressions for data views in SharePoint Designer.

Enabling sorting and grouping

Using the Common Data View Tasks menu for the Data Form Web Part, click the Sorting menu option to specify the sorting expression for the rows in the data view by using the Sort and Group dialog box, as shown in Figure 17.26.

Simply add the fields you want to sort and group by clicking Add to move them to the Sort Order list. Then, click the field to specify the sorting order and grouping settings on the field. You can enable the group header and group footer by using the check boxes, as shown in Figure 17.26.

NOTE   For SharePoint data sources like lists and libraries, the Data Form Web Part currently supports grouping up to seven levels. This means that you can group rows based on the first column in the list, then on the second column, up to seven column levels.

Clicking Advanced Grouping allows you to choose from a number of options, allowing you to create column totals per group, maintain groups while paging, etc.

FIGURE 17.25

The Advanced Condition dialog box

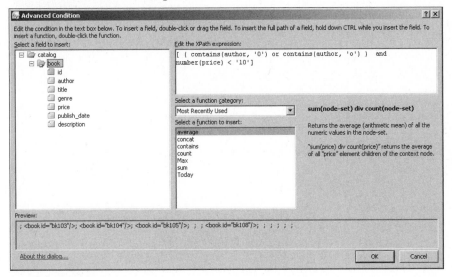

FIGURE 17.26

The Sort and Group dialog box

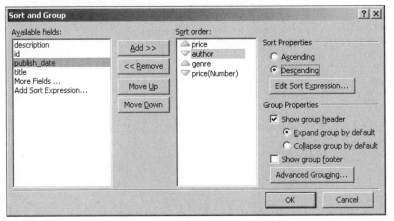

Working with parameters

One of the other cool features that SharePoint Designer provides is the ability to create parameters for use in operations based on user inputs. For example, you can request user interaction on your Web page by using a form and then use parameters to pass user input from the form to a Data Form Web Part to perform operations such as data filtering, sorting, etc.

While this feature is available for use in Data View Web Parts in WSS v2/SPS 2003, the FrontPage 2003 client doesn't provide any user interface to create parameters. The designers have to manually add the parameters in the Data View Web Part code. SharePoint Designer provides designers with the ability to create parameters without having to directly modify the Data Form Web Part code for WSS v3/MOSS sites. You can create a parameter by using the user interface and specify the source for the parameter. The following are the sources that you can use with parameters:

- **Control:** To be able to use user controls, such as text boxes, dropdown menus, etc., placed on the Web page as a source for the parameter value
- **Cookie:** Allows you to use values from an HTTP cookie as a source for the parameter value
- **Form:** Enables you to use the HTML form data as the source for the parameter
- **Query String:** Allows you to use the query strings specified in the URL of the HTTP request as a source for the parameter value
- **Server Variable:** To be able to use the HTTP server variables, such as SERVER_NAME, LOGON_USER, etc., as a value for the parameter

The following exercise illustrates how you can use parameters in the Data Form Web Part to filter data based on user inputs.

In these steps, you create a data view for a data source, which can be filtered based on user selection in a dropdown menu, which is populated from a column in another data source. As a prerequisite to this exercise, you need a couple of related tables in a database — one to use as a data source for the dropdown menu and the other as the data source for the Data Form Web Part:

1. **Create a new ASPX page in your SharePoint Web site by using SharePoint Designer, open it in the Design view, and then place the cursor inside the Web page in the Design view.**

2. **Using the Data Source Library task pane, click the data source that will serve the dropdown list control and then click the Insert Data Source Control menu option.** A data source control is inserted on the Web page based on the nature of the data source. For example, the SQLDataSource control is inserted for a Database Connection. An HTML form is automatically inserted on the page to host the data source control.

3. **Place the cursor at the location inside the HTML form to insert the dropdown list control and then choose Insert ⇨ ASP.NET Controls ⇨ Dropdown List.** A dropdown list control is inserted on the Web page, and the Common DropDownList Tasks menu for the control opens.

4. **Click the Enable AutoPostBack check box in the Common DropDownList Tasks menu.** This ensures that the Web page is refreshed to load data when a selection is made in the dropdown list.

5. **Click Choose Data Source to open the Data Source Configuration Wizard.**

6. **Choose the data source inserted on the page in step 2, the data field to be used as display text, and the data field to be used as the value for the dropdown list and then click OK.** This binds the dropdown list control to the data source control inserted in step 2.

7. **Place the cursor at the location outside the HTML form where you want to insert the data view by using the Data Form Web Part.**

8. **Using the Data Source Library task pane, click the data source for the data view and then click the Show Data menu option to open the Data Source Details task pane, which shows rows of data from the data source.**

9. **Select the columns you want to display in the data view and then choose Insert Selected Fields as ⇨ Multiple Item View.** A data view for the data source is inserted in the Web page and the Common Data View Tasks menu opens.

10. **In the Common Data View Tasks menu, choose the Parameters menu option.** The Data View Parameters dialog box, as shown in Figure 17.27, opens. You use this dialog box to create new parameters for the data view.

11. **Click New Parameter to create a new parameter and then give the parameter a name by using the highlighted list box.**

12. **Using the Parameter Source dropdown menu, select the source for this parameter.** For this exercise, choose Control as the parameter source. This enables the Control ID dropdown menu.

13. **Choose the control ID for the dropdown menu inserted in step 3 and then click OK.** Figure 17.28 shows the Data View Parameters dialog box with a parameter created.

14. **Using the Common Data View Tasks menu, choose the Filter menu option.** The Filter Criteria dialog box opens.

15. **Select the field you want to use for filtering the data view, select the comparison operator, and then choose the parameter you just created in the previous steps, as shown in Figure 17.29.** Also, notice the Create a new parameter option in the Value dropdown menu. This is another access point to create or modify parameters by using the Data View Parameters dialog box.

16. **Click OK, save the Web page, and then preview it in a browser.**

When you select an option in the dropdown menu, the data view is filtered to show only the corresponding rows of data. You can use the concept described above to create multiple parameters and filters based on multiple user inputs.

FIGURE 17.27

The Data View Parameters dialog box

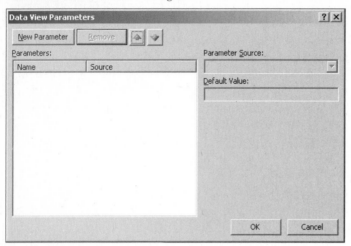

FIGURE 17.28

A parameter created by using the Data View Parameters dialog box

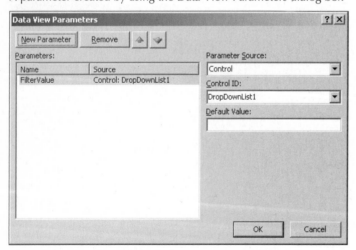

FIGURE 17.29

Creating a filter by using the Filter Criteria dialog box

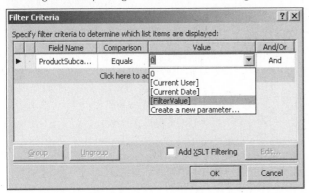

Using advanced XSLT expressions

After you insert a Data Form Web Part on a Web page, you can use the SharePoint Designer XSLT editing interface to apply XSLT formatting to the data that's shown by the data view. You can use XSL to create advanced filtering and sorting expressions, format data fields, and insert data fields using formulae. The user interface for inserting these advanced XSL expressions is similar and is shown in Figure 17.30.

The Select a field to insert list shows the list of available columns from your data source. You can apply XSL functions to these columns by choosing from a list of function categories available in the Select a function category dropdown menu. Also, notice that when you select a function for applying it to the column, a short description and example on how to use the function is presented in the dialog box.

The Edit the XPath expression box shows the expression as it builds and also provides IntelliSense features to assist in authoring the expressions. A preview of the data that results from the XSL expression is shown at the bottom of the dialog box.

NOTE It's important to understand that XSL applied to the Data Form Web Part is recursive. So, if you apply XSL formatting to a single data field value in a column, the formatting is applied to all the data field values in that column.

FIGURE 17.30

The advanced XSLT builder in SharePoint Designer

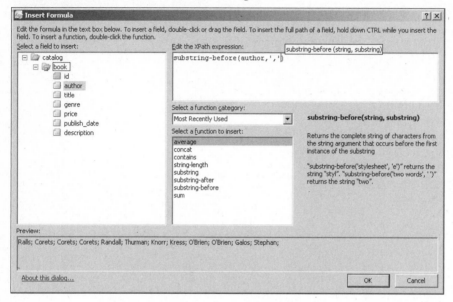

Creating filtering and sorting expressions

You can create advanced XSL expressions for filtering and sorting your data views by using the SharePoint Designer XSL builder interface. For illustration, the following exercise takes you through the steps to filter a data view based on an XSL expression. The idea here is to filter the data view to show only those rows where a column value is less than the average of all the values for the column in the table:

1. **Insert a data view of the data source you want to use for this exercise by using the Data Source Library task pane.**

2. **In the Common Data View Tasks menu, choose the Filter menu option.** The Filter Criteria dialog box opens.

3. **In the Filter Criteria dialog box, click the Advanced button to open the Advanced Condition dialog box for building XSL expressions.**

4. **Using the XSL expression builder, create the XPath expression shown in Figure 17.31.** Keep in mind that you should highlight the column to which you want to apply a function. For example, just by highlighting /catalog/books/price in the Edit the XPath expression box and then selecting average in the Select a function to insert converts the resultant expression to sum(/catalog/book/price) div count(/catalog/book/price).

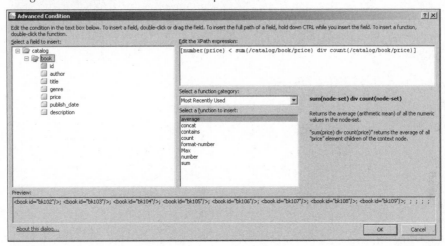

FIGURE 17.31

Using the XPath builder to create filter expressions

NOTE Just clicking on the column in the Select a function to insert box inserts the column name only. If you hold Ctrl and then select the column, the complete XPath for the column is inserted.

5. Click OK twice to implement the filter to the data view.

In the Advanced Condition dialog box, in the Select a function category box, you have the Parameters category. That means you can perform XSL calculations or operations on parameters you're using with your data view to create filters.

For example, prior to filtering the data view based on values of a parameter of Data Time type, you might want to format the parameter value to a specific date format using the FormatDate or FormatDateTime functions in the Date/Time category.

Inserting formulae

Using XSL expressions, you can create new columns in your data view based on calculations performed on the existing columns. For example, you can combine the values of a number of columns to show in a single column. So, if you're storing an address in multiple columns in a table, you can use XSL expressions to combine the values of the address columns and show them as one.

The following exercise shows you how to use XSL expressions to create a new column based on calculation. Follow these steps:

1. Insert a data view of your data source by using the Data Source Library task pane.
2. Click Edit columns in the Common Data View Tasks menu.

3. **In the Available Fields list, scroll to the bottom to find the Add Formula Column and then click Add.** The XPath Expression Builder dialog box opens.

4. **As shown in Figure 17.32, the concat function is used in the Text/String category to combine three columns to be displayed as one.**

5. **Click OK to create a new formula column.**

FIGURE 17.32

Creating formula columns by using XSL expressions

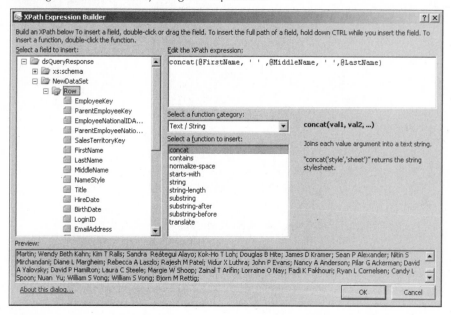

6. **Click OK and then save the Web page.** The new columns added to the data view now have the values in the three columns concatenated to form a single column.

NOTE The column header shows the XSL expression that was used to create the column. However, showing this on a Web page isn't really desirable. So, you can edit the column header text in the Design view. After you change the column header text to the value of your choice, the formula column in the Edit Columns dialog box uses this text as the display name.

Formatting data fields

As shown in Figure 17.33, by using the Common xsl:value-of Tasks menu, which appears when you click the arrow next to a data field value in a data view, you can format the data field value in a number of ways. For example, if you're storing hyperlinks in a column in a table, you can use this menu to format the data field values as hyperlinks.

In the next steps, you use the Common xsl:value-of Tasks menu to format a column of Float or Number data type as currency:

1. **Insert a data view of a data source that has a column (of number data type) that needs to be displayed as currency.**

2. **After you insert the data view, click the arrow on the data field value in a row to open the Common xsl:value-of Tasks menu.**

3. **In the Format as dropdown menu, select Currency to open the Format Number dialog box, as shown in Figure 17.34.**

4. **Choose the symbol you want to display for the currency and then specify other settings for formatting the number.**

5. **Click OK and then save the Web page.**

In the preview of the Web page in the Design view, the formatting is applied to all the data field values in the column.

FIGURE 17.33

Formatting data field values by using the Common xsl:value-of Tasks menu

FIGURE 17.34

Formatting a number data field as currency

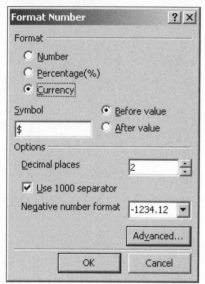

Working with the Conditional Formatting Task Pane

The Data Form Web Part, like its predecessor Front Page 2003, allows you to format rows of data based on conditions. You can apply formatting to rows in your data view when the data in the rows meets a certain criteria. You can also hide or show rows of data based on whether they match a particular condition. This is especially useful in situations when you need to highlight data in your presentations when certain conditions and requirements are met. This feature in SharePoint Designer is called conditional formatting.

Conditional formatting, like most of the formatting features of the Data Form Web Part, is also implemented by using the XSLT formatting. It doesn't mean to change how the data is retrieved from the data source but to apply XSLT to the data retrieved to show, hide, or apply formatting based on the conditions set. You use the familiar Filter Criteria dialog box to create conditions that when met apply the specified formatting to the matching rows of data.

You use the Conditional Formatting task pane to create conditional formatting conditions. As shown in Figure 17.35, the Conditional Formatting task pane by default shows the existing conditions that apply to the selected content on the Web page.

To create a new condition, follow these steps:

1. **Select the HTML component on the Web page on which you want to apply the formatting based on the condition.** For example, you can select the `<tr>` tag in the data view if you want to apply the formatting to the row or the `<td>` tag if you want to apply the formatting to just a column in the data view.

2. **Click Create menu in the Conditional Formatting task pane.** You have three options: Show Content, Hide Content, and Apply Formatting. The Show Content and Hide Content options show or hide the content based on the condition, while Apply Formatting lets you specify the formatting that needs to be applied to the data that needs the condition.

3. **Click the Apply Formatting menu option.** The Condition Criteria dialog box opens, offering the same interface as the Filter Criteria dialog box, which you used earlier in this chapter to create filters on the data view.

4. **Using the Conditions Criteria dialog box, specify the condition that when met applies the formatting to the row of data.**

5. **Click OK.** The Modify Style dialog box opens, which you should be familiar with from using CSS styles.

6. **Use the Modify Style dialog box to specify the formatting that you want to apply to the rows that meet the condition specified in step 4.**

7. **Click OK, save the Web page, and then preview it in a browser.**

The rows to data that matched your condition have the specified formatting applied to them. Similarly, you can use conditional formatting to show or hide content based on conditions.

FIGURE 17.35

The Conditional Formatting task pane

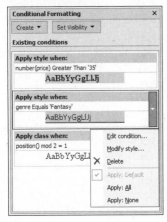

Summary

The Data Form Web Part is one of the most powerful tools provided to you in SharePoint Designer for data retrieval and presentation. With its capabilities to work with almost all SharePoint data source types, the Data Form Web Part becomes one of the most extensible, customizable, and versatile Web parts offered with SharePoint Designer.

This chapter took you through the internals of the Data Form Web Part and discussed how you can create data views and data forms by using the Data Form Web Part. You learned about the recommended methods to create custom list forms for SharePoint lists and libraries. I also showed you how you could use the SharePoint Designer XSLT editing tools to apply advanced filtering, sorting, and formatting.

Chapter 18

Creating Web Part Connections

Web part connections, as the name suggests, is a mechanism to connect Web parts together in a source-target–like arrangement. The source Web part is used to provide parameter values to the target Web part, and based on these values, the target Web part can perform operations on the data it exposes. The source Web part, called the data provider, implements an interface to send rows of data to the target Web part, called the data consumer. SharePoint allows you to identify data consumers placed either on the same page as a data provider or on different Web pages.

While SharePoint Designer provides an advanced user interface to create Web part connections between Web parts on a Web page, the capability to create Web part connections is inherent to SharePoint itself. For example, if you have two custom lists that contain related data in your SharePoint site, you can create a Web part connection between Web parts for these lists using the SharePoint Web site interface in a Web browser.

This chapter discusses how you can connect two or more Web parts by using Web part connections to interface with each other for performing operations such as filtering, sorting, etc. I show you how you can use the SharePoint Web site user interface to create basic Web part connections between two or more Web parts on the same page.

Later, using SharePoint Designer, I talk about how the Web part connections are implemented on Web pages. While SharePoint sites allow you to create basic Web part connections for filtering data, SharePoint Designer abilities regarding Web part connections are unique, as you can use parameter values from the source Web part to perform a number of operations besides just filtering data. As shown in Chapter 17, you can combine advanced XSLT formatting expressions and Web part connections to create heavily customized and branded views of data.

First, follow these steps to create a Web part connection between two Web parts by using the SharePoint (WSS v3) Web site user interface itself:

1. **Create two custom lists on your SharePoint Web site by choosing Site Actions ⇨ Create.** You might not see the Site Actions menu in the SharePoint site if you're not authorized to perform editing operations on the Web site.

2. **Create a column in the source custom list that serves as the parameter to be passed to the target custom list for filtering data.** When the lists are created and some sample data has been inserted into the lists, go back to the home page of the Web site.

3. **Choose Site Actions ⇨ Edit Page to open the Web page in Edit mode.**

4. **Click the Add Web Part bar to open the Add Web Parts Web page, as shown in Figure 18.1, select the custom lists you created in step 1, and then click Add.** The Web parts for the custom lists are inserted on the SharePoint Web page.

5. **On the SourceWebPart, choose Edit ⇨ Connections ⇨ Provide Row To ⇨ TargetWebPart, as shown in Figure 18.2, to open the Configure Connection Web page dialog box.**

6. **In the first screen of the Configure Connection Web page dialog box, choose the column you want to send to the target Web part in the connection for filtering and then click Next.**

7. **Choose the column that contains matching data in the target Web part and then click Next.**

8. **Click the Exit Edit Mode button to commit the changes you made to the Web page in these steps.**

The page is refreshed and the source Web part now has radio buttons that, when selected, filter the target Web part based on the selected column value. The Web part connections make filtering of data by using user input fairly easy to implement by using the SharePoint Web sites.

SharePoint Designer takes the Web part connection abilities provided by SharePoint to the next level by allowing you to create filtered views of data by using Web part connections for data sources other than SharePoint lists and libraries, such as database connections, XML files, BDCs, etc. It does so by providing you with the abilities to create Web part connections between Data Form Web Parts. In fact, you can use SharePoint Designer to connect any two Web parts that support Web part connections. For example, you can have the SharePoint List View Web Part connect to the Data Form Web Part to pass data from a SharePoint list to a non-SharePoint data source, such as a table in a custom database. This allows for greater integration between data sources of various types.

Now that you understand the basic concepts of Web part connections, I take you through some steps to create a Web part connection by using SharePoint Designer and then have a cursory look at the HTML code that makes the Web part connections work.

FIGURE 18.1

Adding Web parts to a SharePoint Web page by using the site user interface

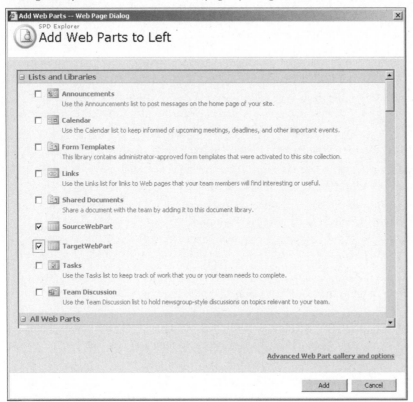

FIGURE 18.2

Connecting Web parts by using the SharePoint user interface

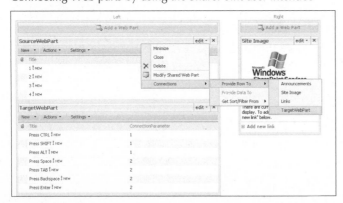

Exploring Web Part Connections

To dive a little deeper to understand how Web part connections work, I take you through the following steps to create a simple Web part connection between a ListViewWebPart and a Data FormWebPart by using SharePoint Designer. Then, I help you explore the key code components that enable the Web part connections:

1. **Create a new ASPX page in SharePoint Designer and then open it in the Design view.**

2. **Place the cursor on the Web page at the location where you want to insert the source Web part.** For this exercise, the source Web part is a ListViewWebPart rendering data from a SharePoint List.

3. **Choose Task Panes ⇨ Web Parts to enable the Web Parts task pane.**

4. **In the Web Parts List, select the SourceWebPart and then click Insert Selected Web part to insert it on the Web page.** This is illustrated in Figure 18.3.

5. **Ensure that the data source you selected for the data view has matching data to filter by using the values from the source Web part.**

6. **Using the Data Source Library and Data Source Details task panes, insert a data view on the Web page.**

7. **Right-click on the source Web part and then choose Web Part Connections from the popup menu to open the Web Part Connections Wizard, as shown in Figure 18.4.**

8. **Using the Choose the action on the source Web Part to use for this connection dropdown menu, select Provide Row To and then click Next.** In the top section of the Web Part Connections Wizard, the details of the connection appear as the connection is built.

9. **On the next screen, click the Connect to a Web Part on this page radio button in the Choose a page containing the Web part for this connection section and then click Next.**

10. **As illustrated in Figure 18.5, select the target Web part and the target action in the Choose the target Web part and action for the connection section and then click Next.** If you have multiple Web parts that support connections on the Web page, you should see them all listed in the Target Web Part listed. Based on the target action selected on the last screen, the options in the next screen change.

11. **Select the matching columns and then click Next.** As shown in Figure 18.6, this screen allows you to match columns in both data sources to filter the data.

FIGURE 18.3

Inserting a ListViewWebPart by using the Web Parts task pane

12. **Click Finish to complete the creation of the Web part connection, save the Web page, and then preview it in a browser.**

When you click the radio button for the row in the source Web part, the target Web part becomes filtered based on the selection. If you click the Code view tab of the Web page where you just inserted the Web parts and connected them by using Web part connections, the HTML code that enables the Web part connections appears.

FIGURE 18.4

Using the Web Part Connections Wizard

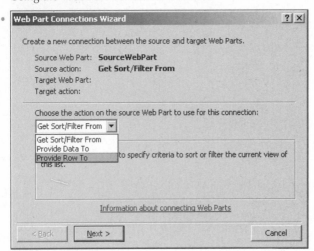

FIGURE 18.5

Choosing the target Web part for the connection

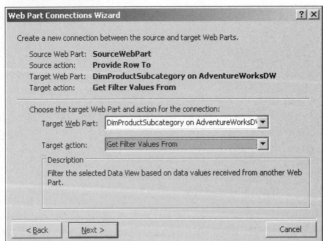

FIGURE 18.6

Matching columns for filtering by using the Web Part Connections Wizard

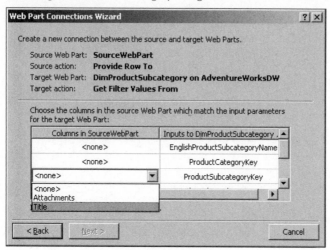

Understanding data providers and data consumers

There are two important sections in the HTML code that enable the Web part connections for the Web page. These sections are illustrated in the following code:

```
<SPWebPartConnections>

<WebPartPages:spWebpartconnection ID="g_
    C81C15B21EA842B0B254CFA49A9A4F9C" ConsumerConnectionPointID="DFWP
    Filter Consumer ID" ConsumerID="g_e14badef_e22f_42ab_b91b_
    a831f878a3e1" ProviderConnectionPointID="ListViewRowProvider_
    WPQ_" ProviderID="g_19a7a140_8d41_4410_ac36_7fa5175e22ee">

<asp:rowtoparameterstransformer ProviderFieldNames="LinkTitle"
    ConsumerFieldNames="@ProductSubcategoryKey" />

</WebPartPages:spWebpartconnection>
</SPWebPartConnections>
```

The `WebPartPages:spWebpartconnection` control stores the relation that establishes the connection between the Web parts. The attributes assigned in this control define which Web part serves as the data provider for the connections and which one is the data consumer. For each connection that you establish between a set of Web parts on the Web page, you get a `WebPartPages:spWebpartconnection` control in the HTML code.

The `asp:rowtoparameterstransformer` lists the matching columns in the two Web parts to be used for comparison.

Investigating the Web part connection string

Looking closely at the `WebPartPages:spWebpartconnection` control shows that the control has its own ID and has the `ConsumerID` and the `ProviderID`:

```
<WebPartPages:spWebpartconnection ID="g_
    C81C15B21EA842B0B254CFA49A9A4F9C" ConsumerConnectionPointID="DFWP
    Filter Consumer ID" ConsumerID="g_e14badef_e22f_42ab_b91b_
    a831f878a3e1" ProviderConnectionPointID="ListViewRowProvider_
    WPQ_" ProviderID="g_19a7a140_8d41_4410_ac36_7fa5175e22ee">
```

The `ConsumerID` matches the `id` attribute of the source Web part on the Web page, and the `ProviderID` matches the `id` attribute of the target Web part. Obviously, if the Web part connection control doesn't find a provider or consumer matching the IDs it has, the control errors out with an error similar to the following: Could not find the connection provider Web Part with ID "g_19a7a140_8d41_4410_ac36_7fa5175e22ee."

CAUTION   **Using the Design view in SharePoint Designer, if you select all and delete the consumer and provider Web parts to insert new ones, the Web part connection control from the old connection might still be left in the Web page code. To avoid errors, ensure that the old Web part connection control is deleted. You can do this by deleting the old Web part connection control in the Code view.**

Managing Web Part Connections

While the exercise in the previous section should have familiarized you with the basic process of creating a Web part connection by using SharePoint Designer, in this section, I discuss some peculiarities that you can exploit while working with the Web part connections on a Web page.

Creating and modifying Web part connections

The Web Part Connections Wizard is the primary interface in SharePoint Designer to create Web part connections between Web parts. You can access the Web Part Connections Wizard either by right-clicking on a Web part and then choosing Web Part Connections from the popup menu or by using the Web Part Connections menu option in the Common Data View Tasks menu.

The Web Part Connections Wizard provides a set of actions available for the source Web part. These actions might change depending on the Web part being used as a source Web part. For example, if the source Web part is a DataFormWebPart, the following source actions are available for use:

- **Get Filter Values From:** Allows you to filter the source Web part based on data received from a target Web part

- **Get Parameters From:** Allows you to use the data sent from the target Web part as input values for parameters being used in the source Web part

- **Send Row of Data To:** Allows you to send data rows to the target Web part

Based on the selection made for the source action, the options available as target actions automatically change to accommodate the source action. For example, if you choose the Send Row of Data To as the source action, the actions available for the target Web part would be Get Filter Values From and Get Parameters From.

To view the existing Web part connections associated with a Web part, simply right-click on it and then choose Web Part Connections from the popup menu. If there are no Web part connections for the Web part, the Web Part Connections Wizard is initiated. However, if the Web part has any Web part connections associated with it, the Web Part Connections dialog box, as shown in Figure 18.7, opens.

When you click Add, the Web Part Connections dialog box links to the Web Part Connections Wizard. This allows you to add new Web part connections to the selected Web part.

If you want to modify the existing Web part connection, select it in the list of Web part connections for the Web part and then click Modify. The Web Part Connections Wizard opens again, this time with all the settings for the Web part connection loaded. You can then change the settings to modify the Web part connection. To remove a Web part connection, simply select it from the list and then click Remove.

FIGURE 18.7

Adding and modifying connections by using the Web Part Connections dialog box

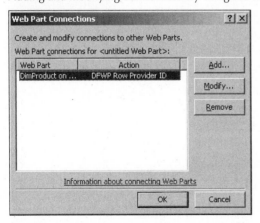

Using cross-page connections

The Web Part Connections Wizard also allows you to create Web part connections between Web parts that exist on separate Web pages in a SharePoint Site. As shown in Figure 18.8, you can choose the Web page inside the site that has the target Web part you want to use for the connection.

When you click Next, the Web parts that support Web part connections and reside on the chosen Web page are available as choices for the target Web part in the Web Part Connections Wizard. From here on, you use the same process to create a Web part connection between Web parts.

Creating parameters

You may have already noticed the power and extensibility that Data Form Web Parts parameters provide. Web part connections help you utilize these parameters to channelize data from the source Web part to the target Web part or vice versa. You can have the parameter values be provided by the source Web part and then use these parameters like you would in the target Web part for filtering, sorting, advanced XSLT expressions, conditional formatting, etc.

When you choose the target action Get Parameters From while creating the Web part connection, you see the screen shown in Figure 18.9.

Clicking the Create a new parameter row opens the Data View Parameters dialog box, where you can create new parameters. You can't change the parameter source because you use the Web part connection as the source for the parameter. As shown in Figure 18.10, after you create the parameters, they're available to match with the columns from the source Web part.

FIGURE 18.8

Creating cross-page connections by using the Web Part Connections Wizard

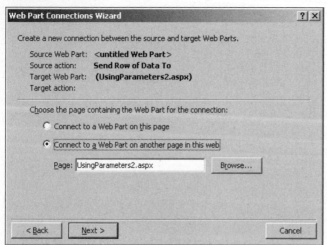

FIGURE 18.9

Creating new parameters for a Web part connection

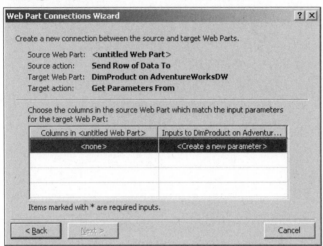

FIGURE 18.10

Matching columns with parameters to identify the source of values

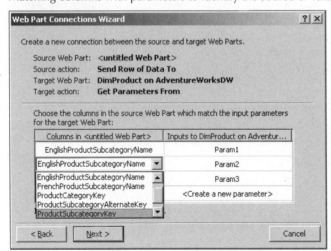

For DataFormWebParts, the Set up conditional formatting on the consumer Web part check box appears on the Finish screen of the Web Part Connections Wizard. Clicking this check box configures the XSL of the data view to enable application of conditional formatting.

Once the Web part connection is created successfully, you can use these parameters created and matched by using the Web Part Connections Wizard to perform filtering and formatting operations on the target Web part. The values of these parameters are made available by the selection made in the source Web part.

NOTE If you're connecting to a Web part on a different page, you only see the parameters already available in the target Web page. To create new parameters, open the Web page connecting the target Web part and then create new parameters by using the Data View Parameters dialog box.

Connecting with the Form Web Part

The Form Web Part is a Web part available in SharePoint that allows you to create simple HTML-based forms that can be used for requesting user input on a Web page. While with the Data Form Web Part in SharePoint Designer you have much more advanced form capabilities, you might just want to use this Web part to create and display an HTML form on a SharePoint site.

The following exercise shows how you can use the Form Web Part to create simple HTML forms by using the SharePoint site interface and then use Web part connections to provide data to and filter another Web part. You don't really need SharePoint Designer for this exercise; however, you can create Web part connections between form Web part and other Web parts with relative ease in SharePoint Designer. Follow these steps:

1. **Open the home page of your SharePoint (WSS v3) Web site and then choose Site Actions ⇨ Edit Page.**

2. **Click the Add Web Part bar to open the Add Web Parts Web dialog box, select the Form Web Part and the target Web part in the list of Web parts, and then click OK.** The Form Web Part is available in the Miscellaneous section in this dialog box.

3. **For the Form Web Part, choose Edit ⇨ Modify Shared Web part to open the Properties pane for the Form Web Part.** This is illustrated in Figure 18.11.

4. **Click the Source Editor button to modify the HTML form associated with the Form Web Part.** The Text Entry Web page dialog box opens.

5. **Change the HTML of the form to suit your requirement.** Notice the default code that exists in the text editor. As shown in the following code, by default, you have an HTML text field `<input type="text" name="T1>` and an HTML button `<input type="button" value="Go" onclick="javascript:_SFSUBMIT_"/>`. When you click the HTML button, a JavaScript function is called that submits the form:

```
<div onkeydown="javascript:if (event.keyCode == 13) _
    SFSUBMIT_"><input type="text" name="T1><input type="button"
    value="Go" onclick="javascript:_SFSUBMIT_"/></div>
```

You might want to keep the HTML button intact to avoid any issues with the Form Web Part. Simply add the HTML tags that make up your form.

6. **Click Save to implement the HTML form changes to the Form Web Part.**

7. On the Form Web Part, choose Edit ⇨ Connections ⇨ Provides Form Values To ⇨ TargetWebPart, as shown in Figure 18.12, to create a Web part connection.

8. Match the form field to the corresponding column in the target Web part to configure the connection and then click Next.

9. Click Exit Edit Mode to save the changes to the Web page.

When you type a value in the Form Web Part and then click Go, the corresponding matching records are displayed in the target Web part. While this is no match for the advanced SharePoint Designer forms, I used this example to illustrate that basic form search capabilities can be implemented using Web part connections right through the SharePoint Web site interface.

NOTE Creating connections between Web parts placed on the list form pages (for example, `dispform.aspx`, `editform.aspx`, etc.) doesn't work beyond one Web part connection. That means you can't create multiple Web part connections on these SharePoint pages.

FIGURE 18.11

Modifying Form Web Part properties

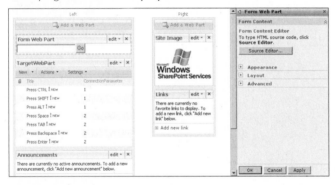

FIGURE 18.12

Creating Web part connections by using the Form Web Part

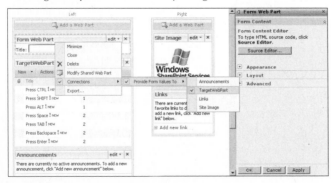

Summary

In this chapter, I discussed the use of Web part connections on SharePoint sites and Web parts. You learned how to use the SharePoint user interface to create Web part connections. Through the facilities that SharePoint Designer provides, you also learned to connect Web parts by using Web part connections. You worked on creating Web part connections that provide input to data view parameters, which can then be used to perform advanced operations on the data views.

Part VI

Developing Workflows

Chapter 19

Understanding Workflow Architecture

Windows SharePoint Services 3.0 (WSS v3) introduces one of the most sought-after features for collaboration-oriented applications called workflows. Workflows provide the backbone for implementing business-driven processes and the logical flow of work. A workflow, in its most basic definition, is a logical process that defines the flow of work in a business entity. You can think of it as a series of steps that take place while implementing a business practice. For example, the chronological order of the steps that occur in a document-approval process may be represented as a workflow where based on a certain set of conditions, an approver decides whether a document should be approved and sent up the chain to be reviewed by the senior approvers or be rejected. A series of steps that need to be executed before a loan application is approved or an insurance claim is accepted could form a workflow process. There are many key pieces to the logical representation of a workflow:

- **Stages:** Stages define the states of an object in a workflow. For example, a document-approval workflow can have a number of stages through which the document passes before reaching the final approval state (which is when the workflow is deemed completed).

- **Events:** Events are the triggers that can be used to start or stop a workflow. For example, the event of a document being submitted for review could be the start of a workflow process.

- **Conditions:** Conditions define the logical clauses that decide what action or operation should be performed in the workflow or whether workflow should move from one stage to another. For example, checking a credit score may be a condition that needs to be determined for moving a loan application workflow to the next stage.

- **Actions:** Actions (or activities) are the operations performed at a given stage in a workflow. Sending an e-mail to a document approver indicating that the document is available for review can be an action that's performed in a stage of a document-approval workflow.

Using these pieces, you can design a workflow process that implements the functional operatives of your business logic. While the aforementioned components have been discussed to elucidate the workflow logical implementation, the actual terminology defining them in SharePoint workflows might differ.

WSS v3 and MOSS 2007 implement the feature of SharePoint workflows. Architecturally, SharePoint workflows are based on the infrastructure provided by the Windows Workflow Foundation, a framework that's a part of Microsoft .NET Framework 3.0. While .NET Framework 3.0 provides the underlying engine that runs the workflows, SharePoint implementation provides a number of sustaining services to this engine. SharePoint Web sites provide a number of out-of-the-box customizable workflows, instances of which you can associate with lists and document libraries for SharePoint Web sites.

Although you can use the Windows Workflow Foundation to develop workflows for Windows Forms and Web-based applications, SharePoint specifically provides you with the feature implementation to quickly develop workflows for SharePoint objects, such as list items, document libraries, etc. SharePoint provides the object model framework that developers can leverage to create workflows for SharePoint Web sites by using developer tools, such as Visual Studio. These workflows can then be deployed to Web servers hosting SharePoint Web sites and configured for use in SharePoint lists and libraries.

SharePoint Designer, leveraging the architecture previously discussed, allows you to create declarative workflows for implementing business logic and processes. This chapter discusses the internals of SharePoint workflow architecture and how SharePoint Designer uses the infrastructure provided by SharePoint and Windows Workflow Foundation to help create business-oriented workflows.

Introducing Workflow Concepts

Most businesses have processes that involve steps or stages in which work is performed. Every stage might have its own logical implementation related to or completely oblivious of other stages. These stages and the actions performed in them form a workflow for a process. To facilitate implementation of such workflows in applications, Microsoft provides a framework for developing workflow-based applications. This framework is part of .NET Framework 3.0 and is called the Windows Workflow Foundation (WF).

Workflow applications, like many business processes are, can be very complex and long-running. They might involve human interactions that are unpredictable and have to accommodate dynamic changes that are inherent in today's business processes. For example, it might take weeks for an approver to review a document and decide what action needs to be taken next in the workflow process. If the workflow application is allowed to keep running for the entire duration while the approver reviews the document, it would just be a waste of resources of the machine on which it's running. There might be many approvers and many more documents. Think of the multiple long-running workflow applications running at the same time on the machine. You can imagine that the computer running these workflow applications will soon run out of all resources.

This and many such design considerations and issues with workflow applications have been innovatively addressed in the WF framework. Like most Microsoft frameworks, WF isn't a workflow application nor does it have a user interface. It's mostly an architectural implementation that provides the class libraries, functions, and a WF runtime engine that facilitate the development and functioning of the workflow applications. Using a development tool, such as Visual Studio, you can develop a Windows- or Web-based workflow application by using the class libraries provided in the WF framework. When an instance of the workflow application runs, the WF framework is loaded into the application's process and provides the runtime engine and services to the workflow instance. In the case of SharePoint, which is a Web-based application, the WF framework is loaded into the Internet Information Services (IIS) worker process where the workflow instance runs.

NOTE A workflow instance is a running state of a workflow application. You might have multiple instances of the same workflow running at the same time with different states. For example, two instances of the same approval workflow may be running when the approval process begins on two documents. The WF framework is responsible for maintaining the states of these workflows without them interfering with each other.

Windows Workflow Foundation provides the runtime engine and services that execute the workflow and provide support for persistence, tracking, transaction, and interaction with other processes.

Exploring the workflow architecture

Technically, a workflow is a set of activities that define the business process for which it's being developed. By default, the WF provides a number of base activities that developers can use to design their workflows. Alternatively, developers can derive workflows from the existing activities and create their own to implement a specific business logic. After the workflow is developed, the WF provides a number of components that help in the execution of the workflow.

Workflow runtime engine

Windows Workflow Foundation makes available a runtime engine responsible for executing WF workflows. This runtime engine is basically a library that can be hosted in any Windows process, including console applications, forms-based applications, Windows Services, ASP.NET Web sites, and Web services. Also, it's customizable and allows developers to have their own version of the runtime with specific implementations.

The runtime engine provides the workflow instances running in the host process with scheduling services and the framework to communicate with the host process and the other processes. The runtime engine uses a number of services to provide workflows with persistence, scheduling, transaction, and tracking services. Figure 19.1 shows an example of a workflow execution architecture.

FIGURE 19.1

A diagrammatical representation of a workflow execution architecture

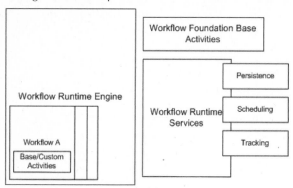

Workflow runtime services

The Workflow runtime engine described previously relies on a number of services when it runs a workflow instance. Although these runtime services are pluggable, which means developers can derive their own implementation of these services, the WF provides out-of-the-box implementations of the runtime services:

- **Persistence:** As indicated earlier, it's innate to workflows that they're long-running applications. A real-time implementation of a business process, such as document approval, can take days, weeks, or even months. Keeping the workflows running while waiting for user input is simply a waste of resources. Persistence services in WF provide the runtime engine with the capabilities to enable workflows to remain active for long periods of time and survive application restarts. While waiting for user input, the state of the workflow instances can be unloaded from memory and serialized into a storage device, such as an SQL database or an XML file. This process is sometimes called dehydration. Whenever the input is received, the workflow runtime engine rehydrates the workflow instances by loading the workflow state back into memory and continues execution of the workflow. While the runtime engine decides when to persist workflow instances, the persistence service decides how and where to save the workflow state.

- **Tracking:** Tracking services provide the runtime engine with the ability to extract and store information about the workflow instances currently running in a host process. Whenever an event occurs during the life cycle of a workflow instance, the tracking framework allows the runtime engine to track a specific field, property, or column and then extract values. For example, the WF tracking service can be use to track when a particular activity in a workflow was started, when it ended, and what the state of the fields were during these events. This information can later be used for display, monitoring, and notification purposes.

As mentioned previously, while the WF provides default implementations for these runtime services, it enables developers to replace the default implementations with their own customization versions. SharePoint in particular uses this nature of workflow runtime services and uses customized implementation of persistence, tracking, notification, and messaging runtime services.

Types of workflows

The Windows Workflow Foundation has been primarily designed to cater to all workflow types in a single architectural implementation. System workflows are the workflow types that don't require or rely on human interaction. While these workflows are easier to implement, they're not the commonly used or desirable ones. Most business processes demand that the workflows entail human interaction at some level. These workflows, commonly referred to as human- or people-driven workflows, depend on or even encourage human participation. Human workflows in general have the following characteristics:

- **The key characteristic of human workflows** is that they're designed to support long-running processes with life cycles measured in days, weeks, and even months. Human intervention implies that the workflow's execution stops at some point of time until an external event, usually triggered by some user interaction or system event, progresses the workflow. The success of the workflow solution is defined by how efficiently it can handle the pause in the activity and resume later.

- **The ability to monitor the state and progress of the workflow** is another key piece. Humans tend to be critical and need data for analysis of the state of a business process. The workflows should be able to display, monitor, and notify the state of the process at durations governed by humans.

While the WF accommodates the previous characteristics in its architecture, it provides the following choices for workflow design:

- **Sequential workflows:** Sequential workflows progress in steps like a flowchart. Based on the conditions encountered, the flow of the process can be directed to perform the associated activities. You can decide whether you want to execute steps one at a time or in parallel. These workflows are characterized by the fact that they have a defined path of execution and have a beginning and an end. Figure 19.2 shows an example of a sequential workflow. Most workflows created by SharePoint Designer fall into this category.

- **State machine workflows:** Unlike the sequential workflows, the state machine workflows transition between various stages or states. Although one state might be considered as a final state, it's not mandatory for the state machine workflows to have an end. The workflows are characterized by providing the ability to the end user to move from one state to another and then back to the previous state. Figure 19.3 shows an example of a state machine workflow.

Workflows can be created by using any .NET programming languages, such as C#, Visual Basic, etc., or defined in XML style by using Extensible Application Markup Language (XAML). While Visual Studio is the development tool for advanced workflow creation, SharePoint Designer provides Web designers with an interface-based designer tool for developing workflows specifically for SharePoint Web sites.

FIGURE 19.2

An example of a sequential workflow

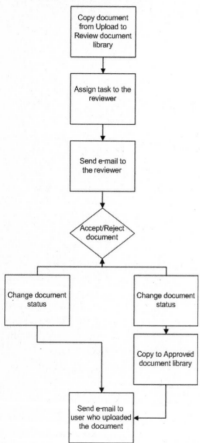

FIGURE 19.3

An example of a state machine workflow

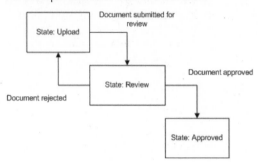

Exploring Workflow Technologies

While the theoretical concepts around Microsoft Workflow technologies have already been discussed in this chapter, this section familiarizes you with some of its practical aspects.

WF is available free with .NET Framework 3.5 and can be downloaded from the Microsoft Web site at http://msdn.microsoft.com/en-us/netframework/aa663328.aspx. It's one of the prerequisites for installing WSS v3 and MOSS 2007. SharePoint has its own implementation of many of the important runtime services provided with WF, such as persistence, tracking, notification, messaging, and roles.

However, it still relies on the WF runtime engine to execute the workflows and call the runtime services when and as required. Also, SharePoint Designer requires that you install WF to be able to use its workflow features. SharePoint Designer uses ASP.NET 2.0 Web services, which SharePoint implements to create, compile, and deploy workflows on SharePoint sites.

Understanding the workflow implementation in Windows SharePoint Services

WSS is one of the most popular implementations of workflow infrastructure provided by WF. Because the primary goal of a SharePoint deployment is to introduce enterprise-level collaboration and process management, workflows provide an important role in completing the SharePoint end-to-end offering in people, document, and information management. MOSS 2007 builds on this infrastructure provided by WSS and offers a number of out-of-the-box workflows for many common scenarios, such as document approval, feedback collection, etc.

WSS provides the hosting infrastructure for the workflow runtime in the IIS 6.0 worker process (w3wp.exe). As discussed earlier, the workflow runtime includes a base set of workflow activities and default implementation for runtime services. WSS builds on these base functionalities and extends them with activities and services specific to SharePoint. By default, the WF runtime engine includes the services for scheduling, persistence, etc., and supports the infrastructure for creating custom runtime services. WSS uses this ability to provide its own version of the default runtime services, such as persistence and tracking, and adds new services for notifications, messaging, transactions, and roles. Figure 19.4 shows an example of a SharePoint workflow architecture.

Workflows created for SharePoint use not only the default workflow activities provided by WF but also make use of the custom activities that SharePoint makes available for interaction with SharePoint lists and libraries. These custom activities can also be used in SharePoint Designer to declaratively create workflows. SharePoint also exposes a workflow object model that developers can use to programmatically design custom workflows.

MOSS builds on the workflow infrastructure provided by WSS and extends the workflow implementation. While WSS only has one out-of-the-box workflow (called Three-States workflow), MOSS provides the following workflows for common scenarios that SharePoint site users can use to create instances of and associate with lists and libraries:

- Approval
- Collect Feedback
- Collect Signatures
- Disposition Approval
- Translation Management

FIGURE 19.4

The diagrammatical representation of a SharePoint workflow architecture

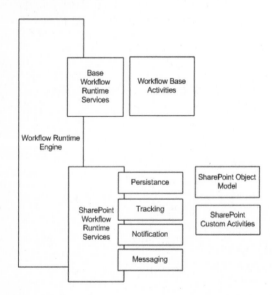

All these workflows are based on WF, but the implementation is obfuscated for the SharePoint users through Web pages that can be used to configure them. SharePoint provides Web pages that can be used to associate these workflows with lists, libraries, or content types, start workflow instances, and interact with the workflows. These workflows are installed on the SharePoint server as features that can be activated on a site basis. Developers can use Visual Studio to create similar workflows and then deploy them to SharePoint servers.

To establish a SharePoint workflow creation life cycle, you must first install the workflow feature (or solution) to a SharePoint Web server and then activate it for a particular site collection in a SharePoint Web application. After deploying the workflow, you can associate the workflow with required lists or libraries. Then, you can create workflow instances that perform the workflow logic on the respective item in the list or library.

While the workflow instance runs, depending on the workflow implementation, it can access a number of SharePoint resources, such as other lists or libraries, task lists, workflow history lists, etc. It's important that the user under whose context the workflow instance begins has appropriate SharePoint permissions for these resources.

Implementing Workflow Association and Initiation

For a workflow to be useable on a SharePoint site, it must first be associated with a list, a library, or a particular content type. As a Web designer, you have to make this choice based on your requirements. After the workflow is associated with a list or a library, an instance of it can be started by firing it manually or setting it to automatically start whenever an item is created or changed.

NOTE Only a single instance of a workflow can be run on a list item at one time. This means that while an instance of a workflow is running on an item, you can't start another instance of the same workflow on the same item. You can, however, start an instance of another workflow on the item. It's recommended that you don't run more than 15 workflow instances on the same item at one time.

You can associate a workflow with the following SharePoint assets:

- **Associate with Lists:** When you associate a workflow with a list, instances of the workflow can be started for the items in the list. The item on which the workflow is running is called the Current Item in the workflow context.

- **Associate with Libraries:** After the workflow is associated with a library, its instances can be run on the document, pictures, etc., that belong to the library.

- **Associate with Content Type:** By allowing you to associate a workflow with a particular content type, SharePoint lets you use a single workflow across multiple lists and libraries that use that content type.

NOTE **Workflows created with SharePoint Designer can't be associated with SharePoint content types.**

Workflows created for SharePoint lists and libraries can be started (or initialized) in the following ways:

- **Automatically when an item is created:** When creating a workflow, you can specify that it should start whenever an item is created in a list or a library.

- **Automatically when an item is updated:** This option triggers an instance of the workflow on an item when the item is changed.

- **Manually:** You can also configure a workflow to be manually started on an item in the list or library. When users start the workflow manually, they're taken to a workflow initiation Web page. The initiation Web page consists of a user interface that can be used to start the workflow. Optionally, designers can also request user input at the start of the workflow by customizing the initiation page to include fields for user input.

SharePoint Designer allows Web designers to choose whether the workflows should be started manually or automatically. You can also design a custom initiation Web page with a form that can be used to request user input. The user input can then be stored in variables that form the workflow data and are used for performing the business logic the workflow is designed for.

Summary

In this chapter, I discussed the internals of a workflow, workflow types, and key concepts around the workflow infrastructure. You learned about the architectural components of the Windows Workflow Foundation, and you became familiar with the workflow runtime engine and services provided by WF to facilitate development of complex workflows. You also learned about the SharePoint implementation of workflow services, workflow association, and initiation.

Chapter 20

Creating Workflows with SharePoint Designer

I f you're a Web designer or an information worker interested in designing workflows on SharePoint sites and don't really want to write custom
code for implementing them, SharePoint Designer may be the ideal tool
for you. You can declaratively create sequential workflows for SharePoint
sites by using Workflow Designer, which is provided with SharePoint
Designer. Workflow Designer, which is available only for SharePoint sites,
both WSS v3 and MOSS, is the tool that SharePoint Designer provides to
create workflows, associate them with SharePoint lists and libraries, check
for errors in workflows, and deploy them to SharePoint sites.

The workflow feature of SharePoint Designer is made possible by the fact
that SharePoint workflows can be compiled at runtime just before the first
time they run on a SharePoint Web site. Using the Workflow Designer interface, Web designers can visually create workflows. Internally, SharePoint
Designer creates some special files that store information about the workflow
configuration and settings made by using the Workflow Designer user interface. SharePoint Designer uploads these files into a special document library
inside a SharePoint Web site. SharePoint Designer also makes use of the
capabilities of SharePoint to associate the workflow with the list or library for
which it's being created. Whenever the first instance of the workflow is
spawned, the workflow is compiled and made available for the rest of the
instances. So, rather than compiling a workflow as a dynamic link library
(.dll) and deploying it on a SharePoint Web server, SharePoint Designer
relies on the just-in-time compiling abilities of the Windows Workflow
Foundation and SharePoint for running the workflows. This nature of the
workflows created by using SharePoint Designer assumes that they only run
on the SharePoint list with which they're associated. Because of this,
SharePoint Designer workflows aren't reusable across lists and libraries.

IN THIS CHAPTER

**Exploring the Workflow
Designer interface**

**Investigating the SharePoint
Designer workflow files**

**Using conditions in Workflow
Designer**

Working with workflow actions

For example, if you want to use a workflow that you created by using SharePoint Designer for one SharePoint list on another, you would really need to re-create that workflow for the other list separately. You won't have the means to reuse the same workflow with multiple lists.

The overall development process of a workflow in Workflow Designer necessitates doing the following:

■ You use SharePoint Designer to open a SharePoint Web site that has user-defined workflows enabled for it.

CROSS-REF   For more on enabling user-defined workflows on a SharePoint site, see Chapter 21.

■ Using Workflow Designer, you begin workflow creation by choosing a SharePoint list or library to which the workflow can be associated.

■ At the very least, you define one step in the workflow by using the predefined conditions and actions that Workflow Designer exposes.

■ When you finish the workflow creation, the created workflow files are deployed to a special document library inside the SharePoint site.

While the terminology around workflow initiation and association was discussed in Chapter 19, you still need to be aware of the following terms from the perspective of designing workflows by using SharePoint Designer:

■ **Step:** To help define a logical sequence of operations that are performed by the workflow, Workflow Designer allows you to break your workflow into steps. This is essentially a mechanism to reduce confusion while creating larger, complex workflows and to help provide a structure to the workflow. Because many workflow processes are divided into logical steps, Workflow Designer allows you to maintain the logical structure of the workflow by using steps.

■ **Condition:** Conditions are rules that you can use for deciding the course of action in a step of a SharePoint Designer workflow. In workflow terminology, a condition is more or less a special kind of activity that can be used to make a decision based on comparison. SharePoint Designer allows you to use predefined conditions available with Windows Workflow Foundation or installed with SharePoint Services to develop a logical if/else flow for performing actions in a workflow step.

■ **Action:** Actions are operations that you can perform in a workflow step. Actions exposed in Workflow Designer are predefined workflow activities installed with SharePoint that are specially designed to provide certain capabilities to workflows for interacting with SharePoint lists and libraries.

Throughout this chapter, the various conditions and actions that Workflow Designer makes available for you to use in workflows are discussed. It's important to understand that these workflow activities and conditions are made available by the SharePoint site that you're working with in

SharePoint Designer. So, you need to always be connected to a workflow-enabled SharePoint site to be able to use SharePoint Designer's workflow tools. Developers can also programmatically create customized conditions and actions and then install them on the SharePoint Web server to be made available in the Workflow Designer interface. Before discussing the various conditions and actions that you can use in Workflow Designer, I familiarize you with the Workflow Designer user interface.

Exploring the Workflow Designer Interface

Workflow Designer is really the first version of a workflow development interface for SharePoint Designer. Choose File ➪ New ➪ Workflow when a SharePoint site is open in SharePoint Designer to access Workflow Designer to create and edit workflows. Besides workflow creation, it also checks for workflow errors and is used to deploy workflows to SharePoint sites. The following points can help you understand the Workflow Designer user interface:

■ The workflow starts whenever an item in the Announcements list is updated or can be started manually.

■ The workflow has two steps that help you check to see if the created date of an item in the Announcements list is older than the current date.

■ If the previous condition is met, the workflow uses the Log to History List action, which is available in Workflow Designer to log a message into the Workflow History List.

NOTE   **The Workflow History List is a special list available in SharePoint to track workflow actions, errors, and problems.**

Follow these steps to create the workflow that performs the previous operation on a WSS v3 Web site. Ensure that the SharePoint site you're using for this exercise has an Announcements list:

1. **Open a SharePoint site in SharePoint Designer and then choose File ➪ New ➪ Workflow to open Workflow Designer.** The first screen of Workflow Designer, as shown in Figure 20.1, is a welcome screen that allows you to pick the SharePoint list or library that you want to associate the workflow with. It also allows you to choose the event that should trigger the start of the workflow.

2. **Specify a name for this workflow.** In the What SharePoint list should this workflow be attached to? dropdown menu, select the Announcements list. Click the Allow this workflow to be manually started for an item and the Automatically start this workflow whenever an item is changed check boxes, as shown in Figure 20.2.

3. **Click Variables to open the Workflow Local Variables dialog box.** You use this dialog box to create variables for storing workflow information.

 These variables (called the workflow data variables) can be used to store the state of
the columns in the SharePoint list or library associated with a workflow for use in
later steps.

4. **Click Add in the Workflow Local Variables dialog box to open the Edit Variable
   dialog box.** Specify a name and the data type for the variable. For this exercise, the data
   type to be used is Date/Time.

FIGURE 20.1

Define your new workflow screen in Workflow Designer

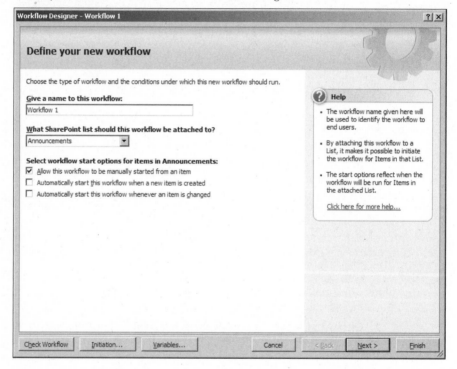

FIGURE 20.2

Choosing the association list and initiation event for a workflow

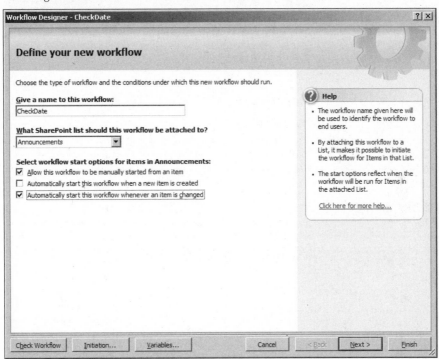

5. **Click OK.** The newly created workflow variable is shown in Figure 20.3.

6. **Click OK to complete the creation of the workflow variable.** This brings you back to the Workflow Designer window.

7. **Click Next to move to the next screen in Workflow Designer.** As illustrated in Figure 20.4, this screen is used to create the steps inside the workflow. In the first step for this workflow, you initialize the workflow variable created in step 4.

FIGURE 20.3

Creating a workflow variable by using the Workflow Local Variables dialog box

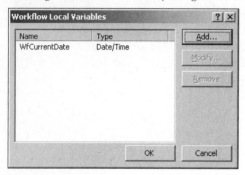

FIGURE 20.4

Creating steps for a workflow

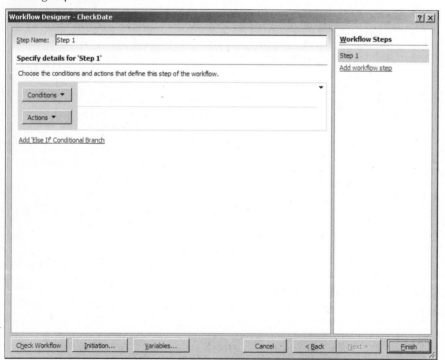

8. **Specify a name for the step by clicking Actions and then clicking the More Actions menu option to open the Workflow Actions dialog box.** As shown in Figure 20.5, the Workflow Actions dialog box lists the available actions in Workflow Designer. This list includes all the default and custom activities that are deployed to the Web server hosting the SharePoint site open in SharePoint Designer. You can use the Select a Category dropdown menu to filter the list of actions based on a particular category.

9. **Choose All Actions in the Select a Category dropdown menu, select the Set Workflow Variable action, and then click Add.** Figure 20.6 shows the interactive description for the Set Workflow Variable action. The Set workflow variable to value description for this action has two links: The workflow variable link allows you to choose the workflow variable that you want to set, and the value link provides the interface to specify a value for the variable. If you click the newly inserted action, you can enable a dropdown that allows you to delete the action or, if you're using multiple actions, you can change the order of the actions.

10. **Click the workflow variable link.** The link changes to a dropdown menu that allows you to choose the existing workflow variable created in step 4 or create a new variable by using the Create a new variable selection. For this exercise, select the workflow variable you created in step 4 from the dropdown menu.

FIGURE 20.5

The Workflow Actions dialog box

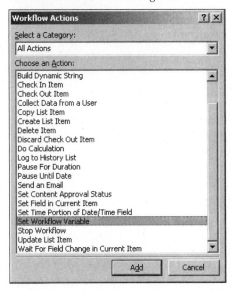

FIGURE 20.6

The Set workflow variable to value description for the Set Workflow Variable action

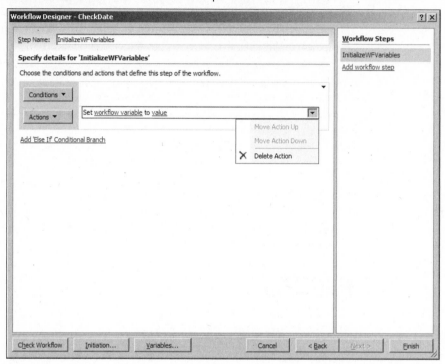

11. **Click the value link.** The link changes to a text field with the ellipsis (…) button and the *fx* button next to it.

12. **Click the ellipsis (…) button to open the Date Value dialog box, click the Current Date radio button, and then click OK.** The completely configured action is displayed in Figure 20.7.

13. **Click the Add workflow step link in the right pane of the Workflow Designer screen to add a new step to the workflow and then specify a name for the step.**

14. **Click Conditions to open a dropdown menu and then choose the Compare any data source condition menu option, as shown in Figure 20.8.** Figure 20.9 displays the interactive description for the Compare any data source condition. The If value equals value description for this condition has three links: The first value link allows you to specify the left operand for the comparison, the equals link allows you to choose the comparison operator, and the second value link allows you to choose the right operand for the comparison. If you click the newly inserted condition, a dropdown menu appears that allows you to delete the condition or, if you're using multiple conditions, change the order of the conditions.

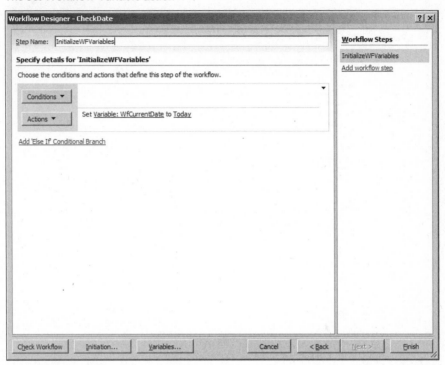

FIGURE 20.7

The Set Workflow Variable action

15. **Click the first value link to specify the left operand.** The link changes into a text field with an *fx* button next to it.

16. **Click the *fx* button to open the Define Workflow Lookup dialog box, as shown in Figure 20.10.** The Define Workflow Lookup dialog box is a commonly used dialog box in Workflow Designer and is used to specify a source of data. The dropdowns in the Define Workflow Lookup dialog box include the following:

   ■ **Source:** This is the list of SharePoint lists and libraries available in the SharePoint site in which the workflow is being created. It also includes the Workflow Data option that allows you to choose the variables that you create in the workflow. The Current Item option makes available the fields on which the item that the workflow (actually an instance of the workflow) is run.

CAUTION Some SharePoint lists and libraries are displayed in this dropdown menu only if they have a list item.

FIGURE 20.8

Choosing a condition to use for a workflow step

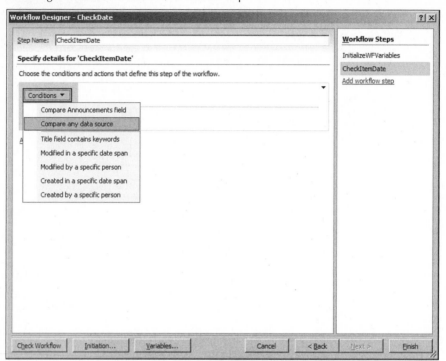

- **Field:** This is the list of columns/fields that exist in the SharePoint list or library selected in the Source dropdown menu. When you select Workflow Data option in the Source dropdown menu, this dropdown shows the list of workflow variables.

17. Select Current Item in the Source dropdown menu, select Created column in the Field dropdown menu, and then OK.

18. Click the value link and then click the *fx* button to open the Define Workflow Lookup dialog box.

19. Select Workflow Data in the Source dropdown menu, select the variable name created in step 4 in the Field dropdown menu, and then click OK.

20. Click the equals link and then select the is less than link, as shown in Figure 20.11.

FIGURE 20.9

The If value equals value description for the Compare any data source condition

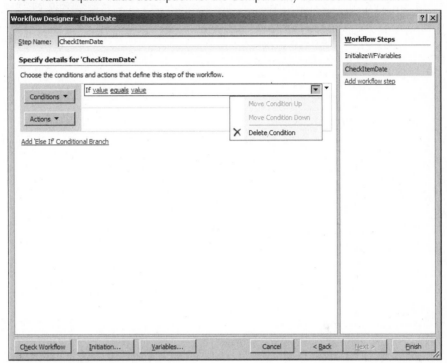

FIGURE 20.10

Defining the source of data by using the Define Workflow Lookup dialog box

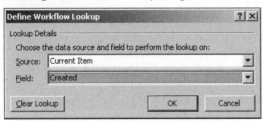

21. Click Actions and then choose the More Actions menu option to open the Workflow Actions dialog box.

FIGURE 20.11

The completed Compare any data source condition

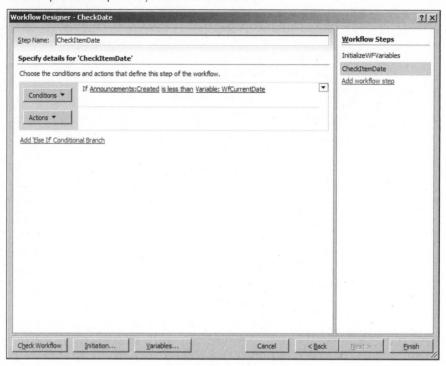

22. **Choose All Actions in the Select a Category dropdown menu, select the Log to History List workflow action, and then click Add.** You should now see the Log this message to the workflow list action description. For this action, the link exists in the this message text.

23. **Click the this message hyperlink that appears in step 22.** The link becomes a text field with an ellipsis (…) button and *fx* button next to it.

24. **Click the *fx* button to open the Define Workflow Lookup dialog box.**

25. **Select Current Item in the Source dropdown menu and select Created field in the Field dropdown menu.** The completed step is displayed in Figure 20.12.

26. **Click Finish.** This checks the workflow for errors, writes the workflow files, creates initiation forms, associates the workflow with the Announcements list, etc.

FIGURE 20.12

The completed workflow step with a condition and action

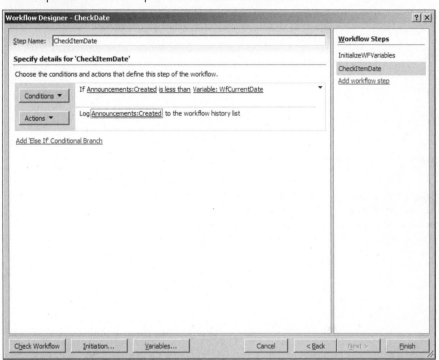

Now that the workflow files have been created and the workflow is associated with the SharePoint list, you can browse to a view of the list in the SharePoint site and then trigger the workflow to start. Remember that you specified that the workflow could be started manually or could be automatically started when an item is updated. To manually start the workflow, right-click the item in the List or Library view and then choose Workflows from the popup menu, as shown in Figure 20.13.

The Workflows page for the list item opens, which displays all the workflows associated with the list. Click the workflow you created in the previous steps to open the workflow initiation page that was created by SharePoint Designer. Clicking Start on the workflow initiation page starts the workflow on the selected item. The SharePoint list where you started appears after you click Start and the workflow initializes. A new column with the workflow name is displayed in the SharePoint list, as shown in Figure 20.14.

FIGURE 20.13

Manually starting a workflow on a SharePoint list item

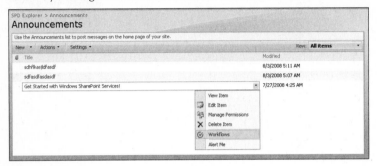

FIGURE 20.14

Viewing the status of the workflow running on an item

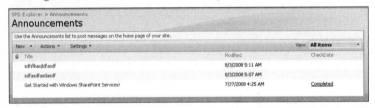

The value of this column for the list item displays the status of the workflow. When the workflow finishes, the status changes to Completed. Clicking the status link opens the Workflow Status Web page, as shown in Figure 20.15.

The workflow status displays the following information about the workflow instance:

- **Workflow Information:** This section indicates the user who ran the workflow instance, the item on which it was run, and the start time and end time.

- **Tasks:** If the workflow is designed to create tasks and assign them to users, you should see those tasks in this view.

- **Workflow History:** This is a special list that stores information about any workflow-related events and errors. You can use SharePoint Designer to log messages into the workflow history list. As shown in Figure 20.15, the Log this message to the workflow history list workflow action creates a comment log in this section with the created date and time of the item on which the workflow created in the above exercise ran on.

While the logic for the workflow for the exercise in this section could have been implemented in many ways in Workflow Designer, this approach was used to help you understand some of the key internals of the SharePoint Designer workflows. The Folder List task pane in SharePoint Designer now shows a `Workflows` folder that contains a number of workflows files generated during the workflow creation process. The next section takes you through the various files that are created by SharePoint Designer to support the workflows.

FIGURE 20.15

The Workflow Status Web page for a workflow

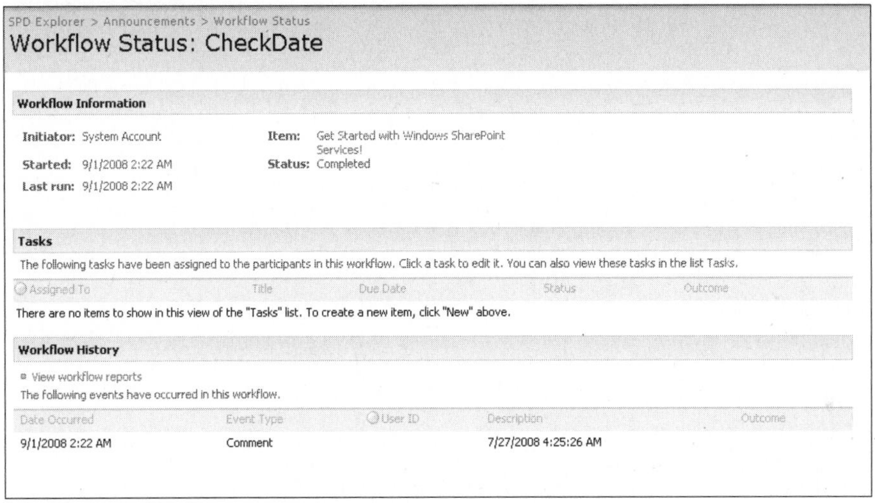

Investigating SharePoint Designer Workflow Files

Whenever you create a workflow by using SharePoint Designer, the workflow files generated in the process are stored in a special document library called Workflows. Unlike other document libraries, this document library doesn't have any forms (for example, `DispForm.aspx`, `EditForm.aspx`, etc.) for interaction. You don't really see this library in the SharePoint user interface. However, in SharePoint Designer, you can see the Workflows document library in the Folder Lists task pane. All workflow files associated with a particular workflow are stored in a folder named after the workflow in the Workflows document library. For the CheckDate workflow you just created in the previous exercise, Figure 20.16 shows the files that now appear in the associated workflow folder.

FIGURE 20.16

Workflow supporting files created by Workflow Designer

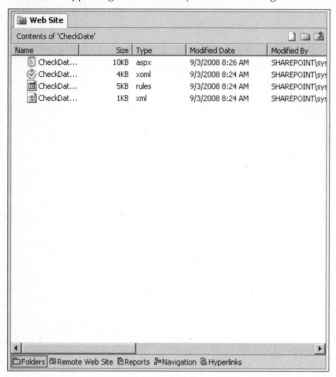

Depending on the settings made for the workflow in Workflow Designer, the number of files in the associated workflow folder might change. However, the file with the `.xoml` extension is the key file that supports workflows.

Workflow markup files

Windows Workflow Foundation allows runtime compilation of workflows that have been created by declaratively specifying the workflow settings in XML files. This means that the workflows don't need to be precompiled and deployed as dynamic link libraries. Instead, developers can define workflow logic by using structured XML. At runtime, the markup files are compiled into a workflow type and then loaded into the Workflow Runtime Engine. SharePoint Designer uses this approach to let Web designers define the workflows on SharePoint sites. Designers use Workflow Designer to choose the activities, initiation, and association settings that they want to use for the workflows. Internally, Workflow Designer writes these settings into XML files by using Extensible Object Markup Language (XOML). These XOML files are then uploaded to the SharePoint site and compiled at runtime to run the workflows.

If you look at the file with the `.xoml.wfconfig.xml` extension, you can easily recognize that this is the binding file that stores information about all the resources needed to run the associated workflow:

```
<WorkflowConfig>
    <Template
        BaseID="{F36F9E51-D396-4256-A7D2-75A89B42EE86}"
        DocLibID="{3FC83390-EC82-4B2D-8E62-982B596F009D}"
        XomlHref="Workflows/CheckDate/CheckDate.xoml"
        XomlVersion="V1.0"
        RulesHref="Workflows/CheckDate/CheckDate.xoml.rules"
        RulesVersion="V1.0"
    >
    </Template>
    <Association
        ListID="{4A716163-0F6C-4931-8FA7-CFE0C7AFEC15}"
        TaskListID="{5B895DF9-D05A-4763-BEF9-83D76E064796}"
        StartManually="true"
        StartOnChange="true"
    >
    </Association>
    <ContentTypes>
    </ContentTypes>
    <Initiation URL="Workflows/CheckDate/CheckDate.aspx">
        <Fields />
        <Parameters></Parameters>
    </Initiation>
</WorkflowConfig>
```

As highlighted in the previous code, just by looking at the contents of this file, the workflow engine can make out the name of the list with which the workflow is associated (`ListID`), the task list to be used for the workflow (`TaskListID`), and whether the workflow should start automatically or when an item is added or changed (`StartManually` and `StartOnChange`). It also stores the reference to the URLs for the workflow XOML file (`XomlHref`), the workflow rules file (`RulesHref`), and the initiation form, if any, which are discussed here:

- **Workflow XOML file:** The workflow XOML file is used to store all the activities (conditions and actions) and workflow variables associated with the workflows.
- **Workflow rules file:** The workflow rules file, the file with the `.xoml.rules` extension, stores the operators and the operands involved in the condition activities being used in the workflow.
- **Workflow initiation form:** This form appears whenever you start the workflow manually. In its most basic form, you click a Start button to begin the workflow.

Double-clicking the XOML file in the Folder List task pane opens Workflow Designer and lets you modify the workflow. Workflow Designer is basically the user interface provided by SharePoint Designer to modify the workflow XOML files without having to know anything about the structured XAML that's used to write these files. If you right-click on the XOML file and then choose Open with ➪ SharePoint Designer (Open as XML) from the popup menu, you can view the XAML code written by Workflow Designer:

```
<ns0:RootWorkflowActivityWithData x:Class="Microsoft.SharePoint.
    Workflow.ROOT" x:Name="ROOT" xmlns="http://schemas.microsoft.com/
    winfx/2006/xaml/workflow" xmlns:x="http://schemas.microsoft.com/
    winfx/2006/xaml" xmlns:ns0="clr-namespace:Microsoft.SharePoint.Wo
    rkflowActions;Assembly=Microsoft.SharePoint.WorkflowActions,
    Version=12.0.0.0, Culture=neutral, PublicKeyToken=null">
    <ns0:RootWorkflowActivityWithData.WorkflowFields>
        <ns0:WorkflowDataField Name="__list" Type="System.String"
    />
        <ns0:WorkflowDataField Name="__item" Type="System.Int32" />
        <ns0:WorkflowDataField Name="__context" Type="Microsoft.
    SharePoint.WorkflowActions.WorkflowContext" />
        <ns0:WorkflowDataField Name="__initParams" Type="Microsoft.
    SharePoint.Workflow.SPWorkflowActivationProperties" />
        <ns0:WorkflowDataField Name="__workflowId" Type="System.
    Guid" />
        <ns0:WorkflowDataField Name="WfCurrentDate" Type="System.
    DateTime" />
        <ns0:WorkflowDataField Name="_x005f_DateTime0"
    Type="System.DateTime" />
        <ns0:WorkflowDataField Name="_x005f_String0" Type="System.
    String" />
    </ns0:RootWorkflowActivityWithData.WorkflowFields>
    <ns0:OnWorkflowActivated WorkflowProperties="{ActivityBind
    ROOT,Path=__initParams}" x:Name="ID1">
        <ns0:OnWorkflowActivated.CorrelationToken>
            <wf0:CorrelationToken Name="refObject"
    OwnerActivityName="ROOT" xmlns:wf0="http://schemas.microsoft.com/
    winfx/2006/xaml/workflow" />
        </ns0:OnWorkflowActivated.CorrelationToken>
    </ns0:OnWorkflowActivated>
    <ns0:ApplyActivation __Context="{ActivityBind ROOT,Path=__
    context}" x:Name="ID2" __WorkflowProperties="{ActivityBind
    ROOT,Path=__initParams}" />
    <SequenceActivity x:Name="ID3" Description="InitializeWFVariable
    s">
        <ns0:CurrentDateActivity x:Name="ID5"
    CurrentDate="{ActivityBind ROOT,Path=_x005f_DateTime0}" />
        <ns0:SetVariableActivity x:Name="ID4" ValueType="System.
    DateTime">
            <ns0:SetVariableActivity.Variable>
                <ActivityBind Name="ROOT"
    Path="WfCurrentDate" />
            </ns0:SetVariableActivity.Variable>
            <ns0:SetVariableActivity.Value>
```

```
                              <ActivityBind Name="ROOT" Path="_x005f_
DateTime0" />
                </ns0:SetVariableActivity.Value>
        </ns0:SetVariableActivity>
</SequenceActivity>
<IfElseActivity x:Name="ID7" Description="CheckItemDate">
        <IfElseBranchActivity x:Name="ID6">
                <IfElseBranchActivity.Condition>
                        <RuleConditionReference ConditionName="__
Rule_ID6" />
                </IfElseBranchActivity.Condition>
                <ns0:LookupActivity ListId="{}{4A716163-0F6C-4931-
8FA7-CFE0C7AFEC15}" x:Name="ID10" FieldName="Created" LookupFunct
ion="LookupFriendlyString" __Context="{ActivityBind ROOT,Path=__
context}" ListItem="{ActivityBind ROOT,Path=__item}">
                        <ns0:LookupActivity.ReturnValue>
                                <ActivityBind Name="ROOT" Path="_
x005f_String0" />
                        </ns0:LookupActivity.ReturnValue>
                </ns0:LookupActivity>
                <ns0:LogToHistoryListActivity x:Name="ID9"
OtherData="{x:Null}" HistoryDescription="{ActivityBind
ROOT,Path=_x005f_String0}" HistoryOutcome="{x:Null}" UserId="0"
Duration="00:00:00" EventId="None" />
        </IfElseBranchActivity>
</IfElseActivity>
</ns0:RootWorkflowActivityWithData>
```

The XML structure of the workflow XOML file is divided into two sections:

■ **WorkflowFields:** This section stores the internal and user-defined workflow variables that are being used for the workflow. For example, as highlighted in the previous code, the user-defined workflow variable (`WfCurrentDate`) and its data type (`System.DateTime`) are stored in this section.

■ **Activities:** After the workflow variables, all the workflow steps are stored as their associated activity type. For example, the workflow step without conditions is stored as `<SequenceActivity>`, and the ones with conditions are stored as `<IfElseActivity>`. All the other actions inside these steps are stored as nested activities. The condition rules are referenced using the `ConditionName`. For example, `<RuleConditionReference ConditionName="_Rule_ID6" />`, which has the ID that's used to pick the condition from the workflow rules file.

NOTE Developers who are well-versed with XAML can directly modify the XAML in these files to change workflow behavior. Given that the workflow associations are respected, these files can be edited in any workflow editor (for example, Visual Studio) and enhanced further. However, if you modify the workflow associated with the customized XAML file in Workflow Designer, you might lose the changes made manually to these files.

Workflow rules files

As indicated previously, the workflow rules files are used to store information about the conditions that are used in the `<IfElseActivity>` defined in the workflow XOML file. The `IfElseActivity` internally references the condition defined in the workflow rules file.

In the workflow rules XML file, there are multiple `<RuleExpressionCondition>` elements; for example, `<RuleExpressionCondition Name="__Rule_ID6>`, one for each condition created in the workflow. Within these elements are described the parameters and methods that define the condition. For example, for the workflow that you created in the previous section, the condition has two parameters: the current item's field (defined `by_context`) and the workflow variable `WfCurrentDate`. The method for the condition is `Compare`.

The same structure is repeated for multiple conditions, and each of them is distinguished by using the `Name` attribute defined in the `<RuleExpressionCondition>` elements. The value of the `Name` parameter is referenced by the appropriate activity in the workflow XOML file.

ASPX forms for initiation and customization

Workflow Designer allows you to create an initiation form that can be used to manually start a workflow associated with a list or library on the SharePoint Web site. The initiation form actually exists on an ASP.NET Web page, which is created by Workflow Designer depending on whether you chose to start the workflow manually. While the basic initiation form created by Workflow Designer contains a Start button that's used to start running a workflow instance on a particular item in a SharePoint list or library, you can design more complex initiation forms by using Workflow Designer.

To create an initiation form to request input from a user before he or she begins the workflow, follow these steps:

1. **While designing a workflow by using Workflow Designer, click the Initiation button.** The Workflow Initiation Parameters dialog box opens. You use this dialog box to create input fields that should be displayed on the initiation form.

2. **Click Add to open the Add Fields dialog box.** Add the fields that you need for requesting user input. Figure 20.17 illustrates several fields added. The fields that you defined in step 1 are available as workflow initiation variables in Workflow Designer for various purposes. You can use the initiation variables to set field values using the Define Workflow Lookup dialog box, as shown in Figure 20.18.

In this manner, you can collect data from the user before the workflow begins. Internally, the user input is stored in workflow initiation variables and can then be used in various workflow actions to set column values in list items, comparisons, etc.

 The workflow initiation variables are stored for reference in the `<Initiation>` section of the `xoml.wfconfig.xml` file.

FIGURE 20.17

Adding fields for user input to a workflow initiation form

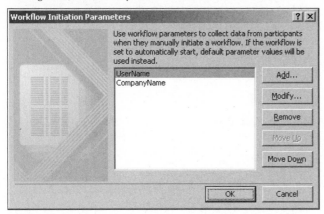

FIGURE 20.18

Using initiation variables in the Define Workflow Lookup dialog box

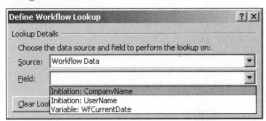

If you open the initiation Web page that Workflow Designer creates for the workflow, you see that the initiation form has been implemented by using the DataFormWebPart. As shown in Figure 20.19, the Design view allows you to open the Common Data View Tasks menu, which you could use to potentially modify the look and feel of an initiation form, such as another DataFormWebPart.

CROSS-REF For more on Data Form Web Parts, see Chapter 17.

However, it's important to note that unlike other DataFormWebParts that you can insert on Web pages by using SharePoint Designer, this DataFormWebPart uses a special data source called SPWorkflowDataSource. The <DataSources> section of the DataFormWebPart inserted on the initiation Web page contains the following code:

```
<DataSources>
        <SharePoint:SPWorkflowDataSource BaseTemplateID="{F36F9E51-
    D396-4256-A7D2-75A89B42EE86}" ListID="{4A716163-0F6C-4931-8FA7-
```

```
CFE0C7AFEC15}" runat="server"="SPWorkflowDataSource2"><SelectPara
meters><WebPartPages:DataFormParameter Name="AssociatedTemplateID"
ParameterKey="AssociatedTemplateID" PropertyName="ParameterValues
"/></electParameters><InsertParameters><WebPartPages:DataFormPara
meter Name="ItemID" ParameterKey="ItemID" PropertyName="Parameter
Values"/><WebPartPages:DataFormParameter
Name="AssociatedTemplateID" ParameterKey="AssociatedTemplateID" P
ropertyName="ParameterValues"/></InsertParameters></SharePoint:SP
WorkflowDataSource>
</DataSources>
```

The Start button that you may see on the DataFormWebPart on the initiation Web page is a Form Action button that has a number of actions associated with it, including a custom action specifically developed for the workflow initiation pages. This is shown in Figure 20.20.

Besides these two dissimilarities, the DataFormWebPart can be modified normally by using SharePoint Designer's editing tools. You can modify the XSLT associated with the DataFormWebPart to change its look and feel, change its layout, or apply conditional formatting to it.

FIGURE 20.19

Viewing the initiation Web page in the Design view

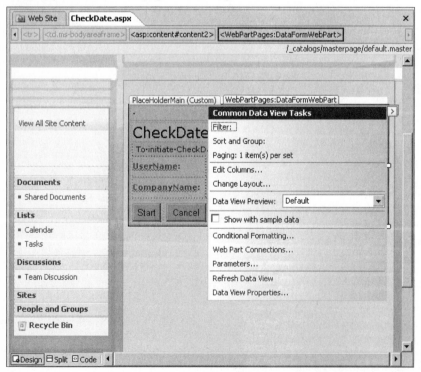

FIGURE 20.20

The Form Actions dialog box for the Start button on the initiation DataFormWebPart

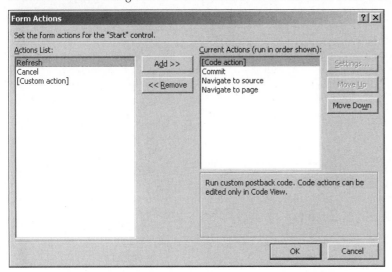

Using Conditions in Workflow Designer

Workflow Designer allows you to work with a number of conditions for setting up branching in a workflow based on the if/else logic. Essentially, this means that based on the result of the condition, the workflow can be branched to perform different operation for each result. Internally, if you review the XOML file created for the workflow, you see that all these conditions are actually rules-based conditions (defined in the .xoml.rules file) used by the IfElseActivity activity.

> **NOTE** SharePoint Designer workflows in the current release aren't capable of looping through the actions. This means that you can't emulate a For-Loop or a Do-While logic by using SharePoint Designer workflows.

Compare List/Library field

Defined by the description "If field equals value," this condition can be used to compare a field in the SharePoint list or library with a constant or a value from anther field or workflow variable. The description has three hyperlinks:

- **Field:** This is a dropdown menu that can be used to choose any of the fields/columns in the list of library.

- **Equals:** Shows a dropdown menu that can be used to choose an operator for the comparison. The dropdown menu has the following operators: equals, not equals, is empty, is not empty, begins with, does not begin with, ends with, does not end with, contains, does not contain, matches regular expression, equals (ignoring case), and contains (ignoring case).

■ **Value:** This can be used to set a new value or choose from a list of existing values (for example, in case of a choice column). Alternatively, you can use the Define Workflow Lookup dialog box to choose a source and field for lookup.

Compare any data source

This condition can be used to compare any field or workflow variable with another. It's defined by the description "If value equals value." The description has three hyperlinks: value, equals, and value. The value hyperlinks can be used to look up a field or workflow variable that forms the left and right operands of the comparison. The equals hyperlink allows you to choose from a set of operators defined by the data type of the operands.

Title field contains keywords

This condition can be used to compare the Title field of the list or library with a value that can be manually set or chosen via the Define Workflow Lookup dialog box.

Modified in a specific date span

This condition is described by using the description "modified between date and date." The date hyperlinks can be used to choose a date value, a field, or a workflow variable for the date/time data type. The condition is used to evaluate whether the current item has been modified between the dates specified by the workflow.

Modified by a specific person

This is defined by using the description "modified by a specific person." This condition is used to find out whether the current item has been modified by a specific person. The specific person hyperlink in the condition's description allows you to specify the user that needs to be used for the comparison. To choose the user for the condition, you can use the Select Users dialog box, as shown in Figure 20.21. The Select Users dialog box can be used to select a single user or group for use in the condition.

While the Select Users dialog box allows you to choose from the existing SharePoint site users, you also can locate contacts from an address book, look up data using the Define Workflow Lookup dialog box, or use the user who created the current item.

NOTE   As the description suggests, the previous conditions can be used to match only a single user or SharePoint Designer group. You can't choose to have the conditions met with multiple users or groups.

Created in a specific date span

Similar to the Modified in a specific date span condition, this condition can be used to check if the current item has been created between the specified dates. The description "created between date and date" has hyperlinks that allow you to specify dates for the comparison.

FIGURE 20.21

Selecting a user for a condition by using the Select Users dialog box

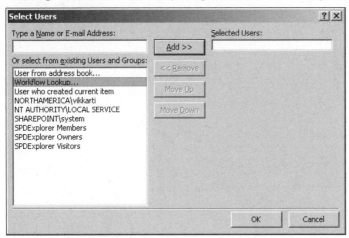

Created by a specific person

Similar to the Modified by a specific person condition, this condition allows you to find out if the current item has been created by a specific person.

 **For more on how these conditions can be used to design complex workflows in Workflow Designer, see Chapter 22.**

Working with Workflow Actions

The list of actions available in Workflow Designer's Workflow Action dialog box by default is a set of predefined activities that are installed with SharePoint on a Web server. Workflow Designer simply provides an interface that helps designers write XAML files. The workflow actions have been designed by keeping in mind the most common operations that designers want to perform on SharePoint list or library items.

Using these workflow actions, you can perform a range of operations, such as creating, copying, and deleting list items; check-in/check-out; discard check-out of list items, perform calculations, send e-mail, perform data-related calculations; delay, pause, or stop workflows; etc. Table 20.1 lists the workflow actions available in Workflow Designer.

TABLE 20.1

Workflow Designer's Workflow Actions

Workflow Action	Description of the Action	Functionality Offered to Workflow
Add Time to Date	Add 0 minutes to date (Output to Variable: date)	Allows you to add a specific amount of time in minutes, hours, days, etc., to a date and then store it in a workflow variable
Assign a Form to a Group	Assign a custom form to these users	Allows you to create a special task with custom fields for user input and then assign it to a specific user. The user can fill out the fields in the task and submit it.
Assign a To-do Item	Assign a to-do item to these users	Assigns a task to the specified user
Build Dynamic String	Store dynamic string in Variable: variable	Provides a string builder user interface that you can use to build a string and then store it in a workflow variable
Check In Item	Check in item in this list with comment: comment	Allows you to check-in an item to a list and supply a comment regarding the check-in
Check Out Item	Check out item in this list	Allows you to check-out an item from a list
Collect Data from a User	Collect data from this user (Output to Variable: collect1)	Allows you to assign a task item to a specific user for collecting input. The data collected can be output to workflow variables.
Copy List Item	Copy item in this list to this list	Allows you to copy an item from one list to another
Create List Item	Create item in this list (Output to Variable: create)	Allows you to create an item in a specified list. Returns the ID of the newly created item in the workflow variable
Delete Item	Delete item in this list	Allows you to delete a list item
Discard Check Out Item	Discard check out of item in this list	Allows you to undo check-out of the specified item in the list
Do Calculation	Calculate value plus value (Output to Variable: calc)	Allows you to perform calculations on two values and then store the result in a workflow variable

Workflow Action	Description of the Action	Functionality Offered to Workflow
Log to History List	Log this message to the workflow history list	Allows you to log messages in the workflow history list
Pause For Duration	Pause for 0 days, 0 hours, 5 minutes	Pauses the workflow for a specified amount of time
Pause Until Date	Pause until this time	Pauses the workflow until the specified date is reached
Send an Email	E-mail this message	Allows you to send an e-mail message to e-mail addresses
Set Content Approval Status	Set content approval status to this status with comments	Allows you to change the content approval status on lists that have content approval enabled
Set Field in Current Item	Set field to value	Sets the value of a field in the current item to a specific value
Set Time Portion of Date/Time Field	Set time as 00:00 for date (Output to Variable: date1)	Allows you to set the time value for a specified date
Set Workflow Variable	Set workflow variable to value	Sets the value of a workflow variable to the value specified by the action
Stop Workflow	Stop the workflow and log this message	Stops the workflow and then logs the specified message in the workflow history list
Update List Item	Update item in this list	Allows you to set a field in a list item to a specific value
Wait for Field Change in Current Item	Wait for field to equal value	Allows you to pause a workflow until a field value in the current time changes to match a specific value

You can choose whether the actions in a particular branch of the workflow should run in a sequence one after the other or run simultaneously in parallel. To make this setting, click the arrow in the top-right corner of the condition box in Workflow Designer. A dropdown menu appears, as shown in Figure 20.22, that allows you to specify whether the actions should run in sequence or in parallel.

CROSS-REF For more real-world workflow scenarios, see Chapter 22.

FIGURE 20.22

Specify whether an action should run in sequence or in parallel

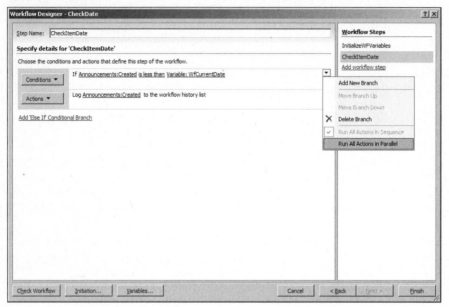

Summary

Workflow Designer is a powerful tool offered by SharePoint Designer to design no-code workflows for SharePoint lists and libraries. It gives Web designers and information workers the ability to use less programming to design workflows based on predefined activities and conditions. You can create and modify workflows, associate them with lists and libraries, check workflows for errors, and then deploy them to a SharePoint site.

Chapter 21

Administrating Workflows

Workflows created by SharePoint Designer depend on SharePoint services provided by WSS v3 and MOSS. If you try to create workflows on a site that's not SharePoint 3.0 (WSS v3 and MOSS), you receive messages indicating the inability of the Web server to support workflows. This dependency of SharePoint Designer workflows on SharePoint requires that you ensure that the workflows are set up properly on a SharePoint Web server.

Workflows available in SharePoint out of the box (for example, Three State, Collect Feedback, etc.) are installed as Features on the SharePoint Web server. Unlike SharePoint Designer workflows, which need to be associated with a particular list before they're deployed to a SharePoint site, these default workflows can be associated with any list by using a SharePoint Web site. You use a SharePoint site user interface to associate these workflows with the list or library of your choice.

NOTE Features is a term used to define a way of implementing a functionality in SharePoint 3.0. Most of the common functions on a SharePoint site, such as lists, document libraries, etc., are implemented as features. The default feature files are stored at `C:\Program Files\Common Files\Microsoft Shared\web server extensions\ 12\TEMPLATE\FEATURES` on the SharePoint Web server. Developers can create and deploy their own custom features to SharePoint servers.

Most of the settings in the SharePoint global and site-level administration Web pages apply to SharePoint out-of-the-box workflows. However, there are some important settings that a Web designer using SharePoint Designer to create declarative workflows should keep in mind. While some workflow settings are available in the SharePoint administration Web pages and can be set by using the site user interface, many settings related to workflows can only be made using `stsadm.exe`, the command-line administration tool for SharePoint.

This chapter takes you through these settings and explains how you can use them to avoid problems when creating workflows in SharePoint Designer. Later in this chapter, I discuss troubleshooting common problems with SharePoint Designer workflows.

Exploring SharePoint Workflow Settings

The SharePoint administration Web pages provide administrators with a number of settings at various levels for managing workflows. These settings are accessible by using the SharePoint Central Administration Web pages of the SharePoint farm and the Site Settings Web pages of a SharePoint site collection or a SharePoint site.

Working with global settings in SharePoint Central Administration

The global settings for workflow management on a SharePoint farm are available at the SharePoint Central Administration Web site. You can access the SharePoint Central Administration Web site on a SharePoint Web server (a Windows Server 2003 machine) by choosing Start ⇨ Administrative Tools ⇨ SharePoint 3.0 Central Administration. The SharePoint Web application level workflow settings are available in the Workflow management section of the Application Management tab. Clicking the Workflow Settings link in the Workflow Management section takes you to the Workflow Settings Web page, as shown in Figure 21.1.

FIGURE 21.1

Web Application–level workflow settings

Central Administration > Application Management > Workflow Settings

Workflow Settings

Change global workflow settings below.

Web Application Select a Web application.	Web Application: **http://spdexplorer/** ▾
User-Defined Workflows Users can assemble new workflows out of building blocks deployed to the site. These workflows cannot add code. They can only reuse code already deployed by the administrator.	Enable user-defined workflows for this site? ⦿ Yes ○ No
Workflow Task Notifications Set options for how users without access to the site are notified of pending workflow tasks.	Alert internal users who do not have site access when they are assigned a workflow task? ⦿ Yes ○ No Allow external users to participate in workflow by sending them a copy of the document? ○ Yes ⦿ No

OK   Cancel

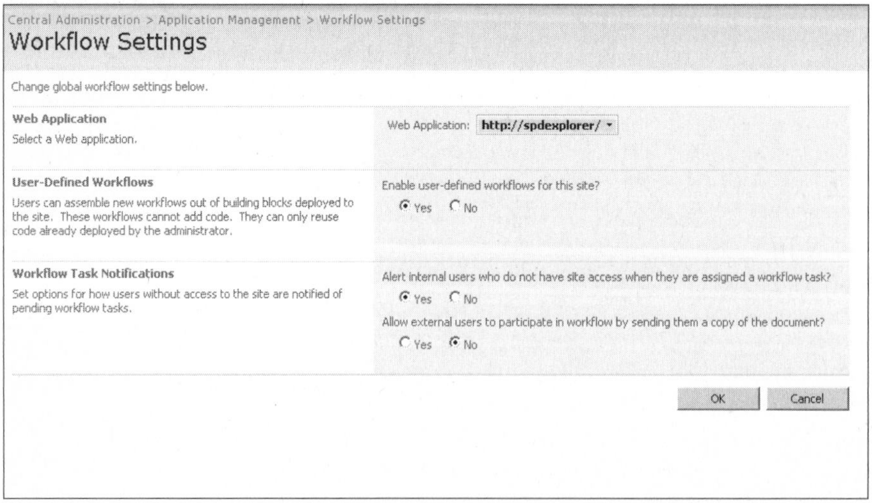

Use the Web Application dropdown menu to choose the SharePoint Web application you want to change the settings for. The Workflow Settings Web page allows you to configure the following settings:

- **User-Defined Workflows:** This setting enables or disables the use of the user-defined workflows on the selected Web application. If you disable user-defined workflows by using this setting for your SharePoint Web application, you can't create new workflows via SharePoint Designer.

- **Workflow Tasks Notifications:** These settings allow you to configure the behavior for the workflow tasks that are assigned to users who don't have access to the SharePoint Web site. The Alert internal users who do not have site access when they're assigned a workflow task? option allows you to send an e-mail to the users, making them aware that a workflow task has been assigned to them. The Allow external users to participate in workflow by sending them a copy of the document? option allows you to configure if the workflow document can be sent to the user in an e-mail for task completion.

If the User-Defined Workflow option is disabled by using the setting described earlier, Web designers using SharePoint Designer can't use or create workflows. You need to keep this setting enabled if you're using SharePoint Designer workflows on your Web site.

Configuring site collection settings

The Site Settings Web page for a SharePoint Web site also has a number of Web pages that can help administrators view the state of workflows. These settings, however, don't show any SharePoint Designer workflow-related data or settings. They can be used to activate or deactivate SharePoint out-of-the-box workflows. You can access the Site Settings page by choosing Site Actions ➪ Site Settings in the top-right corner of the SharePoint site. On the Site Settings Web page, under the Site Collection Administration section, is the Site Collection Feature link. Click this link to open the Site Collection Features Web page, as shown in Figure 21.2, where administrators can activate or deactivate features. This includes the workflow features that are installed by default with SharePoint.

FIGURE 21.2

Checking the activation status of workflow features by using the Site Collection Features Web page

SPDExplorer > Site Settings > Site Features
Site Collection Features

Name		Status
Three-state workflow Use this workflow to track items in a list.	Deactivate	**Active**

Also, the Galleries section on the Site Settings page has the Workflows link, which can be used to view and monitor the status of SharePoint out-of-the-box workflows being used inside the Web site. The status column in this list indicates whether the workflow has been activated on the site for usage, while the association column lists the total number of workflow associations.

Managing content type settings

As indicated previously, workflows created via SharePoint Designer can't be associated with SharePoint site content types. The SharePoint content type settings available in SharePoint sites make sense only for the out-of-the-box SharePoint workflows or custom workflows developed programmatically and deployed to the SharePoint server.

The workflow settings for a particular content type are accessible by using the Content Type settings page. Click the Site Content Types link in the Galleries section of the Site Settings page to access the Content Type settings page. Then, in the list of content types for the Web site, click the content type you want to view the workflow settings for. As shown in Figure 21.3, clicking the Workflow settings link in the Content Type settings page allows you to associate a workflow with the chosen content type.

FIGURE 21.3

Associating workflows with content types

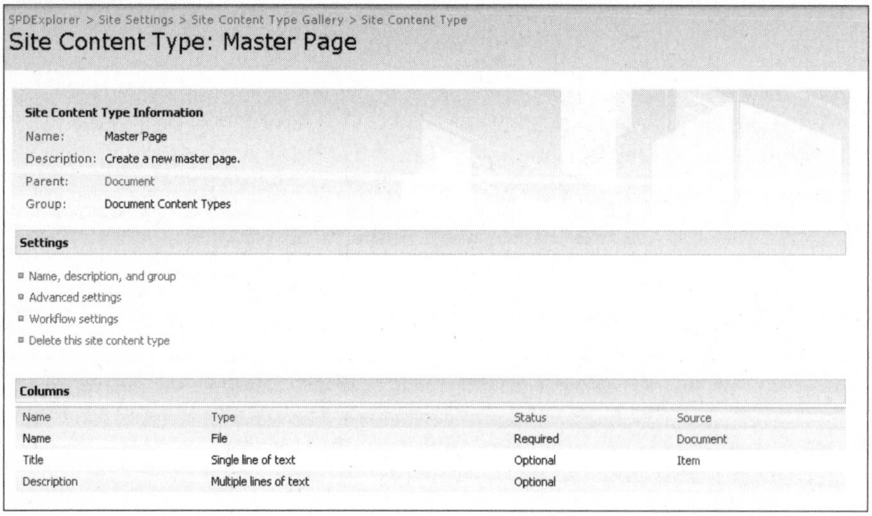

SPDExplorer > Site Settings > Site Content Type Gallery > Site Content Type

Site Content Type: Master Page

Site Content Type Information

Name:	Master Page
Description:	Create a new master page.
Parent:	Document
Group:	Document Content Types

Settings

▪ Name, description, and group
▪ Advanced settings
▪ Workflow settings
▪ Delete this site content type

Columns

Name	Type	Status	Source
Name	File	Required	Document
Title	Single line of text	Optional	Item
Description	Multiple lines of text	Optional	

Only the SharePoint out-of-the-box workflows are available for association with content types. SharePoint Designer workflows aren't available for association here.

Other than the workflow settings described in the previous sections, SharePoint also allows you to configure workflow behavior to a certain extent by providing properties that can be set by using `stsadm.exe`, the command-line SharePoint administration tool. Before you review these properties, it's important for you to understand that workflows generate events that are queued by SharePoint by using an event-queuing mechanism. The SharePoint Timer service (`owstimer.exe`) is responsible for reading this queue and performing operations based on the schedule of the event. For example, when the workflow runtime engine encounters a delay activity (like the Pause for duration action in SharePoint Designer), it logs a workflow event in the SharePoint event queue and then dehydrates the workflow. The SharePoint Timer service repeatedly polls the event queue and, when the appropriate time is reached, assists in rehydrating the workflow. The workflow properties that are discussed in Table 21.1 are useful in tuning the SharePoint event scheduling and polling mechanism. This table lists the workflow-related `stsadm` properties that can be used to change workflow behavior at an application or site level:

TABLE 21.1

Workflow Properties Configurable via the SharePoint stsadm Tool

Property	Description
workflow-eventdelivery-batchsize	Allows you to set the number of workflow jobs that are processed by the SharePoint Timer service. The default value is 100.
workflow-eventdelivery-throttle	Specifies the number of simultaneously active workflows in the memory of the SharePoint server
workflow-eventdelivery-timeout	Can be used to change the time within which a workflow job should run before it's timed out and put back in the queue to be run again
workitem-eventdelivery-batchsize	Specifies the number of items that are processed by the timer job in one batch. The timer job processes the items and determines if they need to be run.
workitem-eventdelivery-throttle	Out of the items that need to be run, this value determines the number of items that are picked up to be run. The rest of the items are run the next time the timer job runs.

continued

TABLE 21.1 *(continued)*	
Property	**Description**
`job-workflow`	Used to configure the SharePoint timer job that delivers the events being queued to the workflows. Can be set to the following values:
	"Every 5 minutes between 0 and 59"
	"Hourly between 0 and 59"
	"Daily at 15:00:00"
	"Weekly between Fri 22:00:00 and Sun 06:00:00"
	"Monthly at 15 15:00:00"
	"Yearly at Jan 1 15:00:00"
`job-workflow-autoclean`	Used to configure the job that runs to clean up the workflow instances and task items that have been completed for a long amount time. The property takes the same values as the `job-workflow`.
`job-workflow-failover`	Used to configure the job that restarts the workflows that have failed due to unforeseeable reasons. The property takes the same values as the `job-workflow`.

The syntax used to get the current value or set new values for these properties by using the `stsadm` command-line tool is as follows:

```
Stsadm -o setproperty -pn -<propertyname> -pv <propertyvalue>
Stsadm -o getproperty -pn -<propertyname> -pv <propertyvalue>
```

Optionally, you can specify a `-url` switch and then use it to target the property setting for a particular SharePoint Web application or site.

Viewing Workflow Reports

MOSS provides SharePoint administrators with the ability to view XML-based reports on workflow usage. Each workflow generates the following reports:

- **Activity Duration Report:** This report provides information about the duration (in hours) for which a particular workflow ran before completion.

- **Cancellation and Error Report:** This report provides information about the workflows that didn't run because they were either cancelled or encountered an error.

The SharePoint site user interface allows administrators to open these XML reports in Excel for review and analysis.

Migrating SharePoint Designer Workflows

Workflows created with SharePoint Designer are associated with a SharePoint list or library by using the list or library's Globally Unique Identifier (GUID). This association is very important for a workflow to initiate properly for the list items. When deciding to migrate lists with workflows created with SharePoint Designer, it's essential to choose a method that maintains the association of the workflow with the list or library's GUID.

> **NOTE** Workflows created by SharePoint Designer are always associated with the particular list or library. To use the workflow with a different list or library, the workflow needs to be remodified in Workflow Designer to choose the new list. So, this section is about the best practices to use to migrate lists and libraries without breaking the associated workflows.

The following are the recommended methods for migrating lists in SharePoint without irreparably losing the workflow associations:

- **Save Site as a Template:** SharePoint allows you to save a Web site as a template. Saving the SharePoint site as a template allows you to reuse the customizations made to the Web site for creating new sites. If you save the SharePoint site where you created your workflows by using SharePoint Designer as a template and then create a new site based on that template, you should be able to reuse the workflows associated with the lists on the new site. It's very important to note that you should include content while saving the site as a template for the workflows to successfully migrate.

- **Content Deployment:** MOSS offers a content management mechanism that allows administrators to deploy content from a source SharePoint farm to a destination farm. This feature, called Content Deployment, can be used to migrate SharePoint Web applications from one server to another. The migration is performed to ensure that the SharePoint workflow associations and functionality are maintained on the destination server.

- **SharePoint backup and restore:** SharePoint backup and restore using the SharePoint Central Administration Web site or using the `stsadm` backup/restore commands ensures that the SharePoint workflows are properly saved and work as expected when the SharePoint site is restored from backup.

- **Databases backup and restore:** If you restore the SharePoint Web applications from SQL server database backups, you should be able to restore the SharePoint Designer workflows to work properly. Restoring the SharePoint Web application from the SQL content database backup is a standard disaster recovery process when the SharePoint server farm is offline due to an unforeseeable problem. The restore ensures that SharePoint Designer maintains the association with the lists or libraries.

Realizing that SharePoint Designer workflows once associated with a SharePoint list or document library need the association to be maintained throughout is important and should help you understand and choose the best migration strategy for your environment. While re-creating the workflows might be the best course of action in some cases, the methods described earlier can assist administrators in planning the backup strategies around SharePoint Designer workflows.

Troubleshooting Workflows

Troubleshooting problems with workflows created by SharePoint Designer can be a daunting task, especially if the workflows become more complex. With multiple activities configured in single steps and a large number of steps in a single workflow, determining the action that causes the problem in workflow execution can be difficult. You might want to keep the following in mind while working on SharePoint Designer workflows:

- When you create workflows for SharePoint lists or libraries by using Workflow Designer, SharePoint Designer makes Web service calls to SharePoint to determine the latest versions of the important SharePoint files. SharePoint Designer then stores a cached copy of these files locally on the computer where it's installed. This location, called the `ProxyAssemblyCache`, is stored on the SharePoint Designer machine at `C:\ Documents and Settings\<username>\Application Data\Microsoft\ SharePoint Designer\ProxyAssemblyCache`. While this is a temporary cache, SharePoint Designer always looks for files inside this folder when creating workflows. If for some reason (such as a version upgrade or solution deployment) the server version of the files changes, SharePoint Designer might not be aware of it and would still use the cached version, which might cause errors and problems in SharePoint Designer while creating workflows. To ensure that SharePoint Designer requests the latest version of files, you can delete the contents of the `ProxyAssemblyCache` folder, which forces SharePoint Designer to request these files again, which helps update the file version.

- If you're troubleshooting a complex SharePoint Designer workflow that has multiple steps, you might want to break it into a smaller workflow to troubleshoot and find the step that's causing the workflow to fail. This approach is useful in quickly eliminating potential problems with the workflow logic.

- Workflows can be resource-intensive. You need to ensure that you test them for performance under a heavy load before deploying them to a production environment. It's also recommended that you break down complex workflows with a lot of steps and branches into smaller multiple workflows. This ensures that the workflows are easier to maintain and troubleshoot.

- Only a single instance of a workflow can run on a particular item at one time. If you have instances of the same workflow overlapping on the same item, the new instances would simply fail to execute. You might want to check scenarios that could lead you into this limitation.

- Avoid/check infinite looping that might happen if you configure a workflow to start on item update and then change the current item within the workflow by using an action. Put checks in place to help the workflow logic to come out of an infinite loop.

> **TIP** A list of most commonly encountered errors when working in SharePoint Designer for creating workflows can be found at http://office.microsoft.com/en-us/ sharepointdesigner/HA102379121033.aspx.

While the SharePoint diagnostics logging (also called Unified Logging Service) can provide you with lots of information for assistance in troubleshooting workflows, you can also enable Windows Workflow Foundation logging to determine the point of failure in a running workflow. Workflow logging can be enabled for a Web application by adding the following code in the Web application's `web.config` file inside the `<system.diagnostics>` section:

```
<system.diagnostics>
    <switches>
        <add name="System.Workflow LogToFile" value="1" />
        <add name="System.Workflow.Runtime" value="All" />
        <add name="System.Workflow.Runtime.Hosting" value="All" />
        <add name="System.Workflow.Runtime.Tracking" value="All" />
        <add name="System.Workflow.Activities" value="All" />
        <add name="System.Workflow.Activities.Rules" value="All" />
    </switches>
</system.diagnostics>
```

After this code is added to the `web.config` file of the SharePoint Web application, a `WorkflowTrace.log` file is created inside the SharePoint Web application's file system for review and analysis. You can expect detailed information and logging for workflows in this log file.

Summary

Workflows created by SharePoint Designer are subject to the same administrative boundaries as the ones that are available out of the box in SharePoint or the ones developed programmatically. However, because the deployment process and compilation of SharePoint Designer workflows are different, many of the SharePoint administration settings don't apply to them. This chapter discussed the various SharePoint site administration settings that apply to workflows created by SharePoint Designer. Along the lines of workflow administration, this chapter also discussed best practices in migrating and troubleshooting workflows created by SharePoint Designer.

Chapter 22

Developing Advanced Workflows

Earlier chapters familiarized you with general Windows Workflow Foundation and SharePoint workflow concepts and introduced you to SharePoint Designer's Workflow Designer and the SharePoint administrative options for workflows. Until now, SharePoint Designer capabilities for designing workflows have been explored in a more generic way to help you understand the complete picture of where SharePoint Designer workflows fit into the larger SharePoint Workflow infrastructure.

This chapter, however, primarily focuses on SharePoint Designer's Workflow Designer capabilities and options for developing advanced workflows declaratively for SharePoint Web sites. Workflow Designer allows you to perform a number of workflow-related tasks by using *conditions* and *actions*. Conditions and actions are just predefined custom workflow activities that are installed on the SharePoint server during initial setup and installation. Workflow Designer provides the user interface to declaratively use these conditions and actions to write workflow files, associate them with SharePoint lists and libraries, and then deploy them to SharePoint sites. These workflow files are then compiled at runtime and executed when the first instance of the workflow is asked to run.

The user interface to configure these conditions and actions is mostly governed by a number of user interface sentences. These sentences are basically user interface descriptions of the conditions and actions. They contain hyperlinks that are access points to a set of dialog boxes and configuration wizards responsible for providing the interface to designers for making settings specific to the conditions or actions. Workflow Designer dialog boxes and wizards provide the user interface for a specific functionality and are used across multiple conditions and actions depending on the feature required. For example, the Define Workflow Lookup is one of the most commonly used dialog boxes and is used by multiple conditions and actions for performing lookups across SharePoint lists and libraries.

The first section in this chapter strives to help you understand these common dialog boxes in Workflow Designer. In later sections in this chapter, I take you through some scenarios that illustrate how easily you can exploit predefined conditions and actions provided in Workflow Designer for designing advanced workflows for SharePoint lists and libraries. You step through exercises that are designed to familiarize you with using conditions and actions in Workflow Designer for designing workflows for real-world scenarios.

Understanding Workflow Designer Common Dialog Boxes

This section is intended to familiarize you with the specific user interface dialog boxes available in Workflow Designer. Many of these dialog boxes are used repeatedly across multiple actions and conditions. Understanding these dialog boxes should help you use them across Workflow Designer in a number of conditions and actions.

CROSS-REF For an overview of Workflow Designer, see Chapter 20.

Using the Workflow Initiation Parameters dialog box

The Workflow Initiation Parameters dialog box is accessible by clicking the Initiation button on the designer surface of Workflow Designer. This dialog box mostly allows you to create initiation variables, values for which can be collected from a user initiating a workflow manually by using an initiation form. As shown in Figure 22.1, the Workflow Initiation Parameters dialog box, accessed by clicking Add, allows you to add fields of a single line of text, multiple lines of text, number, date and time, choice, and yes/no.

When the workflow is saved, these fields are mapped to corresponding input controls in an initiation form. For example, a field of type Choice can be configured to be shown as a dropdown menu on the initiation form.

NOTE It's important to note that if you specify the workflow to start automatically — for example, on item creation or modification — the initiation form isn't displayed to the user by using the workflow. So, the default values set for these initiation parameters are used in that case.

If the workflow is started manually, an initiation form is displayed to the user that has input controls corresponding to the fields created by using the Workflow Initiation Parameters dialog box. Each field is mapped to a workflow initiation variable. When the user submits the form and starts the workflow, the values he or she types in the input controls are saved in the initiation variables in the workflow. These variables can then be used by using the Workflow Data option at various locations in Workflow Designer. In this manner, the Workflow Initiation Parameters dialog box helps implement the initial interaction of the user with the workflow.

FIGURE 22.1

Adding fields using the Workflow Initiation Parameters dialog box

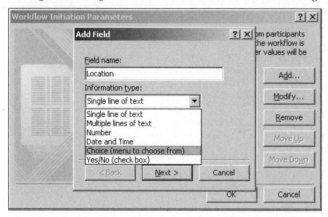

Using the Workflow Local Variables dialog box

The Workflow Local Variables dialog box, available by clicking on the Variables button in Workflow Designer, is Workflow Designer's interface to create, edit, and delete variables that have been defined for a workflow. Workflow variables are pretty useful, as they can be used to store the state of an object, such as a field's value in a SharePoint list item, at a certain point of time. You can then reference the variable at a later point and use the value stored in it to perform the intended operation. As shown in Figure 22.2, the Edit Variable dialog box, accessible by clicking Add in the Workflow Local Variables dialog box, can be used to create and edit workflow variables.

FIGURE 22.2

Creating workflow variables by using the Workflow Local Variables dialog box

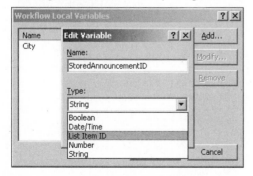

While creating a workflow variable, you can choose the type of data you want to store in the variable. For example, you might want to define the variable type as List Item ID if you want to store the ID of a list item in it for future use.

While the Edit Variable dialog box is accessible by using the Create a new variable option available while binding values to various conditions and actions, the Workflow Local Variables dialog box is the central location to view and manage all workflow variables.

 **NOTE**   The Workflow Local Variables dialog box doesn't display the workflow initiation parameters you defined in the Workflow Initiation Parameters dialog box.

Using the Define Workflow Lookup dialog box

The Define Workflow Lookup dialog box is the most commonly used dialog box in Workflow Designer. This dialog box is the primary interface in Workflow Designer to define a query that returns specific data. The data can then be used to set the value of a workflow variable, for comparison, etc. For example, the Set Workflow Variable action in Workflow Designer displays the Define Workflow Lookup dialog box to choose the field, the value of which should be stored in the workflow variable. In the example shown in Figure 22.3, you're electing to use the ID column in the Shared Documents document library based on the condition that the Approval Status column in the list item has the value 0;#Approved.

FIGURE 22.3

Use the Define Workflow Lookup dialog box to create a lookup query.

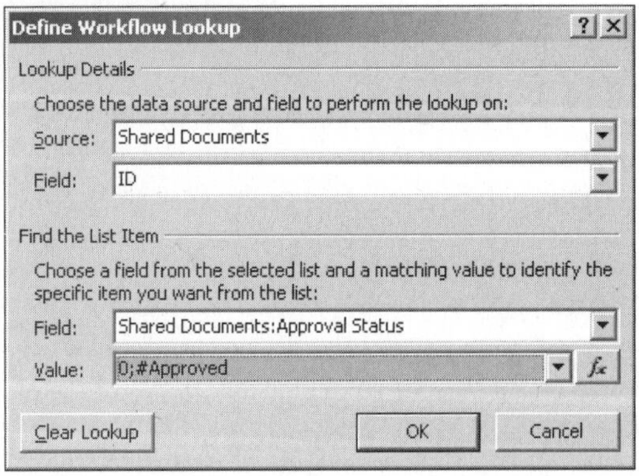

This means that if the Shared Documents document library has a document that has the Approval Status column set to the value 0;#Approved, the value of the ID column of that document would be returned by the lookup. In this manner, the workflow lookup is analogous to an SQL SELECT statement with a WHERE clause. Obviously, in the previous example, there could be multiple documents that have the Approval Status column set to the value 0;#Approved, and the lookup query would then return multiple items. In such a case, the message shown in Figure 22.4 is displayed to indicate that multiple items were returned as the result of the lookup and that the first one is used. Ideally, you should define the workflow lookup in a manner that's guaranteed to return a single item.

This message box displays whether the lookup returns multiple values.

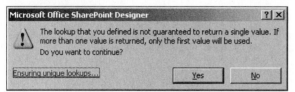

It's also important to note that the Find the List Item section isn't displayed if the item for the lookup is expected to be unique. For example, if you choose Current Item as the value in the Source dropdown menu in the Lookup Details section, the Find the List Item section isn't displayed because it isn't required.

You can use the *fx* button in the Find the List Item section of the Define Workflow Lookup dialog box to perform a second lookup query to determine the value of the field that should be used in the first lookup query. Using the previous example illustration, rather than choosing the value of the Approval Status field from the dropdown menu, if you want to perform a lookup query to get the value to be used, you can use the *fx* button to open another Define Workflow Lookup dialog box and then use it to define the lookup query.

TIP While using the Define Workflow Lookup dialog box, consider the Lookup Details section as the SELECT statement and the Find the List Item section as the WHERE clause. This helps you avoid a lot of confusion while defining lookup queries.

Using the Custom Task Wizard

The Custom Task Wizard is the Workflow Designer interface provided for facilitating task creation. Many workflow actions, such as Collect Data from a User, Assign a To-do Item, etc., depend on tasks that are assigned to specific users. The Custom Task Wizard allows you create these tasks and, for some workflow actions, provides for creating fields for requesting user input.

For example, if you use the Collect Data for a User action in a workflow, clicking the Data hyperlink in the action's sentence opens the Custom Task Wizard. As shown in Figure 22.5, you can use the Custom Task Wizard to create a task with input fields and then assign it to a specific user.

The data collected as the result of the user filling up the form is stored as an item in the Tasks list. The workflow action retrieves the ID of the item created in the Tasks list and then stores it in a workflow variable of type List Item ID. This workflow variable can later be used in the workflow for referencing the data collected from the user.

 The interface of the Custom Task Wizard would be different for the Assign a To-do Item workflow action because the function of this action doesn't require field creation.

FIGURE 22.5

Using the Custom Task Wizard with the Collect Data from a User workflow action

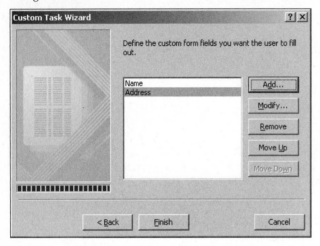

Using the Select Users dialog box

The Select Users dialog box allows you to choose single or multiple users for performing a certain operation in a workflow condition or action. For example, the condition Modified by a Specific Person displays the Select Users dialog box to let you choose the user to be used in the condition. As shown in Figure 22.6, the Select Users dialog box allows you to either manually type the name or e-mail address of the user or choose from a list of users and SharePoint groups. You can specify the user by creating a lookup query by using the Define Workflow Lookup dialog box or choose the user who created the current item.

 Some conditions and actions necessitate that you select only a single user. In such actions, the Select Users dialog box only shows a single-line text field.

To add a user, type the username (or e-mail address) or select the user in the list and then click Add. Or simply double-click your choice in the Select from Existing Users and Groups list. To remove a user, select it in the Selected Users box and then click Remove.

Using the String Builder dialog box

The String Builder dialog box, available in the Build Dynamic String workflow action, is particularly useful for creating dynamic text strings by concatenating values retrieved from lookup queries. The String Builder dialog box, as shown in Figure 22.7, allows you to use the Define Workflow Lookup dialog box to create lookup queries.

FIGURE 22.6

Specifying a user by using the Select Users dialog box

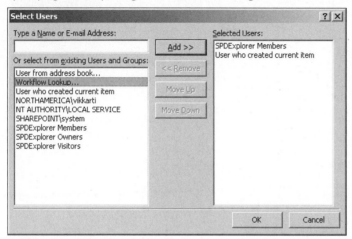

FIGURE 22.7

Using the String Builder dialog box

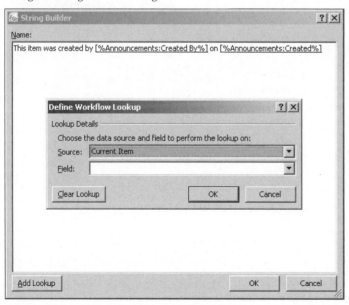

While you can type any text in the text area provided, you click Add Lookup at the bottom of the String Builder dialog box to open the Define Workflow Lookup dialog box for creating the lookup queries.

The values received from these queries can be joined together to form a single text string. This string is then stored in a workflow variable for future use in the workflow. In this manner, the String Builder dialog box is especially useful for creating subject lines for e-mail messages, logging information to history lists, etc.

Using the Define E-mail Message dialog box

The Define E-mail Message dialog box allows you to create an e-mail message for use in the Send an E-mail workflow action. As shown in Figure 22.8, the Define E-mail Message dialog box heavily uses the Select Users and Define Workflow Lookups dialog boxes for specifying the values for the To, CC, and Subject text fields.

TIP You can format advanced formatting and change the look and feel of an e-mail message by adding valid HTML to the body of the message.

The buttons next to the To and CC text fields open the Select Users dialog box, which allows you to specify multiple recipients of an e-mail message. The *fx* button next to the Subject text field opens the Define Workflow Lookup dialog box and allows you to create a lookup query for creating the subject line of the e-mail. Also, the Add Lookup to Body button at the bottom of this dialog box allows you to add dynamic values created by using lookup queries to the body of an e-mail message.

FIGURE 22.8

Using the Define E-mail Message dialog box

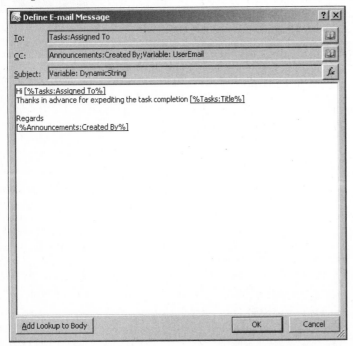

Using the Create New List Item dialog box

Used by the Create List Item workflow action, the Create New List Item dialog box allows you to define the specifics of the list item that's created by the action. As shown in Figure 22.9, the List dropdown menu in the Create New List Item dialog box allows you to specify the SharePoint list or library where the item should be created.

FIGURE 22.9

Using the Create New List Item dialog box to create a new item

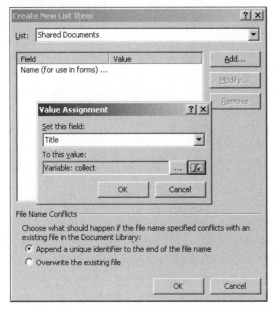

After you choose the list or library, the columns specific to it can be set with appropriate values by using the Value Assignment dialog box, which is accessible by clicking Add. For SharePoint libraries, the File Name Conflicts section is enabled and allows you to choose the course of action in case the item with the same name already exists. You can choose to either append a unique ID at the end of the new item or overwrite the existing item. Once you create the list item, the Create List Item action returns the ID of the newly created item, which is then stored in a workflow variable for future reference in the workflow.

A variant of the Create New List Item dialog box is the Update List Item dialog box, which is used by the Update List Item workflow action to allow for editing a selected list item. As shown in Figure 22.10, the Update List Item dialog box has a Find the List Item section (similar to the Define Workflow Lookup dialog box), which can be used to create a lookup query to determine the item that needs to be updated in the chosen list.

It's important to note that the Update List Item action should be used carefully when designing a workflow that's configured to start automatically on item update. If proper validation checks aren't put in place, you might end up in a workflow that runs in an infinite loop. For example, if you update a list item by using the Update List Item action without specifying any conditions on a workflow configured to automatically start on item update, the workflow keeps triggering itself on every item update. Although the SharePoint server is intelligent enough to terminate running such infinite workflows to avoid system overload, you should keep this behavior in mind while designing workflows.

FIGURE 22.10

Using the Update List Item dialog box to look up and update a list item

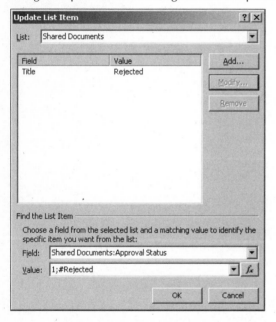

A Workflow Scenario: Document Approval

Approval is one of the most common workflow scenarios. Most processes implement some sort of approval mechanism, as it's innate to the nature of the business implementations to secure approval from senior resources before an operation can be started or continued. Workflow Designer provides Web designers with a number of workflow conditions and actions that can be used to implement approval workflows.

Understanding the scenario

An author working on a document uploads it to the Review document library on the SharePoint site. The act of uploading the document to this library starts a workflow and sends an e-mail to an editor for document review. The editor reviews the document and makes a decision about whether it should be approved or rejected. If the document is approved, it's moved to the Approved document library by using another workflow.

Implementing the scenario by using Workflow Designer

To implement this scenario by using Workflow Designer, follow these steps:

> **NOTE** To successfully send an e-mail, you must properly configure the SharePoint Outgoing e-mail settings.

1. **In a Web browser, open the SharePoint (WSS v3) site where you want to implement this workflow.** First, you need to create two document libraries — Documents for Review and Approved Documents — for storing the documents.

2. **Choose Site Actions ⇨ Create in the SharePoint site to open the Create web page for the web site Web page.**

3. **On the Create page, click Document library in the Libraries section.**

4. **In the new Web page that opens, specify the name Documents for Review for the document library, keep the defaults, and then click Create.** The newly created document library opens in the All Documents view.

5. **Click the Settings action menu and then click Create Column to open the Create Column Web page.** As shown in Figure 22.11, create a column of type Choice with the approval status (for example, Approved, Rejected, etc.) that the document can have.

6. **Click OK.** Using the previous steps, create another document library called Approved Documents with a column that tracks the approval status. After you create the two document libraries, you can start designing the workflow in Workflow Designer.

7. **Open the SharePoint site in SharePoint Designer and then choose File ⇨ New ⇨ Workflow to open Workflow Designer.**

8. **As shown in Figure 22.12, specify a name for the workflow, associate it with the Documents to Review document library, set it to start whenever an item is created, and then click Next.**

9. **Specify a name for the workflow step and then choose the Build Dynamic String workflow action from the More Actions dialog box (which you access by choosing Actions ⇨ More Actions).**

FIGURE 22.11

Creating an approval status column for the document library

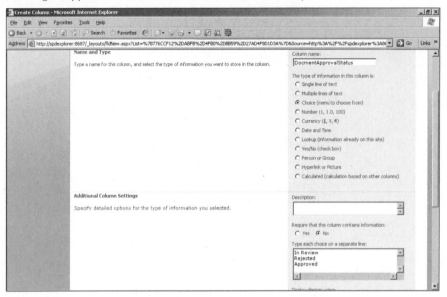

10. **Click the dynamic string hyperlink in the action description sentence Store dynamic string in Variable: Variable1 to open the String Builder dialog box.** You use the String Builder dialog box to create a subject line for the e-mail that's to be sent to an editor when the document is uploaded.

11. **As shown in Figure 22.13, click Add Lookup in the String Builder dialog box to open the Define Workflow Lookup dialog box and then specify the lookup query to retrieve the name of the document being uploaded.**

12. **Using this process, build the dynamic string to be used as the subject line for the e-mail to be sent to an editor.** An example is shown in Figure 22.14.

13. **After the string is complete, click OK to return to Workflow Designer.**

14. **Click Variables to open the Workflow Local Variables dialog box and then rename the Variable1 created automatically to store the dynamic string to a relevant name, as shown in Figure 22.15.**

FIGURE 22.12

Creating the workflow association in Workflow Designer

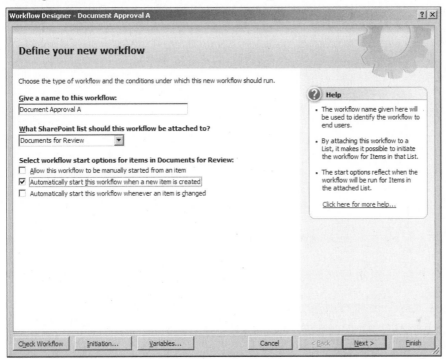

FIGURE 22.13

Using the Define Workflow Lookup dialog box to retrieve the document name

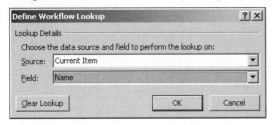

FIGURE 22.14

Building a dynamic string by using the String Builder dialog box

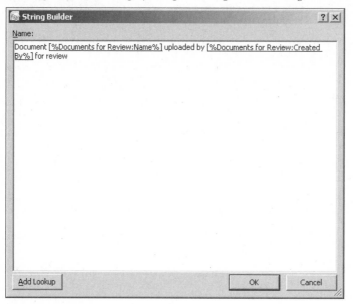

FIGURE 22.15

Renaming the variable for the Build Dynamic String workflow action

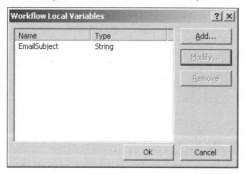

15. Choose Actions ⇨ More Actions to add the Send an E-mail workflow action to the step and then click this message in the workflow action sentence to open the Define E-mail Message dialog box.

16. As shown in Figure 22.16, use the Define E-mail Message dialog box to create an e-mail to be sent to an editor notifying him or her that the document has been uploaded for review.

FIGURE 22.16

Using the Define E-mail Message dialog box to create an e-mail message

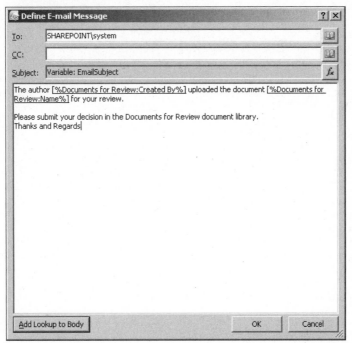

17. **After you create the e-mail message, click OK to return to Workflow Designer.**

18. **Click Check Workflow to check for errors and then click Finish to publish the workflow and associate it with the Documents for Review document library.** Now you can create another workflow for notification and processing once an editor reviews the document and posts his or her decision to the Documents for Review document library. The editor would do so by changing the approval status column. A workflow starts whenever the document is changed, checks whether the status column has been set to a specific value, and performs an action based on the status.

19. **Choose File ⇨ New ⇨ Workflow to open Workflow Designer.** As shown in Figure 22.17, specify the name for the new workflow, associate it with the Documents for Review document library, and then specify it to start whenever an item is changed.

20. **Click Next.**

21. **Choose Conditions ⇨ Compare any data source to use the If value equals value condition sentence, click the first value hyperlink, choose the current item's DocumentApprovalStatus column, and then set the second value hyperlink to Rejected approval status.**

FIGURE 22.17

Creating a secondary workflow for processing based on the approval status

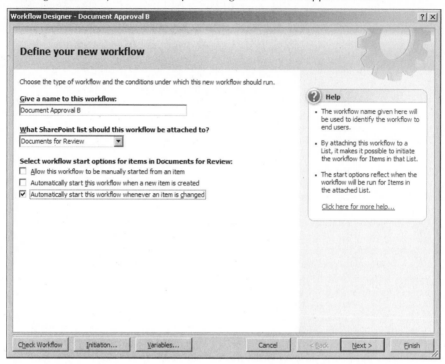

22. **Click the Add Else If Conditional Branch link to add another conditional branch for specifying an Else If condition.** As shown in Figure 22.18, create the conditional statement "If status is rejected, then do this else or do something else."

23. **Using previous steps, use the Build Dynamic String and the Send an E-mail workflow actions to create an e-mail message to notify the author that the document was rejected by the editor.** This is shown in Figure 22.19.

24. **If the document is approved, the document needs to be copied to the Approved Documents document library. To do this, in the Else If branch, choose Actions ➪ More Action and then choose the Copy List Item workflow action.** This places the Copy item in this list to this list action sentence in the Else If branch.

25. **Click the first this list hyperlink.** The Choose List Item dialog box opens, with the Current Item value selected in the List dropdown menu.

26. **Keep the defaults in this dialog box and then click OK.**

FIGURE 22.18

Creating the condition branches for the workflow step

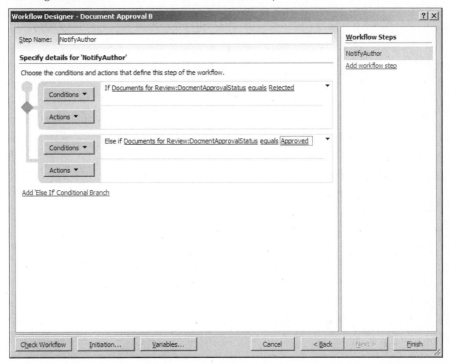

27. **Click the second this list hyperlink in the action sentence and then choose the Approved Documents document library.** The completed sentence is shown in Figure 22.20.

28. **Next, you need to notify the author that the document has been approved. You do this by using the Build Dynamic String and Send an E-mail workflow actions, as used previously in this exercise.** The completed workflow definition is shown in Figure 22.21.

29. **Ensure that the workflow doesn't have any errors and then click Finish to publish the workflow files to the SharePoint site.** As described earlier in the description for this scenario, the first workflow notifies an editor when the author uploads a document to the Documents for Review document library. The second workflow notifies the author when an editor changes the approval status. If the document is approved, the document is copied to the Approved Documents document library.

FIGURE 22.19

Creating a e-mail message for notification

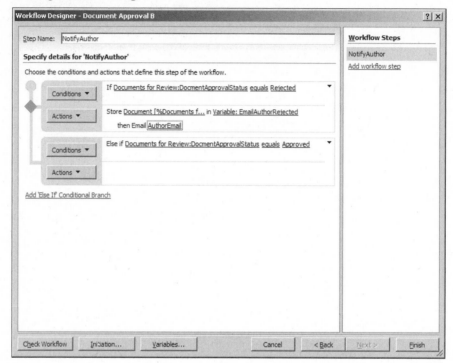

FIGURE 22.20

Configuring the Copy List Item workflow action

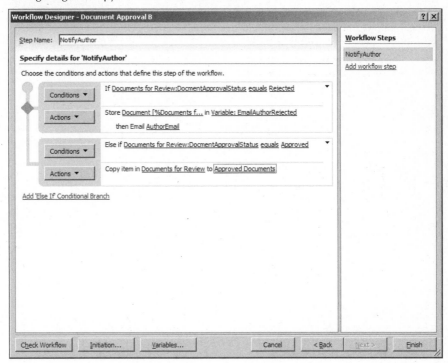

FIGURE 22.21

The process for the second document approval workflow

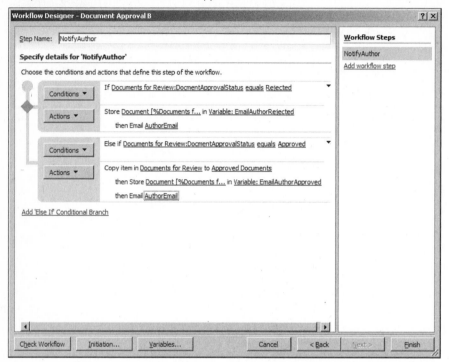

A Workflow Scenario: Newsletters

Workflow Designer allows you to create workflows that can be used to collect information from one or more users. The information collected can then be processed based on the logical requirements of the process. This scenario illustrates the use of the workflow actions provided by Workflow Designer to gather information from users.

Understanding the scenario

The sales department publishes weekly newsletters consisting of content targeted for the employees in the department. Each week, information is collected from subdepartments Sales A, Sales B, and Sales C and is then collated to form a single newsletter that's sent to the entire department. Each subdepartment has a point of contact who's responsible for submitting newsletter content for that subdepartment. Once the newsletter content is collected, it's reviewed by a senior manager and, on approval, subsequently sent to the employees as an e-mail.

Implementing the scenario by using Workflow Designer

Open the SharePoint site where you want to create the list that the workflow uses to store and collate data collected from the users. To implement the preceding scenario using Workflow Designer, follow these steps:

1. Choose Site Actions ⇨ Create to open the Create page.

2. In the Custom Lists section, click Custom List to open the New page, type NewsLetters **in the Name text field, keep the rest of the settings as default, and then click Create.** The newly created NewsLetters list opens in the AllItems view.

3. Choose Site Settings ⇨ Create Column to open the Create Column page.

4. As shown in Figure 22.22, type ContentSalesA **in the Name text field and then choose Multiple lines of text as the type for this column.**

FIGURE 22.22

Creating columns for storing collected newsletter content

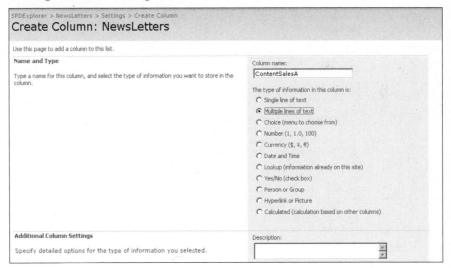

5. Keep the other settings as default and then click Create to create the column.

6. Using the previous steps, create two more columns — ContentSalesB and ContentSalesC — in the NewsLetters list.

7. Open the site in SharePoint Designer and then choose File ⇨ New ⇨ Workflow to open Workflow Designer.

8. **As shown in Figure 22.23, type a name for the workflow, associate it with the NewsLetters list, and then specify for it to start whenever a new item is created.**

9. **Click Variables to open the Workflow Local Variables dialog box.** Here you create three workflow variables — SalesA, SalesB, and SalesC — of type List Item ID for storing the IDs of the tasks created for collecting data from the users. This is shown in Figure 22.24.

10. **After you create the workflow variables, click Next in Workflow Designer.**

11. **Specify a name for the first step.** As shown in Figure 22.25, this step requires that you run all the actions in parallel.

12. **Click the Run All Actions in Parallel menu option.** This ensures that all the users are simultaneously sent the tasks for collecting newsletter content.

FIGURE 22.23

Setting initial settings for the NewsLetters workflow

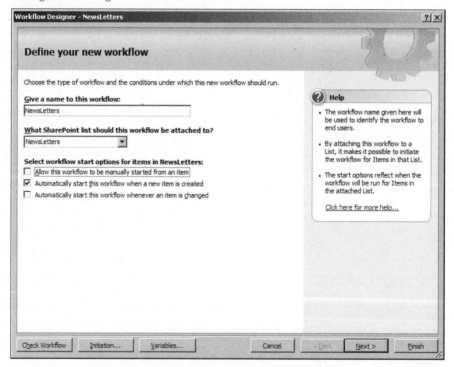

FIGURE 22.24

Creating workflow variables for storing IDs of tasks assigned to users for data collection

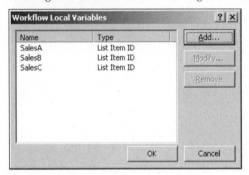

FIGURE 22.25

Running all actions in a step in parallel

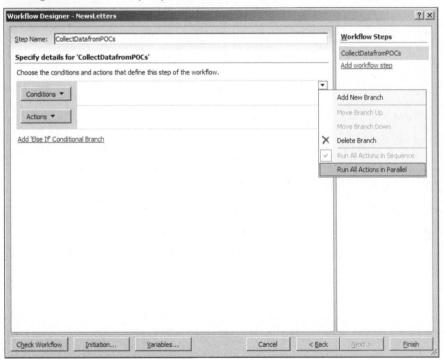

13. **Choose Actions ↪ More Actions and then choose the Collect Data from a User work-flow action.** This shows the Collect data from this user (Output to Variable: collect) action sentence in Workflow Designer. You use this action to send the users task items for collecting newsletter data.

 The workflow is paused until all the task items have been completed.

14. **Click the data hyperlink in the action sentence to open the Custom Task Wizard.** This wizard allows you to create a task that can be assigned to a user for collecting data. The task can have custom fields that map to input boxes, which the user can fill to submit data.

15. **Read the information on the Welcome screen on the Custom Task Wizard and then click Next.**

16. **As shown in Figure 22.26, type a name and description for the task for easy refer-ence later in the workflow.**

FIGURE 22.26

Typing the name and description of the task in the Custom Task Wizard

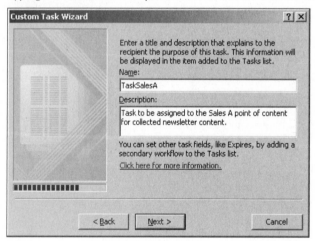

17. **Click Next.**

18. **Click Add to open the Add Field dialog box, create a field called ContentSalesA of type Multiple lines of text, as shown in Figure 22.27, click Next, and then click Finish.**

FIGURE 22.27

Creating fields in tasks by using the Custom Task Wizard

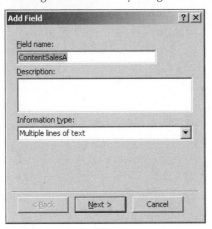

19. **Click Finish to complete the Custom Task Wizard and return to Workflow Designer.**

20. **Click the this user hyperlink to open the Select Users dialog box and then specify the user to whom the task should be assigned.**

21. **Click the Variable: collect hyperlink and select the workflow variable SalesA.** It's important to understand that Collect Data from a User workflow action returns the List Item ID of the task that's assigned to the user. You use the workflow variable to store this List Item ID for future use in the workflow. The completely configured workflow action is shown in Figure 22.28.

22. **Using previous steps, configure two more Collect Data from a User workflow actions for the Sales B and Sales C department.** For this exercise, you can name the tasks TaskSalesB and TasksSalesC and the fields ContentSalesB and ContentSalesC. The completed set of actions is displayed in Figure 22.29.

23. **Click the Add workflow step link in the right pane to add a new workflow step, type a name for the workflow step, and then choose Actions ⇨ More Actions to choose the Update List Item workflow action.** The action sentence for this action is Update item in this list.

24. **Click the this list hyperlink to open the Update List Item dialog box, keep Current Item selected in the List dropdown menu, and then click Add.** The Value Assignment dialog box opens.

FIGURE 22.28

Completed Collect Data from a User workflow action

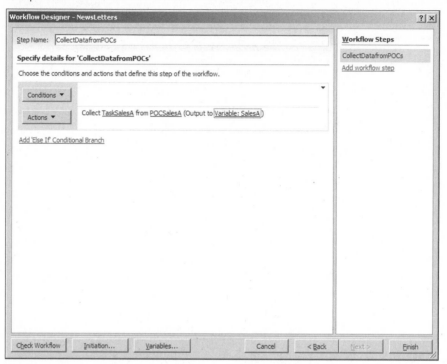

25. In the Set this field dropdown, select ContentSalesA, click the *fx* button to open the Define Workflow Lookup dialog box, and then specify a lookup query to locate the content that the user submitted in the task that was assigned in the previous step. Always keep in mind that at runtime, the workflow can't proceed to this step (Collate Data) until all the tasks in the first step (CollectDataFromPOCs) are completed.

26. To implement the lookup query "Select ContentSalesA field in the Task list item whose List Item ID is equal to the value stored in the Sales A workflow variable" by using the Define Workflow Lookup dialog box, in the Lookup Details section, select Tasks in the Source dropdown menu and ContentSalesA in the Field dropdown menu.

27. In the Find the List Item section, select Tasks:ID in the Field dropdown list box and then click the *fx* button next to the Value text field. Another Define Workflow Lookup dialog box opens.

28. In this Define Workflow Lookup dialog box, select Workflow Data in the Source dropdown menu, Variable: SalesA in the Field dropdown menu. This is shown in Figure 22.30.

29. Click OK. The complete lookup query described in the previous steps is shown in Figure 22.31.

FIGURE 22.29

Creating multiple Collect Data from a User actions for collecting data from multiple users

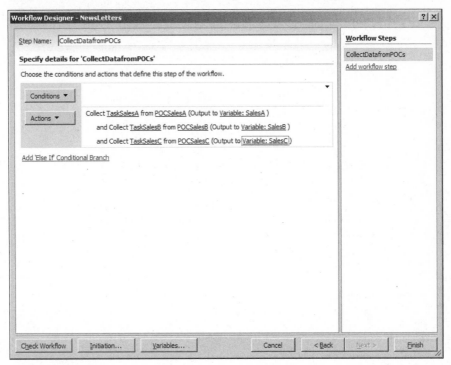

FIGURE 22.30

Defining a complex lookup query by using the Define Workflow Lookup dialog box

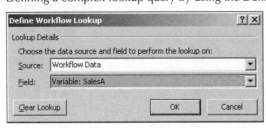

30. Click OK twice to complete the field value assignment.

31. Repeat the previous steps to create value assignments for the ContentSalesB and ContentSalesC columns in the NewsLetters list and then click OK to return to **Workflow Designer.** The completed Update List Item dialog box should look as shown in Figure 22.32.

FIGURE 22.31

The completed workflow lookup query

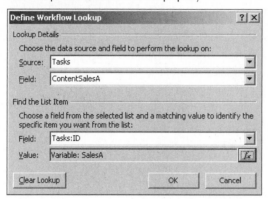

32. **Check the workflow for errors and then click Finish to complete the workflow and deploy it to the SharePoint site.**

In the SharePoint site, you can now initiate the workflow by creating a new item in the NewsLetters list. The workflow should create three task items and then assign them to the specified users. As shown in Figure 22.33, when the user edits the task, he or she is given a choice to complete the task by clicking Complete Task. When all the tasks are completed, the workflow proceeds to the second step and then updates the list item created in the NewsLetters list with the data collected via the tasks from the users.

FIGURE 22.32

The completed Update List Item dialog box for the NewsLetters workflow

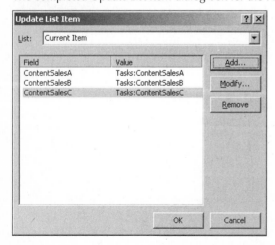

FIGURE 22.33

The completing task in the SharePoint site user interface

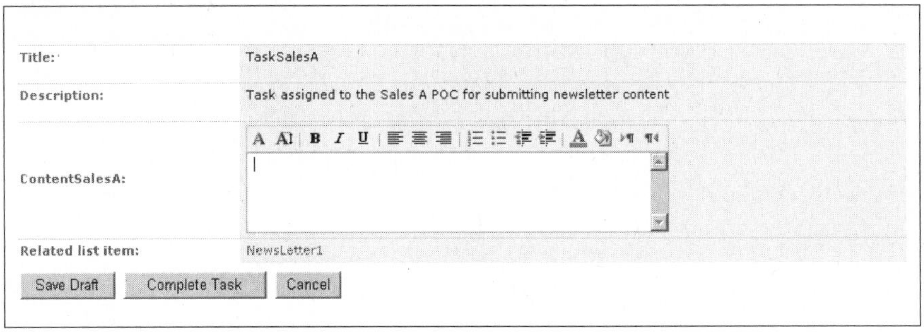

Title:	TaskSalesA
Description:	Task assigned to the Sales A POC for submitting newsletter content
ContentSalesA:	A A B I U ≡ ≡ ≡ ≡ ≡ ≡ ≡ A ⟋ ▸¶ ¶◂
Related list item:	NewsLetter1

[Save Draft] [Complete Task] [Cancel]

Summary

This chapter familiarized you with the rules-based workflow designing model of SharePoint Designer's Workflow Designer. The commonly used dialog boxes, such as Define Workflow Lookup, Select Users, etc., were discussed. Then, you were exposed to the detailed interface aspects and dialog boxes of Workflow Designer through two real-world workflow scenarios.

Part VII

Managing and Publishing Web Sites

Chapter 23

Managing Non-SharePoint Sites

After you develop your Web site project and it's ready for deployment, you most likely need to move it to a Web server that can host the Web site and where it's accessible to its audience. Unless you're remotely authoring directly on a Web site, this task usually involves making a copy of the Web content into the allocated space on the Web server. SharePoint Designer allows for a couple of simple and flexible mechanisms for moving content from one location to another. You can either choose to import and export content or publish Web sites.

Publishing in SharePoint Designer is the process of moving Web site content in a supportable manner from a Web content location to another. You can choose to publish to a remote location or reverse-publish from a remote location to your local computer. Besides publishing, importing, and exporting content from one location to another, SharePoint Designer also provides a Web site packing feature that allows you to package Web sites or portions of Web sites into Web packages that can be unpackaged later at a destination Web content location.

This chapter discusses the various site publishing and management capabilities of SharePoint Designer as applied to non-SharePoint sites. The concept of SharePoint Designer Web publishing doesn't really apply to SharePoint sites, as these sites are authored directly by connecting to the remote SharePoint sites. I talk about how you can import and export Web sites by using Personal Web Packages and publish Web sites by choosing a remote authoring mechanism, such as FTP, WebDAV, FPSE, etc. While you should already be familiar with many of the administrative features of SharePoint Designer to some extent by now, later sections of this chapter take you through the user interface that SharePoint Designer offers for administering non-SharePoint Web sites. To begin with, I discuss the Web site import and export features of SharePoint Designer. After you open your Web site in SharePoint Designer, you can choose to import files and folders or use the Import Web Site Wizard to retrieve files from a file location, a remote Web site, or just an HTTP site on the Internet.

SharePoint Designer's import, export, and publishing features are available through access points in the File menu. You should note that while some of the import and export features in these menus apply to SharePoint sites, the publishing features of SharePoint Designer apply solely to non-SharePoint Web sites.

Importing and Exporting Web Sites

When you choose File ⇨ Import in SharePoint Designer, you can either import files and folders into your Web site or import Web sites that have been packaged into Web Packages by using SharePoint Designer. To import files into your Web site, follow these steps:

1. **Open your Web site in SharePoint Designer.** This can be either your local Web site or a remote Web site residing on a Web server.

2. **Choose File ⇨ Import ⇨ File to open the Import dialog box, as shown in Figure 23.1.**

FIGURE 23.1

The Import dialog box

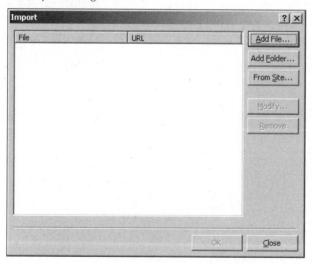

3. **To add files from your local computer to the Web site location, click Add File.**

4. **Choose the files you want to import in the Add Files to Import List dialog box and then click Open.** The files are displayed in the Import dialog box. You can click Add Folder to add a folder (including content) to the import list. Clicking From Site takes you to the Import Web Site Wizard.

5. **Click OK to import the files and folders into your Web site.**

The files and folders you choose to import are now added to your Web site. If the files you're trying to import already exist inside the Web site, a prompt asks whether you want to replace the files.

Using the Import Web Site Wizard

The Import Web Site Wizard, as shown in Figure 23.2, allows you to import content from a number of Web site types into your local Web site. The FPSE or SPS, WebDAV, FTP, and File System options in the Import Web Site Wizard actually link to the Remote Web Site Publishing pane (which is discussed later in this chapter). This means that when you use these options, you're actually publishing content by using the Remote to Local option in the SharePoint Designer Publishing pane.

> **NOTE** It's important to understand that a local Web site in SharePoint Designer import and publishing terms is the Web site that's currently open in SharePoint Designer (using the File ⇨ Open Site dialog box). So, a Web site might actually reside on a Web server but still act as a local Web site for SharePoint Designer, as it was opened directly in SharePoint Designer from the remote location. For example, if your remote Web site is open in SharePoint Designer (using FTP, WebDAV, or FPSE) and you're using the Import Site Web Wizard to import content into it from your local file system, you should see that your local file system is shown as a remote Web site location in SharePoint Designer.

FIGURE 23.2

The Import Web Site Wizard in SharePoint Designer

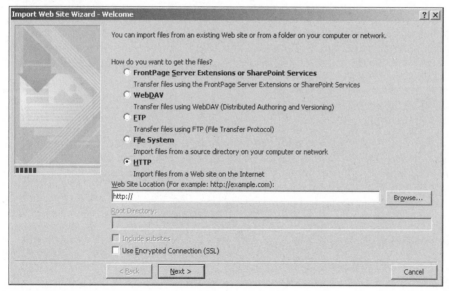

In this section, I take you through the steps for how you can use the Import Web Site Wizard to retrieve content from an HTTP site on the Internet:

1. **Open your Web site in SharePoint Designer.** As discussed before, this could be a Web site that resides locally on your computer or on a remote Web server location.

2. **Choose File ➪ Import ➪ Import Site Wizard.** The Import Web Site Wizard dialog box opens.

3. **Select HTTP in the How do you want to get the files? Section, and in the Web Site Location text field, type the HTTP address of the Web site from which you want to import files.** If you click the Use Encrypted Connection (SSL) check box, the HTTP address changes from `http://` to `https://`.

4. **Click Next.** SharePoint Designer tries to establish a connection with the remote HTTP Internet site you specified in the previous step. If this connection succeeds, you're taken to the next wizard page, where you can choose the location inside your Web site to which you want to import the content.

5. **Click Next.** The Set Import Limits page opens, where you can choose the depth, size, and type of files that you want to import.

6. **Click the Import the home page plus linked pages check box and then type the depth in levels.** The level of depth here implies the depth of hyperlinks that SharePoint Designer browses to while importing files.

7. **Click Next and then click Finish to begin the Import process.** SharePoint Designer starts browsing and then downloads copies of files and images that are accessible at the Internet location.

Creating Personal Web Packages

Personal Web Packages in SharePoint Designer provide for a means to pack up selected content inside your Web site into a package file that you can then send to another location for importing or save as a backup of your Web site. You use the Export Web Package dialog box to create a Web package for your Web site:

1. **Using SharePoint Designer, open the Web site that contains the content you want to export as a Web package.**

2. **Choose File ➪ Export ➪ Personal Web Package to open the Export Web Package dialog box, as shown in Figure 23.3.** The Export Web Package dialog box shows the files and folders of the Web site open in SharePoint Designer in the left list.

3. **Click Show Dependencies to enable the dependency checking section.** Choose Check all dependencies in the Dependency Checking dropdown menu. Now, when you click a file in the folder list, the list of files that the selected file depends on is listed in the list box in the dependency checking section. You can decide which files to include along with the selected file to ensure that the dependencies are maintained when the Web package is imported.

FIGURE 23.3

The Export Web Package dialog box

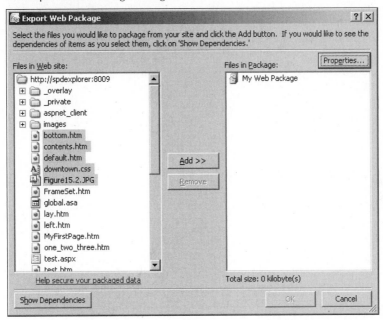

4. **Choose the files you want to export in the package and then click Add to add the files to the Web package.** If you want to export the complete site, choose the topmost folder in the left list and then click Add. Clicking Properties takes you to the Web Package Properties dialog box, which allows you to specify general properties of the Web package and shows any external dependencies.

5. **Click OK to open the File Save dialog box and then save the Web package.**

The Web package file has an .fwp file extension and is mostly a CAB file that contains the files you chose to export and a manifest file that stores the metadata information and dependencies about the files being exported. You can now use this Web package to import content either to an empty Web site or an existing Web site at another location. To import the Web package, choose File ➪ Import ➪ Personal Web Package to open the Import Web Package dialog box, as shown in Figure 23.4.

Simply choose the files and folders you want to import and then click Import. When the import process finishes, you should see the content from the Web package on your Web site.

FIGURE 23.4

The Import Web Package dialog box

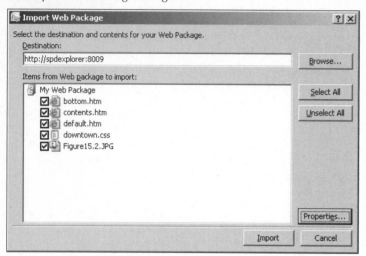

Publishing Web Sites

SharePoint Designer offers a robust and extensive Web content publishing mechanism that allows you to move content to and from a variety of Web server types. Whether your remote Web site location is an FTP, WebDAV, or FPSE site or just a local folder on the file system, publishing interfaces using SharePoint Designer look fairly similar. You can choose to either publish content from a remote to local Web site, a local to remote Web site, or just synchronize contents between two Web site locations.

To publish content, simply choose File ➪ Publish Site or use the Remote Web Site pane in SharePoint Designer. After you specify the location of the remote Web site by using the Remote Web Site Properties dialog box, you're taken to the Publishing pane. It's here that you can choose to either move files to and from one location to another or publish the complete Web site. You can also choose the direction of the publishing in this pane.

Using the Publishing pane

To see the active Publishing pane of SharePoint Designer, you first need to specify the remote location for the publishing operation. If you've never used the publishing interface in SharePoint Designer before, when you choose File ➪ Publish Site, you're taken to the Remote Web Site

Properties dialog box. Otherwise, SharePoint Designer tries to open the last opened remote Web site location in the Publishing pane. To use the Publishing pane, follow these steps:

1. **In SharePoint Designer, open the Web site from where you want to publish content.**

2. **Choose File ⇨ Publish Site to open the Remote Web Site Properties dialog box.**

3. **Choose your remote Web server type, type the location of the remote Web site in this box, and then click OK.** SharePoint Designer tries to connect to the remote site and, if successful, opens the Publishing pane. If a Web site doesn't exist at the location you typed, SharePoint Designer tries to create a Web site at this location.

The Publishing pane, as shown in Figure 23.5, has three main sections: the left section shows the local Web site (the Web site that's currently open in SharePoint Designer); the right section shows the remote Web site (which you specified in the Remote Web Site Properties dialog box); and the bottom section shows the status of the publishing operation and the direction of the publishing.

FIGURE 23.5

The Publishing pane in SharePoint Designer

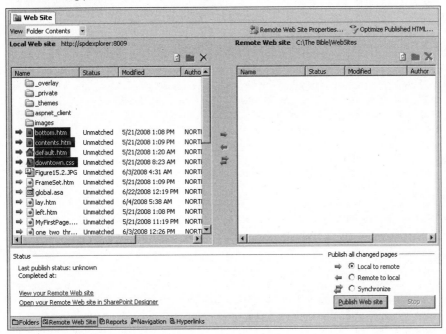

There are multiple ways you can use the left and right sections of the Publishing pane for moving content:

- You can choose files and folders in either section and then click the blue arrows between the sections to move the files.

- You can choose the files and folders in either section and then right-click on Publish Selected Files to publish them.

- You can use the bottom section to specify the direction of the publishing operation: The Local to remote option publishes from the left section to the right section; the Remote to local option publishes from the right section to the left section; and the Synchronize option compares metadata information about files to determine the most updated versions and synchronizes the content on the local and remote Web sites.

In the top-left corner of the Publishing pane is the View dropdown, which allows you to choose from a set of views indicating the files that need publishing. Also, just above the left and right sections, you should see the Refresh and Delete buttons, which can be used to refresh the folder lists and delete files and folders, respectively.

> **NOTE** If you don't want to publish a file or a selection of files, you can use the **Don't Publish menu option (accessible by right-clicking a file and then choosing Don't Publish from the popup menu) to disable publishing for selected files.**

Setting remote Web site properties

When publishing content to existing Web sites, SharePoint Designer compares the metadata information about the files to determine whether the file should be replaced on the destination Web site. The Publishing tab, as shown in Figure 23.6, in the Remote Web Site Properties dialog box allows you to specify a number of settings that SharePoint Designer should consider while determining the files that need to be republished.

The Publishing tab has the following sections that help you configure the publishing mechanism in SharePoint Designer:

- **Publish:** Allows you to choose whether SharePoint Designer should publish the complete Web site or changed content only. The Include subsites check box allows you to specify whether you want to include subsites in the publishing.

- **Changes:** Allows you to specify how SharePoint Designer determines whether a page has changed. If you select Determine changes by comparing the source and destination sites, SharePoint compares the metadata information of the file on the source and destination sites to find out if the file has changed. If you select Use source file timestamps to determine changes since last publish, SharePoint Designer compares the file's last publish timestamp and the modified timestamp to determine whether it should be published again.

■ **Logging:** SharePoint Designer can be set to generate a publishing log file that shows the actions taken during the publishing process. You can use the log file as a report of the publishing process. Once the publishing completes, the bottom section in the Publishing pane shows the link to view the publishing log file.

The Remote Web Site Properties dialog box also has an Optimize HTML tab, as shown in Figure 23.7, which allows you to specify if SharePoint Designer should remove certain elements and HTML comments that are inserted on the Web pages when using SharePoint Designer components.

CAUTION It's important to note that removing HTML comments from Web pages can cause the SharePoint Designer components that depend on these comments to not work in the remote Web site. For example, if you remove all HTML comments, features such as dynamic Web templates, layout tables, etc., might not function when you open the remote Web site for direct editing.

FIGURE 23.6

The Publishing tab in the Remote Web Site Properties dialog box

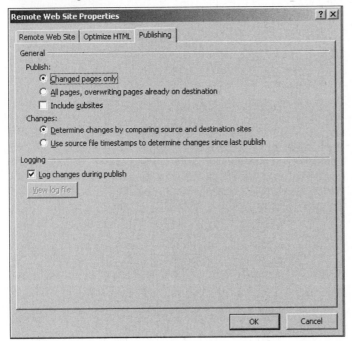

FIGURE 23.7

The Optimize HTML tab in the Remote Web Site Properties dialog box

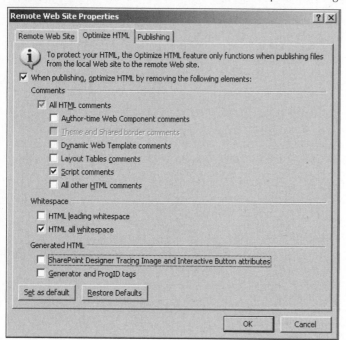

Using Administration Features

While most of the administrative operations on Web sites are performed on a Web server, SharePoint Designer also provides you with some options that either take you to the administrative console on the Web server or let you perform the management operations in the SharePoint Designer user interface itself. For example, if you want to set a Web page as the default home page for your Web site, you don't really need to go to the IIS management console on the Web server to make this change. You can just right-click on the page and then choose Set as Home Page from the popup menu. This automatically makes the Web page the default page for the Web site.

When working with remote Web sites residing on a Web server, you can change Web site server properties by using the Properties menu option available by right-clicking on the site root folder in the Folder List task pane. As shown in Figure 23.8, the Properties dialog box allows you to change the execute permissions for the Web site:

- **Allow scripts to be run:** This option lets you configure the Web site folder to allow for execution of scripts, such as ASP, ASP.NET, etc.

- **Allow files to be browsed:** This option allows you to specify if files in the folder can be browsed to.

- **Allow anonymous uploads to this directory:** Only available if the Allow scripts to be run check box is deselected, this option allows you to specify if anonymous users can upload files to a folder on a Web server.

- **Allow uploaded files to overwrite existing filenames:** Only available if the Allow scripts to be run check box is deselected, this option allows for overwriting if the files being uploaded already exist.

These options are also available on the folders that exist on the Web site. Also, when working with FPSE Web sites, the Convert to Web option is available for folders. This menu option converts a folder into an FPSE-enabled subsite. If you right-click on a subsite, you also have an option to convert the subsite to a folder, which demotes the subsite to a simple folder by deleting FPSE metadata information from it.

FIGURE 23.8

The Properties dialog box for an FPSE Web site

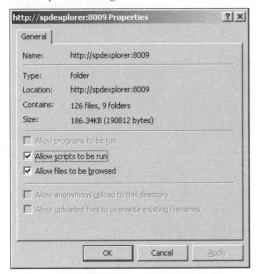

Managing site settings

As discussed earlier, the Site Settings dialog box in SharePoint Designer can be used to find information about the Web site, the type of Web server, and the version of FPSE or SharePoint installed on the site. As shown in Figure 23.9, when working with FPSE sites in SharePoint Designer, the option to remove hidden metadata from the Web site isn't available in the Site Settings dialog box.

FIGURE 23.9

The Site Settings dialog box for an FPSE-enabled Web site

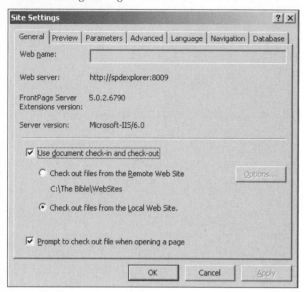

This ensures that an author doesn't inadvertently remove important FPSE metadata information from an FPSE-enabled Web site, thereby causing serious problems with the underlying infrastructure that sustains the Web site.

Recalculating hyperlinks

It's possible that during file move operations, such as import, export, publishing, etc., a network failure may lead to a mismatch in the FPSE hidden metadata for a Web site. This mismatch can cause many features that rely on the hidden metadata to either fail or perform erratically. Recalculate Hyperlinks is a mechanism that FPSE sites offer as a way to repair any broken hyperlinks, FPSE-based components, and hidden metadata of the Web site.

You can easily start the Recalculate Hyperlinks operation by choosing Site ➪ Recalculate Hyperlinks. As the Recalculate Hyperlinks message box indicates, the operation tries to repair all hyperlinks, updates information for all FrontPage components, and synchronizes metadata associated with the Web site.

NOTE   It's advisable to run Recalculate Hyperlinks in situations where you experience rendering and update issues with FrontPage Web components, such as link bars, bars based on navigation structure, etc.

Using Administration options

For FPSE sites, the Site ⇨ Administration menu option is also enabled. This menu option allows you to quickly open some FPSE administration Web pages for performing management tasks:

- **Administration Home:** This takes you to the root FPSE administration Web page for the Web site that you have open in SharePoint Designer.

- **Permissions:** Opens the Permissions administration Web page for FPSE, which allows you to manage users, change FPSE roles, etc.

- **Change Password:** If the user opening the site in SharePoint Designer has been created by using the FPSE administrative pages, this option opens a Web page that allows the user to change his or her password.

- **Backup Web Site:** Available for backward-compatibility, you can use this option to back up your FPSE site.

- **Restore Web Site:** Use this option to restore from a backup that has been created with the Backup Web Site menu option.

Summary

SharePoint Designer allows you to move content from one site to another using a number of mechanisms. You learned to use the SharePoint Designer import/export tools to move Web sites, and you learned how to use the import and export wizards for non-SharePoint sites.

You used the SharePoint Designer publishing features to move Web site content from local to remote as well as remote to local, and you also learned how to synchronize content between Web sites. Again, keep in mind that publishing in SharePoint Designer isn't only for SharePoint sites.

I also took you through the steps to change the properties of Web sites by using SharePoint Designer and discussed a number of administrative features available in SharePoint for non-SharePoint sites.

Chapter 24

Exploring SharePoint Site Management Features

Most SharePoint-related administrative tasks are best performed with SharePoint administration tools, such as the SharePoint Central Administration Web site and the `stsadm.exe` command-line tool. But SharePoint Designer also offers some capabilities in this area that allow SharePoint site designers to quickly perform some basic administrative work, such as backing up sites, saving sites as templates, etc., without having to involve the SharePoint site administrators.

The user interface for SharePoint Designer features that relate to SharePoint site administration, such as import, export, Web packaging, etc., is essentially the same as in the case of non-SharePoint sites. However, some of the menu options that are disabled when working with non-SharePoint sites are enabled and available for use. The process that you follow in SharePoint Designer to import and export content or back up and restore SharePoint sites is mostly similar to non-SharePoint sites. However, there are important considerations to make while using these features with SharePoint sites.

This chapter discusses what you need to keep in mind while using the SharePoint Designer site management features on SharePoint sites. I take you through the import and export, back up and restore, and saving Web sites as templates features. I also talk about how you can save Web parts you modify in SharePoint Designer by exporting them. Later in this chapter, I familiarize you with the concept of Contributor Settings and how it applies to SharePoint Designer when working with SharePoint sites.

It's important to note that while SharePoint Designer offers a set of export and backup features for SharePoint sites, the most recommended means to administer your SharePoint sites is to use the SharePoint administration tools. SharePoint Designer features can be used as a short-term means of quickly backing up or exporting your SharePoint Web sites in a less formal manner.

IN THIS CHAPTER

Importing and exporting SharePoint sites

Using SharePoint backup and restore features

Implementing contributor settings

Also, the SharePoint Designer publishing feature isn't completely applicable to SharePoint Web content. If you publish a SharePoint Web site to a non-SharePoint destination location, SharePoint content, such as lists and document libraries, doesn't work. You have to either export the sites and then import them at the destination location or use the backup and restore features.

Importing and Exporting SharePoint Sites

As in the case of non-SharePoint sites, you can import files and folders into SharePoint sites via the Import dialog box. You can also use the Import Web Site Wizard to import files and folders from remote Web site locations into the SharePoint site. The user interface is similar to the one discussed in the previous chapter and is omitted here in favor of other details.

NOTE When importing content into SharePoint sites from a remote Web site location using FPSE, FTP, WebDAV, etc., the SharePoint Designer interface allows you to move content from the SharePoint site to the remote Web site location. While you can use this interface to move static content, such as HTML pages, pictures, CSS files, etc., any SharePoint-specific content, such as Web part pages, page layouts, etc., shouldn't be moved in this manner.

Exporting Web packages

A better way of moving content between SharePoint sites is to use the Personal Web Packages feature. The user interface for importing and exporting SharePoint sites is essentially the same as for non-SharePoint sites. However, for SharePoint sites, it's important to keep the following points in mind when using the Personal Web Packages feature to export content:

- You should use personal Web packages when you want to use the design and customization of the Web pages, lists, etc., for the SharePoint site at a different location.

- Personal Web packages don't include data associated with SharePoint lists. Also, you can't include subsites and user permissions in the personal Web packages.

- Web packages are useful in special cases when you want to move a specific Web page from one site to another without backing up and restoring the entire Web site.

CAUTION Many lists inside a SharePoint Web site might contain sensitive information, such as confidential documents, user passwords, etc. For protection, you should ensure that these files aren't included in the Web packages. For example, if you've created database connections (stored in the hidden _fpdatasources document library) by using the Data Source Catalog task pane, you might want to exclude them.

The other important thing to consider when using the import/export features of SharePoint Designer is that the destination SharePoint site should be the same version as the source SharePoint site. To avoid mismatches, it's recommended that you use the same site template for the source and destination Web sites. For example, if you're using the Team Site template on the source site, the destination site should also use the Team Site template. You shouldn't import content from a Team Site template–based SharePoint site into a Collaboration template–based SharePoint site.

Using SharePoint site templates

SharePoint site templates allow you to save the structure of the SharePoint site you designed in SharePoint Designer so that new Web sites can reuse the same structure. You should save your Web site as a site template when you want to create new Web sites based on the same layout, look and feel, and customizations.

Choose File ➪ Export ➪ SharePoint Site Template to open the SharePoint administration Save Site as Template Web page, as shown in Figure 24.1, which allows you to save the site as a template (a file with an `.stp` extension) for later use.

NOTE You can click the Include Content check box if you want to include content along with the Web site structure. If you include content, any custom workflows designed with SharePoint Designer are also included in the template. However, keep in mind that there's a limit of 10MB for the size of the template file.

FIGURE 24.1

The Save Site as Template Web page in SharePoint Designer

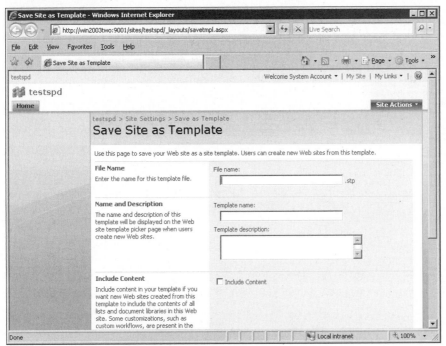

The template file that's created when you save the site as a template is stored in the Site Template Gallery. You need to ensure that you have appropriate permissions to the Site Template Gallery so that you can save the template to the gallery.

Exporting Web parts

One of the really cool features that SharePoint Designer offers is the ability to export Web parts existing on Web pages of a SharePoint Web site, which can then be saved into the Web Part Gallery of the Web site in SharePoint and used on other Web pages. The process of exporting a Web part is simple. Follow these steps:

1. **Open the Web page that has the Web part that you want to import.**

2. **Choose the Web part you want to save and then choose File ⇨ Export ⇨ Save Web Part.** You have the choice to either save the Web part in the Site Gallery or as a file with the extension `.dwp` (or `.Webpart`). This allows you to later add the part to the Web Part Gallery of a SharePoint Web site. When you choose to the save the Web part in the Site Gallery, the Save Web Part to Site Gallery dialog box, as shown in Figure 24.2, opens. This dialog box allows you to specify the display name and description of the Web part that's used in the Web Parts task pane.

FIGURE 24.2

The Save Web Part to Site Gallery dialog box

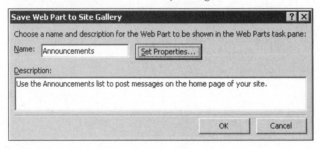

3. **Click OK.** The newly saved Web part is listed in the Web Parts task pane. When you save the Web part, SharePoint Designer automatically opens the Web Parts task pane to show you where the Web part is saved.

NOTE Although you can use this mechanism to save Web parts for later use, it's important to understand that the dependencies of the Web part aren't saved along with the file. For example, if you save a Data Form Web Part by using this option, you must ensure that the database connection that the Web part uses is valid on the Web site where the saved Web part is used.

Using SharePoint Backup and Restore Features

As with non-SharePoint Web sites, the SharePoint Designer backup and restore options for SharePoint sites are available in the Site ⇨ Administration menu. The user interface is pretty straightforward, and you can follow these steps to back up your Web site:

1. In SharePoint Designer, open the Web site you want to back up.

2. Choose Site ⇨ Administration ⇨ Backup Web Site to open the Backup Web Site dialog box, as shown in Figure 24.3.

FIGURE 24.3

The Backup Web Site dialog box

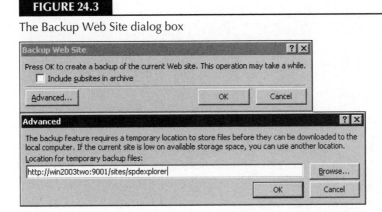

3. You can choose to include subsites by clicking the Include subsites in archive check box. The Advanced button allows you to change the location where the backup files are temporarily stored before they're downloaded to your local machine.

NOTE By default, the SharePoint Designer backup operation stores the backup files in a hidden document library of your SharePoint Web site before they can be downloaded to the SharePoint Designer client machine. After you complete the backup operation, the temporary files (with the extension .snt) inside the SharePoint site are removed. You might still see the temporary files left in case the backup operation fails due to some reason.

4. **When you click OK, you're asked to provide a location where you want to save the backup file.** The backup file is saved with the extension .cmp, which is the abbreviation for Compressed Migration Package.

To restore the Web site to a different location, simply choose Site ⇨ Administration ⇨ Restore Web Site and then specify the location of the backup file. The Restore Web Site dialog box also has an Advanced button that allows you to specify the location of the temporary files and the import log file.

> **CAUTION** It's important to understand that while SharePoint Designer might be able to back up large Web sites, it can only restore backup files that are less than or equal to 24MB. However, you should be able to restore backup files created with SharePoint Designer by using the stsadm.exe command-line tool on the SharePoint Web server.

Implementing Contributor Settings

Contributor Settings is a new offering in SharePoint Designer for SharePoint sites and allows an administrator to lock down SharePoint Designer features, commands, and menus based on the contributor group that the user using SharePoint Designer belongs to. This is particularly useful in scenarios where administrators (or site managers) want to direct their users to perform only site-editing operations of a specific type (such as creating and managing CSS) and not be able to perform any other operations, thereby saving the Web site from an unintentional or inadvertent site modification.

> **NOTE** Contributor Settings isn't a security implementation. It's just a lockdown mechanism that can be used with SharePoint Designer to prevent unintended Web site changes. Only a site administrator can enable or disable Contributor Settings.

The concept of Contributor Settings and the Contributor Mode can be fairly easy to understand if you don't confuse it with SharePoint permissions. This feature is implemented by using Contributor Groups, which can be created in SharePoint Designer and linked to Permission Levels in SharePoint.

Understanding Contributor Settings

To be able to understand Contributor Settings and the Contributor Mode in SharePoint Designer, you need to first understand the concept of permission levels in SharePoint. A *permission level* is basically a bundle of permissions. For example, the Full Control permission level has all the available permissions in it. By default, there are a number of permissions levels available for use with SharePoint sites. You can see the list of available permission levels in your SharePoint site by browsing to the Web site and then choosing Site Actions ⇨ Site Settings ⇨ Modify All Site Settings ⇨ Advanced Permissions. On the Permissions page, choose Settings ⇨ Permission Levels to open the list of permission levels, as shown in Figure 24.4.

FIGURE 24.4

The Permission Levels page in SharePoint Designer

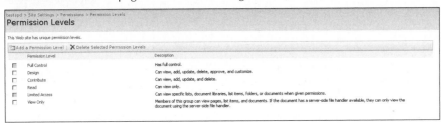

Using this page, you can create new permission levels and then choose the list of permissions available for the permission level. Once the permission level is created, you can associate users (or groups) to a permission level so that the user (or group) has permissions that bundle up in the associated permission level.

In SharePoint Designer, you create contributor groups that are linked to these permission levels. A *contributor group* is basically an object that has a list of SharePoint Designer features, commands, and menu bars enabled for use. Each contributor group is linked to one or more permission levels. By default, SharePoint Designer has three contributor groups: Site Managers (linked to the Full Control permission level); Content Authors (linked to the Contribute permission level); and Web Designers (linked to the Design permission level).

So, the way this mechanism manifests in SharePoint Designer is through the following:

- A user (or group) is added to the SharePoint site with a specific permission level. This could either be any of the default permission levels or a newly created permission level.
- In SharePoint Designer, a contributor group is created and linked to a permission level.
- When a user opens the site in SharePoint Designer with the Contributor Mode turned on, the permission level of the user dictates the contributor group the user should belong to. Based on the contributor groups the user belongs to, the SharePoint Designer interface is enabled or disabled for use.

NOTE Contributor Mode is enabled by default in SharePoint Designer. Because there are three contributor groups created and linked to three permission levels, users accessing SharePoint sites should see the SharePoint Designer features enabled or disabled based on their permission levels.

When you open a SharePoint site that has Contributor Mode enabled for it, the title bar of SharePoint Designer indicates that the Contributor Mode is turned on, as shown in Figure 24.5.

FIGURE 24.5

SharePoint Designer with the Contributor Mode turned on

Microsoft Office SharePoint Designer (Contributor Mode)

The Contributor task pane is also enabled, which indicates that the contributor settings are turned on, allows you to view your Contributor Settings, and shows the tasks you previously performed using SharePoint Designer.

Configuring contributor group properties

You work with the Contributor Settings in SharePoint Designer via the Site ➪ Contributor Settings menu. This menu opens the Contributor Settings dialog box, as shown in Figure 24.6, which allows you to create or modify contributor groups, manage region types, and toggle Contributor Settings off and on.

FIGURE 24.6

The Contributor Settings dialog box

The three contributor groups that are created by default in SharePoint Designer are shown in the Manage Contributor Groups section. To create a new contributor group, follow these steps:

1. **In the Contributor Settings dialog box, click Add in the Manage Contributor Groups section.** This opens the Contributor Group Properties dialog box, as shown in Figure 24.7. The left pane in this dialog box lists all the areas in SharePoint Designer where the features can be enabled or disabled.

2. Type the name and description for the contributor group by using the Group name and Group description text fields.

3. In the SharePoint site permission levels section, choose the permission levels you want to link the contributor group to and then click Link.

4. Using the various options, such as Folders, Formatting, etc., in the list on the left, choose the features that you want to enable in SharePoint Designer for the contributor group. By default, all features are enabled. You can deselect the available check boxes to disable features.

You can use the Manage Region Types section in the Contributor Settings dialog box to create region types that can be associated with content regions in Master Pages by using the Manage Content Region menu option, as shown in Figure 24.8. After a content region is associated with a region type, a user can make only those modifications to the content of the content region that are considered valid according to the associated region type.

FIGURE 24.7

The Contributor Group Properties dialog box

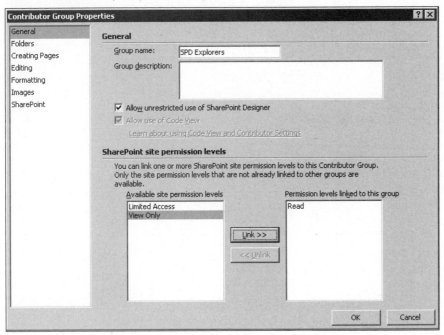

While creating region types, you can specify if the settings should be inherited from the contributor group. Otherwise, you can override the inheritance and then specify your own settings for enabling and disabling features.

FIGURE 24.8

Using master page content regions with region types

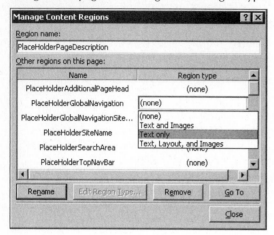

Summary

In this chapter, I discussed a number of site management features for SharePoint sites exposed by SharePoint Designer.

You learned about the SharePoint Designer capabilities to import and export content into SharePoint sites. You also learned how you can export sites as templates and save Web parts. I also discussed SharePoint Designer's backup and restore capabilities.

Finally, I took you through the Contributor Settings feature of SharePoint Designer, which can be used to lock SharePoint Designer menus and command bars based on user permissions, and I also explained how to manage content regions in master pages.

Chapter 25

Reporting for Web Sites

Reporting features of SharePoint Designer for sites have mostly been carried over from FrontPage 2003. You have the capability to view reports related to usage of FrontPage components on the targeted Web site, information about hyperlinks, various problems, and usage-related information. However, SharePoint Designer adds to these reporting features by providing task panes that have the ability to generate reports related to the Web site's accessibility and conformation to various Web standards, compatibility with various browser schemas, and CSS reporting.

This chapter focuses on the SharePoint Designer Reports pane, which allows administrators and site developers to view information and reports about their Web sites and helps in performing analysis based on site usage, problems encountered, and components and features used. I also talk about the various Web standards of accessibility that SharePoint Designer can compare your Web site content against and generate reports that help you determine the standards your Web site adheres to. Usage Reporting, one of the most popular features of FrontPage reporting that SharePoint Designer also inherits, is also discussed later in this chapter. I show you how to set up usage reporting in SharePoint sites and use the usage data through the SharePoint Designer reporting interface.

The Reports pane in SharePoint Designer is accessible through the Site menu. Here, you can view reports detailing the site summary, recent files, style sheets, hyperlinks, and usage data. The interface is fairly simple, and the reports are shown in a tabular format that can be filtered and worked upon for analysis. Before you actually begin working with the Reports pane in SharePoint Designer, I want to take you through the settings that you can configure for the Reports pane. You can access the settings for the Reports pane by using the Application Options dialog box (Tools ⇨ Application Options).

The Reports View tab, as shown in Figure 25.1, in the Application Options dialog box allows you to define settings for the reports. You can specify the following settings in the Reports View tab:

- **General:** Allows you to specify the number of days that determine whether a file on the Web site is considered recent or old, set the number of seconds a page should take to load to consider it a slow page, and set the connection speed for consideration when generating reports

- **Usage:** Allows you to specify the number of months the usage report should be based upon

FIGURE 25.1

The Reports View tab in the Application Options dialog box

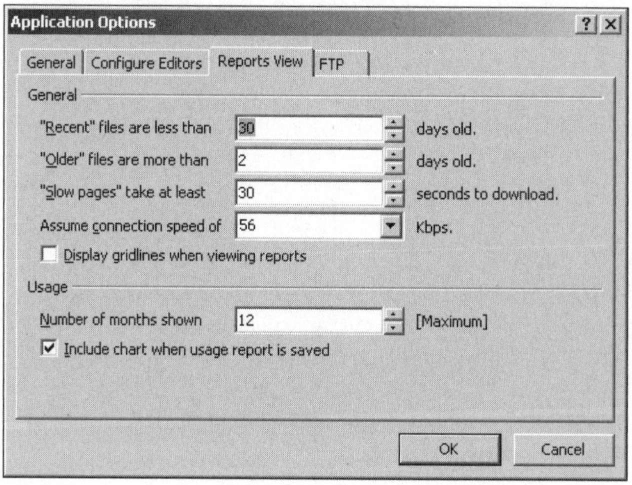

Using the Reports Pane

The Reports pane is mostly a tabular representation of data collected from the site metadata information, Web server log files, etc., which is formatted to indicate various operations that have been performed on the Web site in the recent past. You can use the following steps to generate and access your Web site's reports:

1. **In Sharepoint Designer, choose Site ⇨ Reports ⇨ Site Summary to open the Reports pane in the Site Summary view.** This view, as shown in Figure 25.2, is the generic view that contains links to other views in the Reports pane.

2. **Click the All Files link in the Site Summary report.** You're redirected to the All Files view of the Reports pane. Here, you can see a tabular structure of your Web page content, which can be filtered to categorize the information displayed. For example, if you want to view the files that were modified on a certain date, you can just click the Modified Date column arrow and then click Custom. Then, you can use the Custom AutoFilter dialog box to specify the filter criteria (the required modified date in this case) and reduce the amount of data displayed. After you apply a filter, the filter dropdown arrow changes to a blue color to indicate that the view has been filtered on the corresponding column.

3. **Save the report generated by SharePoint Designer by choosing File ⇨ Save As.** By default, the report is saved as an HTML file.

In this manner, you can generate a number of reports by using the SharePoint Designer Reports pane. For example, if you want to create a list of recently changed files, simply choose Reports ⇨ Files ⇨ Recently Changed Files. SharePoint Designer automatically creates a report for you based on the settings you made in the Reports tab in the Application Options dialog box. You can then save this report by choosing File ⇨ Save As and then use the report for reporting and analysis.

FIGURE 25.2

The Site Summary view in SharePoint Designer

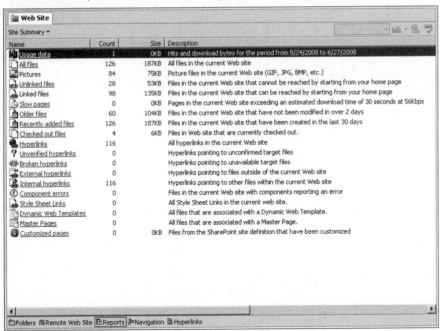

Using Site-Reporting Features

SharePoint Designer allows you to generate a number of reports in the Reports pane. This section discusses some of the commonly used report views.

Files reports

If you choose Site ➪ Reports ➪ Files, a number of views for reports related to recently added, changed, and old files appear. In the Reports pane, you can switch between views by clicking the view name in the top-left corner. If you choose the Recently Added Files, Recently Changed Files, or Old Files menu option, a Days dropdown menu is enabled in the top-right corner of the Reports pane. You can use this dropdown menu to bypass the settings for days you made in the Reports View tab in the Application Options dialog box.

> **NOTE**   The Checkout Status view is enabled for Web sites that support checking-in and checking-out files. For example, you can use the Checkout Status view for an FPSE site that has check-in/check-out enabled for it.

Shared content reports

The report views in this section focus on providing reports that can help developers understand the usage of various types of shared resources, such as master pages, style sheets, and dynamic Web templates. It also helps you create a report that indicates the pages in SharePoint sites that have been customized by using SharePoint Designer.

> **TIP**   You can use the customized reports view in SharePoint Designer to find out which pages have been un-ghosted in SharePoint sites. Then, you can use this report view to either reset a selection of pages to site definition or just use it for analysis and reporting.

The following steps indicate how easy it is in SharePoint Designer to determine the number of customized pages in a SharePoint site:

1. Open a SharePoint site for which you want to know the amount of pages that have been un-ghosted or customized.

2. Choose Site ➪ Reports ➪ Shared Content ➪ Customized Pages to open the Customized Pages reports view.

3. For each page that has been customized in SharePoint Designer, a Yes appears in the Customized column.

4. Filter the Customized column for Yes values.

5. Choose File ➪ Save As to save the report. You can also right-click a customized Web page in this report and then choose Reset to Site Definition from the popup menu to re-ghost them.

 When you re-ghost pages that have been customized by using SharePoint Designer, you lose all customizations made in SharePoint Designer.

Problems reports

The reports in this view can help you determine broken hyperlinks as well as components and pages that are considered slow:

- **Unlinked Pages:** Shows the Web pages other pages on the Web site don't have hyperlinks to

- **Slow Pages:** Shows the list of pages that are considered slow based on the settings in the Reports View tab in the Application Options dialog box

- **Hyperlinks:** Generates a report of broken hyperlinks. When you switch to this view, SharePoint Designer tries to verify all hyperlinks for your Web site. If you click Yes, it tries to find out if the hyperlink is valid. The result of the validation shows in the reports view. You can also edit and fix broken hyperlinks by right-clicking on the broken hyperlink in the reports view and then choosing Edit Hyperlink from the popup menu. This opens the Edit Hyperlink dialog box, as shown in Figure 25.3, which allows you to specify the new hyperlink and then choose whether you want to make changes to this hyperlink on all pages or on selected pages only.

- **Components Errors:** Determines if there are any errors on the various Web components being used on the Web site. The error is displayed in the Error column of the report.

FIGURE 25.3

Fixing broken hyperlinks using the Hyperlinks reports view

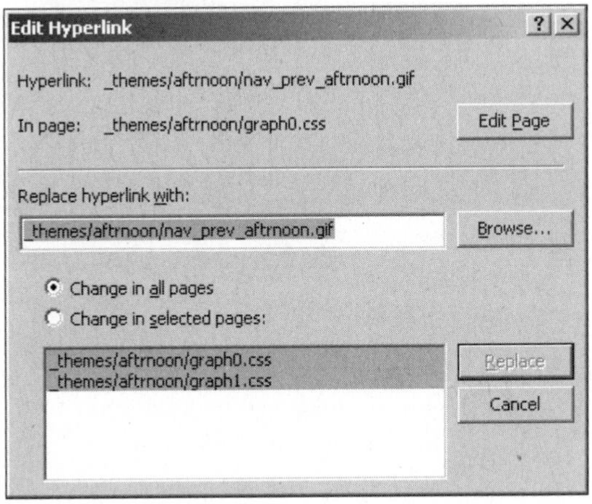

Exploiting Usage-Reporting Features

One of the cool features that SharePoint Designer exposes is the ability to consume usage data from the Web server for a Web site and then generate report views indicating usage information, such as page hits, visiting users, and the Web browsers and operating systems being used to access the Web site. However, because this feature relies on the Web server usage data, you have to ensure that this data is generated and available for use at the Web server. Fortunately, FPSE and SharePoint allow for accumulation of usage data at the Web server.

Enabling usage reporting for Web sites

To enable the generation of usage data on an FPSE site, you have to perform some administrative work on the Web server. On Windows 2003 servers, FPSE 2002 allows for the creation of usage data by using the `owsadm` command-line tool. For example, to create usage data for a Web site that has the IIS identifier 87257621, you can use the following command: `C:\Program Files\ Common Files\Microsoft Shared\Web server extensions\50\bin>owsadm -o usage -p /lm/w3svc/87257621`.

 **For more information on how to generate usage data on FPSE sites, visit this Web site: http://support.microsoft.com/kb/889363.**

Once the usage data has been created, you can open the site in SharePoint Designer to view the usage reports that are generated based on the usage data created on a Web server. Figure 25.4 shows a sample of the usage data for an FPSE site. You might need to refresh the Web site or recalculate hyperlinks to have SharePoint Designer generate the usage for you once the usage data has been created for the Web site. The usage data is stored in the _vti_pvt folder of the FPSE site in the form of XML documents.

CROSS-REF **For more on Recalculate Hyperlinks, see Chapter 23.**

For SharePoint sites, you need to configure usage processing on the SharePoint server by using the SharePoint Central Administration Web site.

 **For more information on how to enable usage processing on SharePoint sites, visit this Web site: http://support.microsoft.com/kb/825541.**

Working with usage data

Once the usage processing is configured and the usage data is available for a Web site, it's very simple in SharePoint Designer to generate reports for usage analysis. Choose Site ⇨ Reports ⇨ Usage reports view to examine the usage data for your site. Usage data can be exposed to provide the following information:

- Usage summary, which can be generated on a weekly, monthly, or daily basis
- Page hits, which can be determined on a daily, weekly, or monthly basis
- List of users visiting the Web site as well as the browsers and operating systems being used to visit the site
- Referring URLs to the Web site pages inside the Web site

 **NOTE** For SharePoint sites, the first 20 visiting users are displayed separately, along with their usernames, in the reports. The rest of the users are combined in the All Others row.

FIGURE 25.4

The usage data for an FPSE site

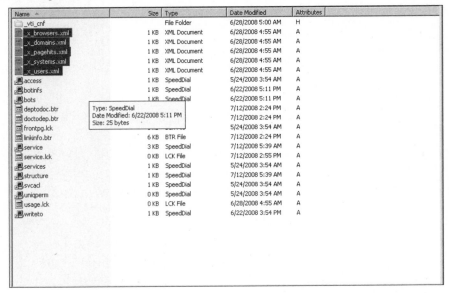

Conforming to Web Standards

While designing Web sites, you have to always keep the audience in mind. In a general case, if you're developing for a wider audience, you have to keep in mind that your Web site is accessible with the same fidelity for different desktops, screen resolutions, and browsers and provides functionality to support devices and software meant for users with disabilities. SharePoint Designer provides you with ways to determine whether a Web site or Web page that you create adheres to the standards developed for accessibility.

Understanding accessibility standards

SharePoint Designer allows you to check whether content of your Web site conforms to the following standards for the accessibility of content on the Web:

- **WCAG Priority 1:** Web Content Accessibility Guidelines (WCAG) is a set of guidelines determining the accessibility of Web content. It's suggested that the Priority 1 guidelines must be met in order for the Web content to appear on a Web site, and if ignored, the content would not be accessible to a set of users and groups.

- **WCAG Priority 2:** The WCAG 2.0 draft lists a set of accessibility requirements that should be met by Web content creators and if ignored would make it difficult for users to access the site.

- **Access Board Section 508:** This is the U.S. government standard for accessibility. All U.S. government bodies adhere to this standard to determine if a service or content section is technically compliant.

The general idea for these standards for Internet-based content is to ensure that software that provides assistance to people with disabilities can access/read the content clearly.

Using the Accessibility Checker

You use the Accessibility Checker, as shown in Figure 25.5, to provision settings for checking the accessibility of a Web site. Follow these steps:

1. **Choose Tools ➪ Accessibility Reports to open the Accessibility Checker dialog box.** You use this dialog box to specify the standard you want to compare your Web site with.

2. **Choose All Pages to run the check on all Web content inside the Web site.** If you have any Web pages open or chosen, the option to run the check on open or chosen content is also available.

3. **By default, all the standards are enabled.** If you want to disable checking for one of these, just deselect the corresponding check box.

4. **Specify whether you want to see errors or warnings or if you want to perform manual checking of the standards.**

5. **Click OK.**

The Accessibility task pane opens, listing errors, warnings, etc., related to the content of the Web site. You can use this pane to perform actions on the resulting rows of Web pages and content that don't adhere to the accessibility standard you chose. The warnings in this case are generally recommendations that SharePoint Designer makes if it encounters an implementation that can be improved to match the standard completely.

FIGURE 25.5

The Accessibility Checker in SharePoint Designer

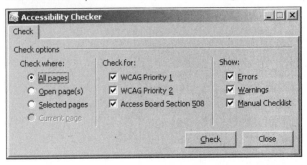

Working in the Accessibility task pane

The Accessibility task pane provides you with the location on the Web pages where SharePoint Designer finds a problem matching with the selected accessibility standard. As shown in Figure 25.6, the table shows the page and the line number on the page where the issue exists and also mentions the nature of the problem in the Problem Summary column. You can filter or arrange this report by dropping the column headers in the task pane.

FIGURE 25.6

The report for a site in the Accessibility task pane

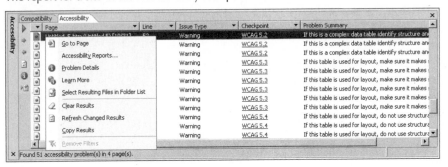

If you right-click on an issue depicted in the report, a popup menu appears, offering the following options:

- **Go to Page:** Opens the page where the issue has been detected

- **Accessibility Report:** Opens the Accessibility Checker to run the report again

- **Problem Details:** Displays a description box with the details of the issue discovered

- **Learn More:** Opens the W3C recommendation Web site and directs to the location associated with the suggestions

- **Select Resulting Files in Folder List:** Chooses the files in the Folder List to perform additional operations on

- **Clear Results:** Clears the Accessibility task pane

- **Refresh Changed Results:** Refreshes the results for changes made to the Web site since the last check was run

- **Copy Results:** Allows you to copy results to the Clipboard

The taskbar in the left corner of the task pane has a Generate HTML Reports button that allows you to create an HTML checklist of the issues found, which you can save or print out and use for tracking the changes and fixes made to the Web site based on the report.

Using Compatibility Reports

While the Accessibility Checker looks for inconsistencies with the Web site's accessibility, the Compatibility Checker allows you to check whether your Web content is compatible with a particular browser version or schema, XHTML, CSS version, or Document Type Declaration on the page.

Working with the Compatibility Checker

You can access the Compatibility Checker by choosing Tools ➪ Compatibility Reports. As shown in Figure 25.7, the Compatibility Checker allows you to choose a version of HTML, XHTML, or browser scheme and then validates the documents against that version. It checks for incompatible tags, attributes, and other implementations on the Web pages of a Web site.

You can also choose a version of CSS that you want to check compatibility against. The Compatibility Checker is particularly useful in situations where you're designing against a particular schema or version and want to ensure that your content correctly renders in the chosen version.

> **NOTE** The errors that appear in the Compatibility Report generated by SharePoint Designer don't always mean that the Web pages on which these errors appear are useless. These errors are an indication that the code doesn't completely match the chosen schema, and the browser might switch to a backward-compatibility mode to render the component. A number of SharePoint Designer components might show up as error components in these reports. There are times when you can just choose to live with the incompatibility in favor of the functionality obtained.

FIGURE 25.7

The Compatibility Checker in SharePoint Designer

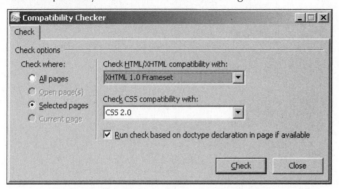

Using the compatibility task pane

The report generated for the pages selected in the Compatibility Checker is shown in the Compatibility task pane. The interface is mostly similar to the Accessibility task pane, and you can view the errors and incompatibilities found on the Web pages of a Web site by looking at the problem description in the task pane table. Like the Accessibility task pane, the Compatibility task pane also allows you to save a copy of the report generated by creating an HTML file, which can be used as a reference task list.

Summary

As discussed in this chapter, while SharePoint Designer inherits many of its reporting capabilities from FrontPage 2003, it has a number of cool features for planning the accessibility and compatibility of Web sites.

SharePoint Designer offers a number of reports that can be used to determine the state and usage of the Web sites. It relies on the Web server type for usage reports.

You can use the Accessibility Checker to find out if there are issues related to accessibility on your Web pages. SharePoint Designer generates reports that provide information and suggestions about how you can conform to the chosen accessibility standards.

SharePoint Designer also offers a Compatibility Checker that allows you to determine whether your Web pages are compatible with a certain HTML, XHTML, or CSS schema.

Index

Symbols

A